N JUMP MANGA

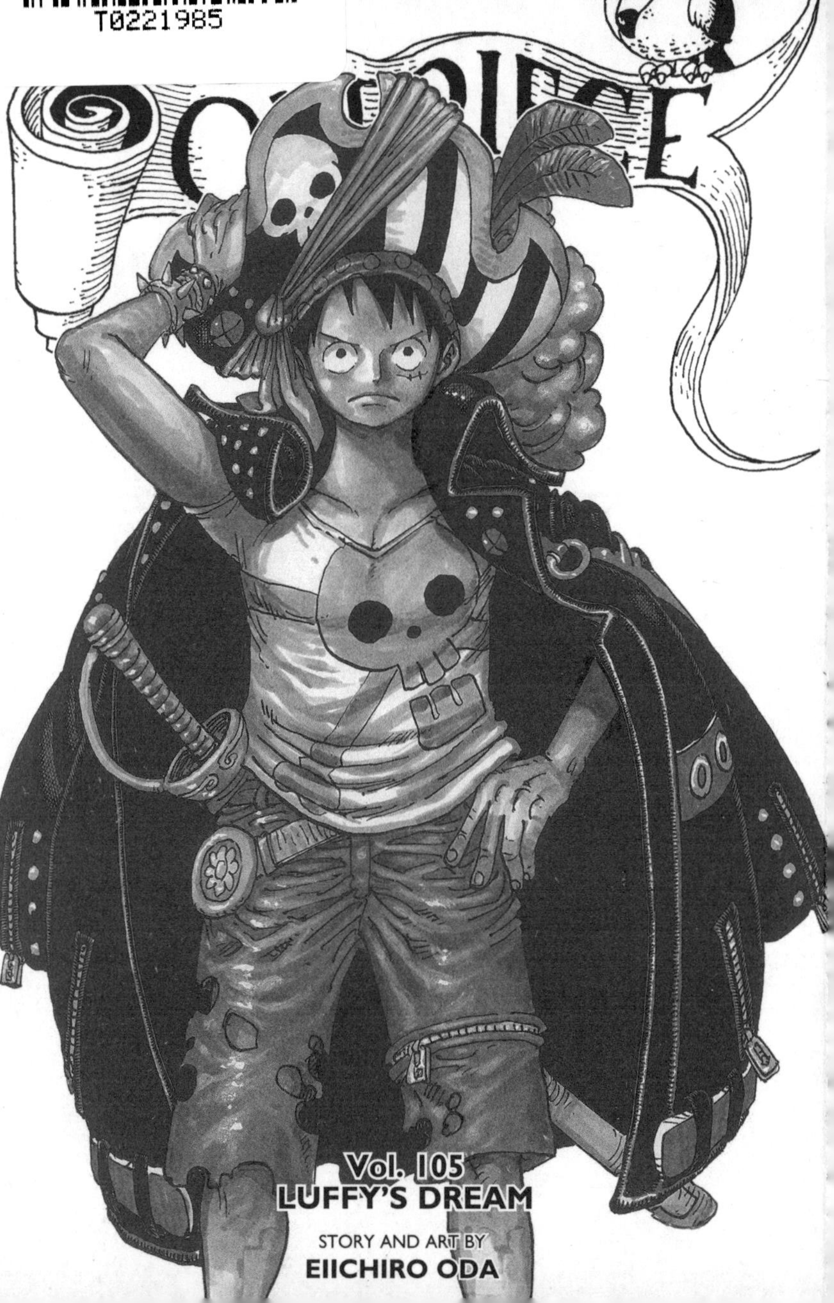

Vol. 105
LUFFY'S DREAM

STORY AND ART BY
EIICHIRO ODA

The Straw Hat Crew

Tony Tony Chopper

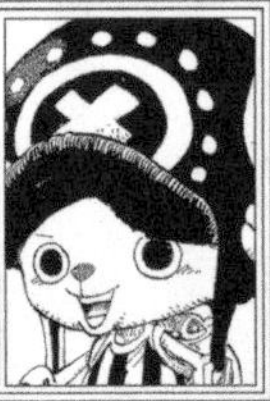

Studied powerful medicines in the Birdie Kingdom as he waited to rejoin the crew.

Ship's Doctor, Bounty: 100 berries

Roronoa Zolo

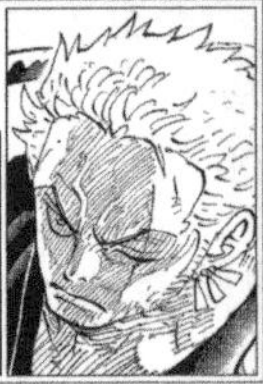

Swallowed his pride on Gloom Island and trained under Mihawk before rejoining Luffy.

Fighter, Bounty: 320 million berries

Nico Robin

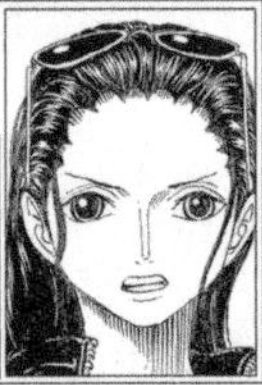

Spent time on the island of Baltigo with Dragon, Luffy's father and leader of the Revolutionary Army.

Archeologist, Bounty: 130 million berries

Nami

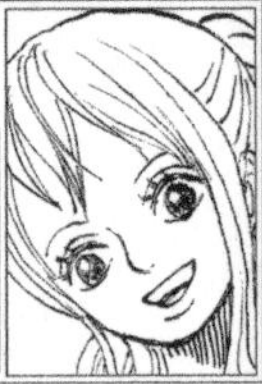

Learned about the climates of the New World on Weatheria, a Sky Island that studies the atmosphere.

Navigator, Bounty: 66 million berries

Franky

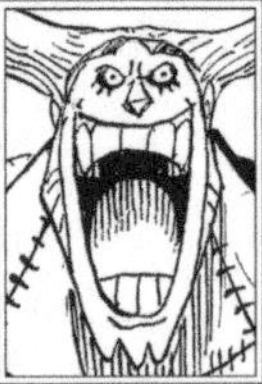

Upgraded himself into "Armored Franky" in the Future Land, Baldimore.

Shipwright, Bounty: 94 million berries

Usopp

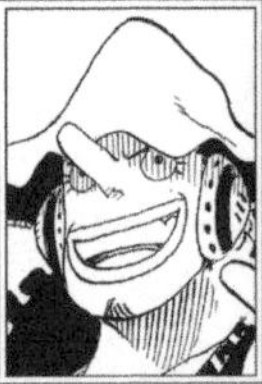

Received Heraclesun's lessons on the Bowin Islands in his quest to be the "king of the snipers."

Sniper, Bounty: 200 million berries

Brook

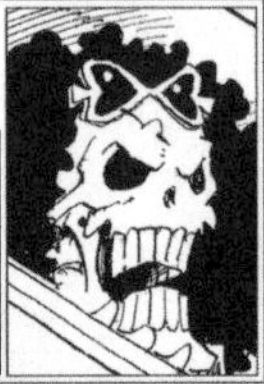

Originally captured by Long-Arm bandits for a freak show, he is now the mega-star "Soul King" Brook.

Musician, Bounty: 83 million berries

Sanji

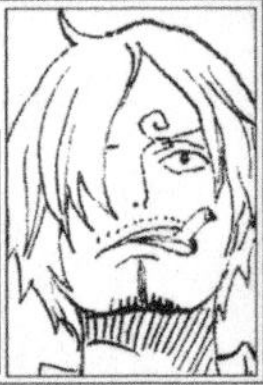

Honed his skills fighting with the masters of Newcomer Kenpo in the Kamabakka Kingdom.

Cook, Bounty: 330 million berries

Jimbei, First Son of the Sea [Former Warlord]

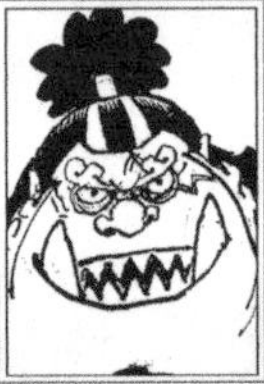

A man loyal to the code. Acted as rear guard against Big Mom to help Luffy escape, then rejoined before the raid.

Helmsman, Bounty: 438 million berries

The story of ONE PIECE 1»105

The Four Emperors

Monkey D. Luffy

A young man dreaming of being the Pirate King. After two years of training he rejoins his friends in search of the New World!

Captain, Bounty: 3 billion berries

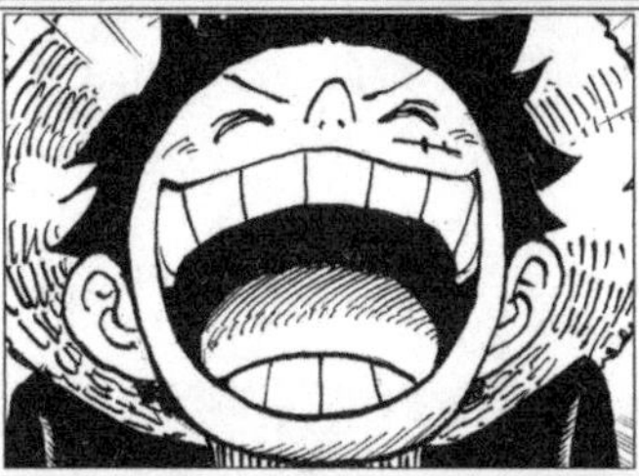

Red-Haired Shanks

One of the Four Emperors. Waits for Luffy in the "New World," the second half of the Grand Line.

Captain of the Red-Haired Pirates

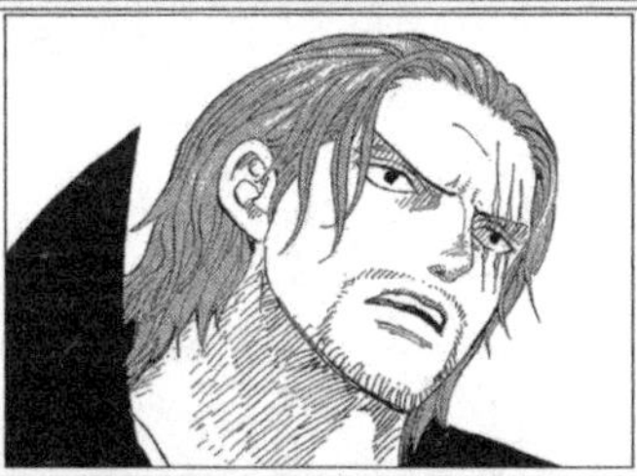

Marshall D. Teech

Former member of the Whitebeard Pirates. Fled after killing a crewmate. Rose from a Warlord to an Emperor.

Commodore of the Blackbeard Pirates

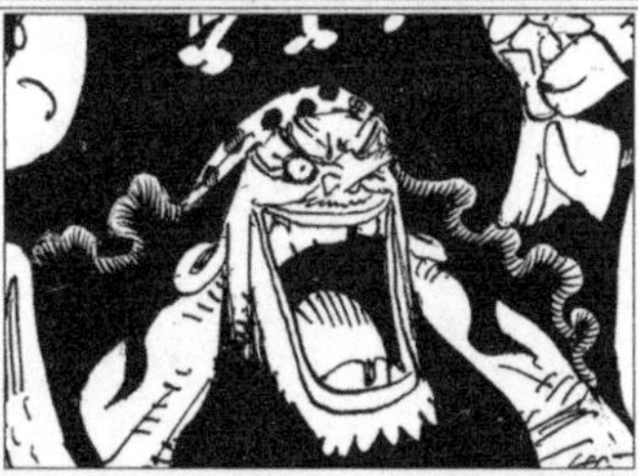

Buggy the Genius Jester

Was a swabbie with the Roger Pirates along with Shanks. An Emperor of the Sea at last!!

Chairman of Buggy's Delivery

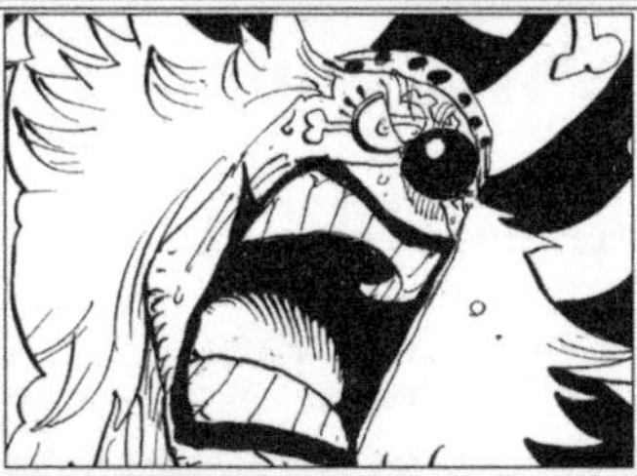

Land of Wano (Kozuki Clan)

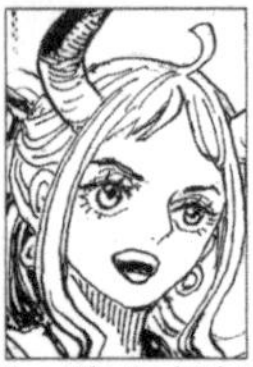

Yamato (Alias: Kozuki Oden)

Kaido's Daughter

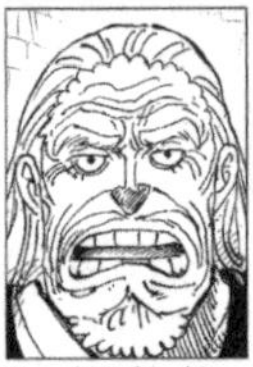

Kozuki Sukiyaki

Former Shogun (Tenguyama Hitetsu)

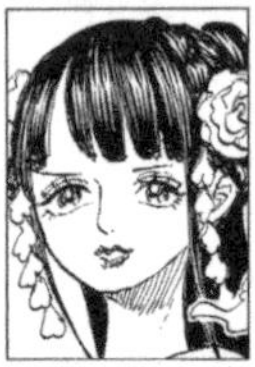

Kozuki Hiyori (Komurasaki)

Momonosuke's Little Sister

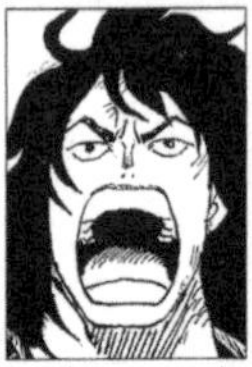

Kozuki Momonosuke

Daimyo (Heir) to Kuri in Wano

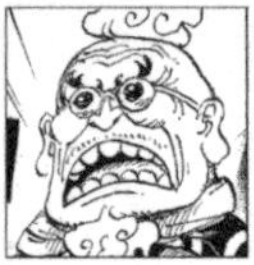

Hyogoro the Flower

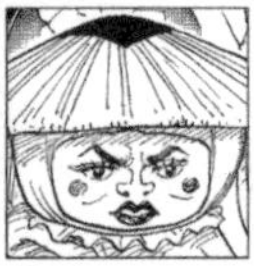

Shinobu

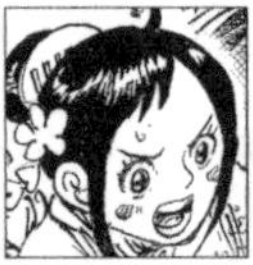

Otama

Akazaya Nine

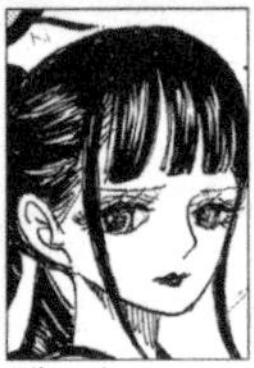

Kikunojo

Samurai of Wano

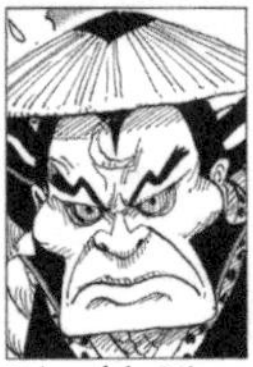

Raizo of the Mist

Ninja of Wano

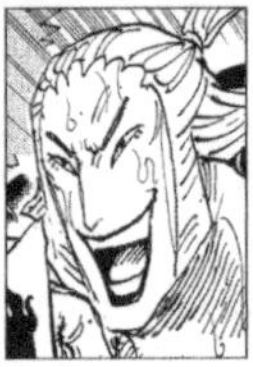

Denjiro

Formerly Kyoshiro the Money Changer

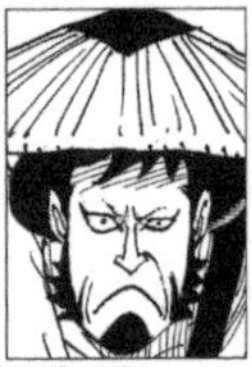

Foxfire Kin'emon

Samurai of Wano

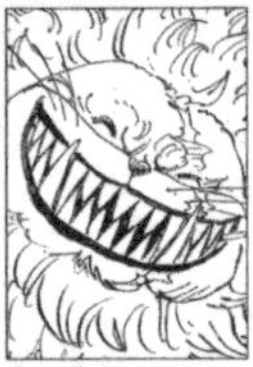

Cat Viper

King of the Night, Mokomo

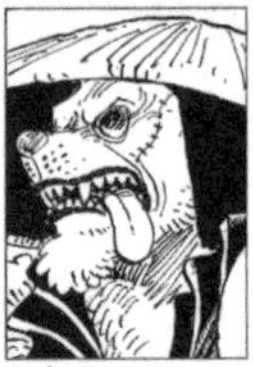

Duke Dogstorm

King of the Day, Mokomo

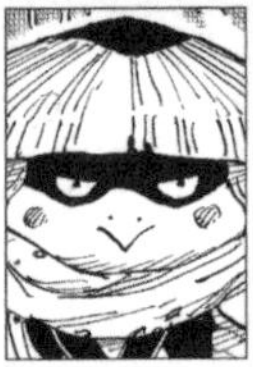

Kawamatsu

Samurai of Wano

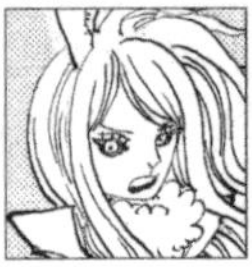

Carrot

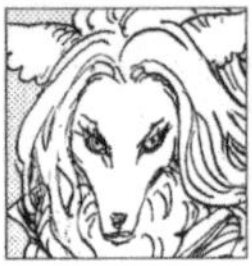

Wanda

enemy officers, and takes down Big Mom! All that's left is Luffy's battle with Kaido, where the extreme level of combat causes the Gum-Gum Fruit to awaken, activating Gear Five and helping Luffy win!!

Momonosuke announces his intent to lead Wano. While peace has arrived in the country at last, the world picture is greatly unbalanced by the shocking defeat of two Emperors. And with his bounty jumping ever higher, Luffy's era as an Emperor of the Sea begins...

The story of ONE PIECE 1»105

Navy

Akainu (Sakazuki)

Fleet Admiral, Navy HQ

Ryokugyu (Aramaki)

Admiral, Navy HQ

Revolutionary Army

Sabo

Chief of Staff, Rev. Army

Heart Pirates

Trafalgar Law

Captain, Heart Pirates

Kid Pirates

Eustass Kid

Captain, Kid Pirates

Killer

Fighter, Kid Pirates

Marco the Phoenix

Former 1st Div. Leader, Whitebeard Pirates

Scratchmen Apoo

Captain, On-Air Pirates

Story

After two years of hard training, the Straw Hat pirates are back together, first at the Sabaody Archipelago and then through Fish-Man Island to their next stage: the New World!!

Luffy and crew join with Momonosuke's faction in order to defeat Kaido, one of the Four Emperors. With all the allies in place, the raid on Onigashima begins!! Despite the disaster of Big Mom allying with Kaido, the alliance defeats the

Vol. 105
LUFFY'S DREAM

CONTENTS

Chapter 1056: Cross Guild		007
Chapter 1057: The End		025
Chapter 1058: New Emperors		043
Chapter 1059: The Matter Involving Captain Koby		061
Chapter 1060: Luffy's Dream		078
Chapter 1061: Future Island Egghead		099
Chapter 1062: Adventure in the Land of Science		115
Chapter 1063: My Only Family		133
Chapter 1064: Egghead Labophase		149
Chapter 1065: Six Vegapunks		166

Chapter 1056:
CROSS GUILD

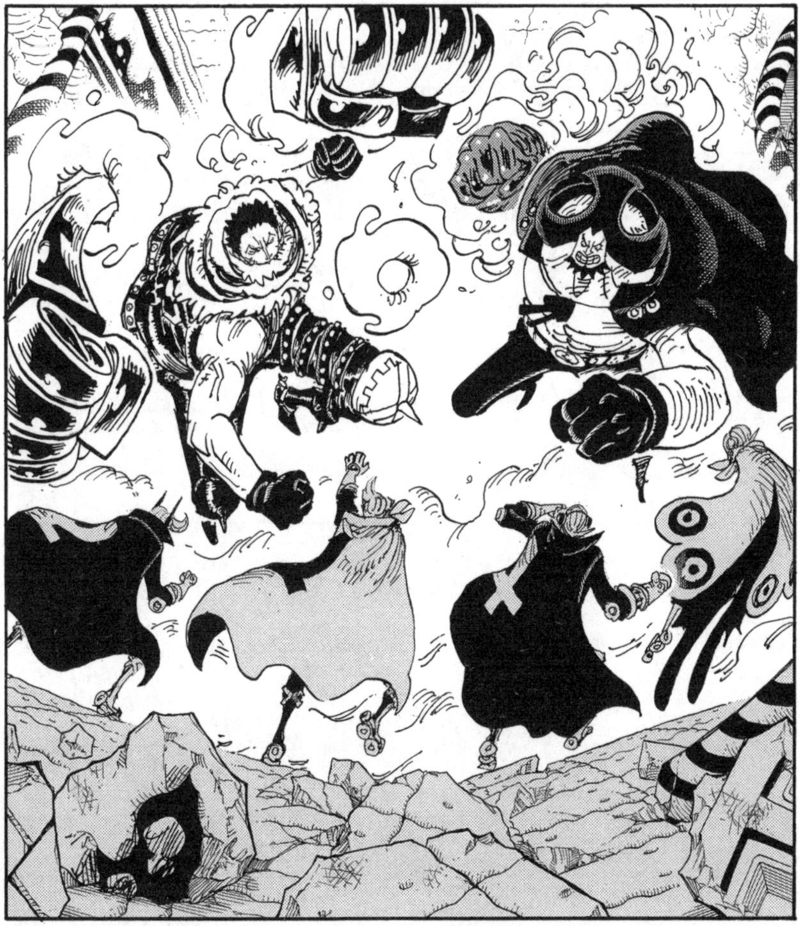

GERMA 66'S AHH... AN EMOTIONLESS EXCURSION,
VOL. 15: "KATAKURI AND OVEN ARRIVE!!"

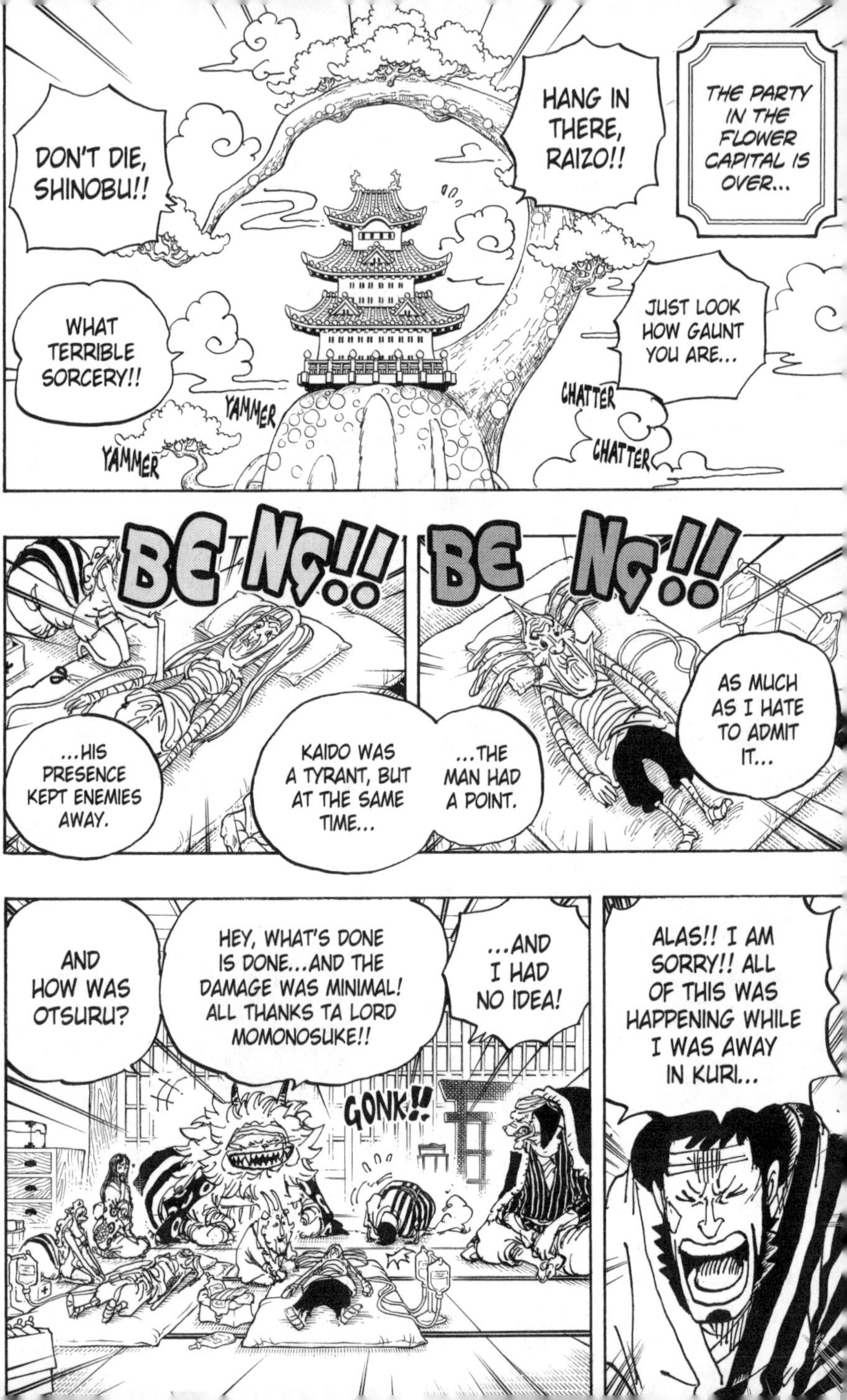
THE PARTY IN THE FLOWER CAPITAL IS OVER...
HANG IN THERE, RAIZO!!
DON'T DIE, SHINOBU!!
JUST LOOK HOW GAUNT YOU ARE...
CHATTER
CHATTER
YAMMER
YAMMER
WHAT TERRIBLE SORCERY!!
BENG!!
AS MUCH AS I HATE TO ADMIT IT...
...THE MAN HAD A POINT.
BENG!!
KAIDO WAS A TYRANT, BUT AT THE SAME TIME...
...HIS PRESENCE KEPT ENEMIES AWAY.
ALAS!! I AM SORRY!! ALL OF THIS WAS HAPPENING WHILE I WAS AWAY IN KURI...
...AND I HAD NO IDEA!
HEY, WHAT'S DONE IS DONE...AND THE DAMAGE WAS MINIMAL! ALL THANKS TA LORD MOMONOSUKE!!
GONK!!
AND HOW WAS OTSURU?

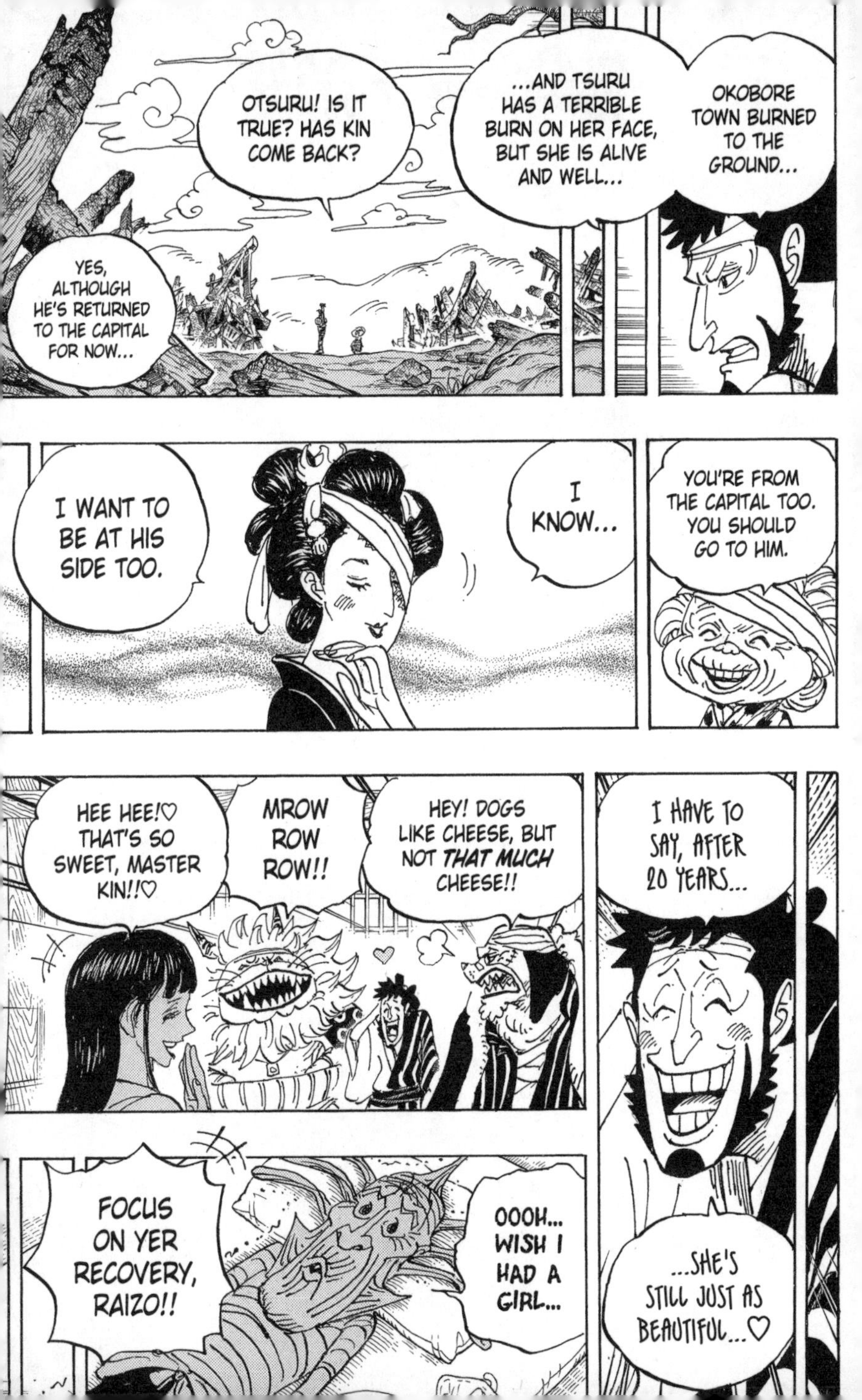
OKOBORE TOWN BURNED TO THE GROUND...
...AND TSURU HAS A TERRIBLE BURN ON HER FACE, BUT SHE IS ALIVE AND WELL...
OTSURU! IS IT TRUE? HAS KIN COME BACK?
YES, ALTHOUGH HE'S RETURNED TO THE CAPITAL FOR NOW...
YOU'RE FROM THE CAPITAL TOO. YOU SHOULD GO TO HIM.
I KNOW...
I WANT TO BE AT HIS SIDE TOO.
I HAVE TO SAY, AFTER 20 YEARS...
...SHE'S STILL JUST AS BEAUTIFUL...♡
HEY! DOGS LIKE CHEESE, BUT NOT *THAT MUCH* CHEESE!!
MROW ROW ROW!!
HEE HEE!♡ THAT'S SO SWEET, MASTER KIN!!♡
OOOH... WISH I HAD A GIRL...
FOCUS ON YER RECOVERY, RAIZO!!

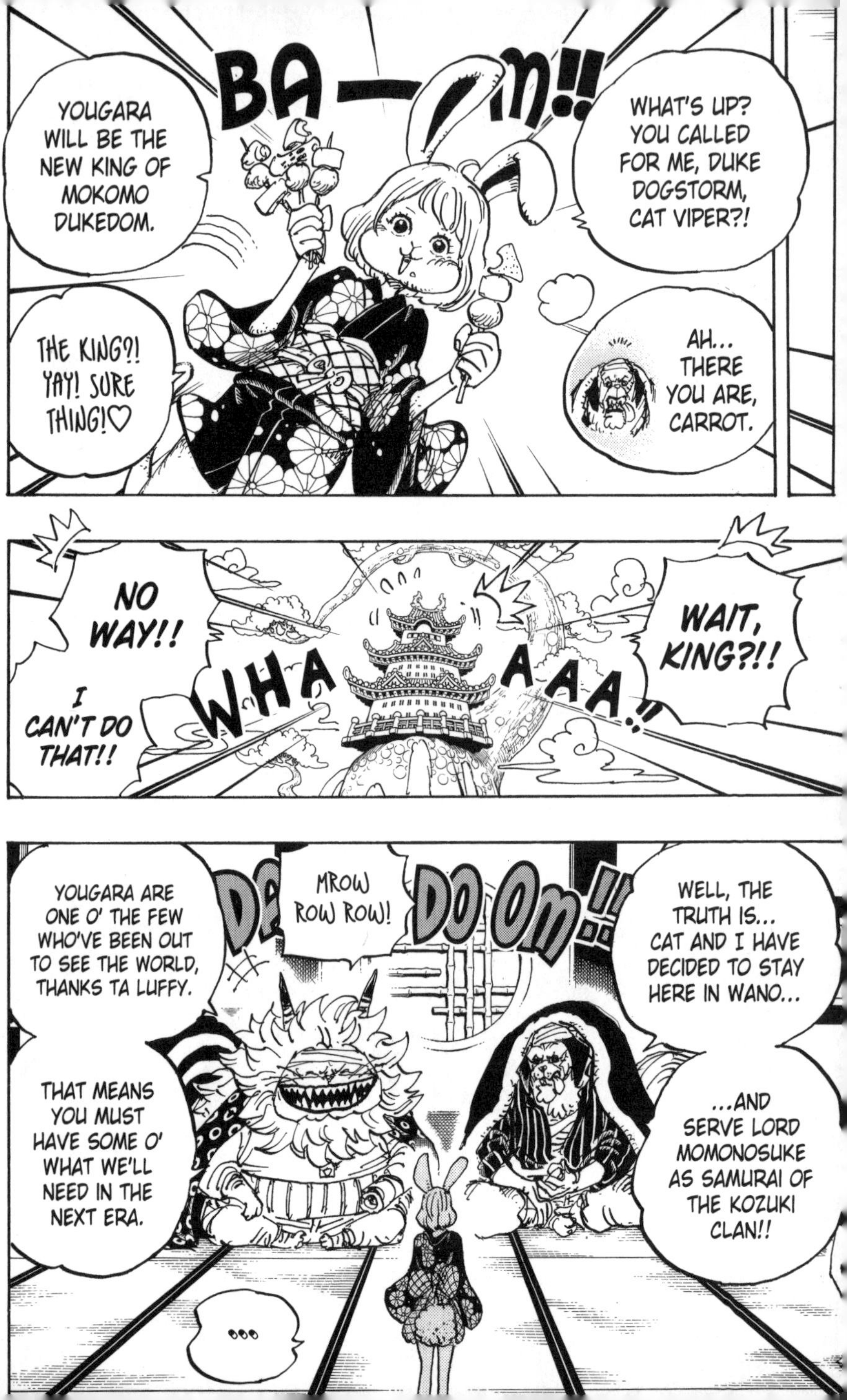

BA—N!!
WHAT'S UP? YOU CALLED FOR ME, DUKE DOGSTORM, CAT VIPER?!
AH... THERE YOU ARE, CARROT.
YOUGARA WILL BE THE NEW KING OF MOKOMO DUKEDOM.
THE KING?! YAY! SURE THING!♡
WAIT, KING?!!
WHAAAA!!
NO WAY!!
I CAN'T DO THAT!!
WELL, THE TRUTH IS... CAT AND I HAVE DECIDED TO STAY HERE IN WANO...
...AND SERVE LORD MOMONOSUKE AS SAMURAI OF THE KOZUKI CLAN!!
DADOOM!!
MROW ROW ROW!
YOUGARA ARE ONE O' THE FEW WHO'VE BEEN OUT TO SEE THE WORLD, THANKS TA LUFFY.
THAT MEANS YOU MUST HAVE SOME O' WHAT WE'LL NEED IN THE NEXT ERA.
...

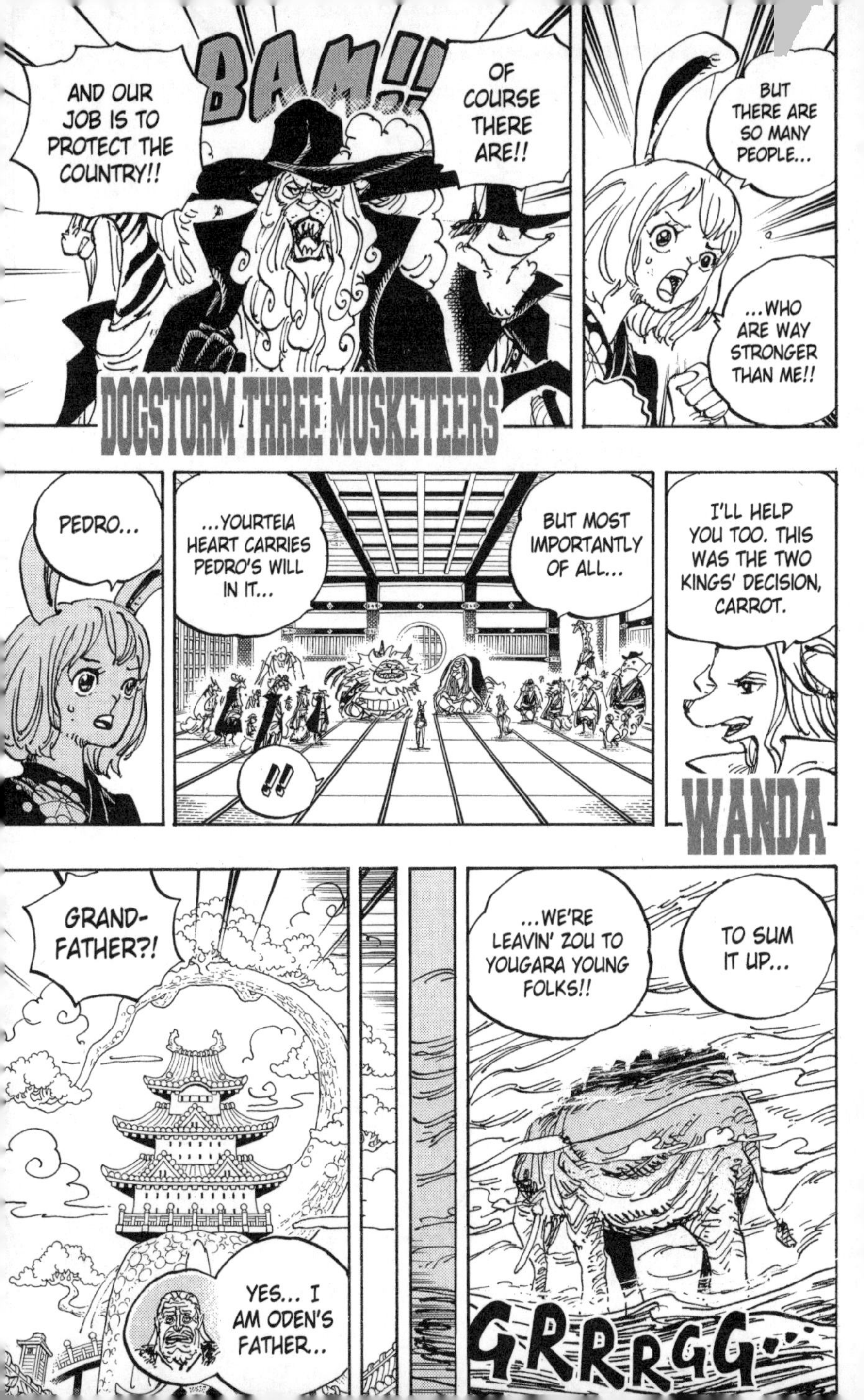
BUT THERE ARE SO MANY PEOPLE...
...WHO ARE WAY STRONGER THAN ME!!
OF COURSE THERE ARE!!
BAM!!
AND OUR JOB IS TO PROTECT THE COUNTRY!!
DOGSTORM THREE MUSKETEERS
I'LL HELP YOU TOO. THIS WAS THE TWO KINGS' DECISION, CARROT.
WANDA
BUT MOST IMPORTANTLY OF ALL...
...YOURTEIA HEART CARRIES PEDRO'S WILL IN IT...
!!
PEDRO...
TO SUM IT UP...
...WE'RE LEAVIN' ZOU TO YOUGARA YOUNG FOLKS!!
GRRRGG
GRAND-FATHER?!
YES... I AM ODEN'S FATHER...

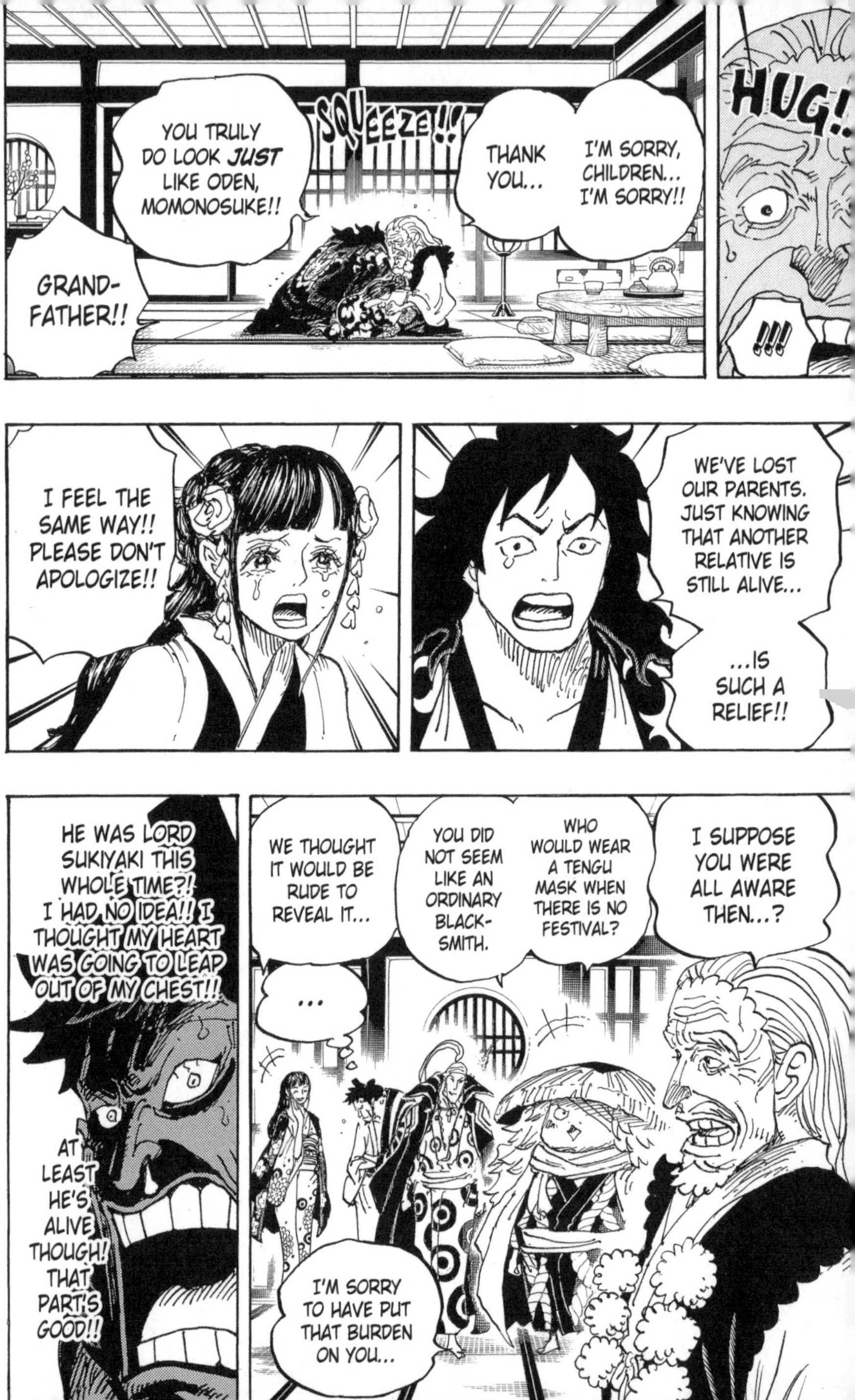
HUG!!
!!!
I'M SORRY, CHILDREN... I'M SORRY!!
THANK YOU...
SQUEEZE!!
YOU TRULY DO LOOK **JUST** LIKE ODEN, MOMONOSUKE!!
GRAND-FATHER!!
WE'VE LOST OUR PARENTS. JUST KNOWING THAT ANOTHER RELATIVE IS STILL ALIVE...
...IS SUCH A RELIEF!!
I FEEL THE SAME WAY!! PLEASE DON'T APOLOGIZE!!
I SUPPOSE YOU WERE ALL AWARE THEN...?
WHO WOULD WEAR A TENGU MASK WHEN THERE IS NO FESTIVAL?
YOU DID NOT SEEM LIKE AN ORDINARY BLACK-SMITH.
WE THOUGHT IT WOULD BE RUDE TO REVEAL IT...
...
I'M SORRY TO HAVE PUT THAT BURDEN ON YOU...
HE WAS LORD SUKIYAKI THIS WHOLE TIME?! I HAD NO IDEA!! I THOUGHT MY HEART WAS GOING TO LEAP OUT OF MY CHEST!!
AT LEAST HE'S ALIVE THOUGH! THAT PART'S GOOD!!

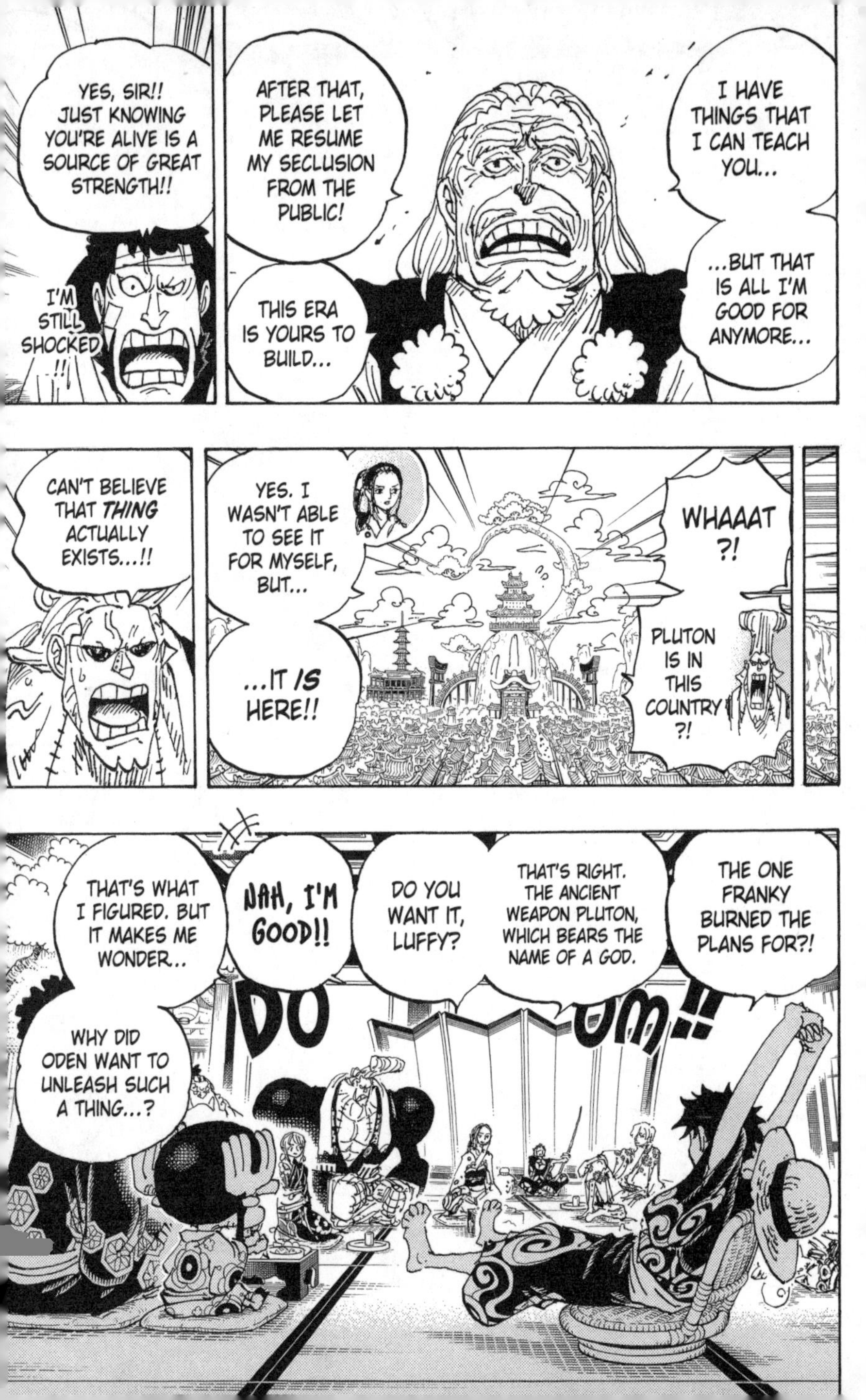
I HAVE THINGS THAT I CAN TEACH YOU...
...BUT THAT IS ALL I'M GOOD FOR ANYMORE...
AFTER THAT, PLEASE LET ME RESUME MY SECLUSION FROM THE PUBLIC!
THIS ERA IS YOURS TO BUILD...
YES, SIR!! JUST KNOWING YOU'RE ALIVE IS A SOURCE OF GREAT STRENGTH!!
I'M STILL SHOCKED!!
WHAAAT?!
PLUTON IS IN THIS COUNTRY?!
YES. I WASN'T ABLE TO SEE IT FOR MYSELF, BUT...
...IT *IS* HERE!!
CAN'T BELIEVE THAT *THING* ACTUALLY EXISTS...!!
THE ONE FRANKY BURNED THE PLANS FOR?!
THAT'S RIGHT. THE ANCIENT WEAPON PLUTON, WHICH BEARS THE NAME OF A GOD.
DO YOU WANT IT, LUFFY?
NAH, I'M GOOD!!
THAT'S WHAT I FIGURED. BUT IT MAKES ME WONDER...
WHY DID ODEN WANT TO UNLEASH SUCH A THING...?
DO
OM!!

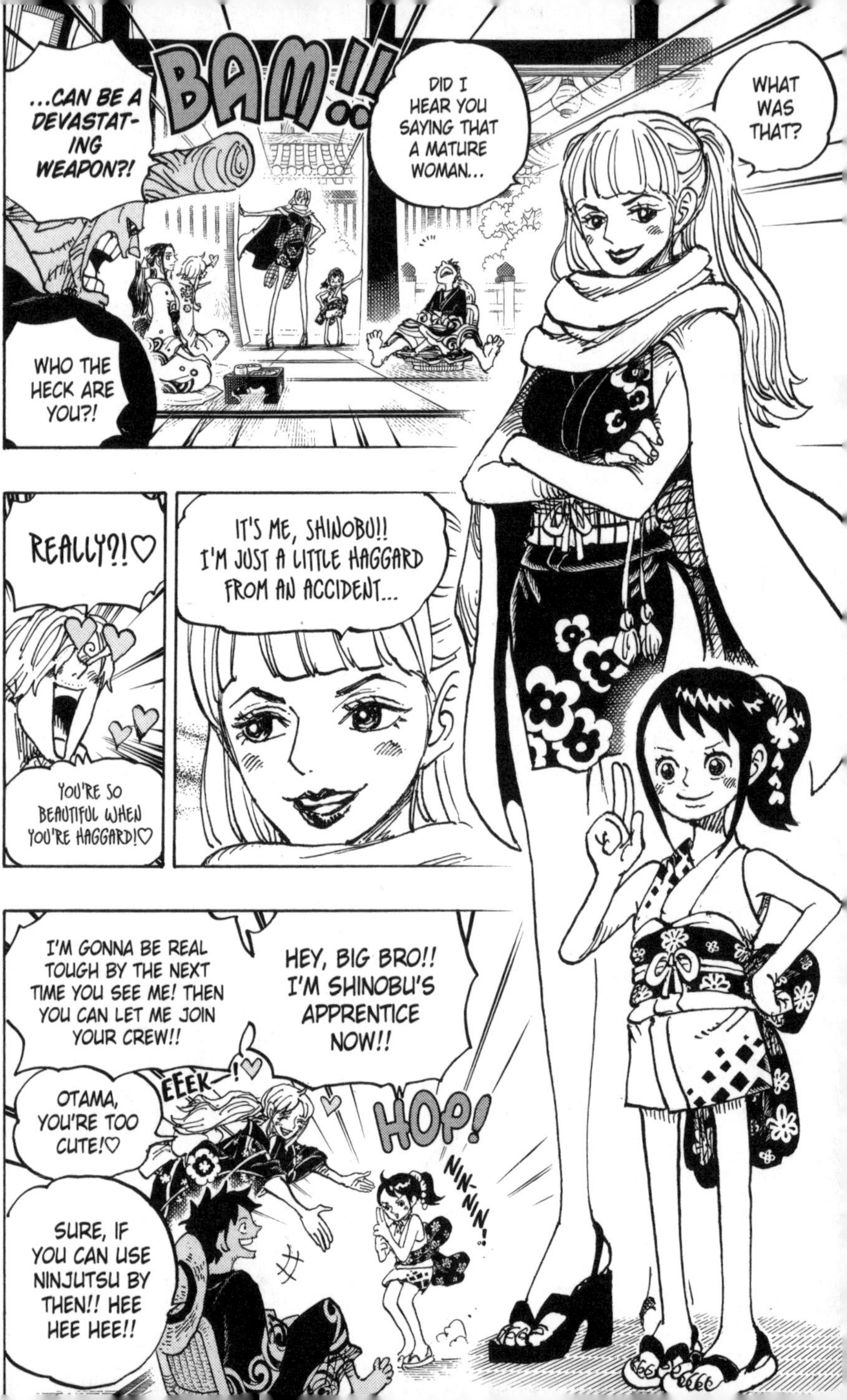
WHAT WAS THAT?
DID I HEAR YOU SAYING THAT A MATURE WOMAN...
BAM!!
...CAN BE A DEVASTATING WEAPON?!
WHO THE HECK ARE YOU?!
IT'S ME, SHINOBU!! I'M JUST A LITTLE HAGGARD FROM AN ACCIDENT...
REALLY?!♡
YOU'RE SO BEAUTIFUL WHEN YOU'RE HAGGARD!♡
HEY, BIG BRO!! I'M SHINOBU'S APPRENTICE NOW!!
I'M GONNA BE REAL TOUGH BY THE NEXT TIME YOU SEE ME! THEN YOU CAN LET ME JOIN YOUR CREW!!
HOP!
NIN-NIN!
EEEK—!♡
OTAMA, YOU'RE TOO CUTE!♡
SURE, IF YOU CAN USE NINJUTSU BY THEN!! HEE HEE HEE!!

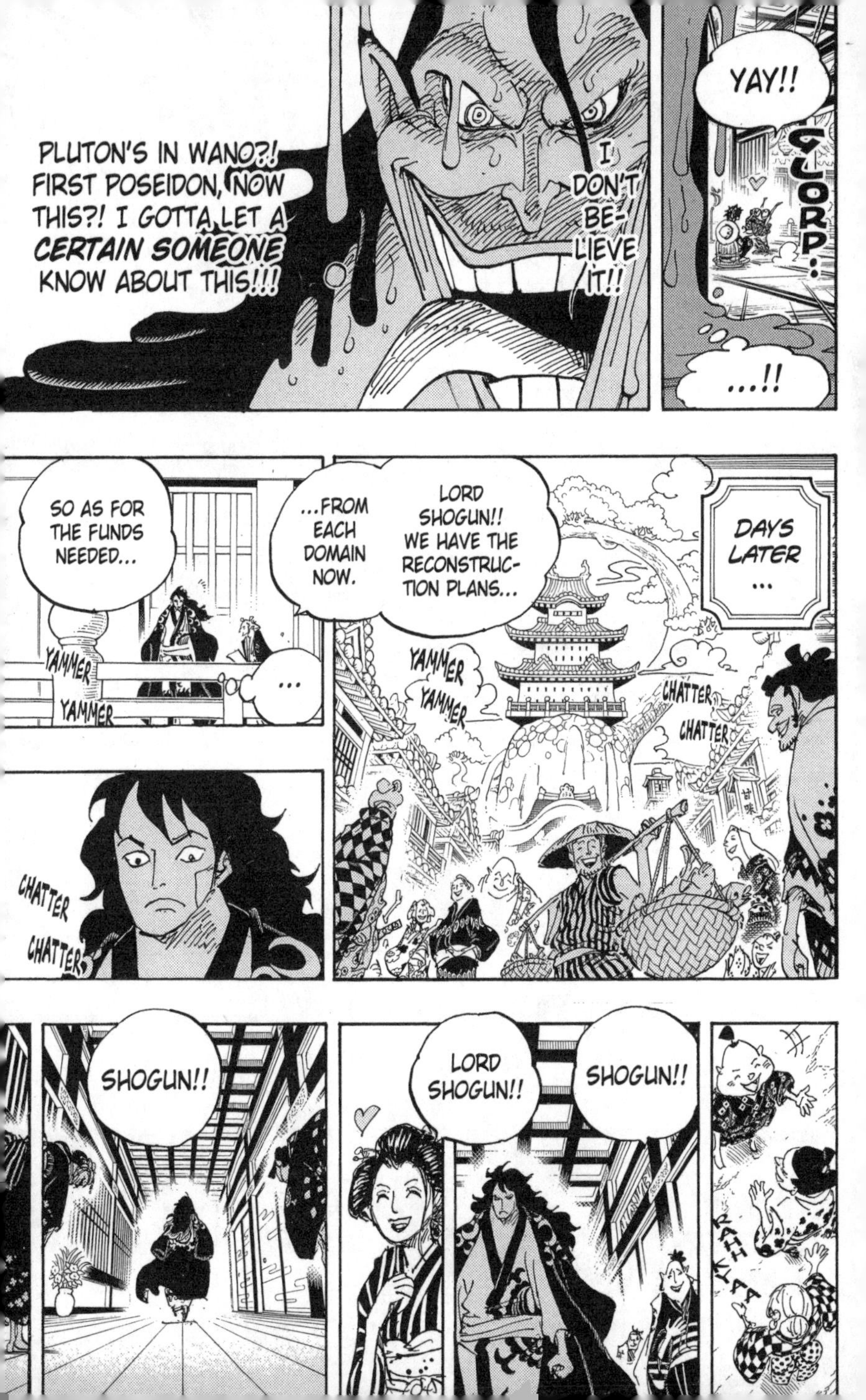
YAY!!
GLORP..
...!!
I DON'T BE-LIEVE IT!!
PLUTON'S IN WANO?! FIRST POSEIDON, NOW THIS?! I GOTTA LET A *CERTAIN SOMEONE* KNOW ABOUT THIS!!!
DAYS LATER ...
LORD SHOGUN!! WE HAVE THE RECONSTRUCTION PLANS...
...FROM EACH DOMAIN NOW.
YAMMER YAMMER
CHATTER CHATTER
SO AS FOR THE FUNDS NEEDED...
...
YAMMER YAMMER
CHATTER CHATTER
KYAAAH
SHOGUN!!
LORD SHOGUN!!
SHOGUN!!

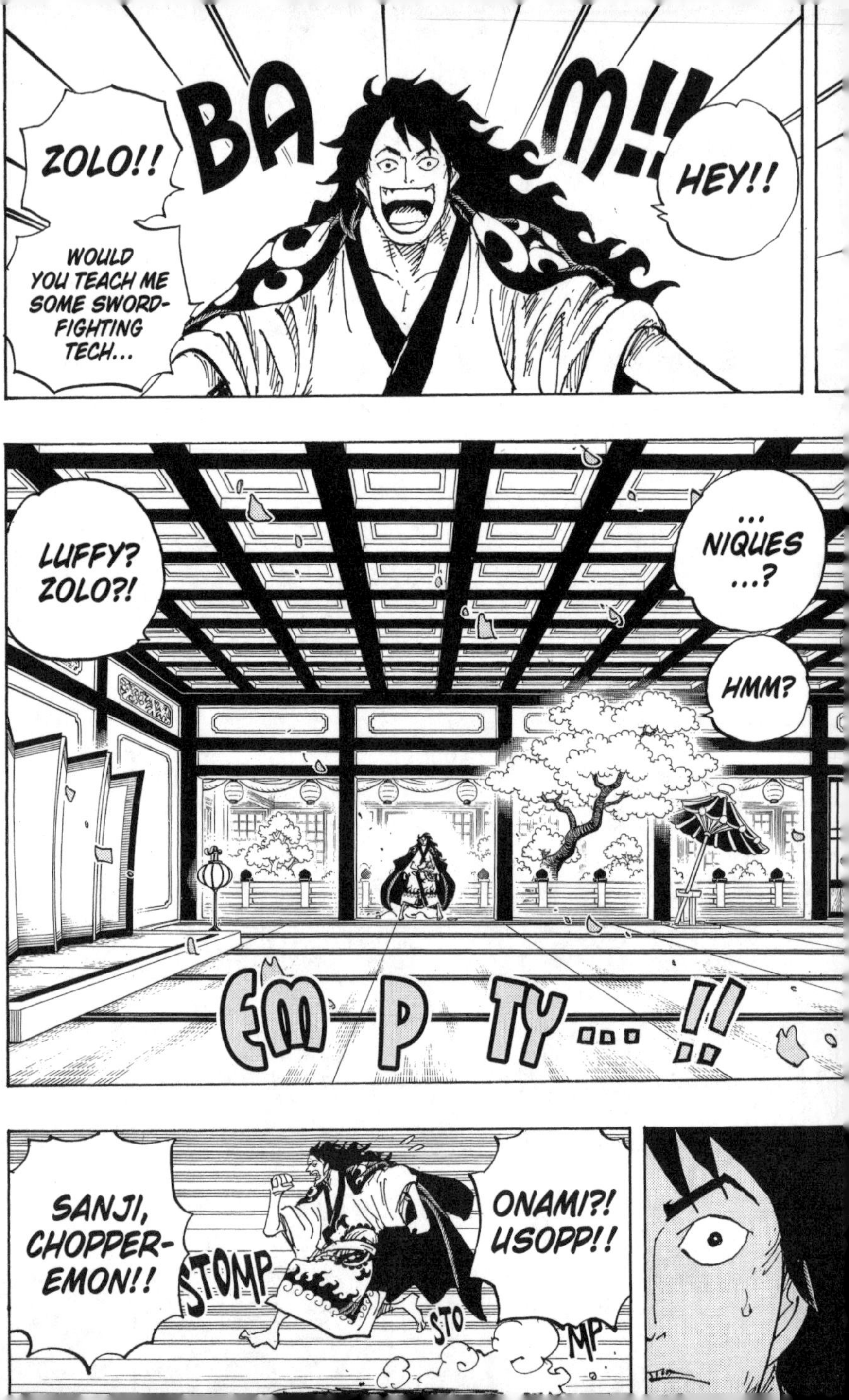
HEY!!
BAM!!
ZOLO!!
WOULD YOU TEACH ME SOME SWORD-FIGHTING TECH...
... NIQUES ...?
HMM?
LUFFY? ZOLO?!
EMPTY...!!
ONAMI?! USOPP!!
SANJI, CHOPPER-EMON!!
STOMP
STOMP

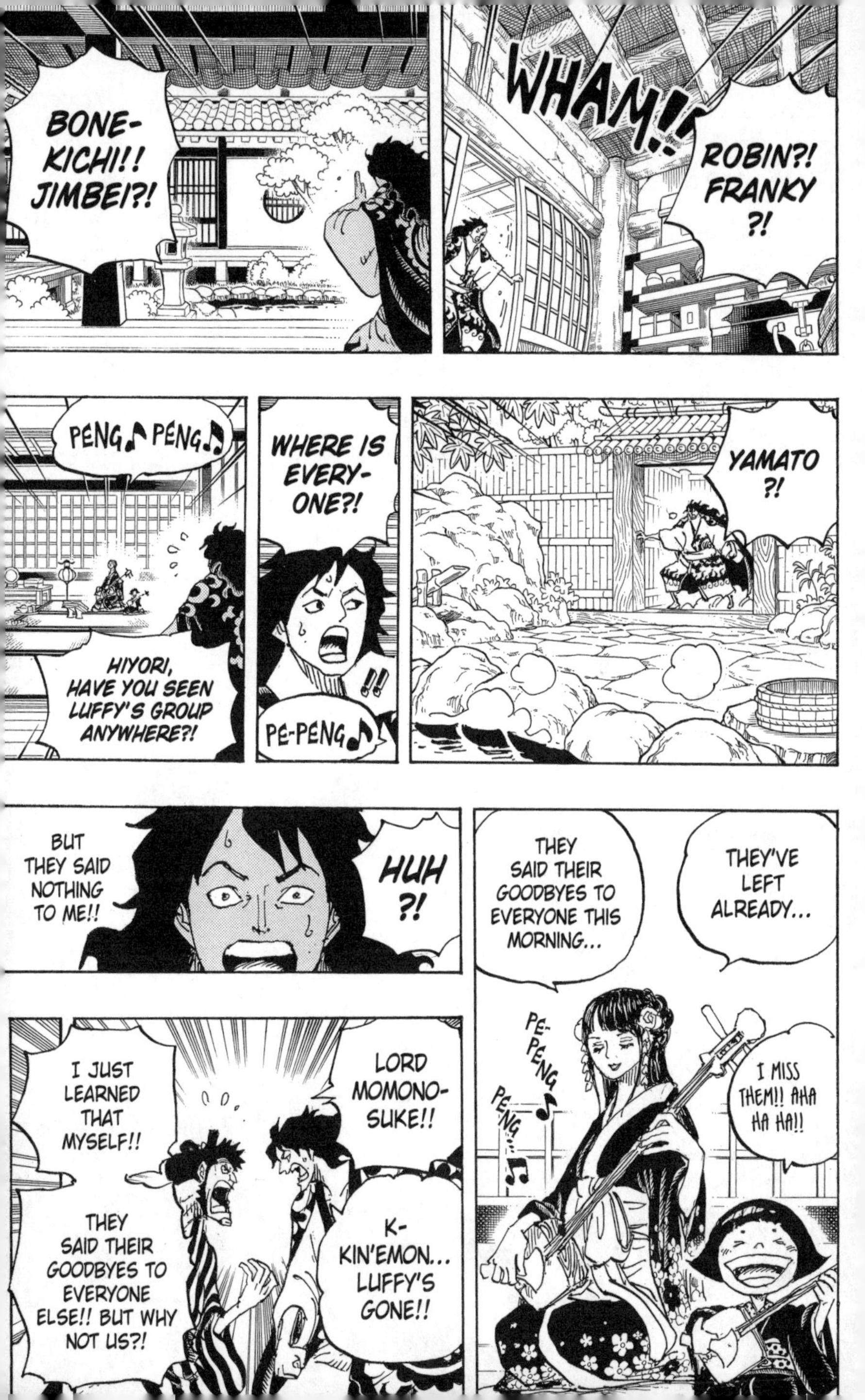
WHAM!!
ROBIN?! FRANKY ?!
BONE-KICHI!! JIMBEI?!
YAMATO ?!
WHERE IS EVERY-ONE?!
!!
PE-PENG♪
PENG♪ PENG♪
HIYORI, HAVE YOU SEEN LUFFY'S GROUP ANYWHERE?!
THEY'VE LEFT ALREADY...
THEY SAID THEIR GOODBYES TO EVERYONE THIS MORNING...
PE-PENG♪
PENG♪
I MISS THEM!! AHA HA HA!!
HUH ?!
BUT THEY SAID NOTHING TO ME!!
LORD MOMONO-SUKE!!
I JUST LEARNED THAT MYSELF!!
K-KIN'EMON... LUFFY'S GONE!!
THEY SAID THEIR GOODBYES TO EVERYONE ELSE!! BUT WHY NOT US?!

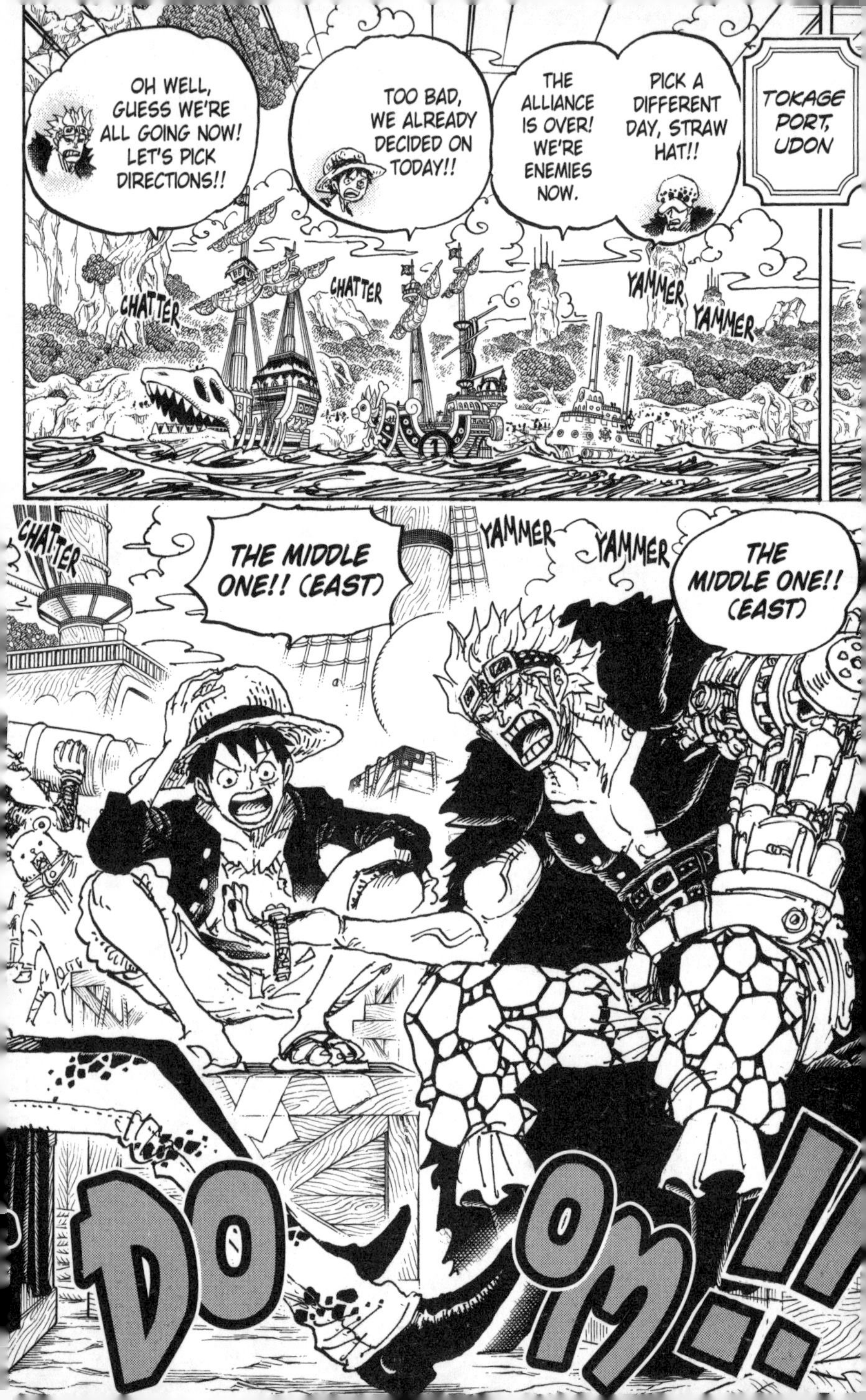
TOKAGE PORT, UDON
PICK A DIFFERENT DAY, STRAW HAT!!
THE ALLIANCE IS OVER! WE'RE ENEMIES NOW.
TOO BAD, WE ALREADY DECIDED ON TODAY!!
OH WELL, GUESS WE'RE ALL GOING NOW! LET'S PICK DIRECTIONS!!
YAMMER
YAMMER
CHATTER
CHATTER
THE MIDDLE ONE!! (EAST)
YAMMER
YAMMER
THE MIDDLE ONE!! (EAST)
CHATTER
DOOM!!

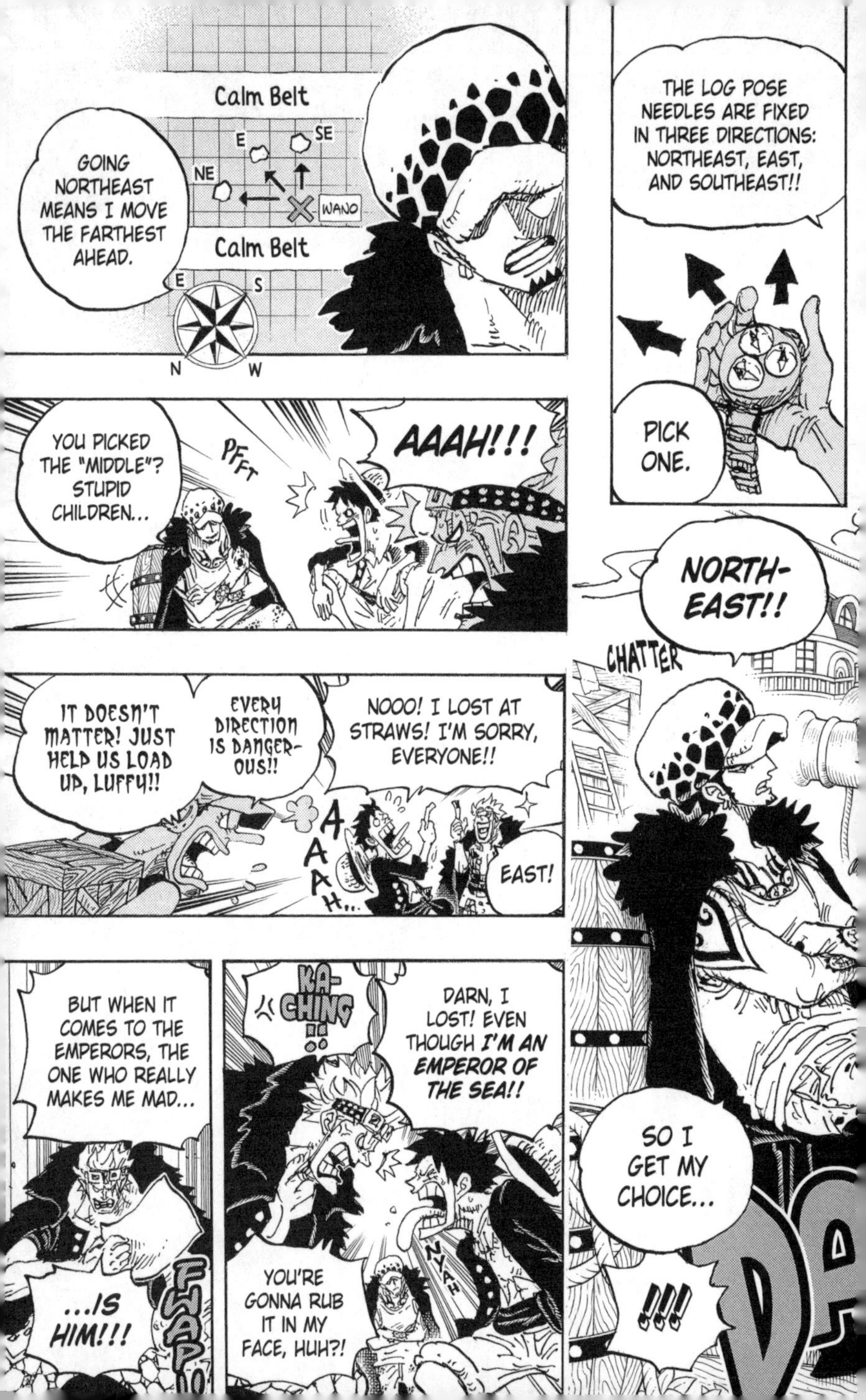
THE LOG POSE NEEDLES ARE FIXED IN THREE DIRECTIONS: NORTHEAST, EAST, AND SOUTHEAST!!
PICK ONE.
NORTH-EAST!!
CHATTER
SO I GET MY CHOICE...
!!!
Calm Belt
SE
E
NE
WANO
Calm Belt
E
S
N
W
GOING NORTHEAST MEANS I MOVE THE FARTHEST AHEAD.
AAAH!!!
PFFT
YOU PICKED THE "MIDDLE"? STUPID CHILDREN...
NOOO! I LOST AT STRAWS! I'M SORRY, EVERYONE!!
EAST!
AAAH...
EVERY DIRECTION IS DANGER-OUS!!
IT DOESN'T MATTER! JUST HELP US LOAD UP, LUFFY!!
DARN, I LOST! EVEN THOUGH *I'M AN EMPEROR OF THE SEA!!*
KA-CHING!!
NYAH
YOU'RE GONNA RUB IT IN MY FACE, HUH?!
BUT WHEN IT COMES TO THE EMPERORS, THE ONE WHO REALLY MAKES ME MAD...
...IS HIM!!!
FWAP

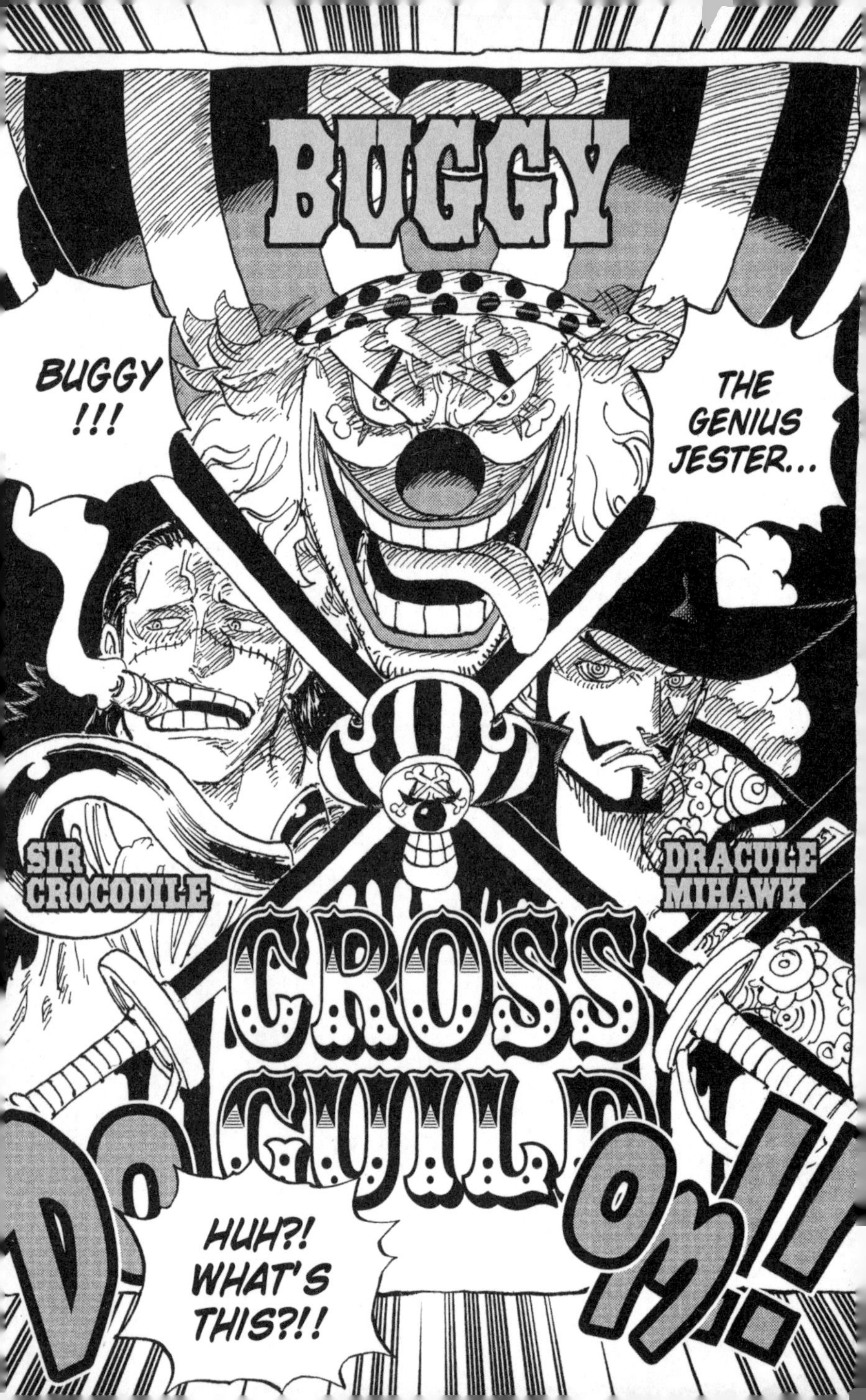
BUGGY
THE GENIUS JESTER...
BUGGY!!!
DRACULE MIHAWK
SIR CROCODILE
CROSS GUILD
DOOM!!
HUH?! WHAT'S THIS?!!

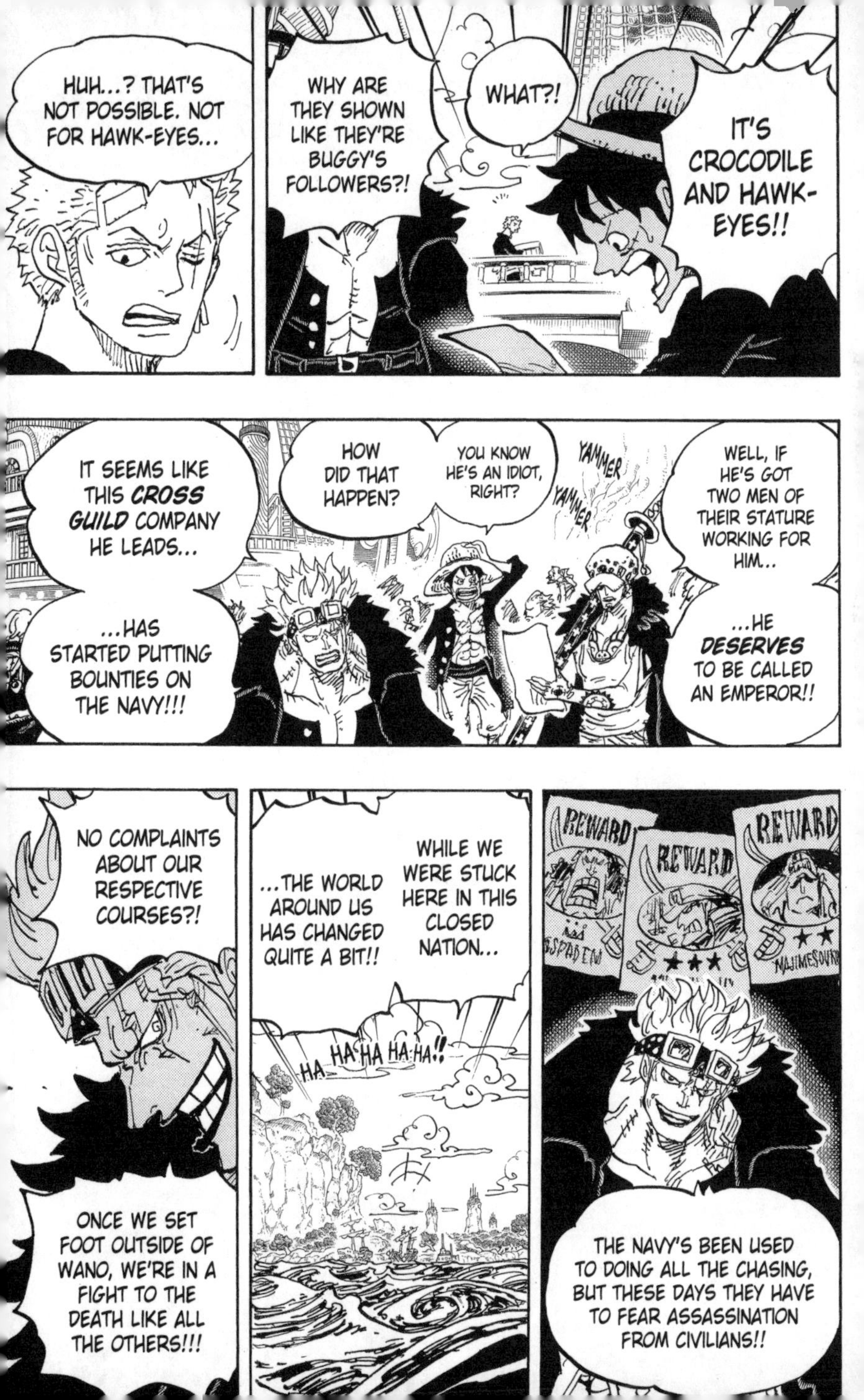
IT'S CROCODILE AND HAWK-EYES!!
WHAT?!
WHY ARE THEY SHOWN LIKE THEY'RE BUGGY'S FOLLOWERS?!
HUH...? THAT'S NOT POSSIBLE. NOT FOR HAWK-EYES...
WELL, IF HE'S GOT TWO MEN OF THEIR STATURE WORKING FOR HIM...
...HE ***DESERVES*** TO BE CALLED AN EMPEROR!!
YAMMER
YAMMER
YOU KNOW HE'S AN IDIOT, RIGHT?
HOW DID THAT HAPPEN?
IT SEEMS LIKE THIS ***CROSS GUILD*** COMPANY HE LEADS...
...HAS STARTED PUTTING BOUNTIES ON THE NAVY!!!
REWARD
REWARD
REWARD
THE NAVY'S BEEN USED TO DOING ALL THE CHASING, BUT THESE DAYS THEY HAVE TO FEAR ASSASSINATION FROM CIVILIANS!!
WHILE WE WERE STUCK HERE IN THIS CLOSED NATION...
...THE WORLD AROUND US HAS CHANGED QUITE A BIT!!
HA HA HA HA HA!!
NO COMPLAINTS ABOUT OUR RESPECTIVE COURSES?!
ONCE WE SET FOOT OUTSIDE OF WANO, WE'RE IN A FIGHT TO THE DEATH LIKE ALL THE OTHERS!!!

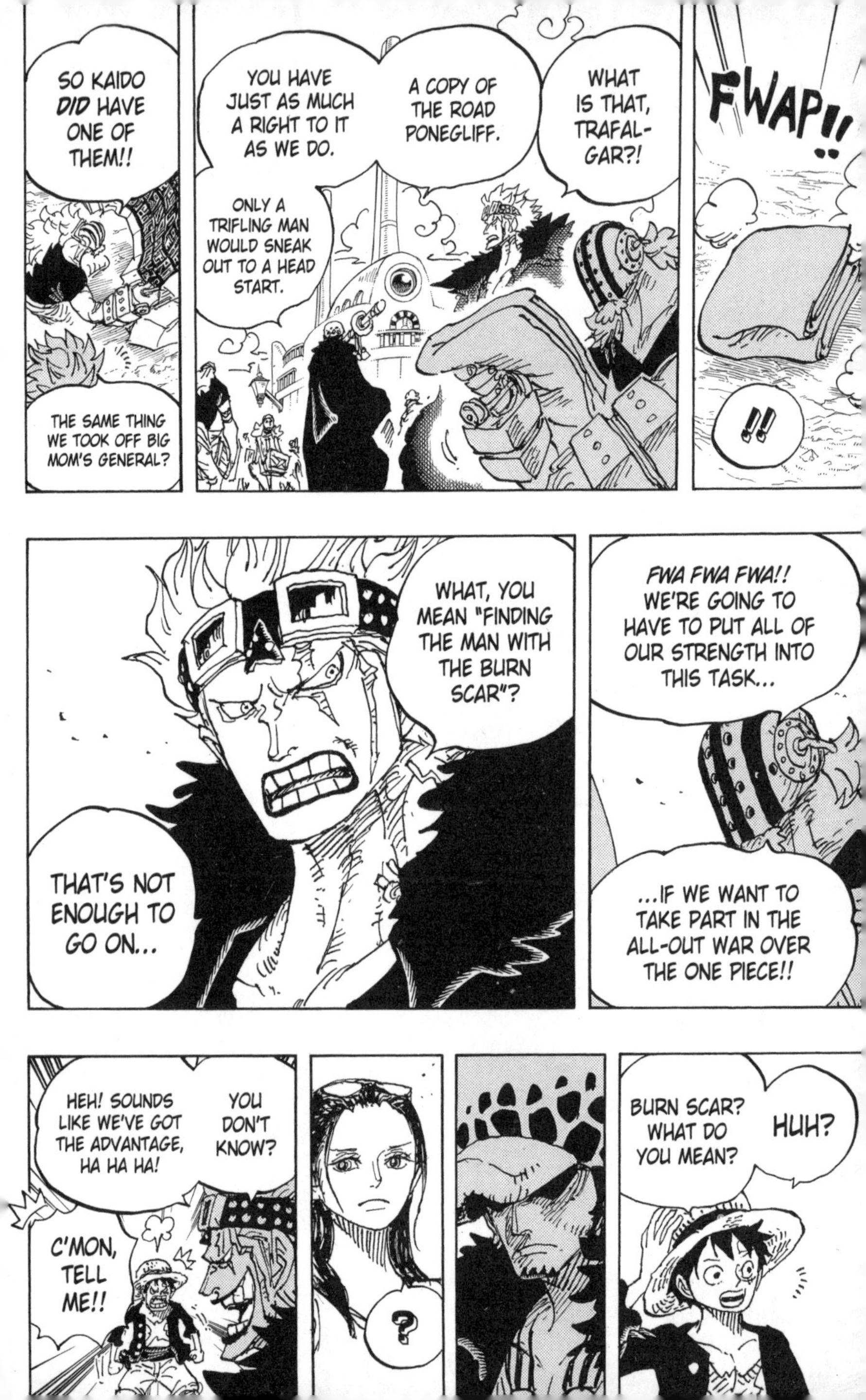
FWAP!!
!!
WHAT IS THAT, TRAFALGAR?!
A COPY OF THE ROAD PONEGLIFF.
YOU HAVE JUST AS MUCH A RIGHT TO IT AS WE DO.
ONLY A TRIFLING MAN WOULD SNEAK OUT TO A HEAD START.
SO KAIDO *DID* HAVE ONE OF THEM!!
THE SAME THING WE TOOK OFF BIG MOM'S GENERAL?
FWA FWA FWA!! WE'RE GOING TO HAVE TO PUT ALL OF OUR STRENGTH INTO THIS TASK...
...IF WE WANT TO TAKE PART IN THE ALL-OUT WAR OVER THE ONE PIECE!!
WHAT, YOU MEAN "FINDING THE MAN WITH THE BURN SCAR"?
THAT'S NOT ENOUGH TO GO ON...
HUH?
BURN SCAR? WHAT DO YOU MEAN?
?
YOU DON'T KNOW?
HEH! SOUNDS LIKE WE'VE GOT THE ADVANTAGE, HA HA HA!
C'MON, TELL ME!!

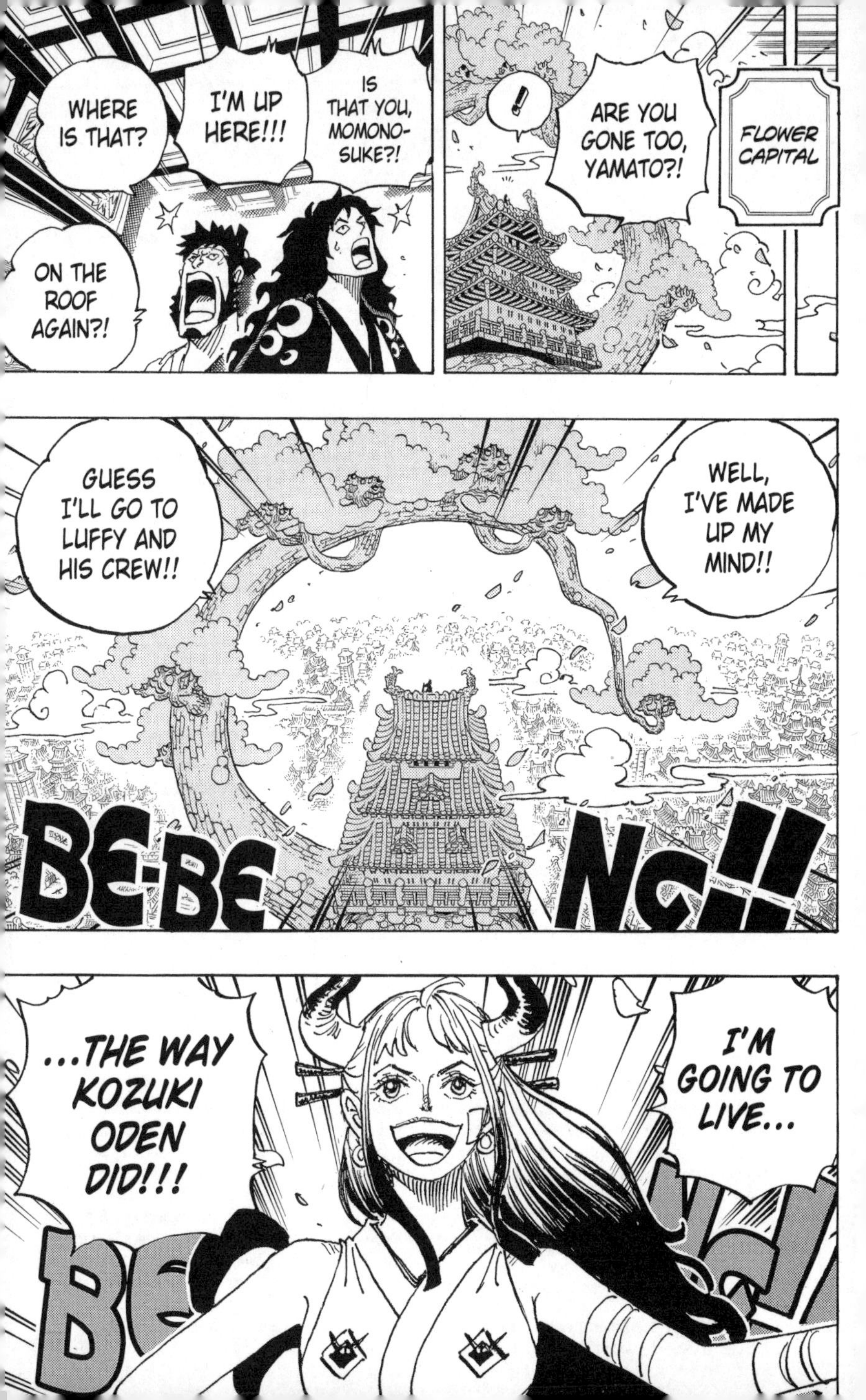
FLOWER CAPITAL
!
ARE YOU GONE TOO, YAMATO?!
IS THAT YOU, MOMONOSUKE?!
I'M UP HERE!!!
WHERE IS THAT?
ON THE ROOF AGAIN?!
WELL, I'VE MADE UP MY MIND!!
GUESS I'LL GO TO LUFFY AND HIS CREW!!
BE-BENG!!
I'M GOING TO LIVE...
...THE WAY KOZUKI ODEN DID!!!

SBS Question Corner

質問コーナー

(Shin Bucho, Tochigi)

Q: Today's the big concert for our princess, the wonderful Uta, so let's all lead a cheer for her!

U-T-A! U-T-A! U-T-A!
It's-time-to! Be-gin-the! S-B-S!!!

--Tokomon

A: It's-time-to! Be-gin-the! S-B-S has already begun!!

Q: Odacchi… You're really good at drawing!! Odacchi… You're really good at drawing!! x6
I wrote that down because I was bored.

--Chopami

A: Awww, that's so sweet. Thanks, byeeee.

DIABLE...
... JAMBE.

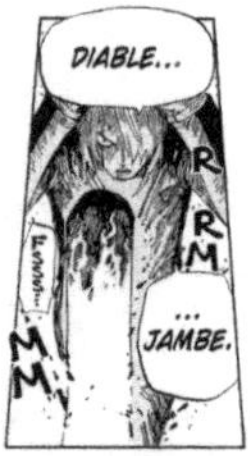

Q: Oda Sensei, why does fire come out of Sanji's feet?

--T. Ura

A: Because it's way cooler than if farts came out of his feet. Thanks, byeeee. Write again pleeeease.

Q: My question is about Sanji's eyebrow. In volume 102, chapter 1031, it reversed itself, but in volume 103, chapter 1044, it's back to normal. Why did it go back?

--Roof

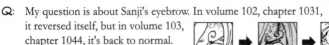

Ch. 1029 Ch. 1031 Ch. 1044

A: Well spotted! Yes, his eyebrow does change. Going back to the Whole Cake Island arc, all of Sanji's siblings were born with superhuman capabilities and hardy skin called an "exoskeleton," due to the bloodline element manipulation performed on them. But because of Sanji's mother's resistance, he was born as a regular human. Let's look at his siblings' eyebrows.

Reiju Ichiji Niji Yonji

⬅ Each of them has the "double-six" eyebrows, like Yonji. It's the opposite of Sanji's. So, in his case, the raid suit caused the power of science to manifest in him. Sanji already had an abnormal resistance to flame to begin with. That was a strange little event, wasn't it? Let's see where this takes him.

Chapter 1057:
THE END

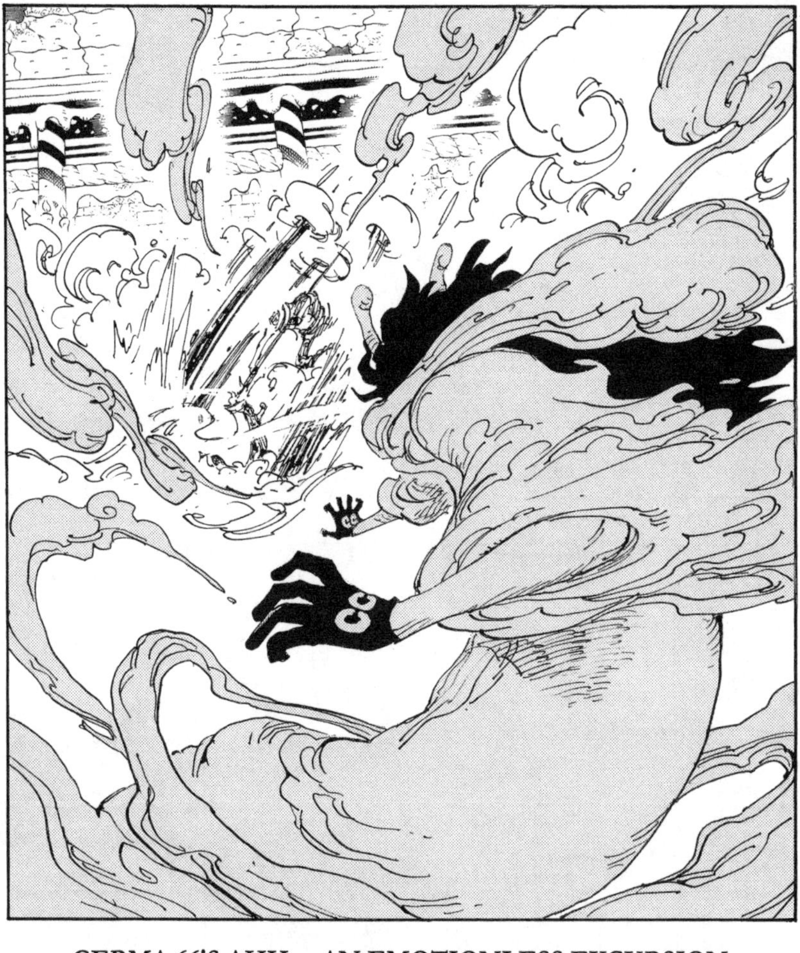

GERMA 66'S AHH... AN EMOTIONLESS EXCURSION,
VOL. 16: "CAESAR'S POISON GAS ATTACK!!"

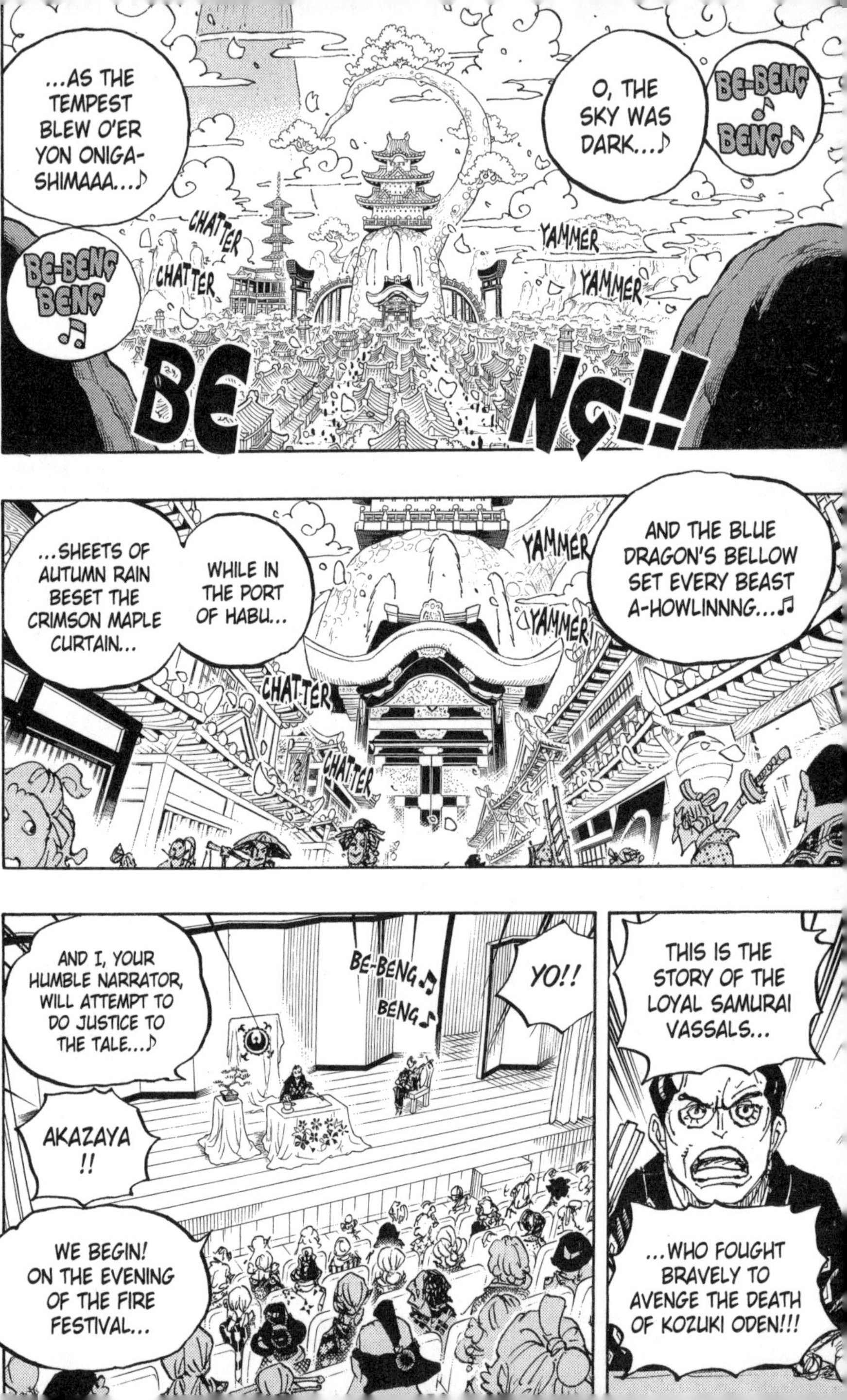
BE-BENG ♪ BENG♪
O, THE SKY WAS DARK...♪
YAMMER
YAMMER
...AS THE TEMPEST BLEW O'ER YON ONIGA-SHIMAAA...♪
CHATTER
CHATTER
BE-BENG BENG ♪
BENG!!
AND THE BLUE DRAGON'S BELLOW SET EVERY BEAST A-HOWLINNNG...♫
YAMMER
YAMMER
WHILE IN THE PORT OF HABU...
...SHEETS OF AUTUMN RAIN BESET THE CRIMSON MAPLE CURTAIN...
CHATTER
CHATTER
THIS IS THE STORY OF THE LOYAL SAMURAI VASSALS...
...WHO FOUGHT BRAVELY TO AVENGE THE DEATH OF KOZUKI ODEN!!!
YO!!
BE-BENG♫ BENG♪
AND I, YOUR HUMBLE NARRATOR, WILL ATTEMPT TO DO JUSTICE TO THE TALE...♪
AKAZAYA !!
WE BEGIN! ON THE EVENING OF THE FIRE FESTIVAL...

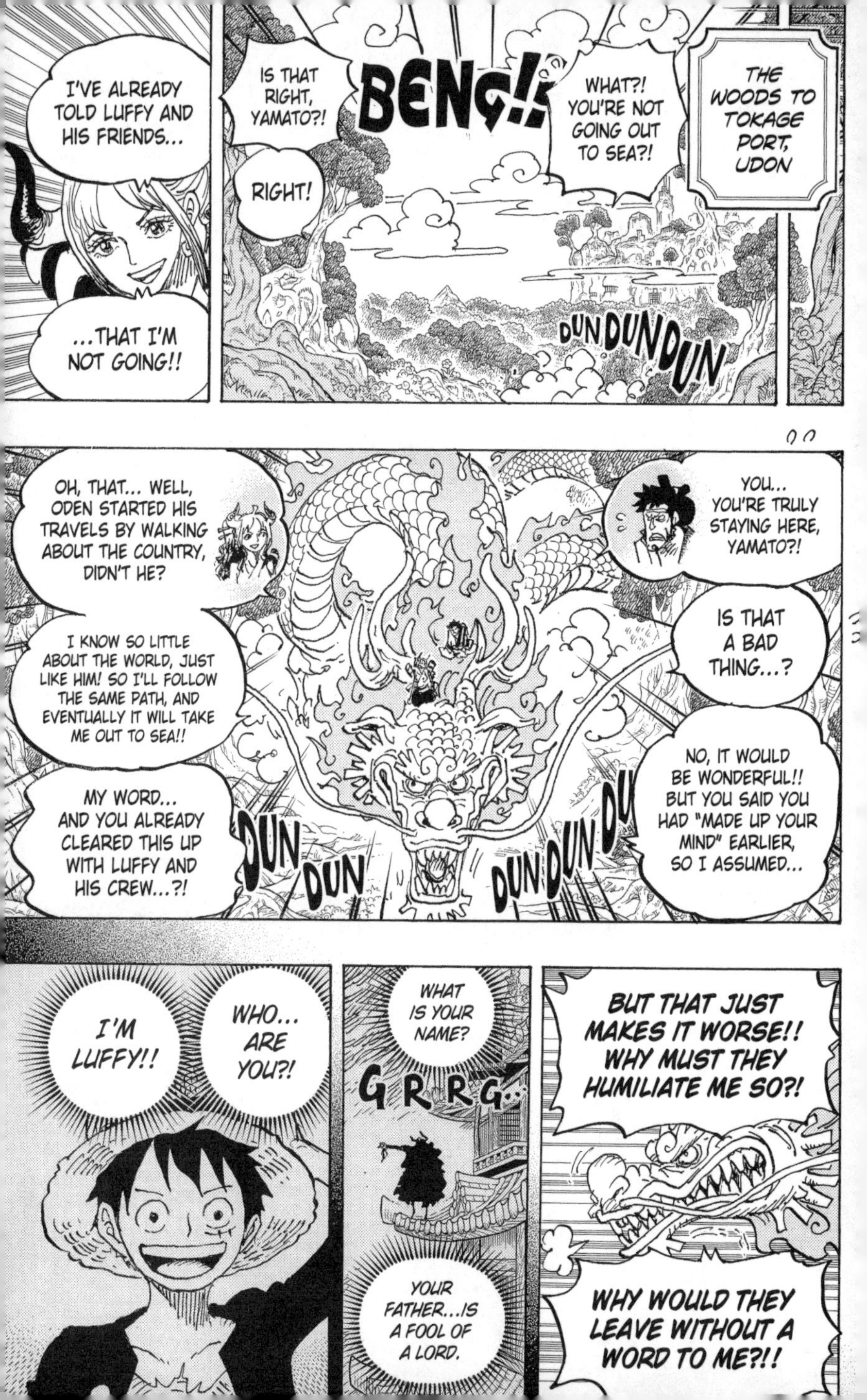
THE WOODS TO TOKAGE PORT, UDON
WHAT?! YOU'RE NOT GOING OUT TO SEA?!
BENG!!
IS THAT RIGHT, YAMATO?!
RIGHT!
DUN DUN DUN DUN
I'VE ALREADY TOLD LUFFY AND HIS FRIENDS...
...THAT I'M NOT GOING!!
YOU... YOU'RE TRULY STAYING HERE, YAMATO?!
IS THAT A BAD THING...?
NO, IT WOULD BE WONDERFUL!! BUT YOU SAID YOU HAD "MADE UP YOUR MIND" EARLIER, SO I ASSUMED...
DUN DUN DUN DU
OH, THAT... WELL, ODEN STARTED HIS TRAVELS BY WALKING ABOUT THE COUNTRY, DIDN'T HE?
I KNOW SO LITTLE ABOUT THE WORLD, JUST LIKE HIM! SO I'LL FOLLOW THE SAME PATH, AND EVENTUALLY IT WILL TAKE ME OUT TO SEA!!
MY WORD... AND YOU ALREADY CLEARED THIS UP WITH LUFFY AND HIS CREW...?!
DUN DUN
BUT THAT JUST MAKES IT WORSE!! WHY MUST THEY HUMILIATE ME SO?!
WHY WOULD THEY LEAVE WITHOUT A WORD TO ME?!!
WHAT IS YOUR NAME?
GRRG..
YOUR FATHER...IS A FOOL OF A LORD.
WHO... ARE YOU?!
I'M LUFFY!!

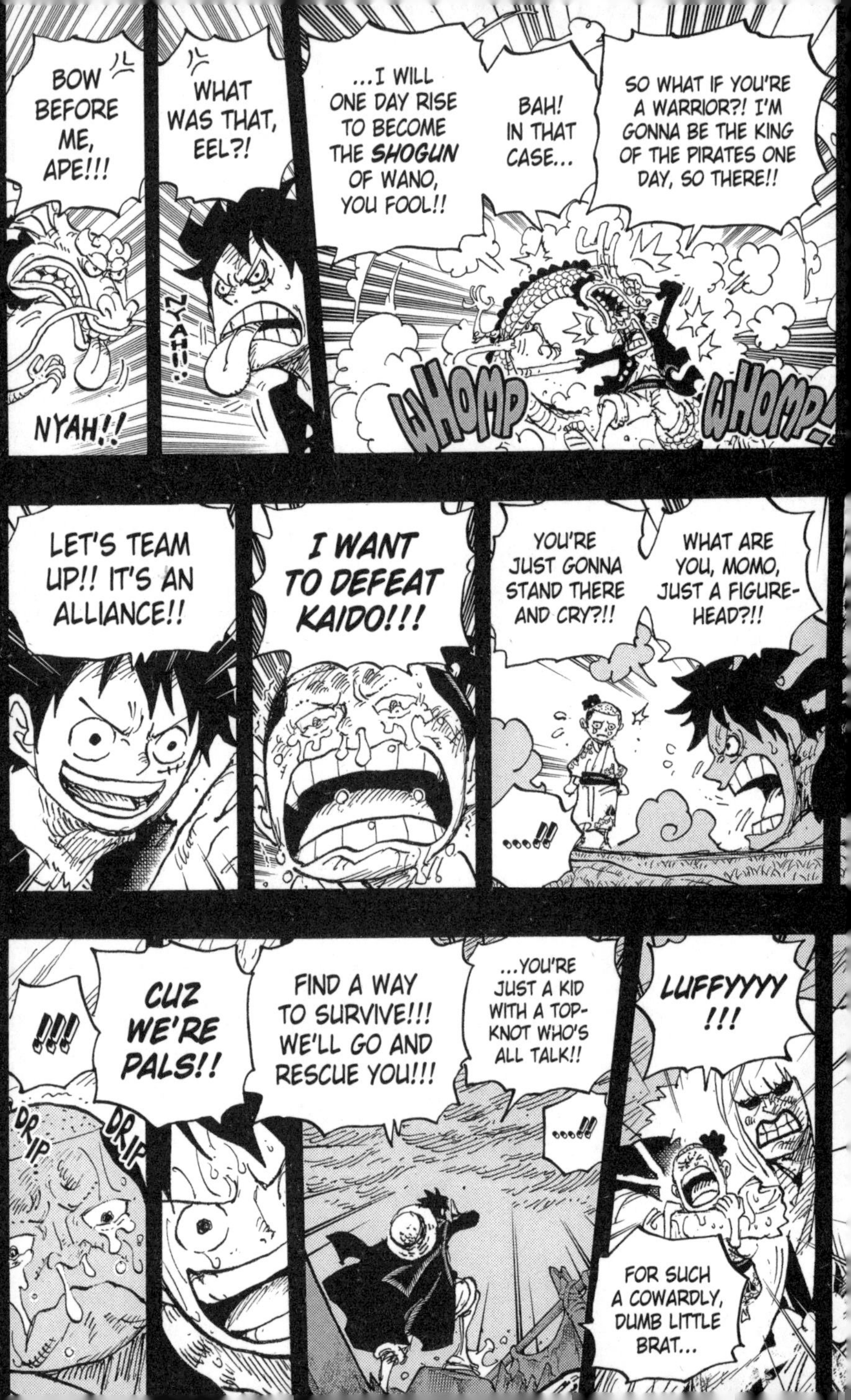
SO WHAT IF YOU'RE A WARRIOR?! I'M GONNA BE THE KING OF THE PIRATES ONE DAY, SO THERE!!
BAH! IN THAT CASE...
...I WILL ONE DAY RISE TO BECOME THE SHOGUN OF WANO, YOU FOOL!!
WHOMP
WHOMP!
WHAT WAS THAT, EEL?!
NYAHI!!
BOW BEFORE ME, APE!!!
NYAH!!
WHAT ARE YOU, MOMO, JUST A FIGURE-HEAD?!!
YOU'RE JUST GONNA STAND THERE AND CRY?!!
...!!
I WANT TO DEFEAT KAIDO!!!
LET'S TEAM UP!! IT'S AN ALLIANCE!!
LUFFYYYY!!!
FOR SUCH A COWARDLY, DUMB LITTLE BRAT...
...YOU'RE JUST A KID WITH A TOP-KNOT WHO'S ALL TALK!!
...!!
FIND A WAY TO SURVIVE!!! WE'LL GO AND RESCUE YOU!!!
CUZ WE'RE PALS!!
DRIP
!!!
DRIP

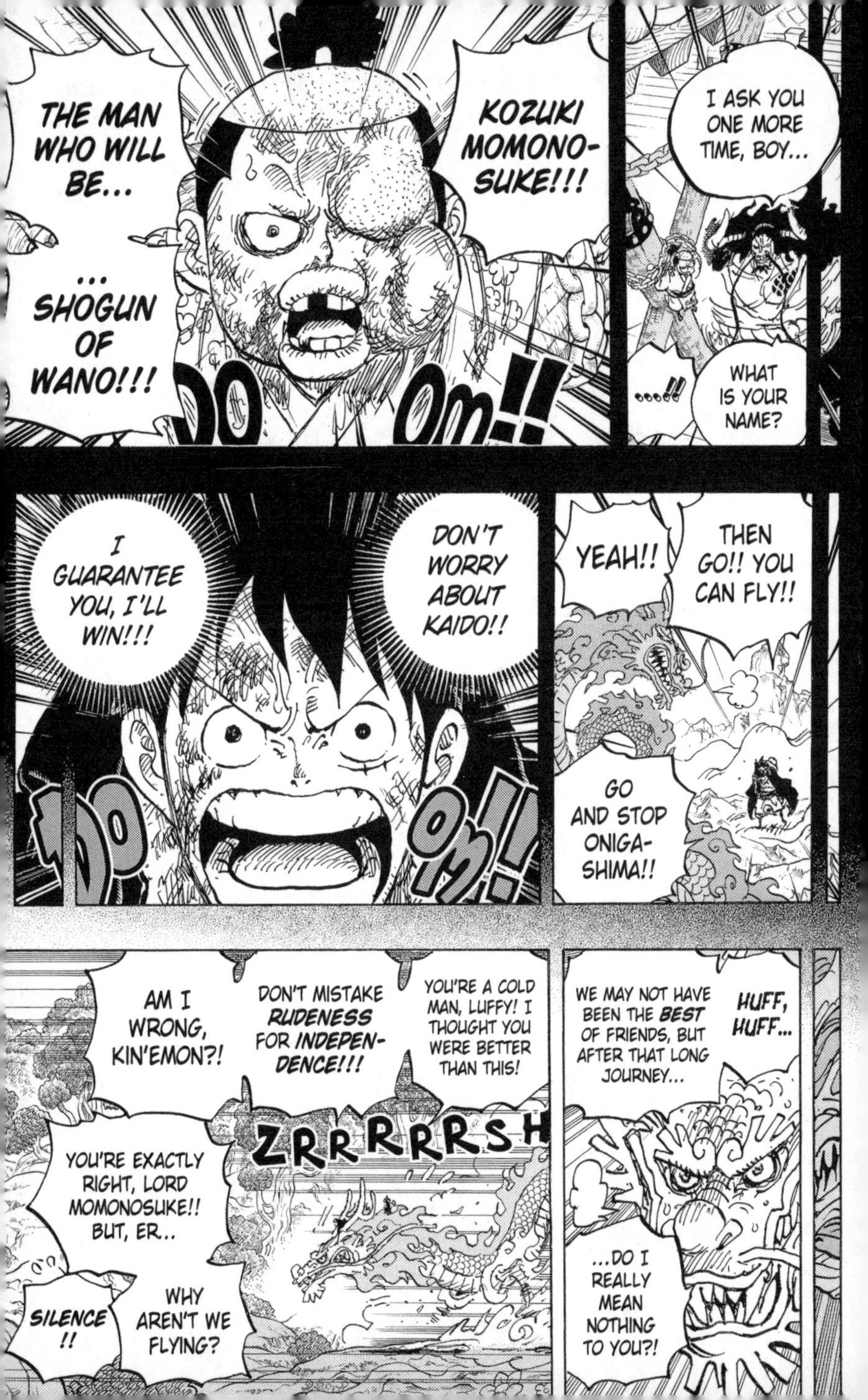

I ASK YOU ONE MORE TIME, BOY...
WHAT IS YOUR NAME?
...!!
KOZUKI MOMONOSUKE!!!
THE MAN WHO WILL BE...
...SHOGUN OF WANO!!!
DOOM!!
THEN GO!! YOU CAN FLY!!
YEAH!!
GO AND STOP ONIGASHIMA!!
DON'T WORRY ABOUT KAIDO!!
I GUARANTEE YOU, I'LL WIN!!!
DOOM!!
HUFF, HUFF...
WE MAY NOT HAVE BEEN THE *BEST* OF FRIENDS, BUT AFTER THAT LONG JOURNEY...
...DO I REALLY MEAN NOTHING TO YOU?!
YOU'RE A COLD MAN, LUFFY! I THOUGHT YOU WERE BETTER THAN THIS!
DON'T MISTAKE *RUDENESS* FOR *INDEPENDENCE!!!*
AM I WRONG, KIN'EMON?!
ZRRRRRSH
YOU'RE EXACTLY RIGHT, LORD MOMONOSUKE!! BUT, ER...
WHY AREN'T WE FLYING?
SILENCE!!

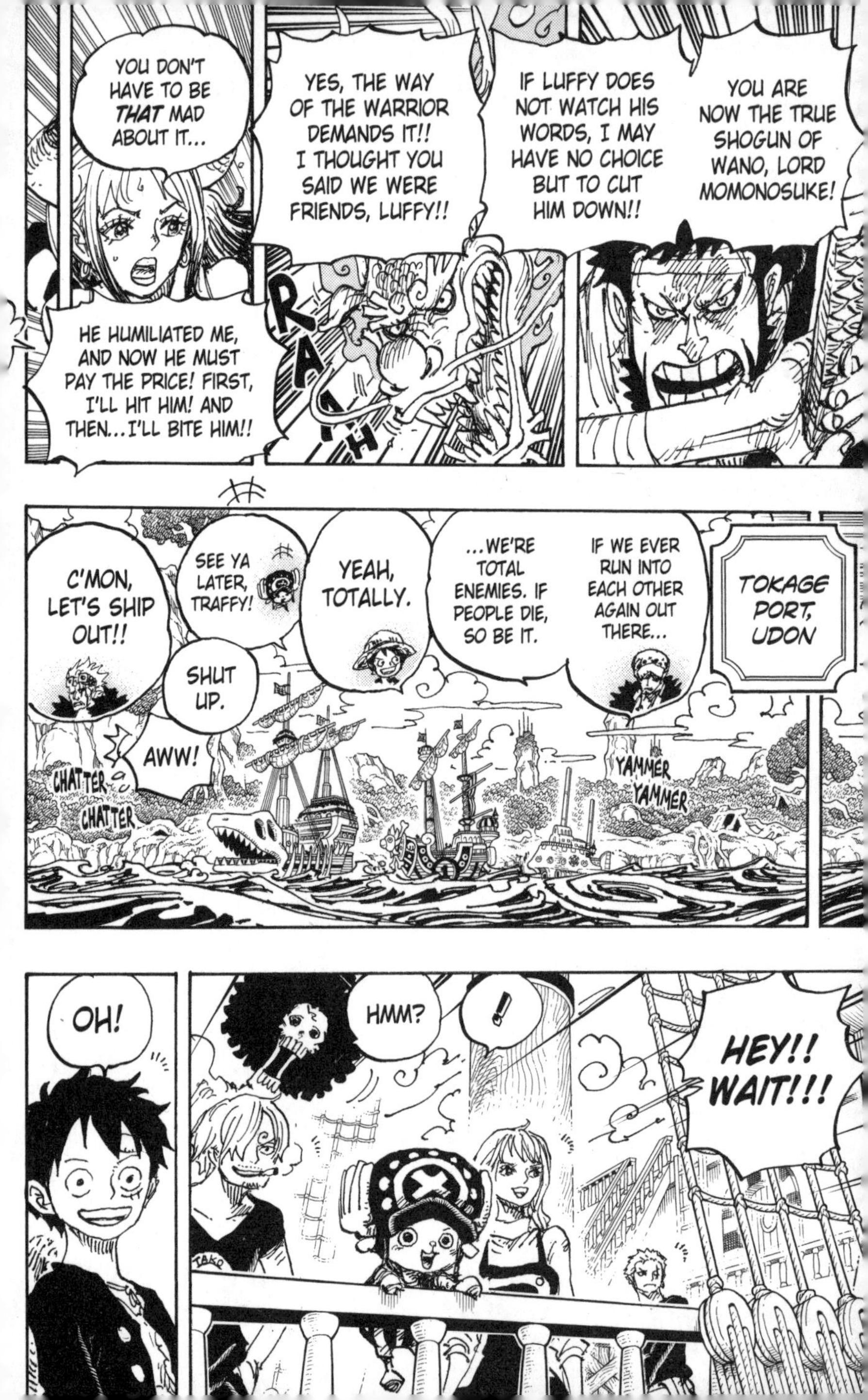
YOU ARE NOW THE TRUE SHOGUN OF WANO, LORD MOMONOSUKE!
IF LUFFY DOES NOT WATCH HIS WORDS, I MAY HAVE NO CHOICE BUT TO CUT HIM DOWN!!
YES, THE WAY OF THE WARRIOR DEMANDS IT!! I THOUGHT YOU SAID WE WERE FRIENDS, LUFFY!!
RAAH
YOU DON'T HAVE TO BE *THAT* MAD ABOUT IT...
HE HUMILIATED ME, AND NOW HE MUST PAY THE PRICE! FIRST, I'LL HIT HIM! AND THEN...I'LL BITE HIM!!
TOKAGE PORT, UDON
IF WE EVER RUN INTO EACH OTHER AGAIN OUT THERE...
...WE'RE TOTAL ENEMIES. IF PEOPLE DIE, SO BE IT.
YEAH, TOTALLY.
YAMMER YAMMER
SEE YA LATER, TRAFFY!
SHUT UP.
C'MON, LET'S SHIP OUT!!
AWW!
CHATTER CHATTER
HEY!! WAIT!!!
!
HMM?
OH!

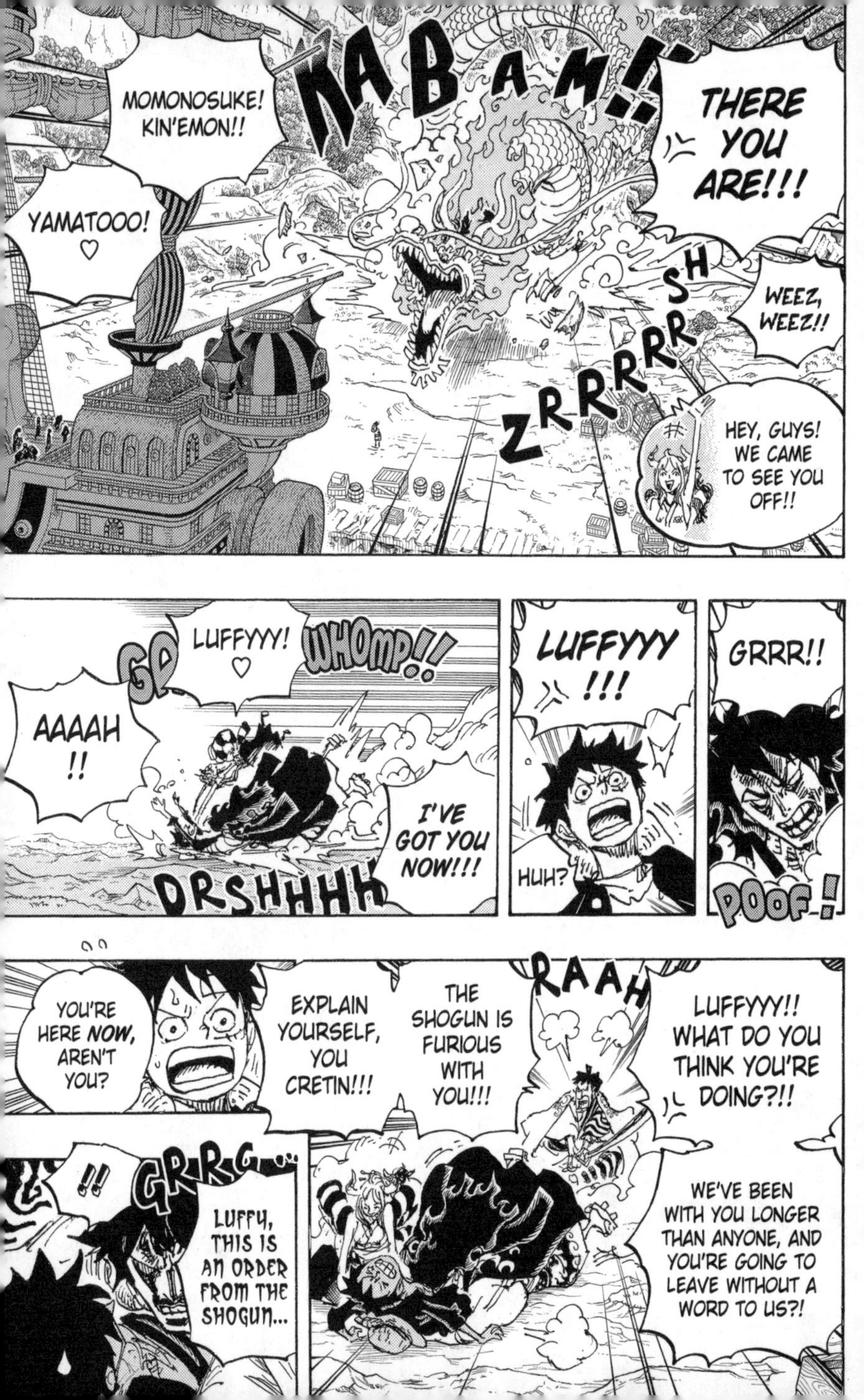
THERE YOU ARE!!!
KABAM!!
MOMONOSUKE! KIN'EMON!!
WEEZ, WEEZ!!
ZRRRRRSH
YAMATOOO! ♡
HEY, GUYS! WE CAME TO SEE YOU OFF!!
GRRR!!
POOF!!
LUFFYYY !!!
HUH?
WHOMP!!
LUFFYYY! ♡
AAAAH !!
I'VE GOT YOU NOW!!!
DRSHHHH
LUFFYYY!! WHAT DO YOU THINK YOU'RE DOING?!!
RAAH
THE SHOGUN IS FURIOUS WITH YOU!!!
EXPLAIN YOURSELF, YOU CRETIN!!!
YOU'RE HERE *NOW*, AREN'T YOU?
WE'VE BEEN WITH YOU LONGER THAN ANYONE, AND YOU'RE GOING TO LEAVE WITHOUT A WORD TO US?!
GRRG...
!!
LUFFY, THIS IS AN ORDER FROM THE SHOGUN...

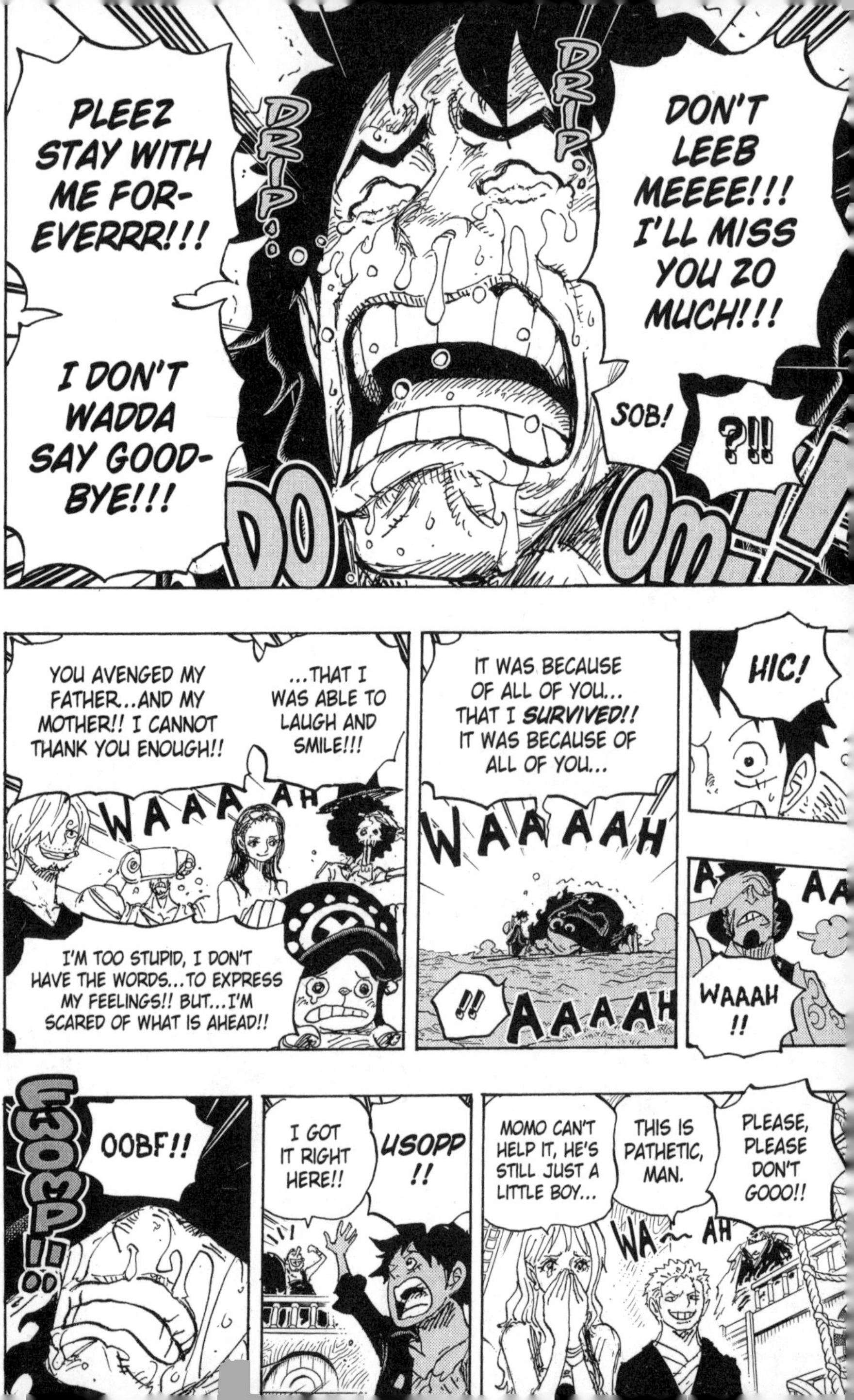

DON'T LEEB MEEEE!!! I'LL MISS YOU ZO MUCH!!!
DRIP.
DRIP.
PLEEZ STAY WITH ME FOR-EVERRR!!!
SOB!
?!!
I DON'T WADDA SAY GOOD-BYE!!!
DOOM!!
HIC!
AA AA
WAAAH !!
IT WAS BECAUSE OF ALL OF YOU... THAT I ***SURVIVED!!*** IT WAS BECAUSE OF ALL OF YOU...
WAAAAAH
AAAAH
!!
...THAT I WAS ABLE TO LAUGH AND SMILE!!!
YOU AVENGED MY FATHER...AND MY MOTHER!! I CANNOT THANK YOU ENOUGH!!
WAAAAH
I'M TOO STUPID, I DON'T HAVE THE WORDS...TO EXPRESS MY FEELINGS!! BUT...I'M SCARED OF WHAT IS AHEAD!!
PLEASE, PLEASE DON'T GOOO!!
THIS IS PATHETIC, MAN.
MOMO CAN'T HELP IT, HE'S STILL JUST A LITTLE BOY...
WA~AH
USOPP !!
I GOT IT RIGHT HERE!!
OOBF!!
FWOMP!!

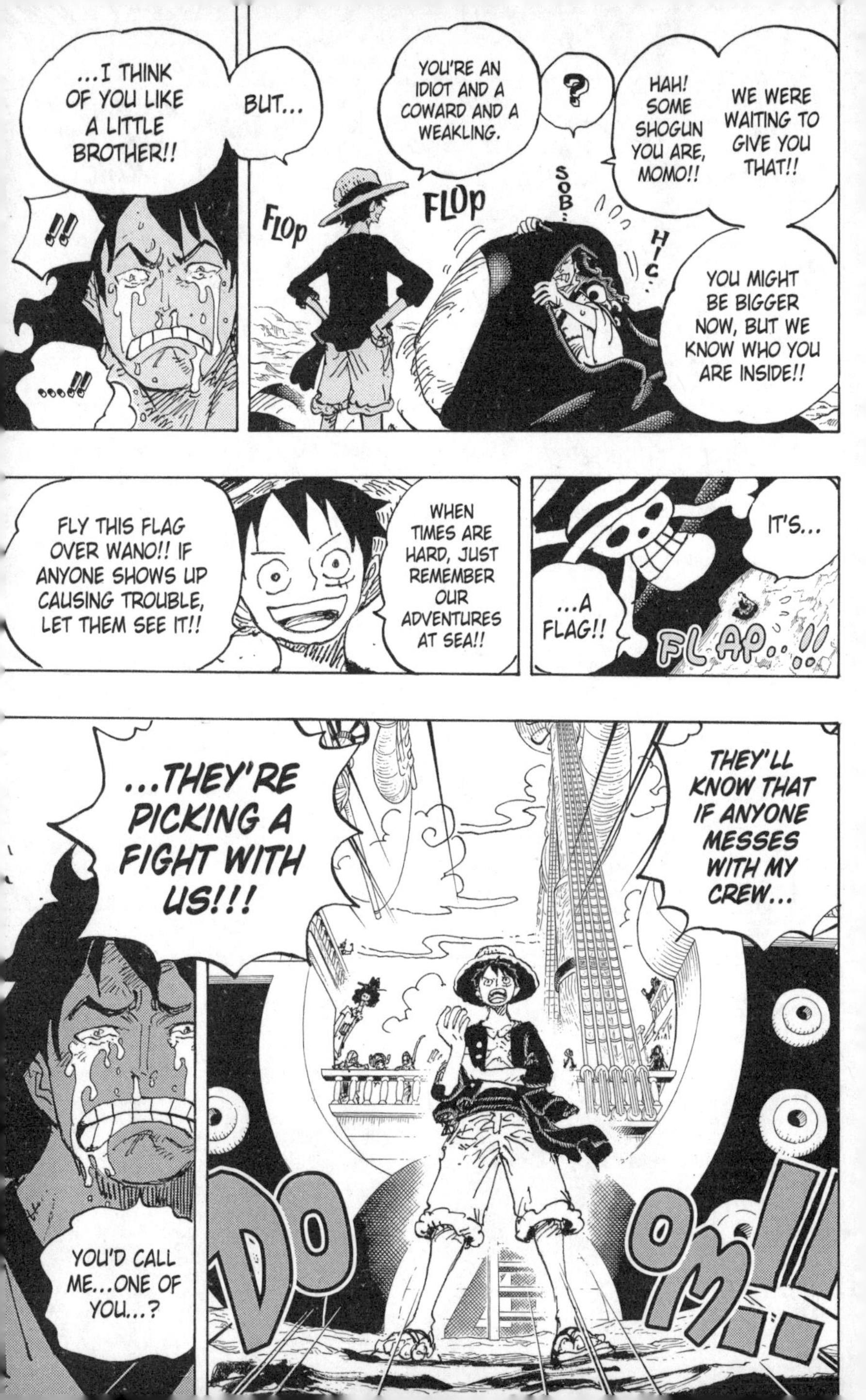
YOU'RE AN IDIOT AND A COWARD AND A WEAKLING.
?
HAH! SOME SHOGUN YOU ARE, MOMO!!
WE WERE WAITING TO GIVE YOU THAT!!
FLOP
FLOP
SOB...
HIC...
YOU MIGHT BE BIGGER NOW, BUT WE KNOW WHO YOU ARE INSIDE!!
BUT...
...I THINK OF YOU LIKE A LITTLE BROTHER!!
!!
....!!
IT'S...
...A FLAG!!
FLAP..!!
FLY THIS FLAG OVER WANO!! IF ANYONE SHOWS UP CAUSING TROUBLE, LET THEM SEE IT!!
WHEN TIMES ARE HARD, JUST REMEMBER OUR ADVENTURES AT SEA!!
THEY'LL KNOW THAT IF ANYONE MESSES WITH MY CREW...
...THEY'RE PICKING A FIGHT WITH US!!!
DOOM!!
YOU'D CALL ME...ONE OF YOU...?

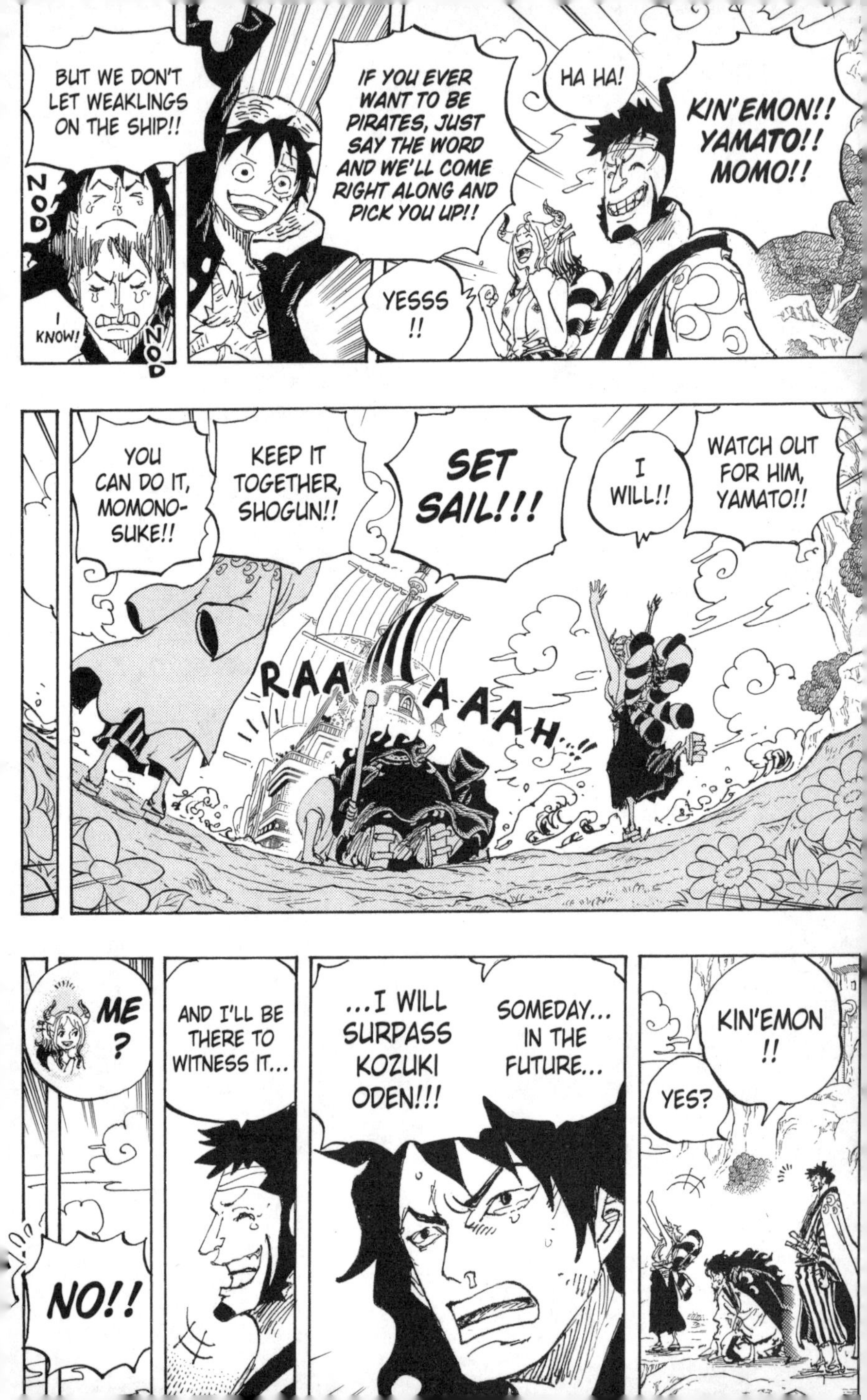
KIN'EMON!! YAMATO!! MOMO!!
HA HA!
IF YOU EVER WANT TO BE PIRATES, JUST SAY THE WORD AND WE'LL COME RIGHT ALONG AND PICK YOU UP!!
YESSS !!
BUT WE DON'T LET WEAKLINGS ON THE SHIP!!
NOD
I KNOW!
NOD
WATCH OUT FOR HIM, YAMATO!!
I WILL!!
SET SAIL!!!
KEEP IT TOGETHER, SHOGUN!!
YOU CAN DO IT, MOMONO-SUKE!!
RAAAAAAH...!!
KIN'EMON !!
YES?
SOMEDAY... IN THE FUTURE...
...I WILL SURPASS KOZUKI ODEN!!!
AND I'LL BE THERE TO WITNESS IT...
ME ?
NO!!

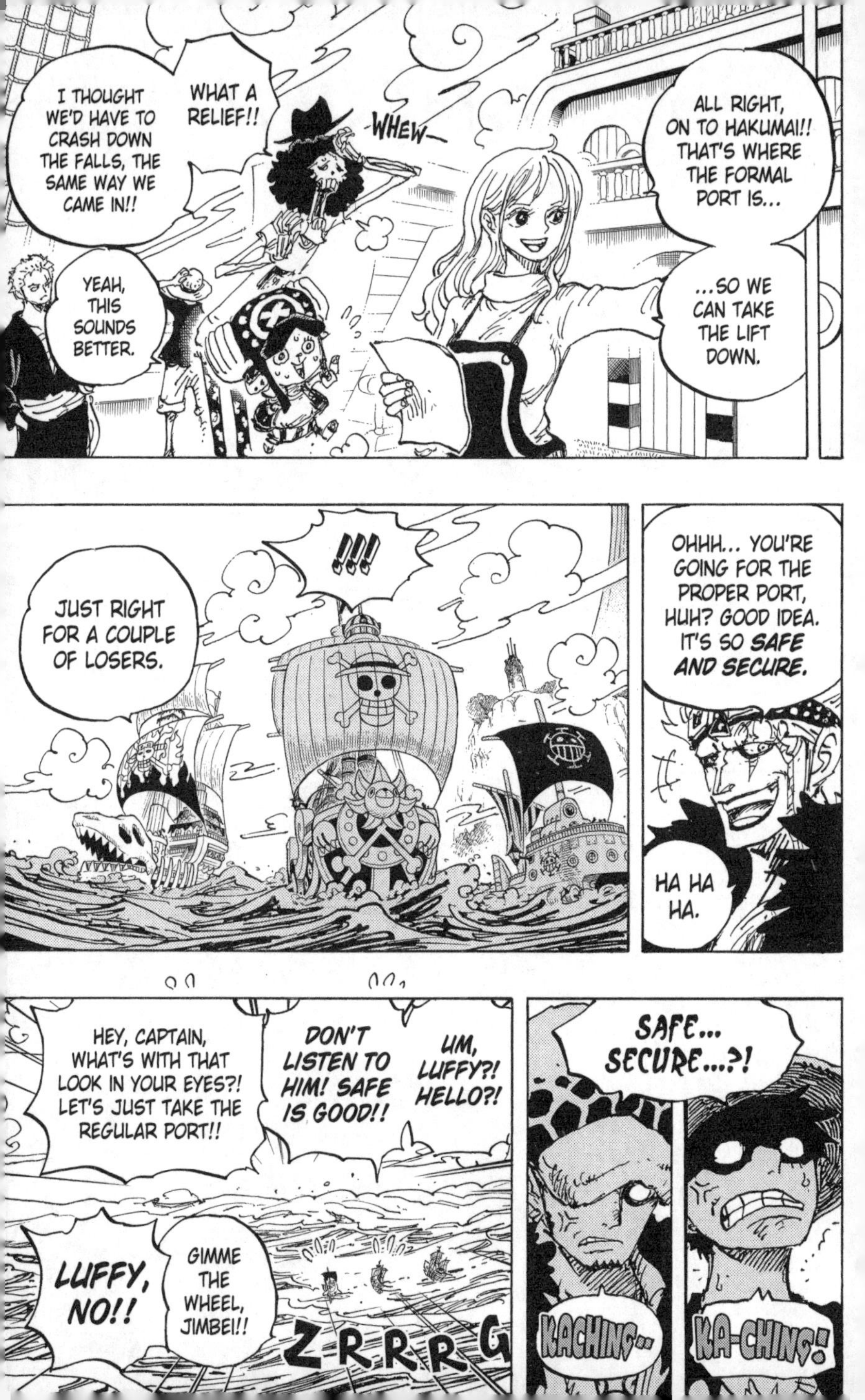
ALL RIGHT, ON TO HAKUMAI!! THAT'S WHERE THE FORMAL PORT IS...
...SO WE CAN TAKE THE LIFT DOWN.
WHAT A RELIEF!!
-WHEW-
I THOUGHT WE'D HAVE TO CRASH DOWN THE FALLS, THE SAME WAY WE CAME IN!!
YEAH, THIS SOUNDS BETTER.
OHHH... YOU'RE GOING FOR THE PROPER PORT, HUH? GOOD IDEA. IT'S SO SAFE AND SECURE.
HA HA HA.
!!!
JUST RIGHT FOR A COUPLE OF LOSERS.
SAFE... SECURE...?!
KA-CHING!
KACHING..
UM, LUFFY?! HELLO?!
DON'T LISTEN TO HIM! SAFE IS GOOD!!
HEY, CAPTAIN, WHAT'S WITH THAT LOOK IN YOUR EYES?! LET'S JUST TAKE THE REGULAR PORT!!
GIMME THE WHEEL, JIMBEI!!
LUFFY, NO!!
Z-R-R-R-G

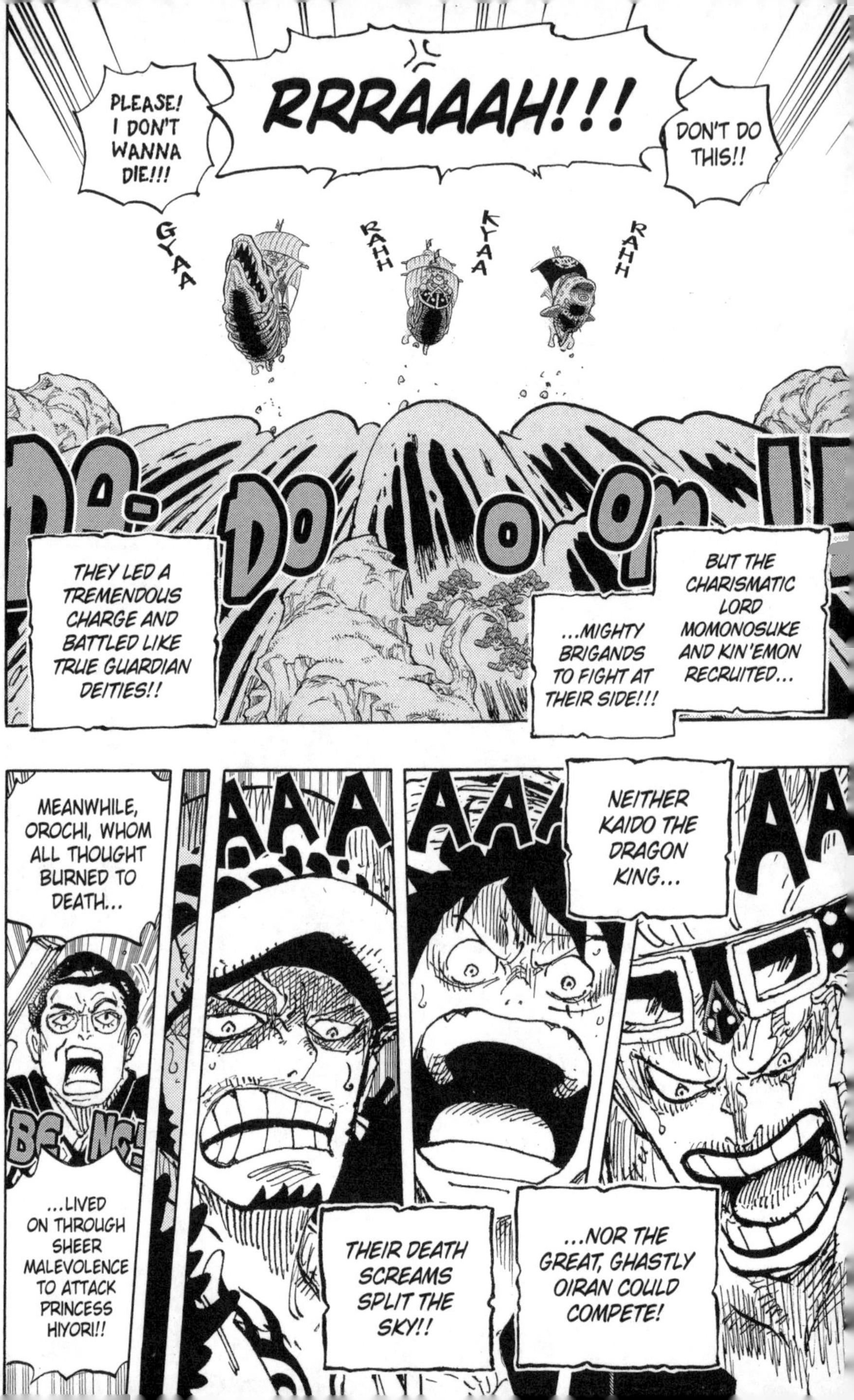
DON'T DO THIS!!
RRRAAAH!!!
PLEASE! I DON'T WANNA DIE!!!
RAHH
KYAA
RAHH
GYAA
BUT THE CHARISMATIC LORD MOMONOSUKE AND KIN'EMON RECRUITED...
...MIGHTY BRIGANDS TO FIGHT AT THEIR SIDE!!!
THEY LED A TREMENDOUS CHARGE AND BATTLED LIKE TRUE GUARDIAN DEITIES!!
NEITHER KAIDO THE DRAGON KING...
AAAAAAAA
...NOR THE GREAT, GHASTLY OIRAN COULD COMPETE!
THEIR DEATH SCREAMS SPLIT THE SKY!!
MEANWHILE, OROCHI, WHOM ALL THOUGHT BURNED TO DEATH...
...LIVED ON THROUGH SHEER MALEVOLENCE TO ATTACK PRINCESS HIYORI!!

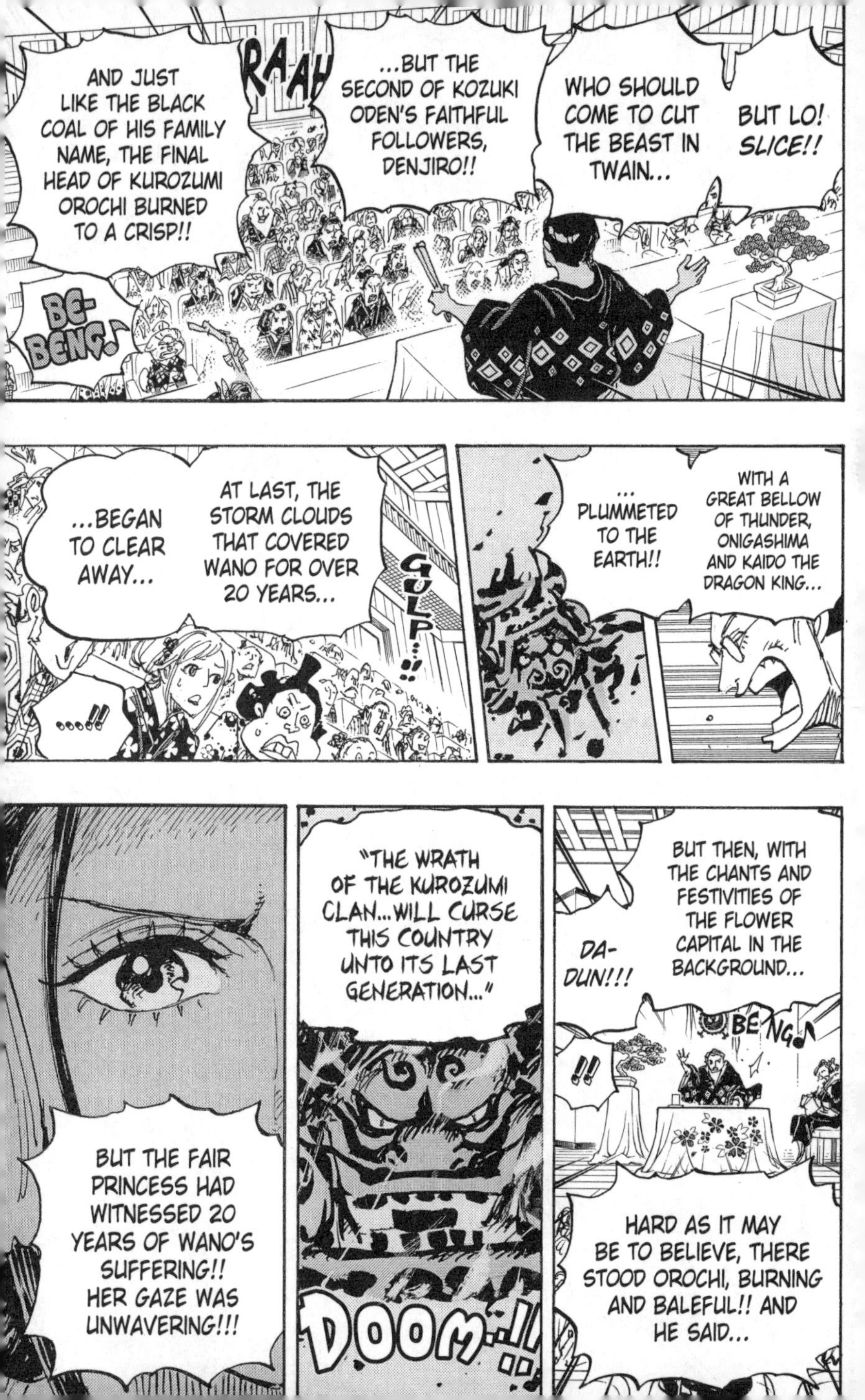
BUT LO! SLICE!!
WHO SHOULD COME TO CUT THE BEAST IN TWAIN...
...BUT THE SECOND OF KOZUKI ODEN'S FAITHFUL FOLLOWERS, DENJIRO!!
RAAH
AND JUST LIKE THE BLACK COAL OF HIS FAMILY NAME, THE FINAL HEAD OF KUROZUMI OROCHI BURNED TO A CRISP!!
BE-BENG♪
WITH A GREAT BELLOW OF THUNDER, ONIGASHIMA AND KAIDO THE DRAGON KING...
...PLUMMETED TO THE EARTH!!
AT LAST, THE STORM CLOUDS THAT COVERED WANO FOR OVER 20 YEARS...
GULP...!!
...BEGAN TO CLEAR AWAY...
...!!
BUT THEN, WITH THE CHANTS AND FESTIVITIES OF THE FLOWER CAPITAL IN THE BACKGROUND...
DA-DUN!!!
BENG♪
!!
HARD AS IT MAY BE TO BELIEVE, THERE STOOD OROCHI, BURNING AND BALEFUL!! AND HE SAID...
"THE WRATH OF THE KUROZUMI CLAN...WILL CURSE THIS COUNTRY UNTO ITS LAST GENERATION..."
DOOM...!!
BUT THE FAIR PRINCESS HAD WITNESSED 20 YEARS OF WANO'S SUFFERING!! HER GAZE WAS UNWAVERING!!!

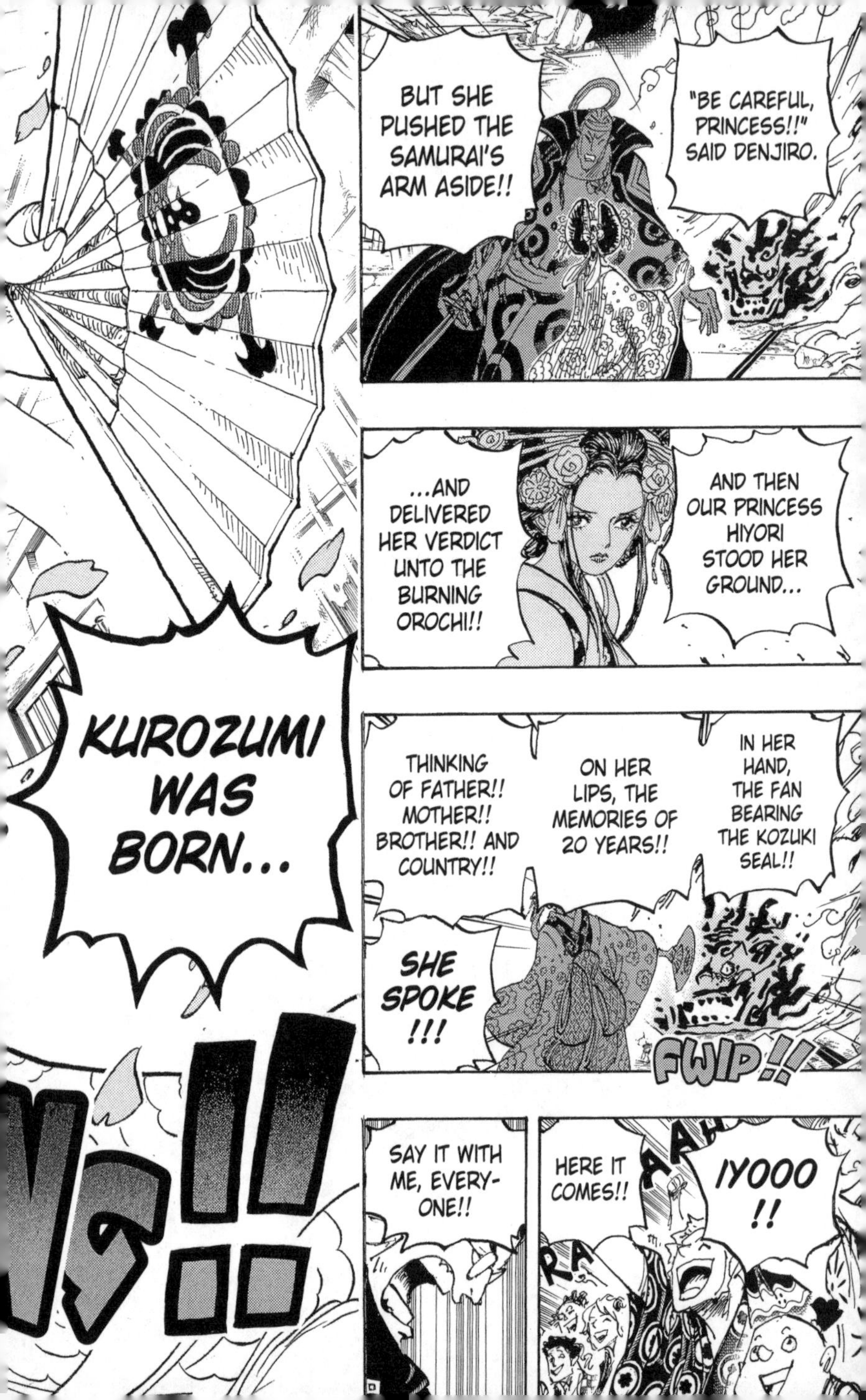

"BE CAREFUL, PRINCESS!!" SAID DENJIRO.
BUT SHE PUSHED THE SAMURAI'S ARM ASIDE!!
AND THEN OUR PRINCESS HIYORI STOOD HER GROUND...
...AND DELIVERED HER VERDICT UNTO THE BURNING OROCHI!!
IN HER HAND, THE FAN BEARING THE KOZUKI SEAL!!
ON HER LIPS, THE MEMORIES OF 20 YEARS!!
THINKING OF FATHER!! MOTHER!! BROTHER!! AND COUNTRY!!
FWIP!!
SHE SPOKE!!!
IYOOO!!
HERE IT COMES!!
SAY IT WITH ME, EVERY-ONE!!
KUROZUMI WAS BORN...

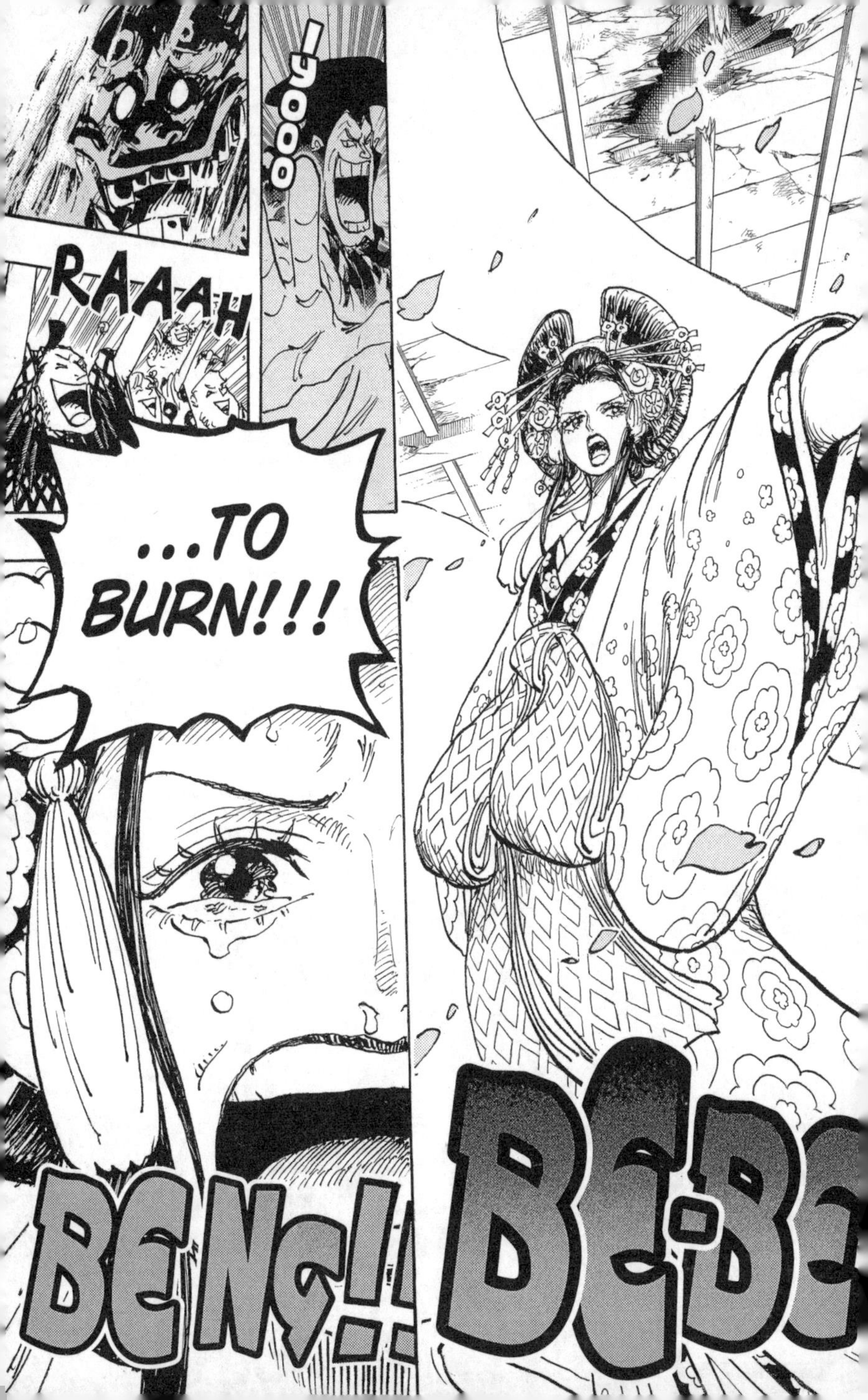
BE-BE
IYOOOO
RAAAH
...TO BURN!!!
BENG!!

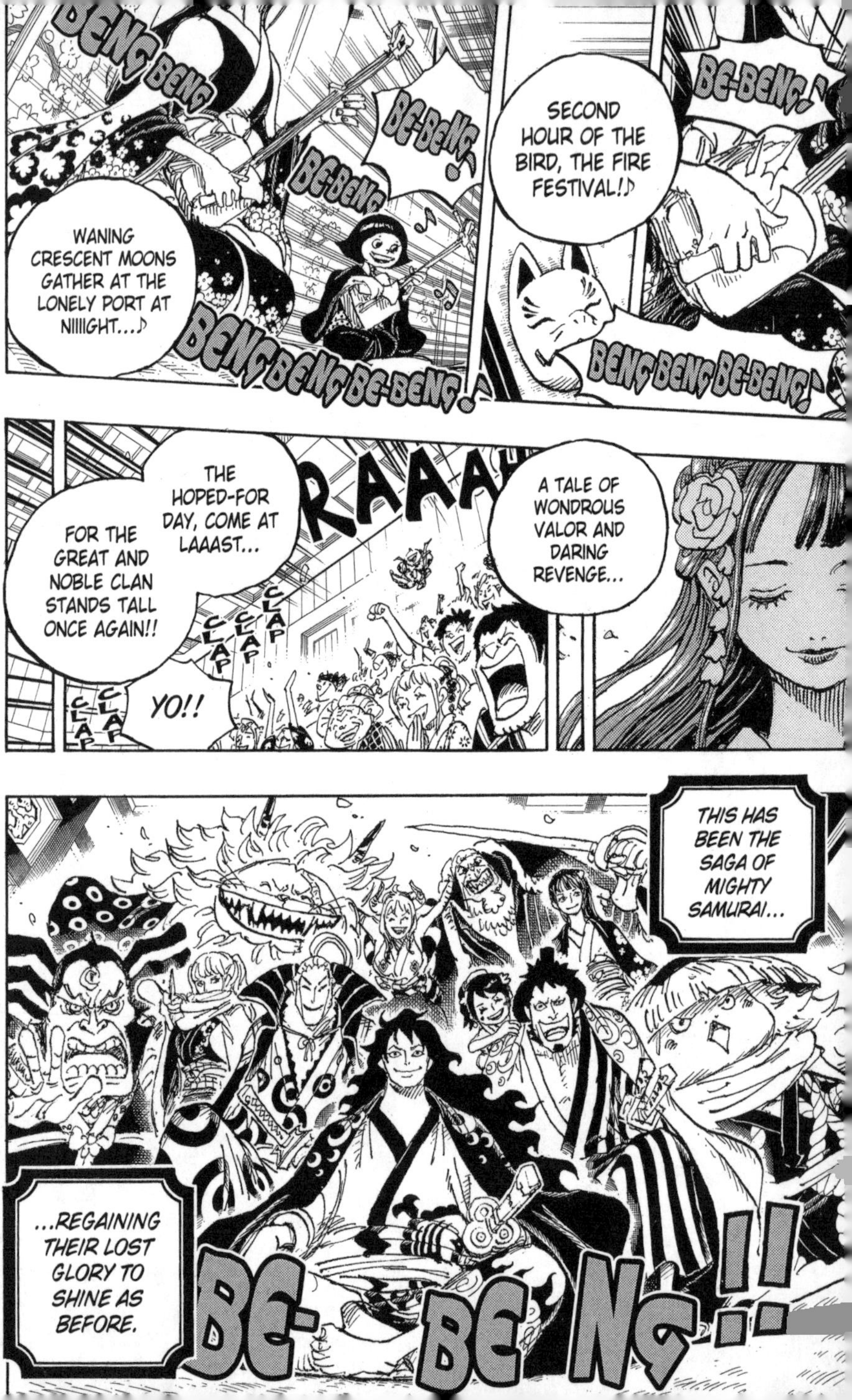
BE-BENG♪
SECOND HOUR OF THE BIRD, THE FIRE FESTIVAL!♪
BENG BENG BE-BENG♪
BENG BENG
BE-BENG♪
BE-BENG
WANING CRESCENT MOONS GATHER AT THE LONELY PORT AT NIIIIGHT...♪
BENG BENG BE-BENG♪
A TALE OF WONDROUS VALOR AND DARING REVENGE...
RAAA
THE HOPED-FOR DAY, COME AT LAAAST...
FOR THE GREAT AND NOBLE CLAN STANDS TALL ONCE AGAIN!!
CLAP CLAP CLAP
CLAP CLAP
YO!!
THIS HAS BEEN THE SAGA OF MIGHTY SAMURAI...
...REGAINING THEIR LOST GLORY TO SHINE AS BEFORE.
BE-BENG!!

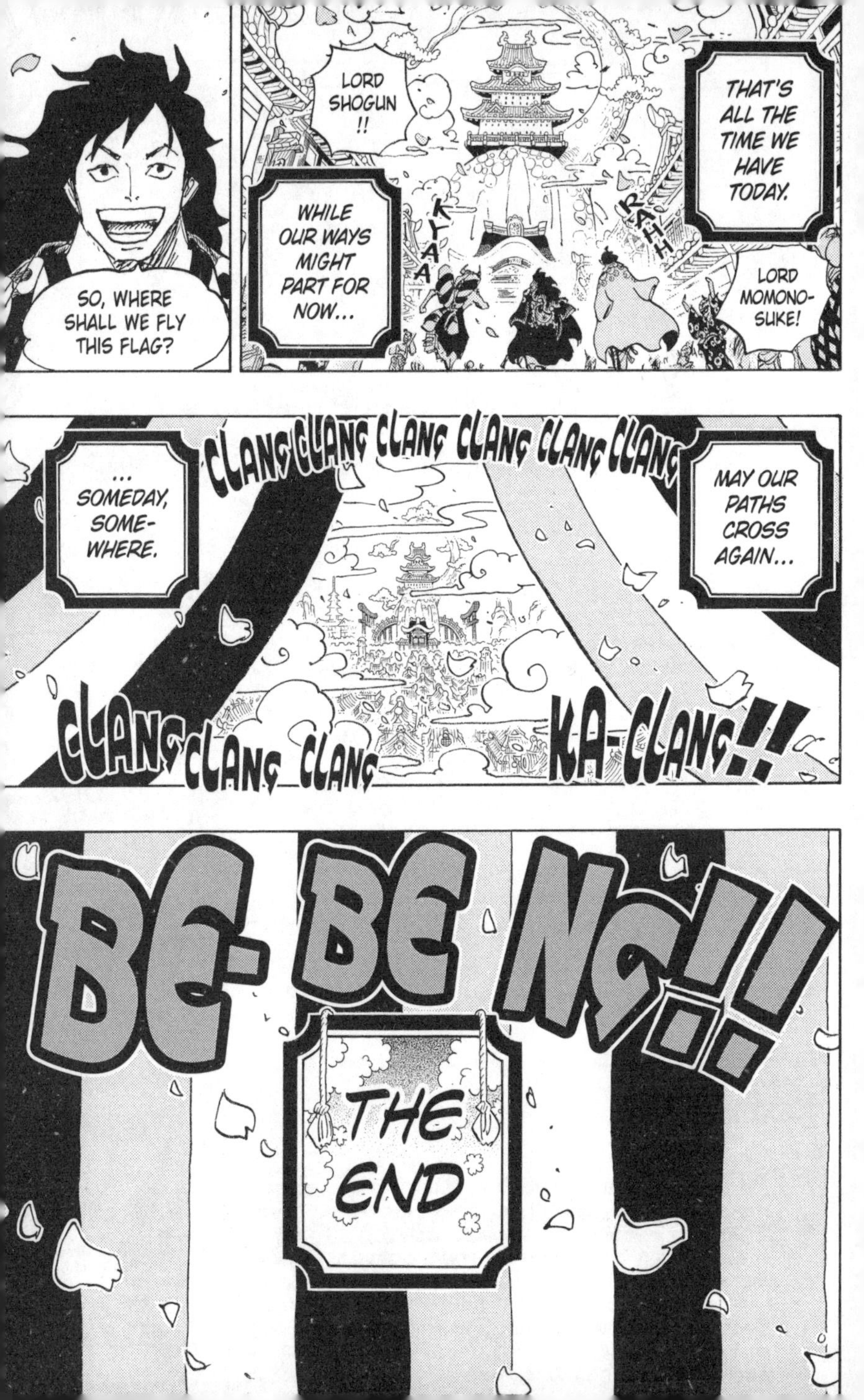
THAT'S ALL THE TIME WE HAVE TODAY.
LORD SHOGUN!!
RAHH
LORD MOMONOSUKE!
WHILE OUR WAYS MIGHT PART FOR NOW...
KYAA
SO, WHERE SHALL WE FLY THIS FLAG?
MAY OUR PATHS CROSS AGAIN...
CLANG CLANG CLANG CLANG CLANG CLANG
...SOMEDAY, SOMEWHERE.
KA-CLANG!!
CLANG CLANG CLANG
BE-BENG!!
THE END

SBS Question Corner

エス
ビー
エス
質問コーナー

(I ♡ OP, Ishikawa)

Q: Hello. I love *One Piece.* I heard the Wano arc is over. It's really sad that the people who ate the failed Devil Fruits can only laugh now, so I was hoping Chopper would make a medicine that cures them before the Straw Hats sail away. It's too sad for Killer that all he does is laugh. Please take care of this, Master Oda.

--Hiromi M.

WHEE

A: Thank you for this very considerate letter. It's really horrible to be unable to mourn, or do anything but laugh, just after your parent has died. But I don't think Chopper has the ability to make that medicine yet. Some things in life you just can't stop, and this is one of them. But honestly, I laughed when the Kid Pirates stuck together and said, "We'll be a cheerful pirate crew" after the sad news about Killer. It's great to be able to look on the bright side of life when things are depressing. I believe in the strength of the people of Wano!!

FWA FWA
FWA!!
YEAH.
FWA FWA
FWA FWA!!

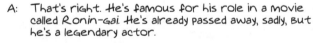

Q: Is Ryokugyu based on the real-life actor Yoshio Harada? He was so cool, my nose started bleeding.

--Match & Takeshi

A: That's right. He's famous for his role in a movie called *Ronin-gai.* He's already passed away, sadly, but he's a legendary actor.

Q: Is there an actor who serves as a model for Director Kurouma (Tensei) of the Naval Bureau of Investigation, who was introduced in chapter 1054?

--Jinbe

A: Tensei is modeled after an actor named Akira Kobayashi. Incidentally, I realized that by putting all of my favorite legendary actors in the upper echelon of the Navy, I was creating a problem--everyone's going to end up with black hair! So that's why I didn't fill in his hair. I'm not making Ryokugyu's hair black either. If you're familiar with my personal film bible, *Battles Without Honor and Humanity,* the scene of Akainu and Kurouma speaking to one another as equals is super exciting! They're awesome!!

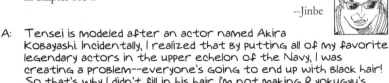

Chapter 1058:
NEW EMPERORS

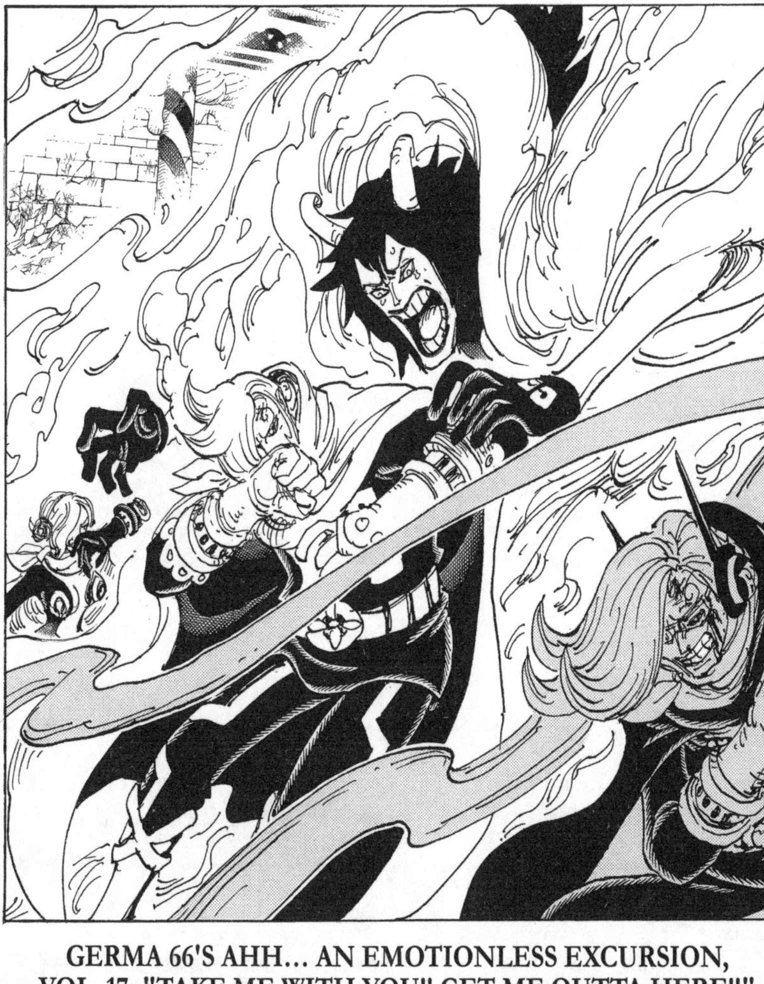

GERMA 66'S AHH... AN EMOTIONLESS EXCURSION,
VOL. 17: "TAKE ME WITH YOU!! GET ME OUTTA HERE!!"

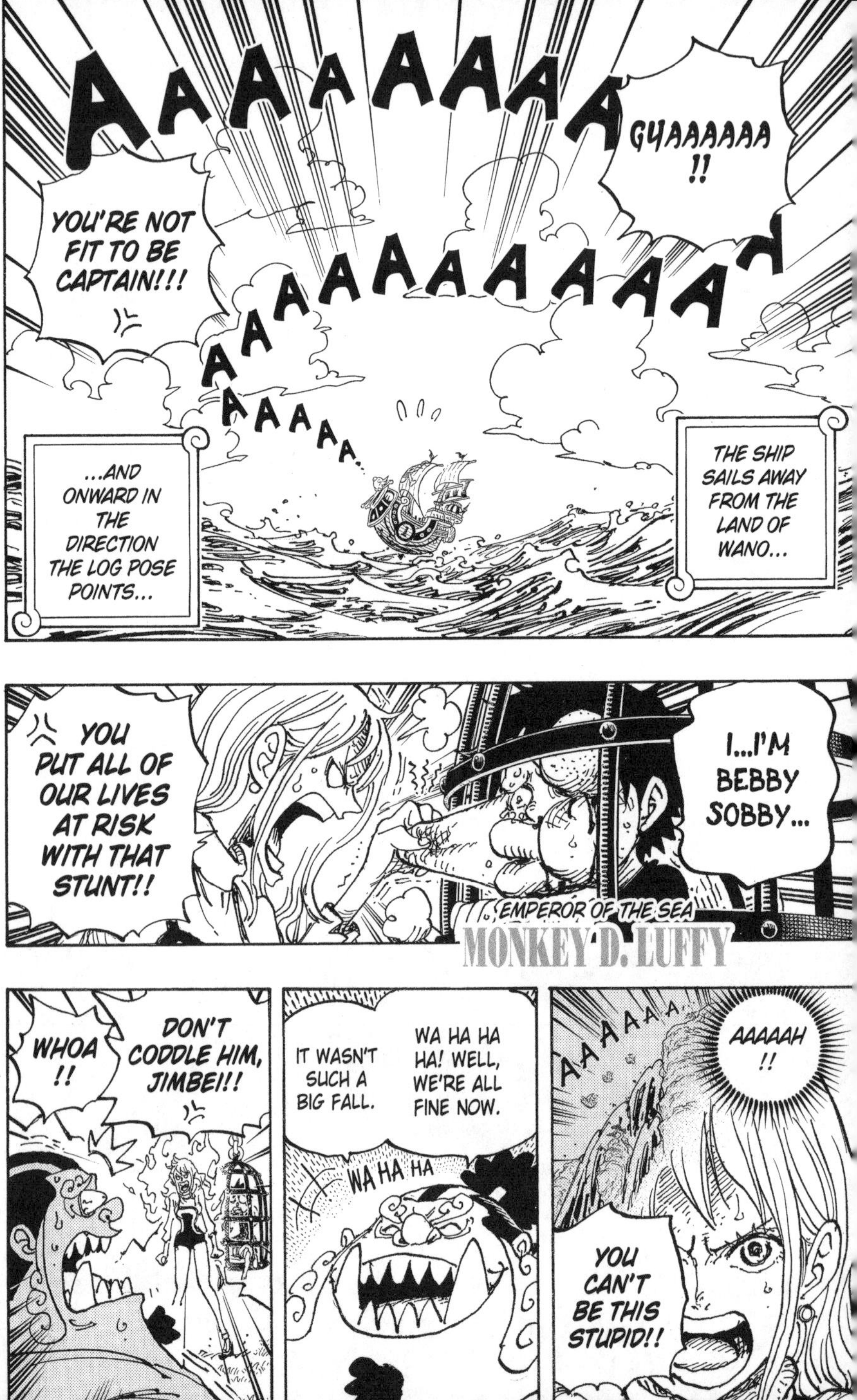
GUAAAAAA!!
AAAAAAAA
YOU'RE NOT FIT TO BE CAPTAIN!!!
AAAAAAAAAAAAAAA...
THE SHIP SAILS AWAY FROM THE LAND OF WANO...
...AND ONWARD IN THE DIRECTION THE LOG POSE POINTS...
I...I'M BEBBY SOBBY...
EMPEROR OF THE SEA
MONKEY D. LUFFY
YOU PUT ALL OF OUR LIVES AT RISK WITH THAT STUNT!!
AAAAAH!!
AAAAAA
YOU CAN'T BE THIS STUPID!!
WA HA HA HA! WELL, WE'RE ALL FINE NOW.
IT WASN'T SUCH A BIG FALL.
WA HA HA
DON'T CODDLE HIM, JIMBEI!!
WHOA!!

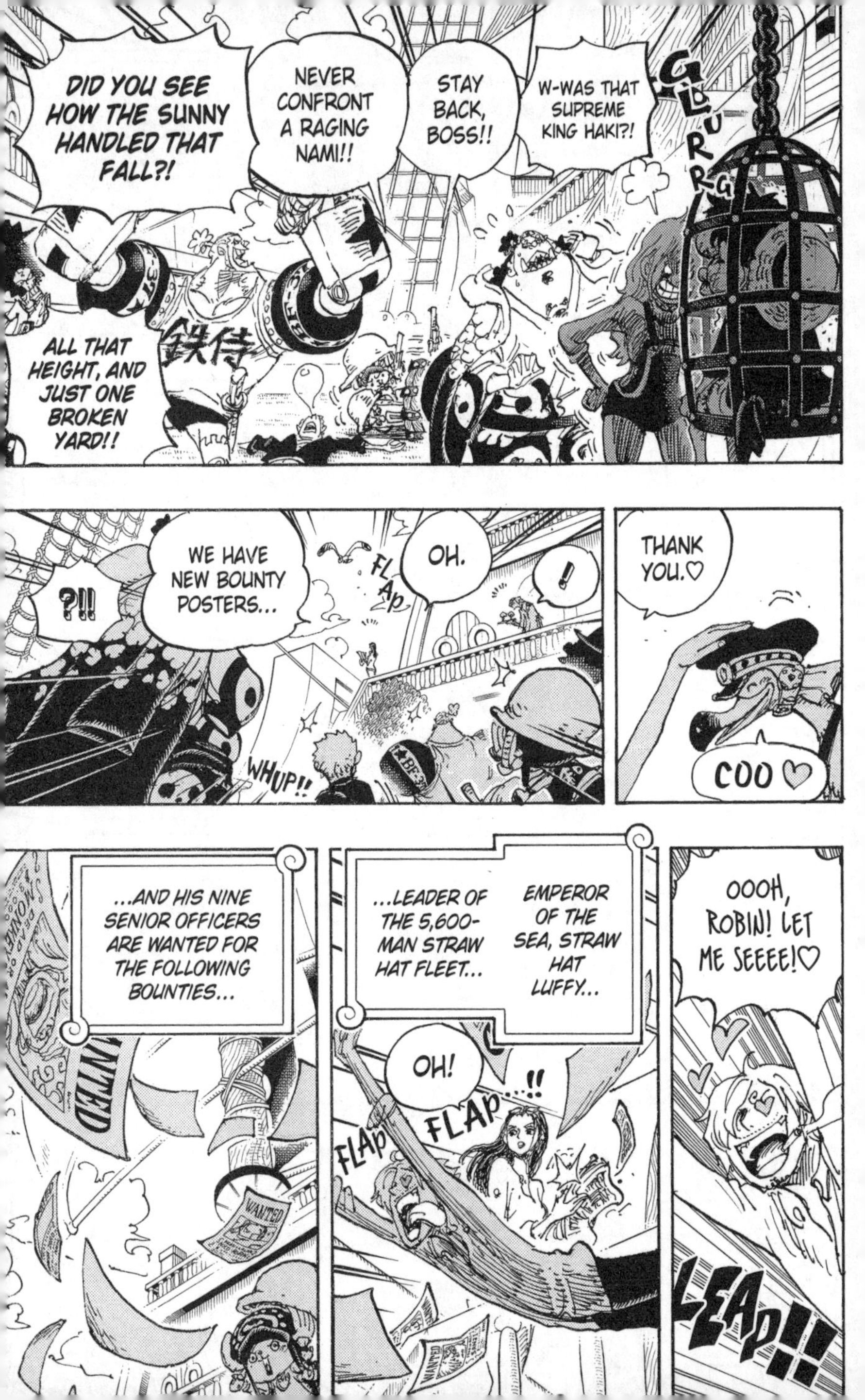
GLURRRG
W-WAS THAT SUPREME KING HAKI?!
STAY BACK, BOSS!!
NEVER CONFRONT A RAGING NAMI!!
DID YOU SEE HOW THE SUNNY HANDLED THAT FALL?!
鉄侍
ALL THAT HEIGHT, AND JUST ONE BROKEN YARD!!
THANK YOU.♡
COO♡
!
OH.
FLAP
WE HAVE NEW BOUNTY POSTERS...
?!!
WHUP!!
OOOH, ROBIN! LET ME SEEEE!♡
LEAP!!
EMPEROR OF THE SEA, STRAW HAT LUFFY...
...LEADER OF THE 5,600-MAN STRAW HAT FLEET...
OH!
FLAP...!!
FLAP
FLAP
...AND HIS NINE SENIOR OFFICERS ARE WANTED FOR THE FOLLOWING BOUNTIES...
WANTED

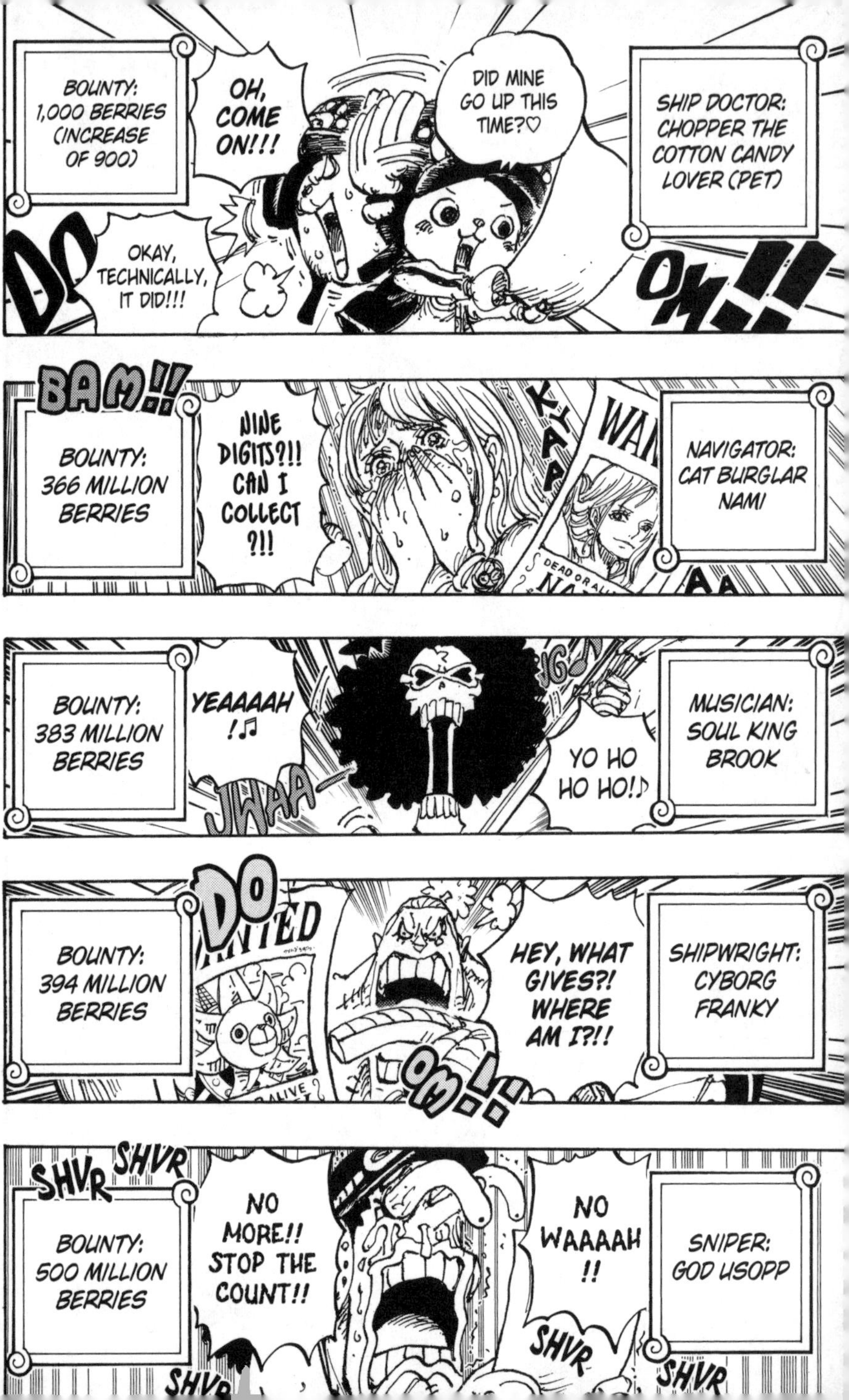
SHIP DOCTOR: CHOPPER THE COTTON CANDY LOVER (PET)
DID MINE GO UP THIS TIME?♡
OM!!
BOUNTY: 1,000 BERRIES (INCREASE OF 900)
OH, COME ON!!!
DO
OKAY, TECHNICALLY, IT DID!!!
NAVIGATOR: CAT BURGLAR NAMI
KYAA
NINE DIGITS?!! CAN I COLLECT ?!!
BAM!!
BOUNTY: 366 MILLION BERRIES
MUSICIAN: SOUL KING BROOK
YO HO HO HO!♪
YEAAAAH !♫
BOUNTY: 383 MILLION BERRIES
JWAA
SHIPWRIGHT: CYBORG FRANKY
HEY, WHAT GIVES?! WHERE AM I?!!
DO
OM!!
BOUNTY: 394 MILLION BERRIES
SNIPER: GOD USOPP
NO WAAAAH !!
SHVR
SHVR
NO MORE!! STOP THE COUNT!!
SHVR
SHVR
BOUNTY: 500 MILLION BERRIES
SHVR

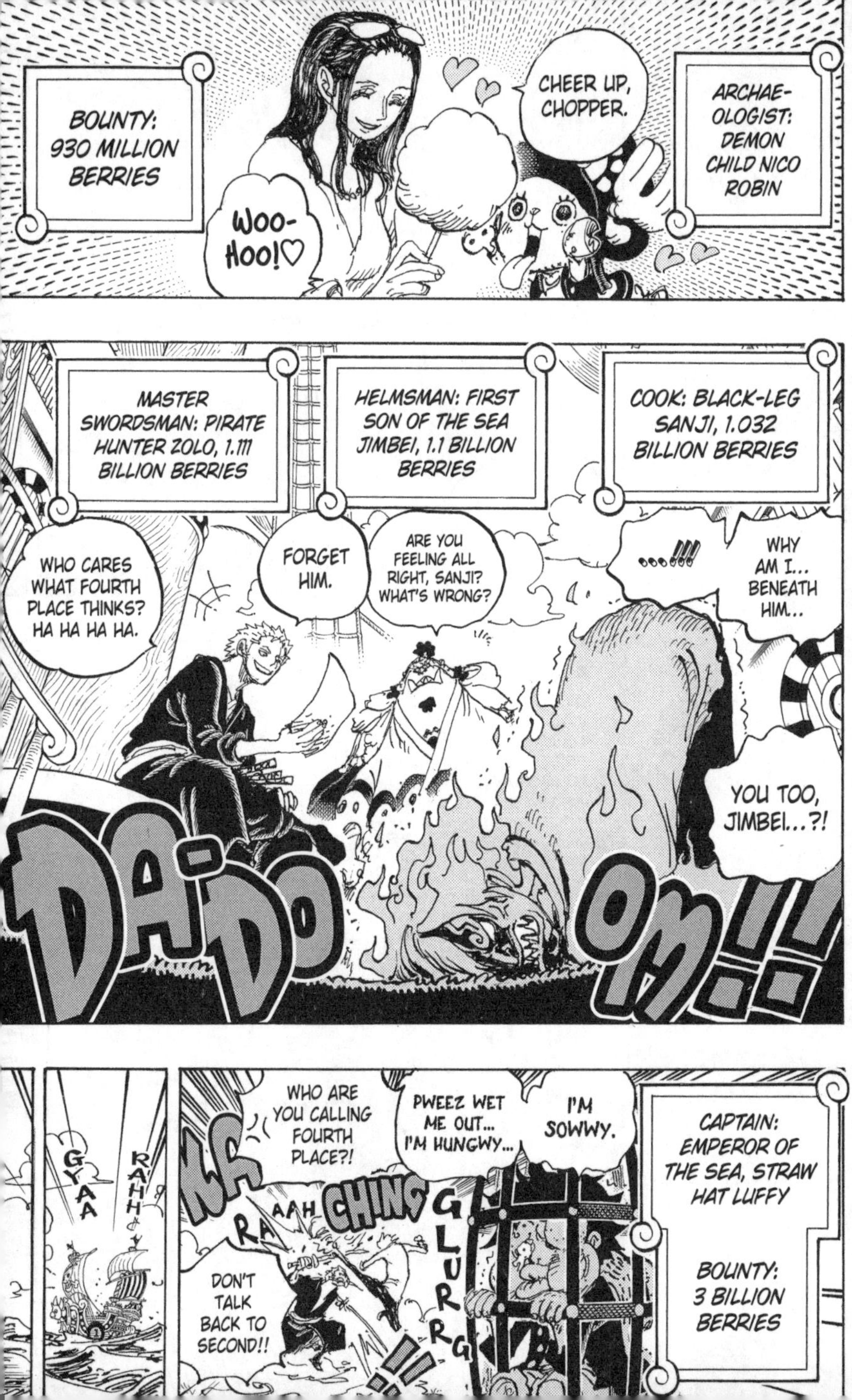
ARCHAE-OLOGIST: DEMON CHILD NICO ROBIN
CHEER UP, CHOPPER.
BOUNTY: 930 MILLION BERRIES
WOO-HOO!♡
COOK: BLACK-LEG SANJI, 1.032 BILLION BERRIES
HELMSMAN: FIRST SON OF THE SEA JIMBEI, 1.1 BILLION BERRIES
MASTER SWORDSMAN: PIRATE HUNTER ZOLO, 1.111 BILLION BERRIES
WHY AM I... BENEATH HIM..
...!!!
ARE YOU FEELING ALL RIGHT, SANJI? WHAT'S WRONG?
FORGET HIM.
WHO CARES WHAT FOURTH PLACE THINKS? HA HA HA HA.
YOU TOO, JIMBEI...?!
DA-DOOM!!
CAPTAIN: EMPEROR OF THE SEA, STRAW HAT LUFFY
BOUNTY: 3 BILLION BERRIES
I'M SOWWY.
PWEEZ WET ME OUT... I'M HUNGWY...
WHO ARE YOU CALLING FOURTH PLACE?!
CHING
GLURRG
RAAAH
DON'T TALK BACK TO SECOND!!
RAHH
GYAA

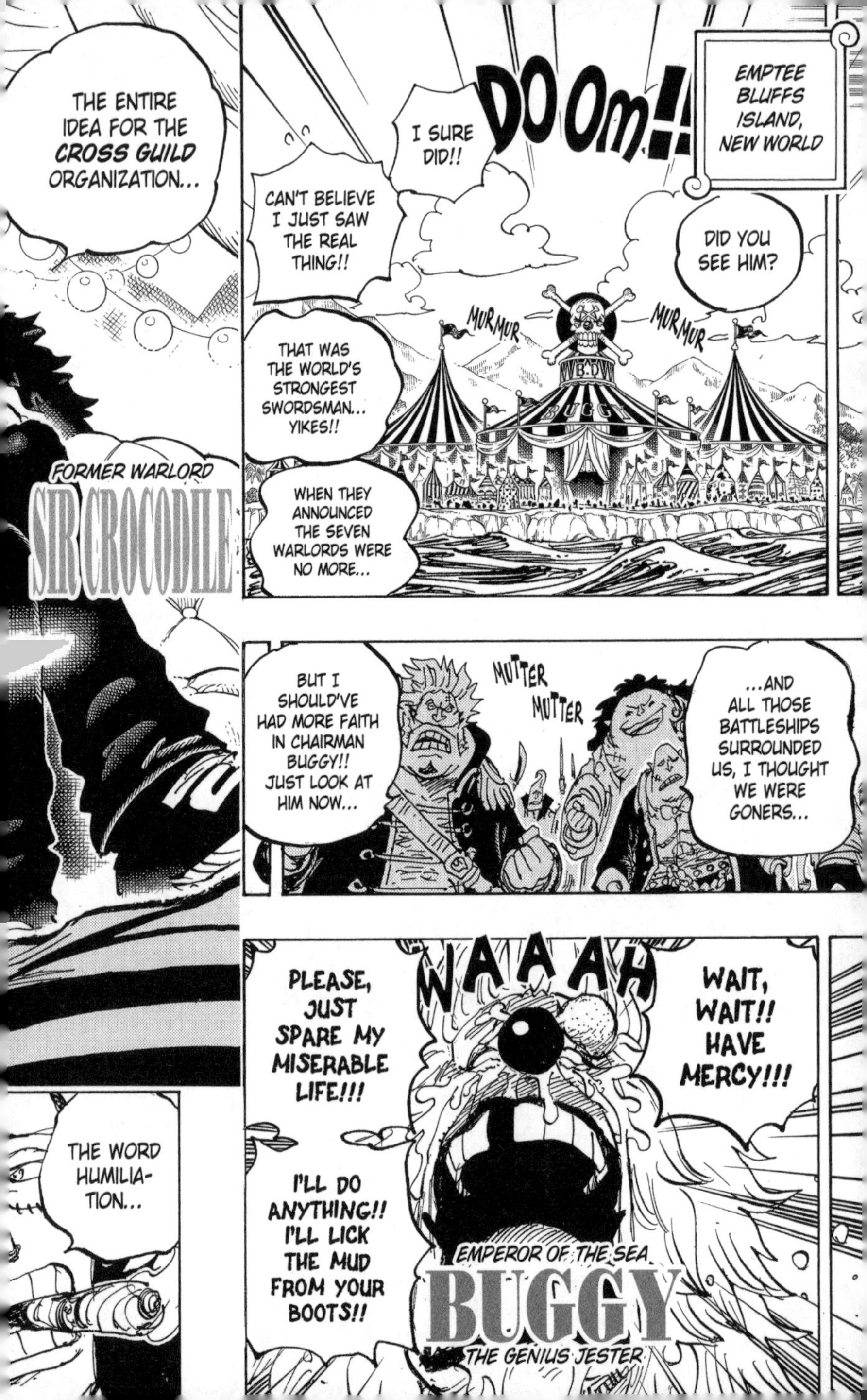
EMPTEE BLUFFS ISLAND, NEW WORLD
DOOM!!
DID YOU SEE HIM?
I SURE DID!!
CAN'T BELIEVE I JUST SAW THE REAL THING!!
MURMUR
MURMUR
B.D
BUGGY
THAT WAS THE WORLD'S STRONGEST SWORDSMAN... YIKES!!
WHEN THEY ANNOUNCED THE SEVEN WARLORDS WERE NO MORE...
...AND ALL THOSE BATTLESHIPS SURROUNDED US, I THOUGHT WE WERE GONERS...
MUTTER MUTTER
BUT I SHOULD'VE HAD MORE FAITH IN CHAIRMAN BUGGY!! JUST LOOK AT HIM NOW...
WAIT, WAIT!! HAVE MERCY!!!
WAAAH
PLEASE, JUST SPARE MY MISERABLE LIFE!!!
I'LL DO ANYTHING!! I'LL LICK THE MUD FROM YOUR BOOTS!!
EMPEROR OF THE SEA
BUGGY
THE GENIUS JESTER
THE ENTIRE IDEA FOR THE CROSS GUILD ORGANIZATION...
FORMER WARLORD
SIR CROCODILE
THE WORD HUMILIATION...

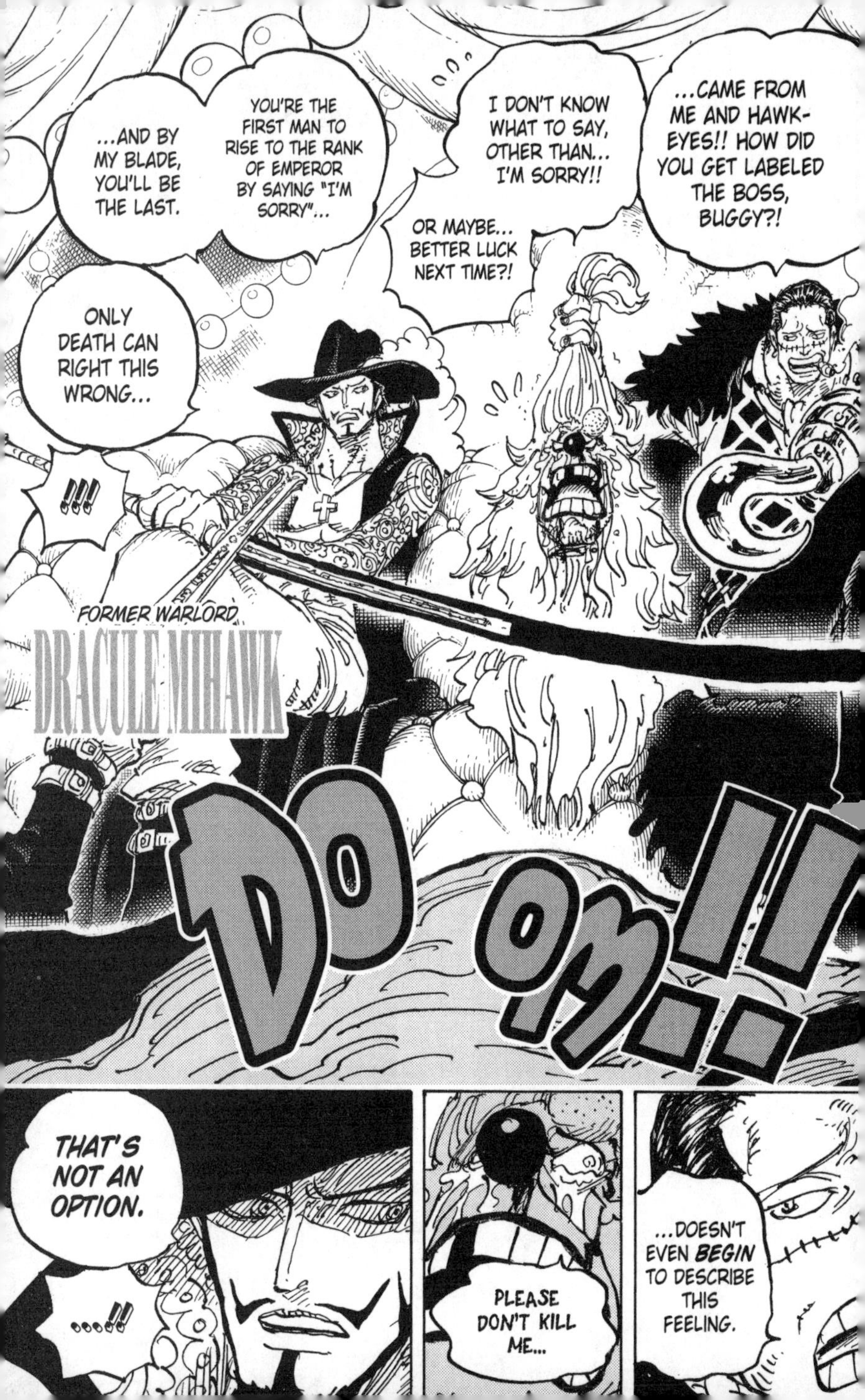
...CAME FROM ME AND HAWK-EYES!! HOW DID YOU GET LABELED THE BOSS, BUGGY?!
I DON'T KNOW WHAT TO SAY, OTHER THAN... I'M SORRY!!
OR MAYBE... BETTER LUCK NEXT TIME?!
YOU'RE THE FIRST MAN TO RISE TO THE RANK OF EMPEROR BY SAYING "I'M SORRY"...
...AND BY MY BLADE, YOU'LL BE THE LAST.
ONLY DEATH CAN RIGHT THIS WRONG...
!!!
FORMER WARLORD
DRACULE MIHAWK
DOOM!!
...DOESN'T EVEN BEGIN TO DESCRIBE THIS FEELING.
PLEASE DON'T KILL ME...
THAT'S NOT AN OPTION.
...!!

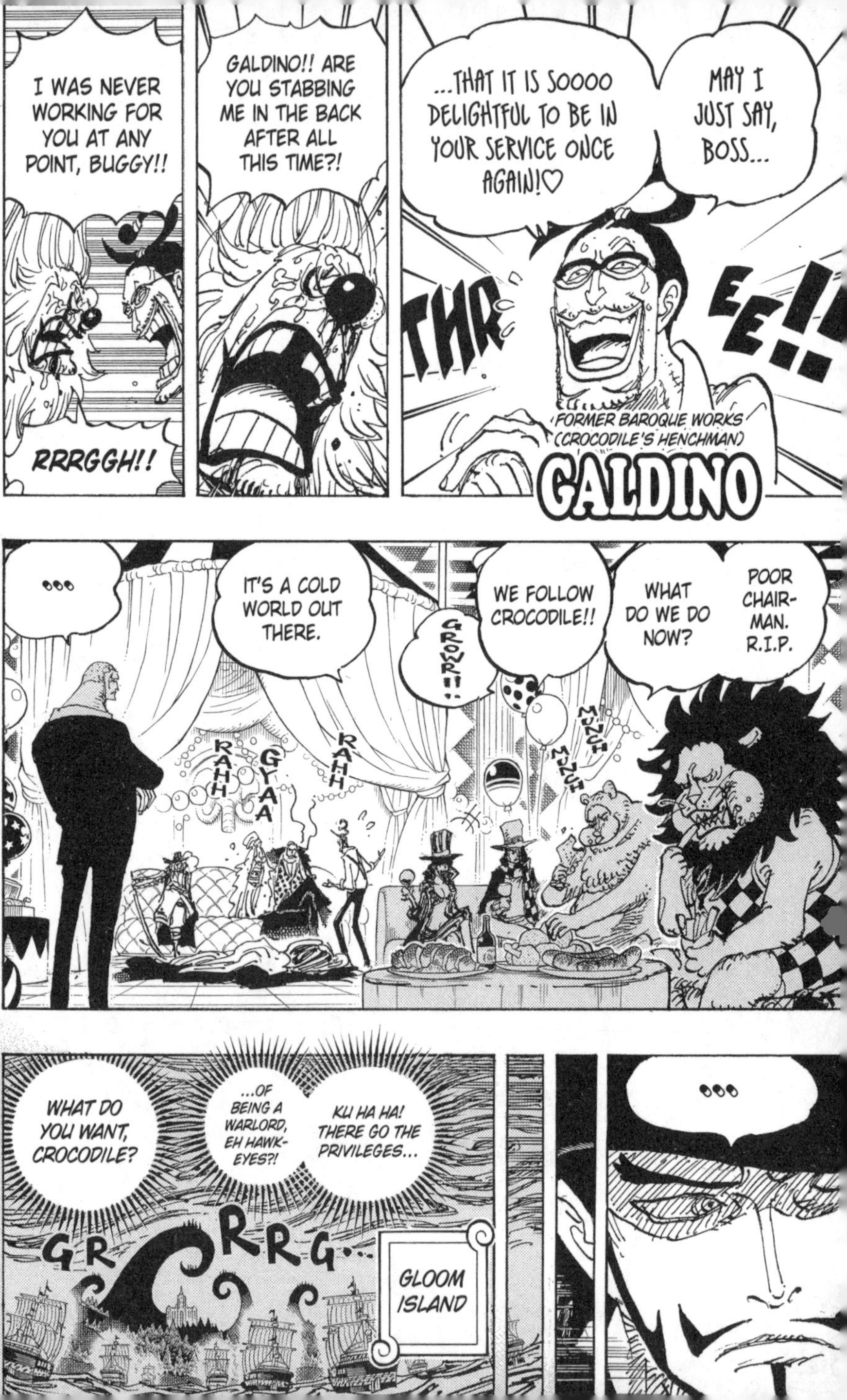
MAY I JUST SAY, BOSS...
...THAT IT IS SOOOO DELIGHTFUL TO BE IN YOUR SERVICE ONCE AGAIN!♡
THR EE!!
FORMER BAROQUE WORKS (CROCODILE'S HENCHMAN)
GALDINO
GALDINO!! ARE YOU STABBING ME IN THE BACK AFTER ALL THIS TIME?!
I WAS NEVER WORKING FOR YOU AT ANY POINT, BUGGY!!
RRRGGH!!
POOR CHAIR-MAN. R.I.P.
WHAT DO WE DO NOW?
WE FOLLOW CROCODILE!!
MUNCH
MUNCH
GROWR!!
IT'S A COLD WORLD OUT THERE.
RAHH
GYAA
RAHH
...
...
KU HA HA! THERE GO THE PRIVILEGES...
...OF BEING A WARLORD, EH HAWK-EYES?!
WHAT DO YOU WANT, CROCODILE?
GRRRG...
GLOOM ISLAND

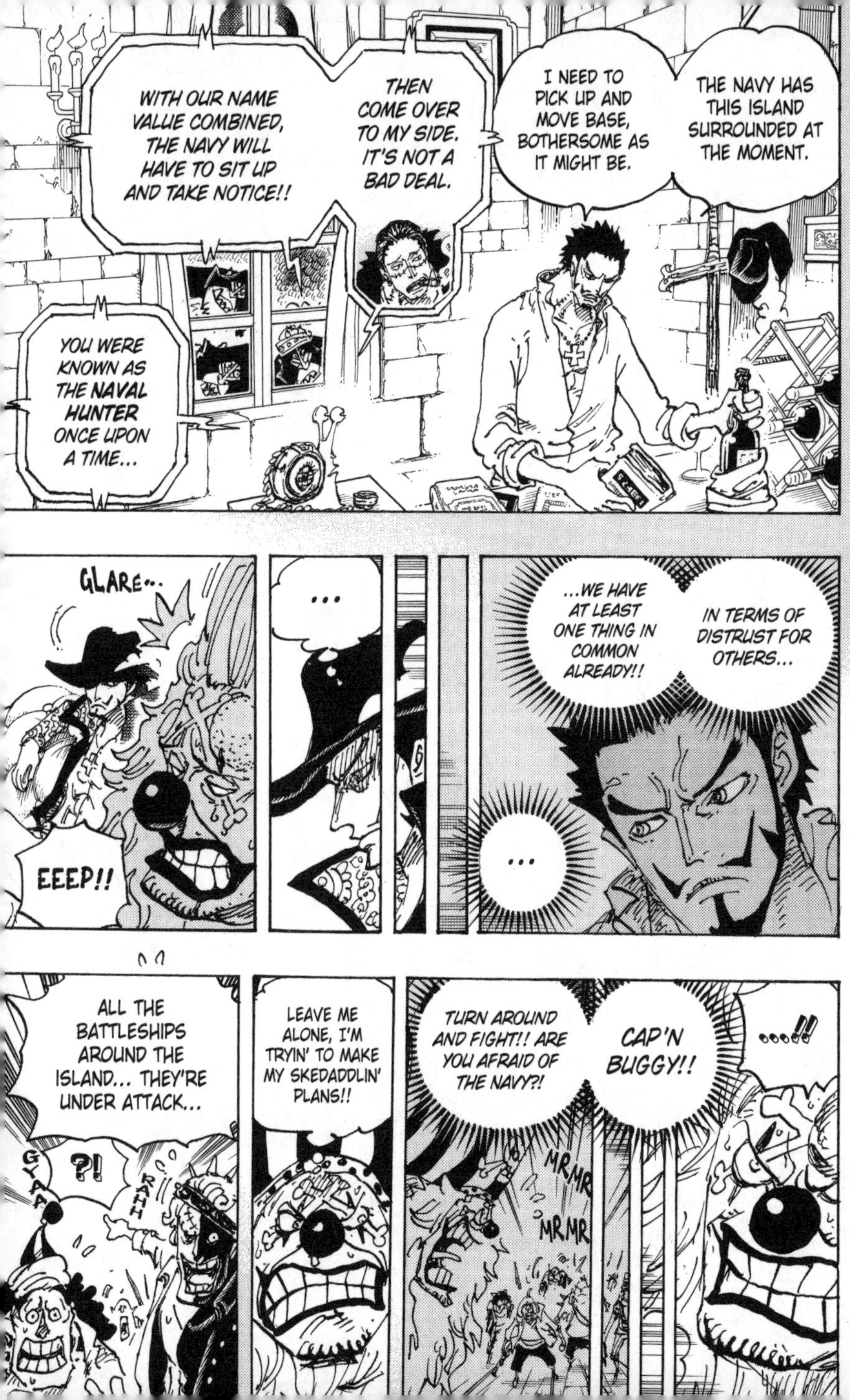
THE NAVY HAS THIS ISLAND SURROUNDED AT THE MOMENT.
I NEED TO PICK UP AND MOVE BASE, BOTHERSOME AS IT MIGHT BE.
THEN COME OVER TO MY SIDE. IT'S NOT A BAD DEAL.
WITH OUR NAME VALUE COMBINED, THE NAVY WILL HAVE TO SIT UP AND TAKE NOTICE!!
YOU WERE KNOWN AS THE NAVAL HUNTER ONCE UPON A TIME...
IN TERMS OF DISTRUST FOR OTHERS...
...WE HAVE AT LEAST ONE THING IN COMMON ALREADY!!
...
...
GLARE...
EEEP!!
...!!
CAP'N BUGGY!!
TURN AROUND AND FIGHT!! ARE YOU AFRAID OF THE NAVY?!
MR MR
MR MR
LEAVE ME ALONE, I'M TRYIN' TO MAKE MY SKEDADDLIN' PLANS!!
ALL THE BATTLESHIPS AROUND THE ISLAND... THEY'RE UNDER ATTACK...
?!
GYAA
RAHH

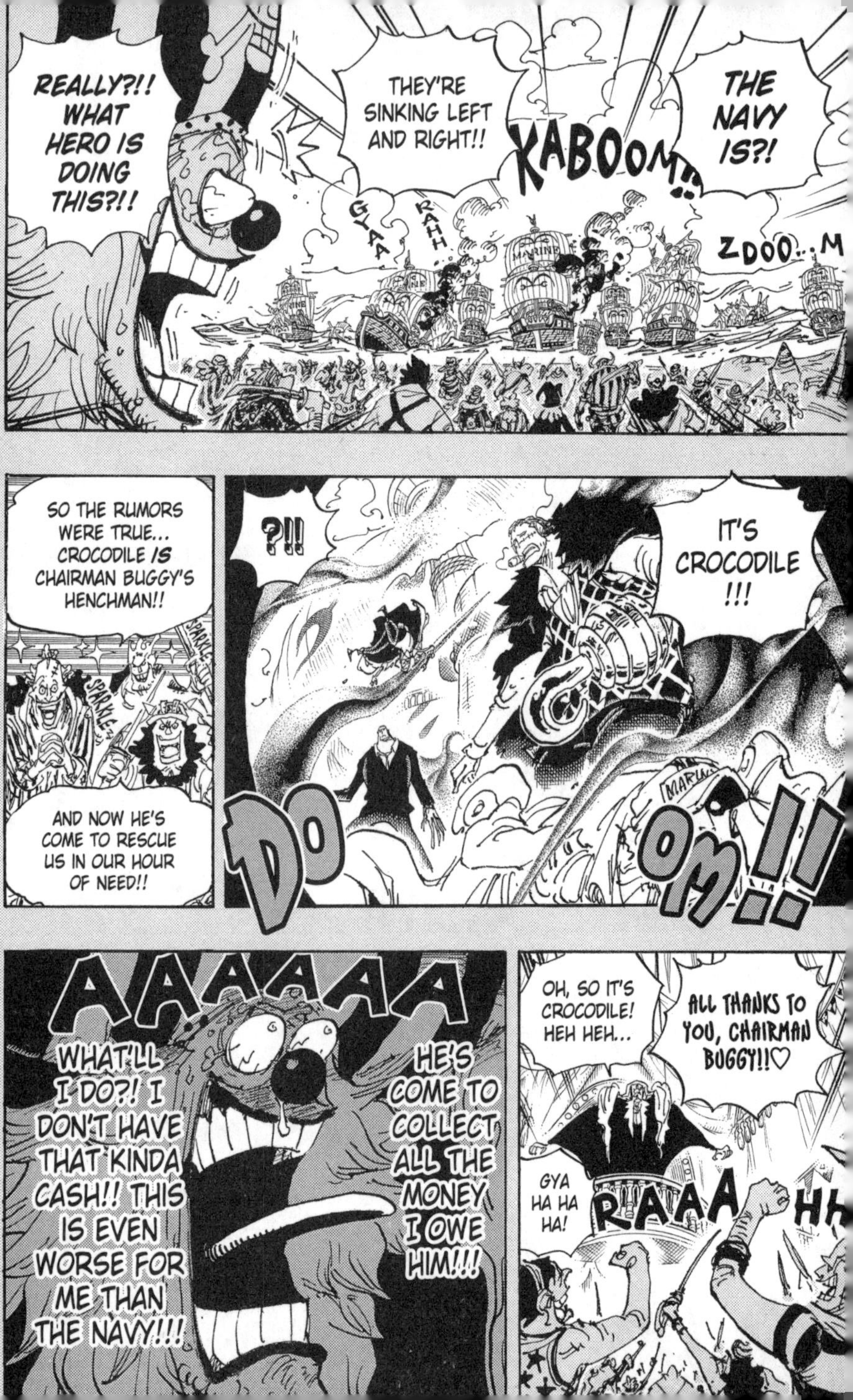
THE NAVY IS?!
KABOOM!!
THEY'RE SINKING LEFT AND RIGHT!!
ZDOO...M
RAHH
GYAA
REALLY?!! WHAT HERO IS DOING THIS?!!
IT'S CROCODILE!!!
?!!
DOOM!!
SO THE RUMORS WERE TRUE... CROCODILE *IS* CHAIRMAN BUGGY'S HENCHMAN!!
SPARKLE
SPARKLE
AND NOW HE'S COME TO RESCUE US IN OUR HOUR OF NEED!!
ALL THANKS TO YOU, CHAIRMAN BUGGY!!♡
OH, SO IT'S CROCODILE! HEH HEH...
RAAAHH
GYA HA HA HA!
AAAAAA
HE'S COME TO COLLECT ALL THE MONEY I OWE HIM!!!
WHAT'LL I DO?! I DON'T HAVE THAT KINDA CASH!! THIS IS EVEN WORSE FOR ME THAN THE NAVY!!!

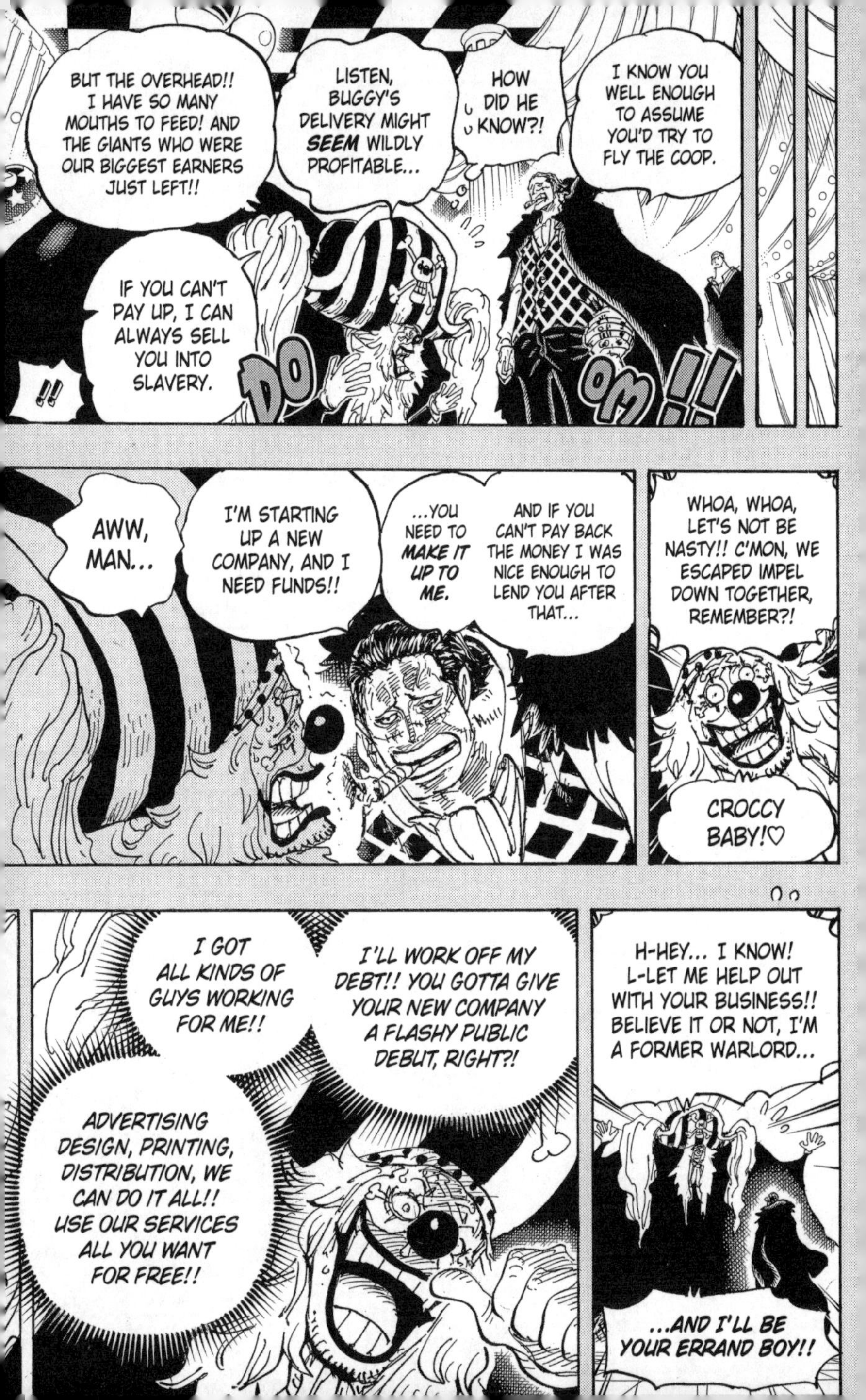
I KNOW YOU WELL ENOUGH TO ASSUME YOU'D TRY TO FLY THE COOP.
HOW DID HE KNOW?!
LISTEN, BUGGY'S DELIVERY MIGHT SEEM WILDLY PROFITABLE...
BUT THE OVERHEAD!! I HAVE SO MANY MOUTHS TO FEED! AND THE GIANTS WHO WERE OUR BIGGEST EARNERS JUST LEFT!!
IF YOU CAN'T PAY UP, I CAN ALWAYS SELL YOU INTO SLAVERY.
!!
DOOM!!
WHOA, WHOA, LET'S NOT BE NASTY!! C'MON, WE ESCAPED IMPEL DOWN TOGETHER, REMEMBER?!
CROCCY BABY!♡
AWW, MAN...
I'M STARTING UP A NEW COMPANY, AND I NEED FUNDS!!
AND IF YOU CAN'T PAY BACK THE MONEY I WAS NICE ENOUGH TO LEND YOU AFTER THAT...
...YOU NEED TO MAKE IT UP TO ME.
H-HEY... I KNOW! L-LET ME HELP OUT WITH YOUR BUSINESS!! BELIEVE IT OR NOT, I'M A FORMER WARLORD...
...AND I'LL BE YOUR ERRAND BOY!!
I'LL WORK OFF MY DEBT!! YOU GOTTA GIVE YOUR NEW COMPANY A FLASHY PUBLIC DEBUT, RIGHT?!
I GOT ALL KINDS OF GUYS WORKING FOR ME!!
ADVERTISING DESIGN, PRINTING, DISTRIBUTION, WE CAN DO IT ALL!! USE OUR SERVICES ALL YOU WANT FOR FREE!!

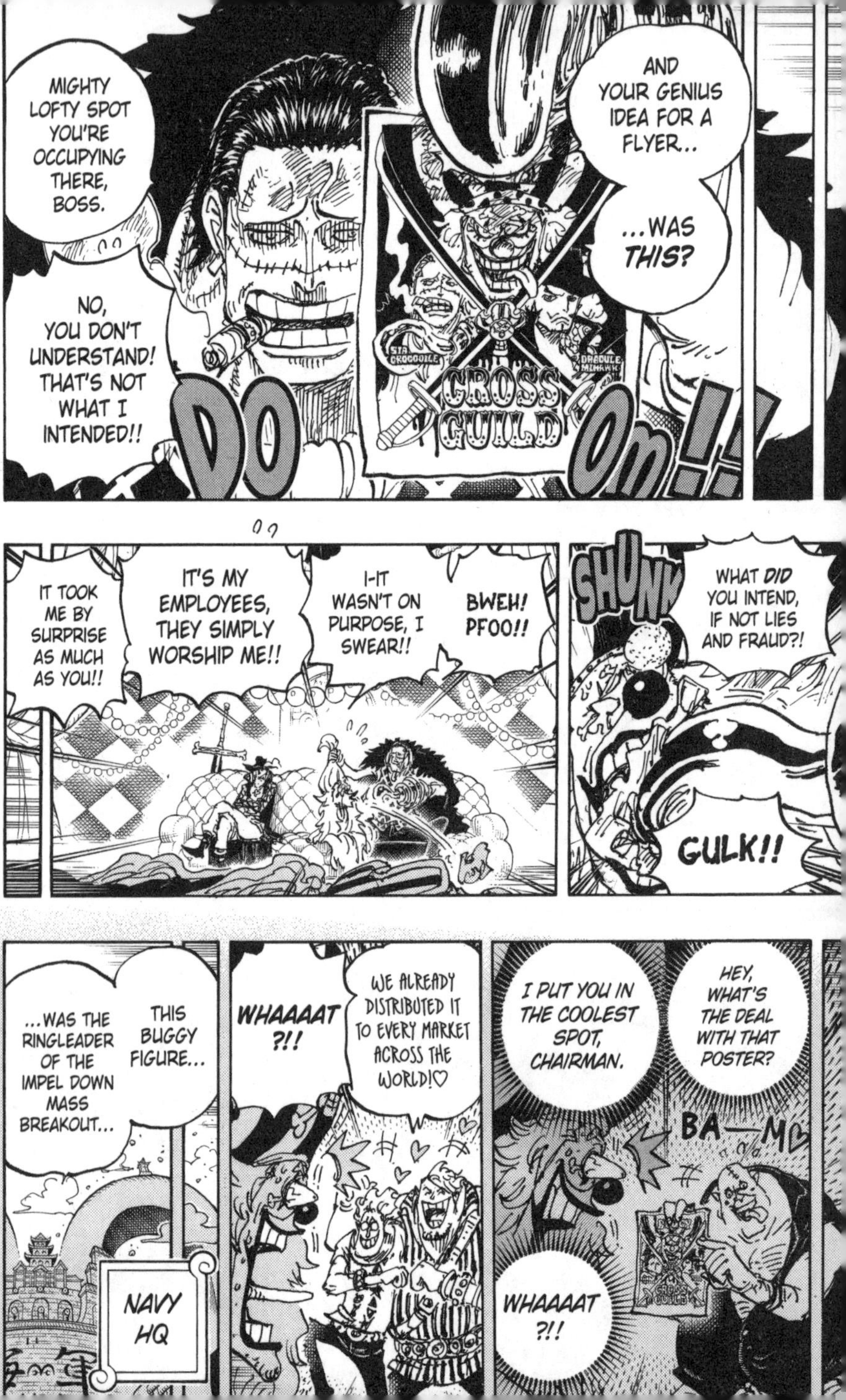
AND YOUR GENIUS IDEA FOR A FLYER...
...WAS *THIS?*
MIGHTY LOFTY SPOT YOU'RE OCCUPYING THERE, BOSS.
SIR CROCODILE
DRACULE MIHAWK
CROSS GUILD
DOOM!!
NO, YOU DON'T UNDERSTAND! THAT'S NOT WHAT I INTENDED!!
SHUNK
WHAT *DID* YOU INTEND, IF NOT LIES AND FRAUD?!
GULK!!
BWEH! PFOO!!
I-IT WASN'T ON PURPOSE, I SWEAR!!
IT'S MY EMPLOYEES, THEY SIMPLY WORSHIP ME!!
IT TOOK ME BY SURPRISE AS MUCH AS YOU!!
HEY, WHAT'S THE DEAL WITH THAT POSTER?
I PUT YOU IN THE COOLEST SPOT, CHAIRMAN.
BA—M♡
WHAAAAT ?!!
WE ALREADY DISTRIBUTED IT TO EVERY MARKET ACROSS THE WORLD!♡
WHAAAAT ?!!
THIS BUGGY FIGURE...
...WAS THE RINGLEADER OF THE IMPEL DOWN MASS BREAKOUT...
NAVY HQ

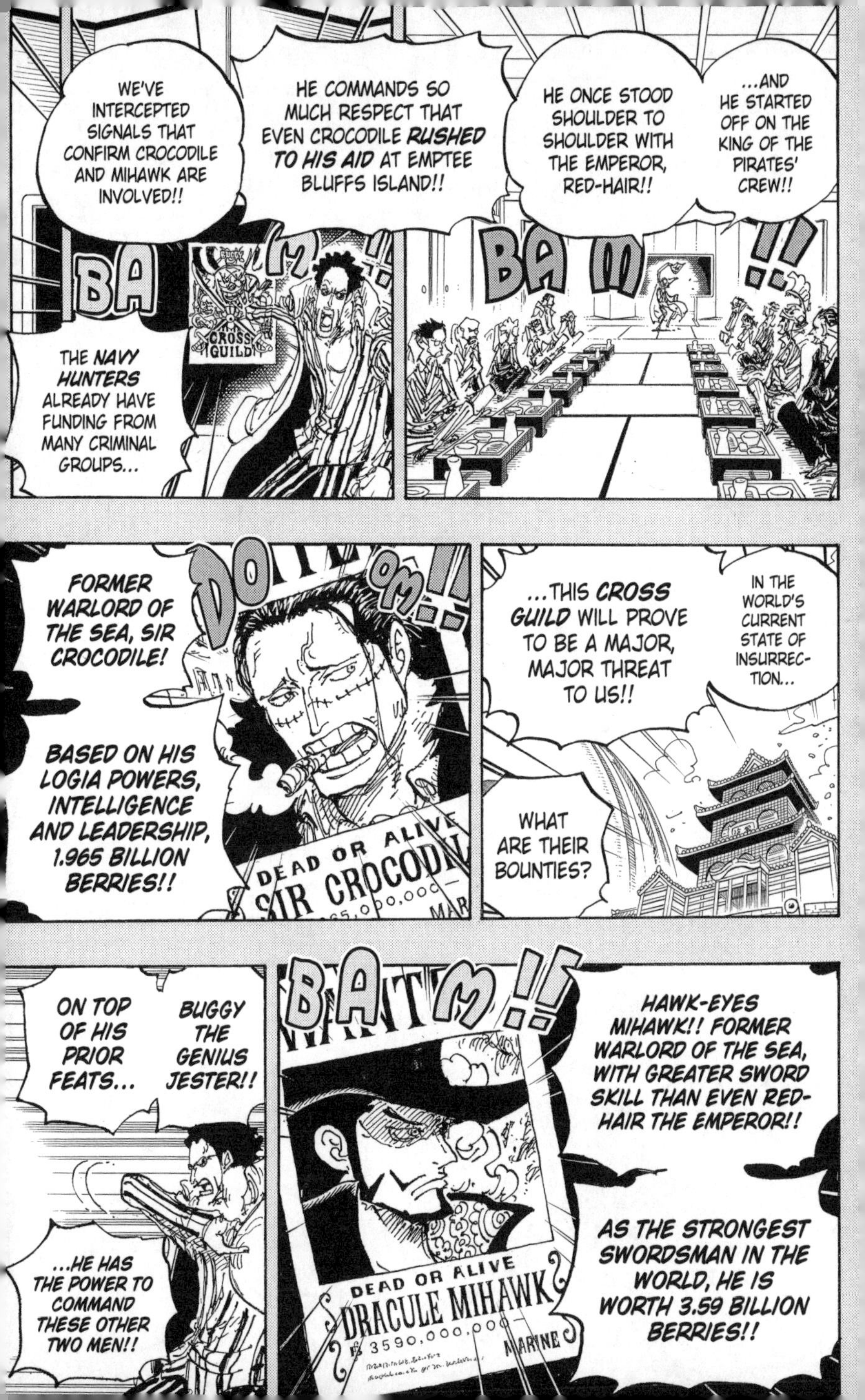
HE ONCE STOOD SHOULDER TO SHOULDER WITH THE EMPEROR, RED-HAIR!!
...AND HE STARTED OFF ON THE KING OF THE PIRATES' CREW!!
BAM!!
HE COMMANDS SO MUCH RESPECT THAT EVEN CROCODILE RUSHED TO HIS AID AT EMPTEE BLUFFS ISLAND!!
WE'VE INTERCEPTED SIGNALS THAT CONFIRM CROCODILE AND MIHAWK ARE INVOLVED!!
BAM!!
CROSS GUILD
THE NAVY HUNTERS ALREADY HAVE FUNDING FROM MANY CRIMINAL GROUPS...
IN THE WORLD'S CURRENT STATE OF INSURREC-TION...
...THIS CROSS GUILD WILL PROVE TO BE A MAJOR, MAJOR THREAT TO US!!
WHAT ARE THEIR BOUNTIES?
DOOM!!
FORMER WARLORD OF THE SEA, SIR CROCODILE!
BASED ON HIS LOGIA POWERS, INTELLIGENCE AND LEADERSHIP, 1.965 BILLION BERRIES!!
DEAD OR ALIVE
BAM!!
HAWK-EYES MIHAWK!! FORMER WARLORD OF THE SEA, WITH GREATER SWORD SKILL THAN EVEN RED-HAIR THE EMPEROR!!
AS THE STRONGEST SWORDSMAN IN THE WORLD, HE IS WORTH 3.59 BILLION BERRIES!!
DEAD OR ALIVE
DRACULE MIHAWK
฿3590,000,000
MARINE
BUGGY THE GENIUS JESTER!!
ON TOP OF HIS PRIOR FEATS...
...HE HAS THE POWER TO COMMAND THESE OTHER TWO MEN!!

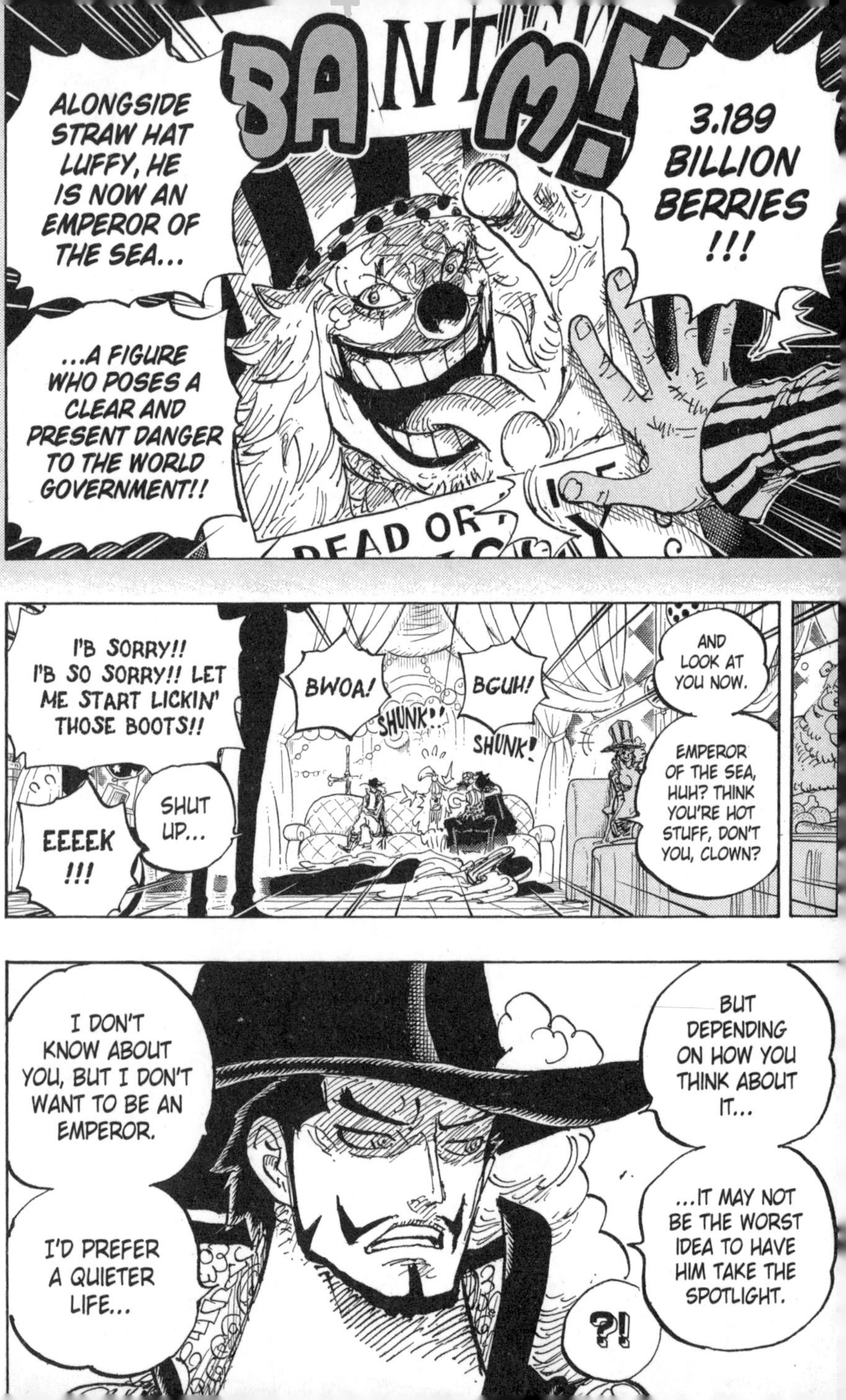
BANTM!
3.189 BILLION BERRIES!!!
ALONGSIDE STRAW HAT LUFFY, HE IS NOW AN EMPEROR OF THE SEA...
...A FIGURE WHO POSES A CLEAR AND PRESENT DANGER TO THE WORLD GOVERNMENT!!
DEAD OR
AND LOOK AT YOU NOW.
EMPEROR OF THE SEA, HUH? THINK YOU'RE HOT STUFF, DON'T YOU, CLOWN?
BGUH!
SHUNK!
BWOA!
SHUNK!?!
I'B SORRY!! I'B SO SORRY!! LET ME START LICKIN' THOSE BOOTS!!
SHUT UP...
EEEEK!!!
BUT DEPENDING ON HOW YOU THINK ABOUT IT...
...IT MAY NOT BE THE WORST IDEA TO HAVE HIM TAKE THE SPOTLIGHT.
?!
I DON'T KNOW ABOUT YOU, BUT I DON'T WANT TO BE AN EMPEROR.
I'D PREFER A QUIETER LIFE...

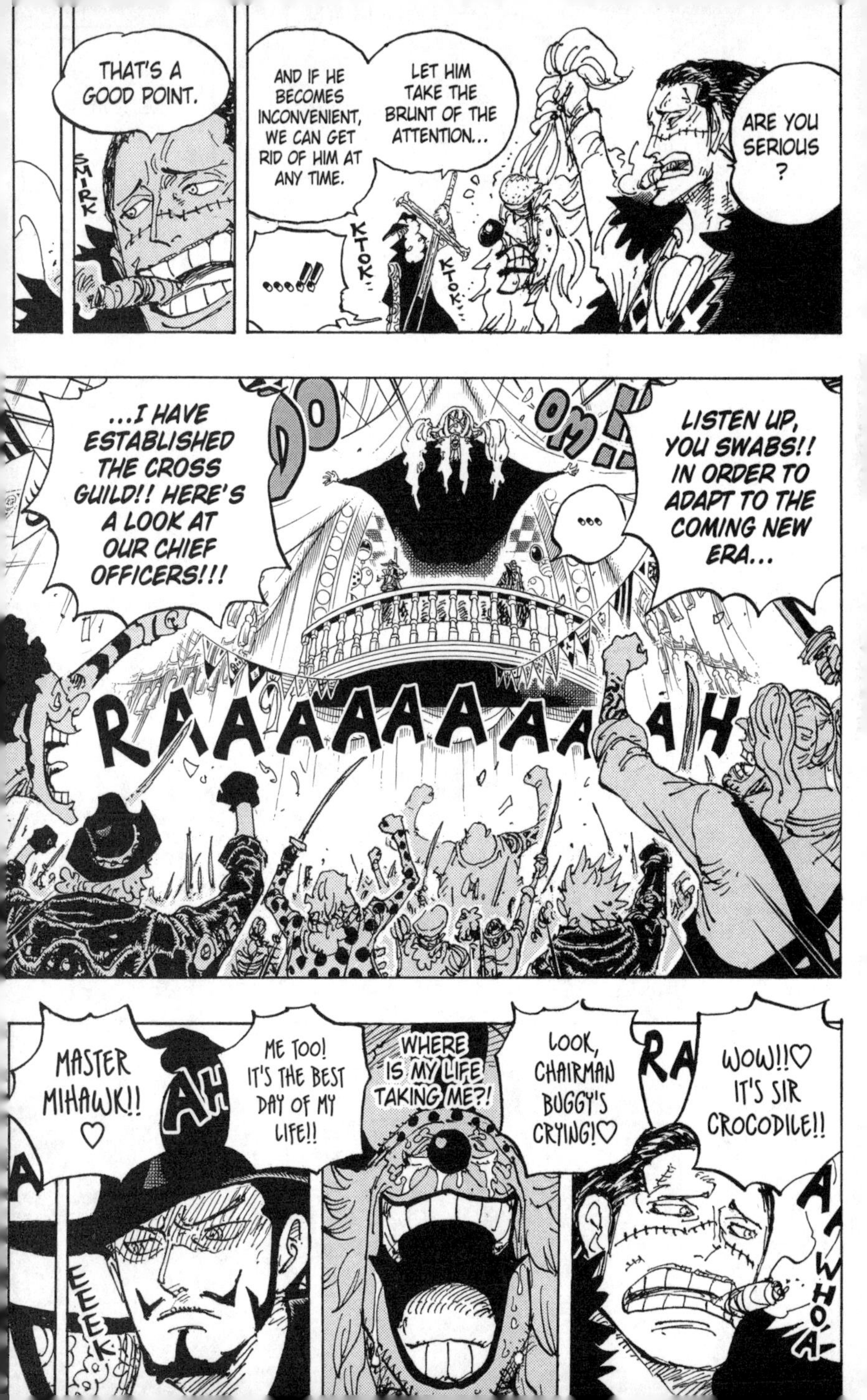
ARE YOU SERIOUS?
LET HIM TAKE THE BRUNT OF THE ATTENTION...
AND IF HE BECOMES INCONVENIENT, WE CAN GET RID OF HIM AT ANY TIME.
KTOK
KTOK
......!!
THAT'S A GOOD POINT.
SMIRK
LISTEN UP, YOU SWABS!! IN ORDER TO ADAPT TO THE COMING NEW ERA...
...
...I HAVE ESTABLISHED THE CROSS GUILD!! HERE'S A LOOK AT OUR CHIEF OFFICERS!!!
RAAAAAAAAAH
WOW!!♡ IT'S SIR CROCODILE!!
LOOK, CHAIRMAN BUGGY'S CRYING!♡
WHOA
WHERE IS MY LIFE TAKING ME?!
ME TOO! IT'S THE BEST DAY OF MY LIFE!!
MASTER MIHAWK!! ♡
AH
EEEEK

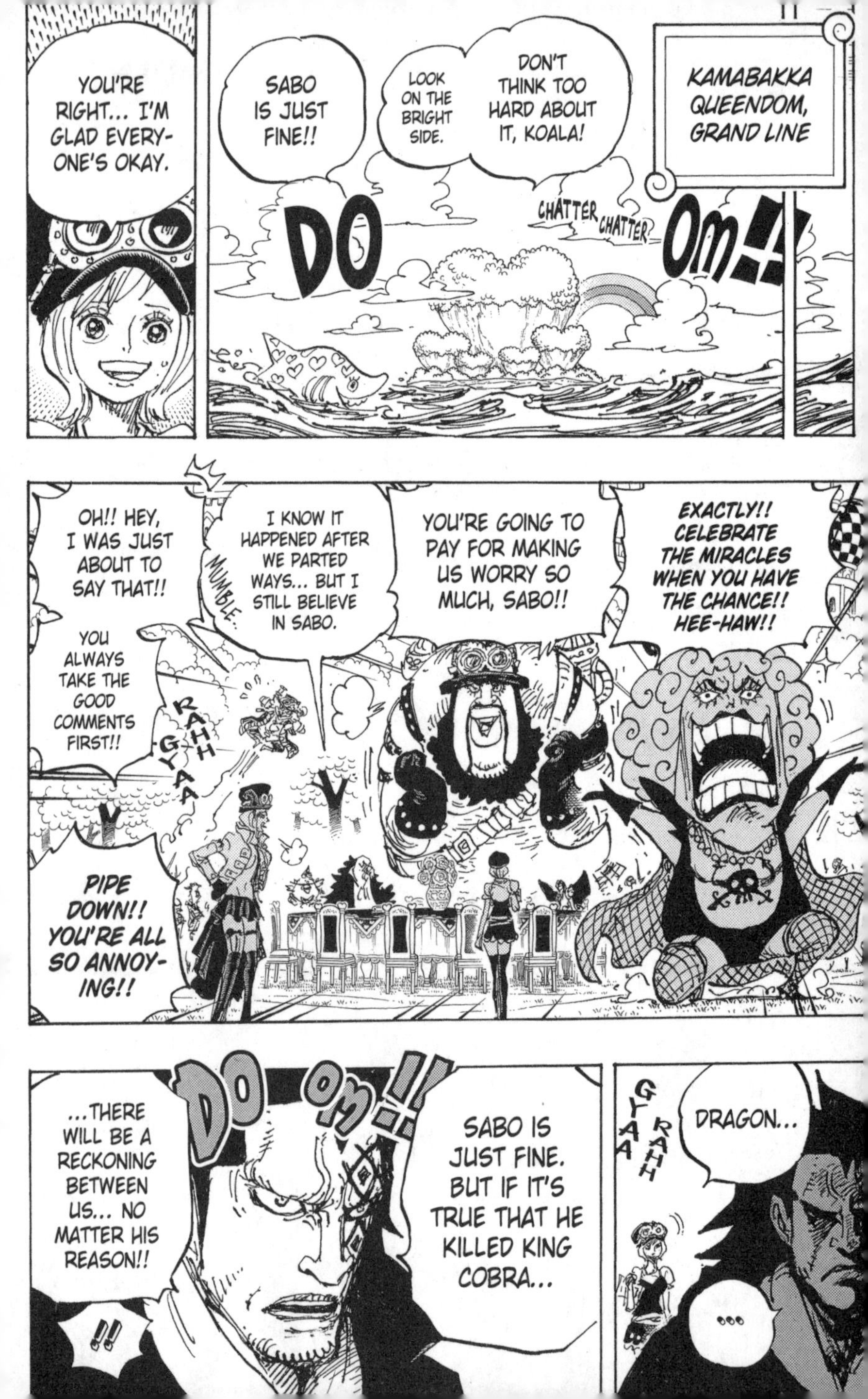
KAMABAKKA QUEENDOM, GRAND LINE
DON'T THINK TOO HARD ABOUT IT, KOALA!
LOOK ON THE BRIGHT SIDE.
SABO IS JUST FINE!!
CHATTER CHATTER
DOOM!!
YOU'RE RIGHT... I'M GLAD EVERYONE'S OKAY.
EXACTLY!! CELEBRATE THE MIRACLES WHEN YOU HAVE THE CHANCE!! HEE-HAW!!
YOU'RE GOING TO PAY FOR MAKING US WORRY SO MUCH, SABO!!
I KNOW IT HAPPENED AFTER WE PARTED WAYS... BUT I STILL BELIEVE IN SABO.
MUMBLE...
OH!! HEY, I WAS JUST ABOUT TO SAY THAT!!
YOU ALWAYS TAKE THE GOOD COMMENTS FIRST!!
RAHH
GYAA
PIPE DOWN!! YOU'RE ALL SO ANNOYING!!
DRAGON...
GYAA
RAHH
...
SABO IS JUST FINE. BUT IF IT'S TRUE THAT HE KILLED KING COBRA...
DOOM!!
...THERE WILL BE A RECKONING BETWEEN US... NO MATTER HIS REASON!!
!!

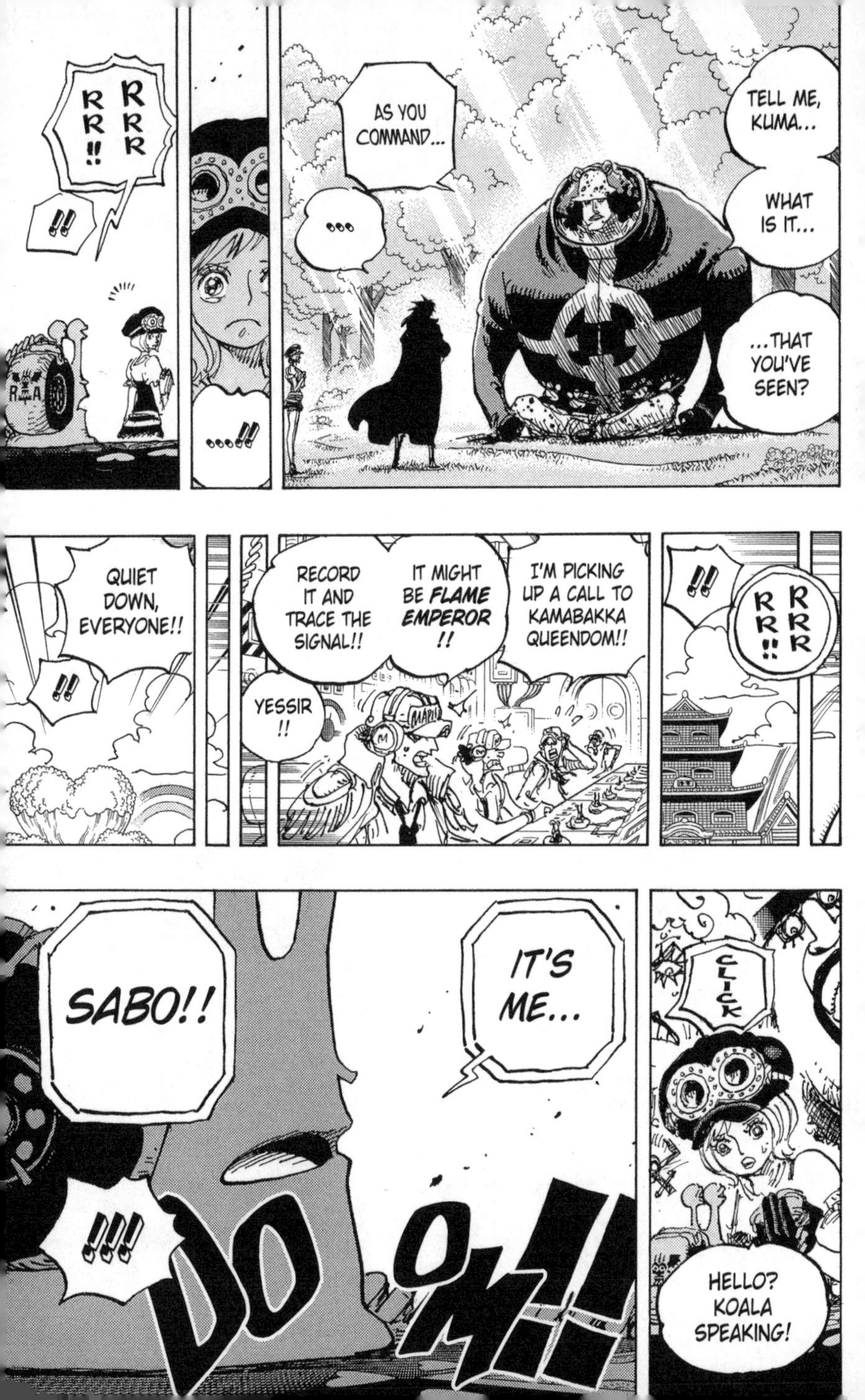
TELL ME, KUMA...
WHAT IS IT...
...THAT YOU'VE SEEN?
AS YOU COMMAND...
...
...!!
RRR RR!!
!!
RRR RR!!
!!
I'M PICKING UP A CALL TO KAMABAKKA QUEENDOM!!
IT MIGHT BE FLAME EMPEROR!!
RECORD IT AND TRACE THE SIGNAL!!
YESSIR!!
QUIET DOWN, EVERYONE!!
!!
CLICK
HELLO? KOALA SPEAKING!
IT'S ME...
SABO!!
!!!
DOOM!!

SBS Question Corner

質問コーナー
SBS
えす びー えす

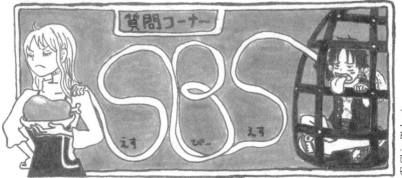

(F Chie, Tokyo)

Q: Do the later members to join the crew (Robin, Franky, Brook, Jimbei) ever hear about the earlier adventures in the East Blue from the more senior members (like Usopp)? I'm really curious about this!

--Seito

A: Some things they know, some things they don't. Let's break it down by their personalities. Luffy and Zolo don't really talk about the past. Nami, Sanji and Chopper will tell you if you ask them. And Usopp will tell you stories unprompted. Of course, the adults are smart enough to see through his lies, so if they're really curious, they'll ask Nami, Sanji or Chopper. For the most part, however, the Straw Hat Crew are a bunch of folks who don't care too much about each others' pasts.

Q: In chapter 1045, Kaido mentions "comic strips." Does that mean the concept of manga doesn't exist in the world of *OP?* What?! You mean Kaido hasn't read *One Piece?!*

--Kei

FSHOOO
THUD..
IT'S LIKE SOMETHING FROM A COMIC STRIP...

A: You hear the terms "storybook" and "comic strip" pop up in *One Piece* from time to time. Storybooks are just what you'd expect, but you can think of "comic strips" as being the manga of the *OP* world. They don't have the custom of including dialogue in speech bubbles, so instead there are narrative boxes by the art that have prose text and quotations from the characters. Some of the most famous comic strips are *Sora, Warrior of the Sea, Mastiff-oenix, Pokaemon, Monkey Ball,* and *Marco-san.*

There are all kinds out there.

Chapter 1059: THE MATTER INVOLVING CAPTAIN KOBY

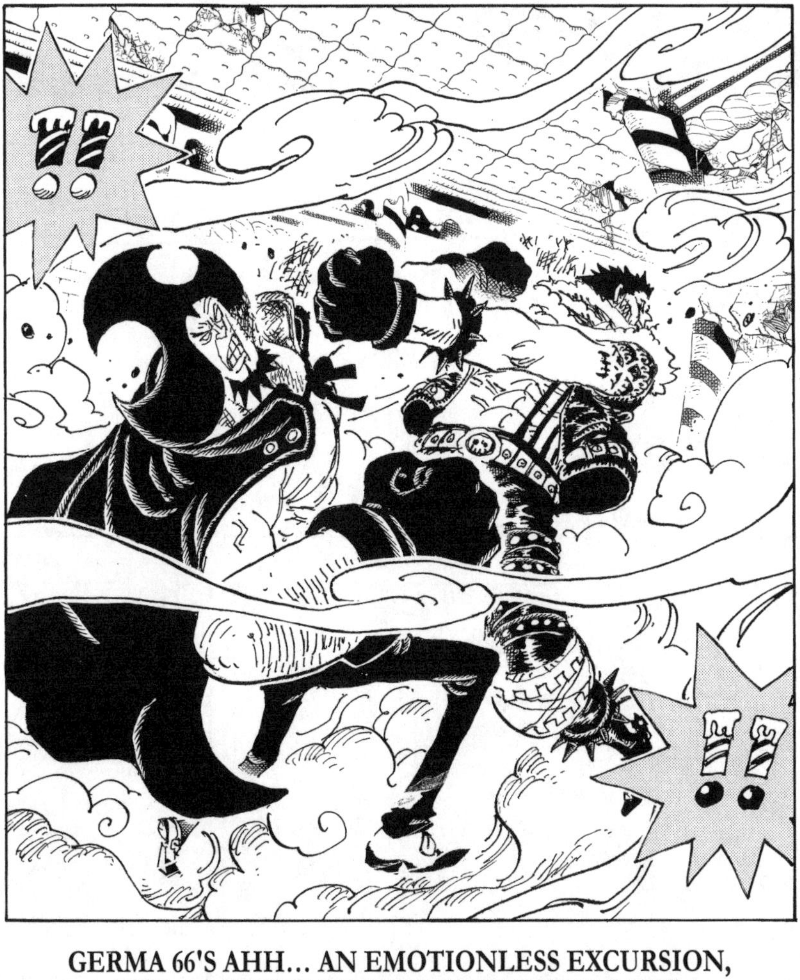
!!
!!

GERMA 66'S AHH… AN EMOTIONLESS EXCURSION, VOL. 18: "CAESAR'S HALLUCINATION GAS!!"

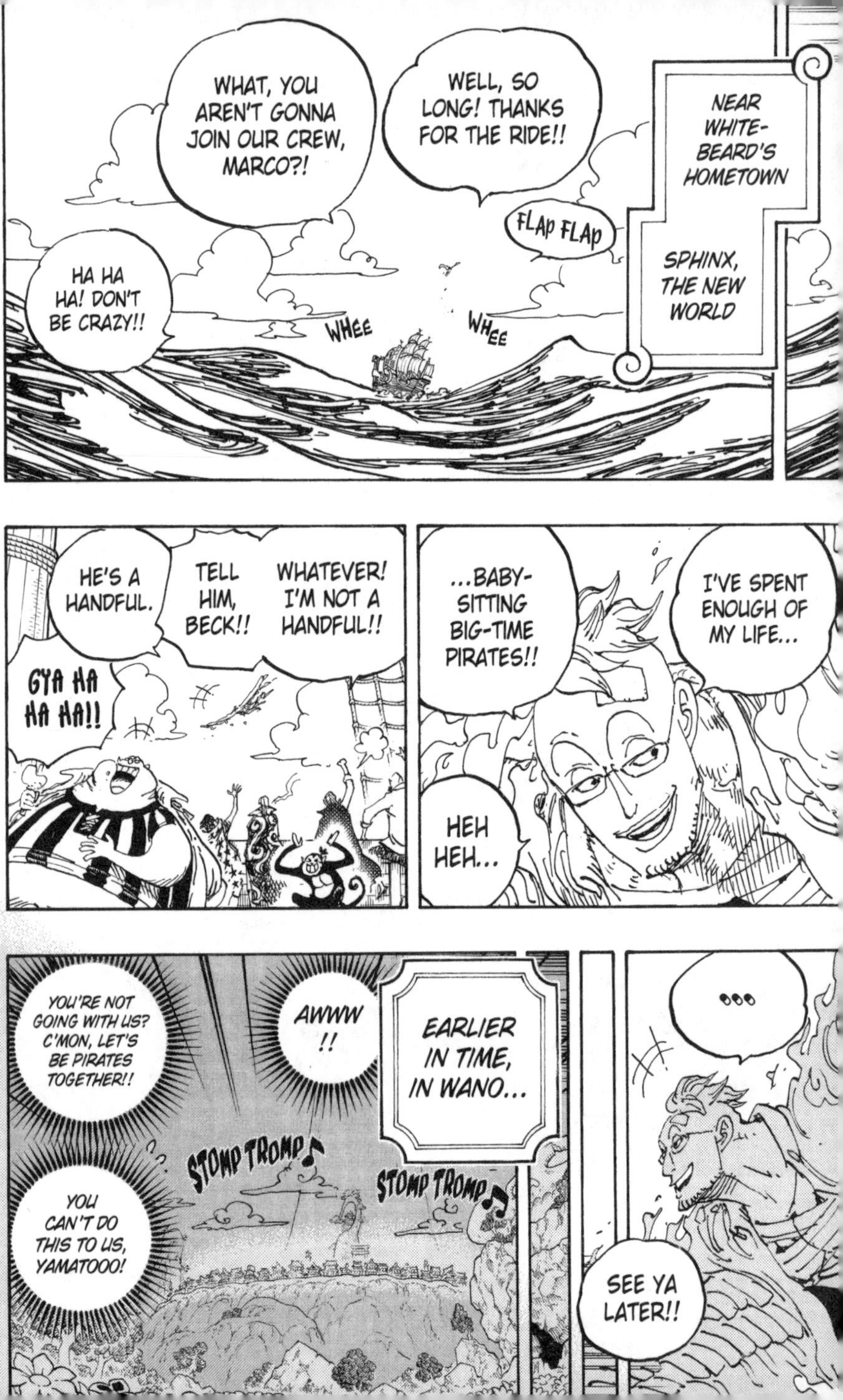
NEAR WHITE-BEARD'S HOMETOWN
SPHINX, THE NEW WORLD
WELL, SO LONG! THANKS FOR THE RIDE!!
FLAP FLAP
WHAT, YOU AREN'T GONNA JOIN OUR CREW, MARCO?!
WHEE
WHEE
HA HA HA! DON'T BE CRAZY!!
I'VE SPENT ENOUGH OF MY LIFE...
...BABY-SITTING BIG-TIME PIRATES!!
HEH HEH...
WHATEVER! I'M NOT A HANDFUL!!
TELL HIM, BECK!!
HE'S A HANDFUL.
GYA HA HA HA!!
...
SEE YA LATER!!
EARLIER IN TIME, IN WANO...
AWWW !!
YOU'RE NOT GOING WITH US? C'MON, LET'S BE PIRATES TOGETHER!!
STOMP TROMP
STOMP TROMP
YOU CAN'T DO THIS TO US, YAMATOOO!

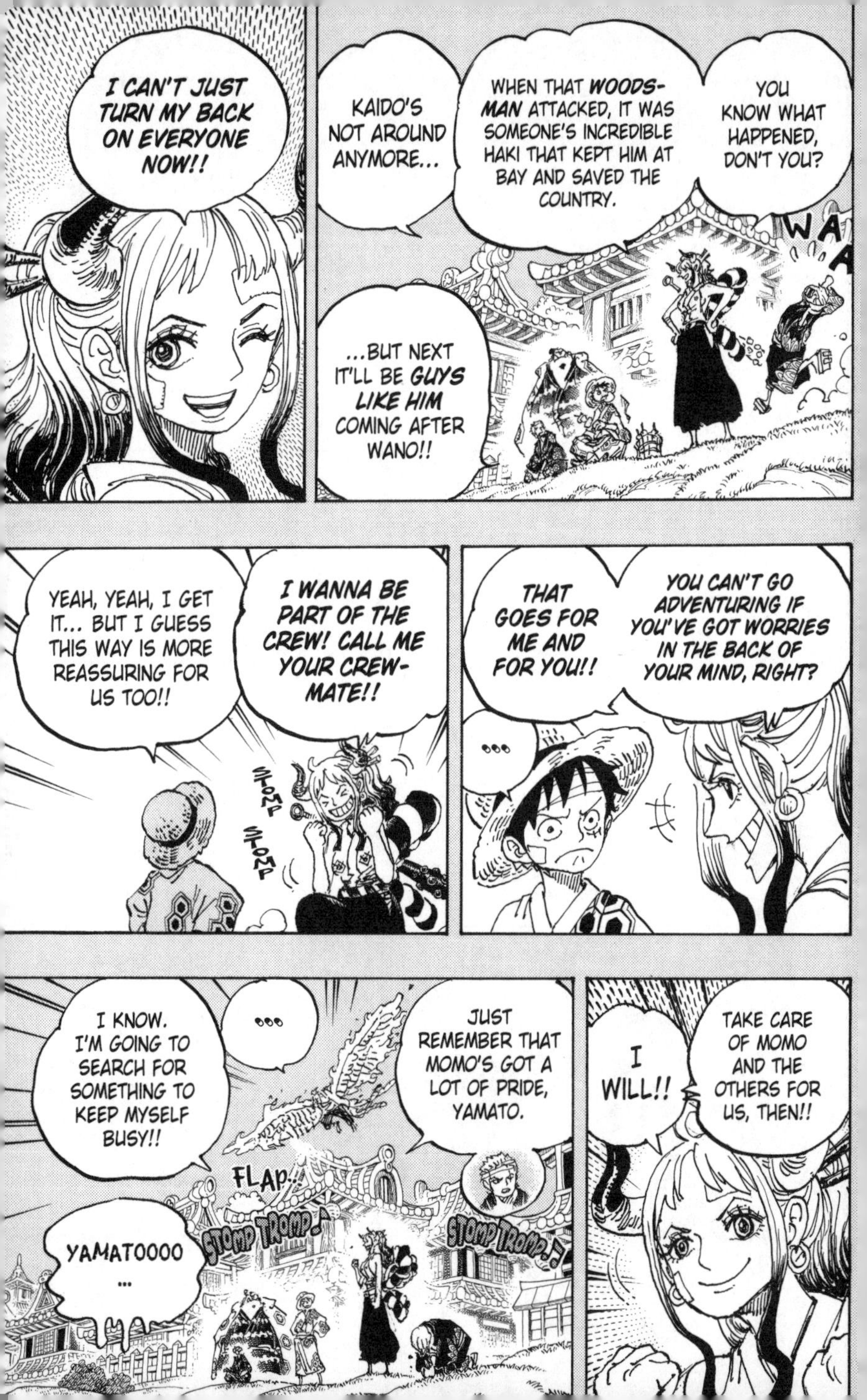
YOU KNOW WHAT HAPPENED, DON'T YOU?
WHEN THAT WOODS-MAN ATTACKED, IT WAS SOMEONE'S INCREDIBLE HAKI THAT KEPT HIM AT BAY AND SAVED THE COUNTRY.
KAIDO'S NOT AROUND ANYMORE...
...BUT NEXT IT'LL BE GUYS LIKE HIM COMING AFTER WANO!!
WA A
I CAN'T JUST TURN MY BACK ON EVERYONE NOW!!
YOU CAN'T GO ADVENTURING IF YOU'VE GOT WORRIES IN THE BACK OF YOUR MIND, RIGHT?
THAT GOES FOR ME AND FOR YOU!!
...
I WANNA BE PART OF THE CREW! CALL ME YOUR CREW-MATE!!
YEAH, YEAH, I GET IT... BUT I GUESS THIS WAY IS MORE REASSURING FOR US TOO!!
STOMP
STOMP
TAKE CARE OF MOMO AND THE OTHERS FOR US, THEN!!
I WILL!!
JUST REMEMBER THAT MOMO'S GOT A LOT OF PRIDE, YAMATO.
...
I KNOW. I'M GOING TO SEARCH FOR SOMETHING TO KEEP MYSELF BUSY!!
FLAP..
STOMP TROMP
STOMP TROMP
YAMATOOOO ...

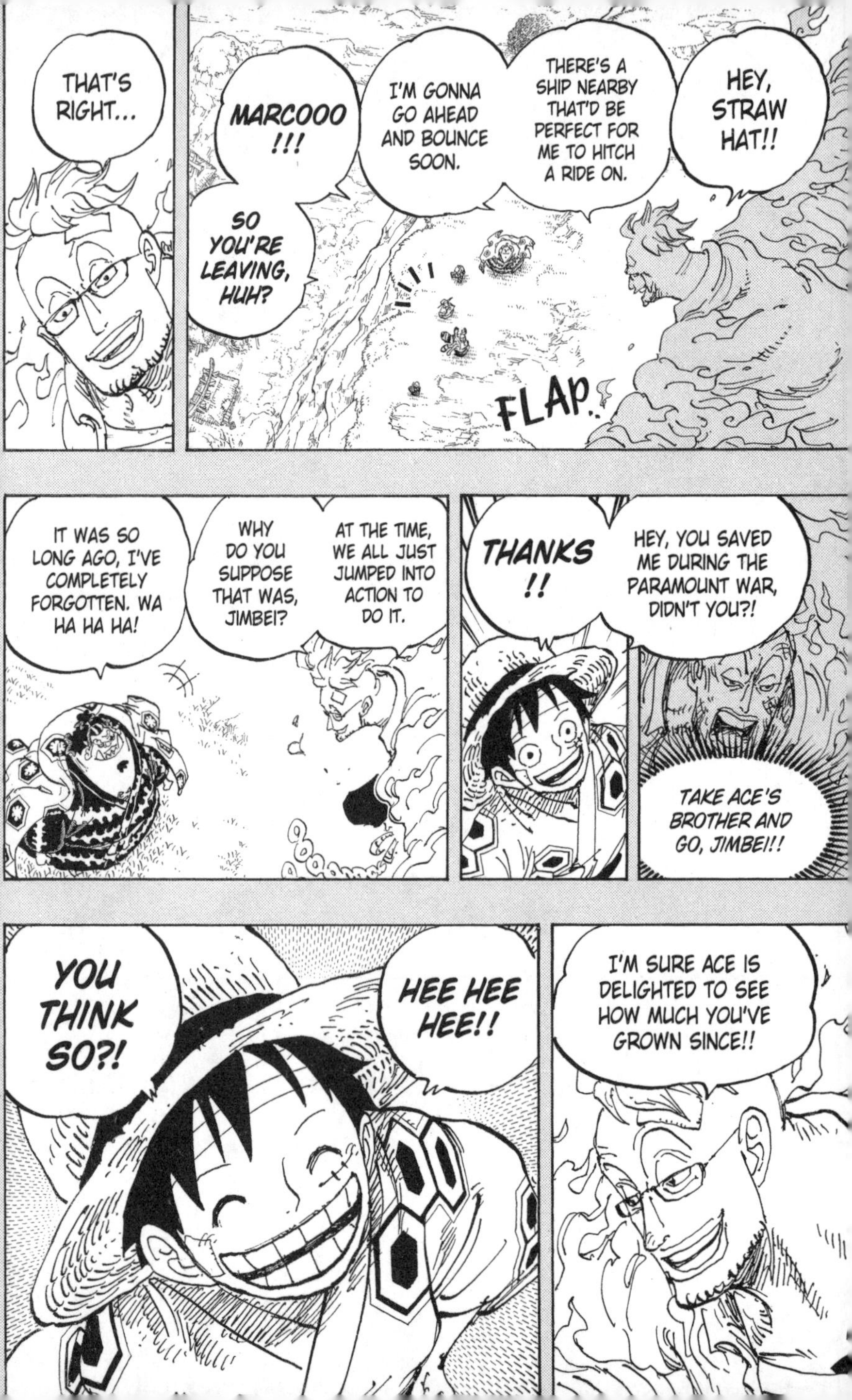
HEY, STRAW HAT!!
THERE'S A SHIP NEARBY THAT'D BE PERFECT FOR ME TO HITCH A RIDE ON.
I'M GONNA GO AHEAD AND BOUNCE SOON.
MARCOOO!!!
SO YOU'RE LEAVING, HUH?
FLAP..
THAT'S RIGHT...
HEY, YOU SAVED ME DURING THE PARAMOUNT WAR, DIDN'T YOU?!
THANKS!!
TAKE ACE'S BROTHER AND GO, JIMBEI!!
AT THE TIME, WE ALL JUST JUMPED INTO ACTION TO DO IT.
WHY DO YOU SUPPOSE THAT WAS, JIMBEI?
IT WAS SO LONG AGO, I'VE COMPLETELY FORGOTTEN. WA HA HA HA!
I'M SURE ACE IS DELIGHTED TO SEE HOW MUCH YOU'VE GROWN SINCE!!
HEE HEE HEE!!
YOU THINK SO?!

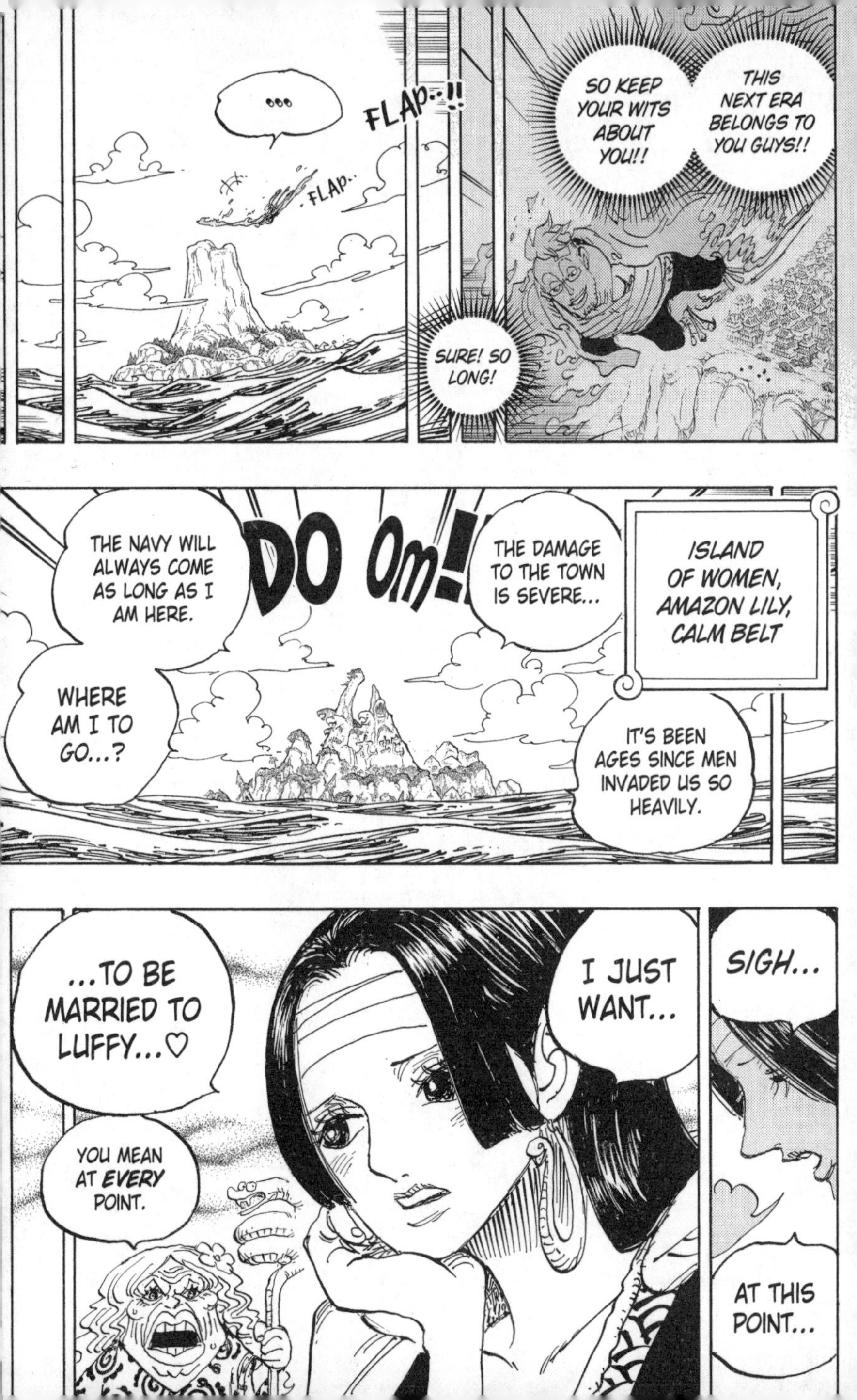
THIS NEXT ERA BELONGS TO YOU GUYS!!
SO KEEP YOUR WITS ABOUT YOU!!
SURE! SO LONG!
FLAP..!!
...
FLAP..
ISLAND OF WOMEN, AMAZON LILY, CALM BELT
THE DAMAGE TO THE TOWN IS SEVERE...
IT'S BEEN AGES SINCE MEN INVADED US SO HEAVILY.
DOOM!!
THE NAVY WILL ALWAYS COME AS LONG AS I AM HERE.
WHERE AM I TO GO...?
SIGH...
AT THIS POINT...
I JUST WANT...
...TO BE MARRIED TO LUFFY...♡
YOU MEAN AT EVERY POINT.

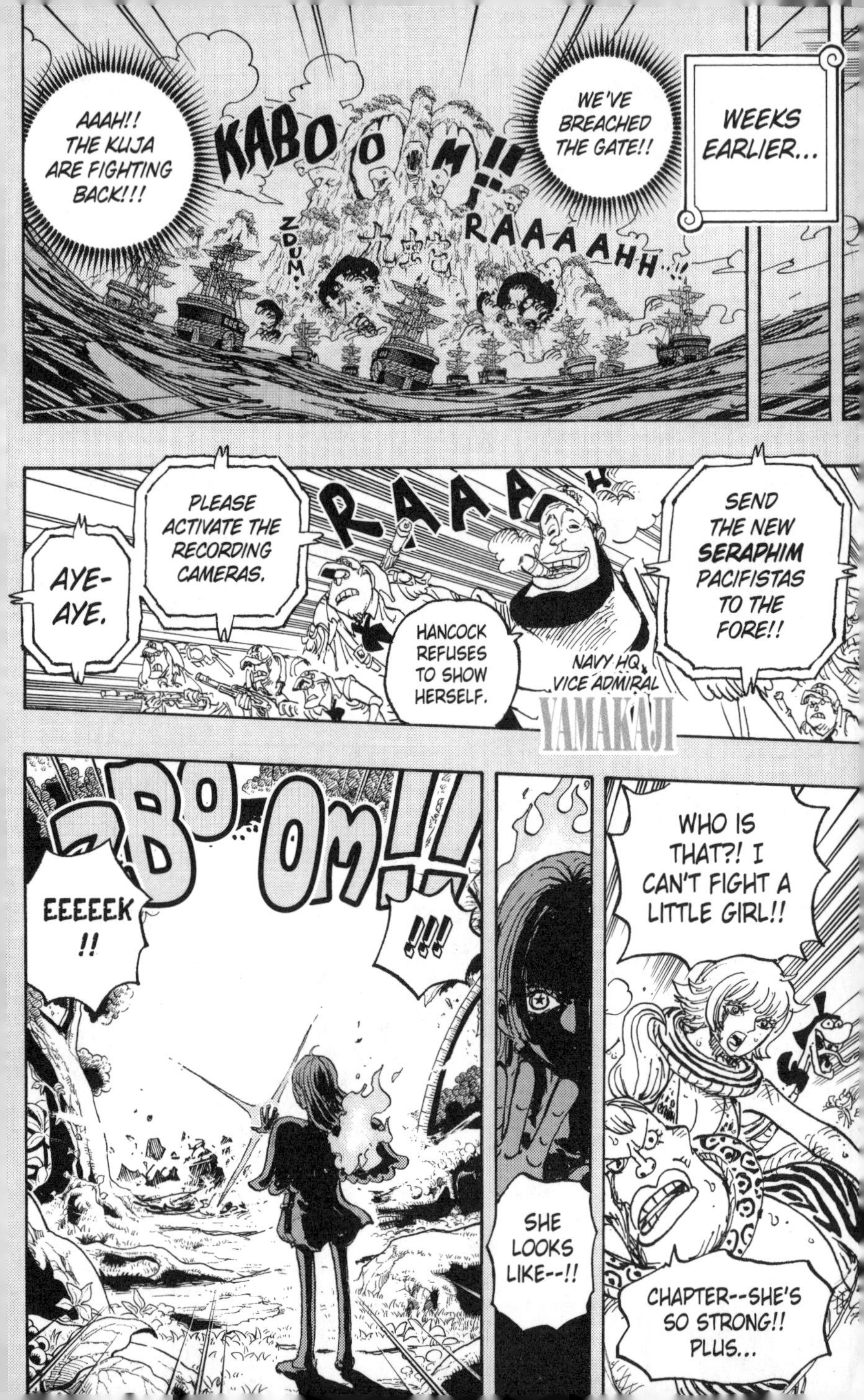
WEEKS EARLIER...
WE'VE BREACHED THE GATE!!
KABOOM!!
RAAAAAHH..!!
AAAH!! THE KUJA ARE FIGHTING BACK!!!
ZDUM
SEND THE NEW SERAPHIM PACIFISTAS TO THE FORE!!
NAVY HQ VICE ADMIRAL
YAMAKAJI
HANCOCK REFUSES TO SHOW HERSELF.
RAAAH
PLEASE ACTIVATE THE RECORDING CAMERAS.
AYE-AYE.
WHO IS THAT?! I CAN'T FIGHT A LITTLE GIRL!!
CHAPTER--SHE'S SO STRONG!! PLUS...
SHE LOOKS LIKE--!!
BOOM!!
!!!
EEEEEK !!

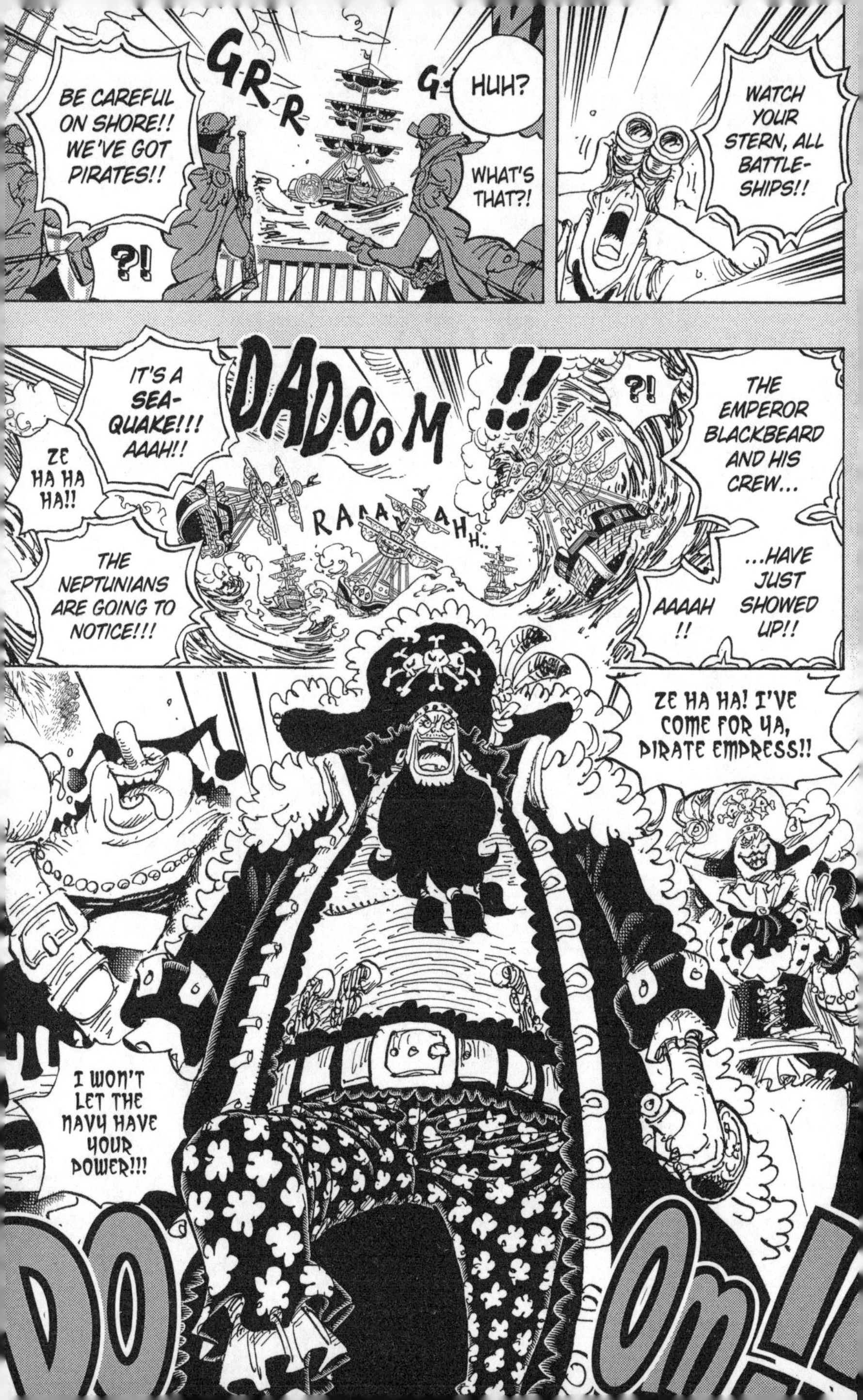
WATCH YOUR STERN, ALL BATTLE-SHIPS!!
HUH?
G-R-R G-
BE CAREFUL ON SHORE!! WE'VE GOT PIRATES!!
WHAT'S THAT?!
?!
THE EMPEROR BLACKBEARD AND HIS CREW...
?!
...HAVE JUST SHOWED UP!!
AAAAH!!
DADOOM!!
IT'S A SEA-QUAKE!!! AAAH!!
ZE HA HA HA!!
RAAAAAHH..
THE NEPTUNIANS ARE GOING TO NOTICE!!!
ZE HA HA! I'VE COME FOR YA, PIRATE EMPRESS!!
I WON'T LET THE NAVY HAVE YOUR POWER!!!
DOOM!!

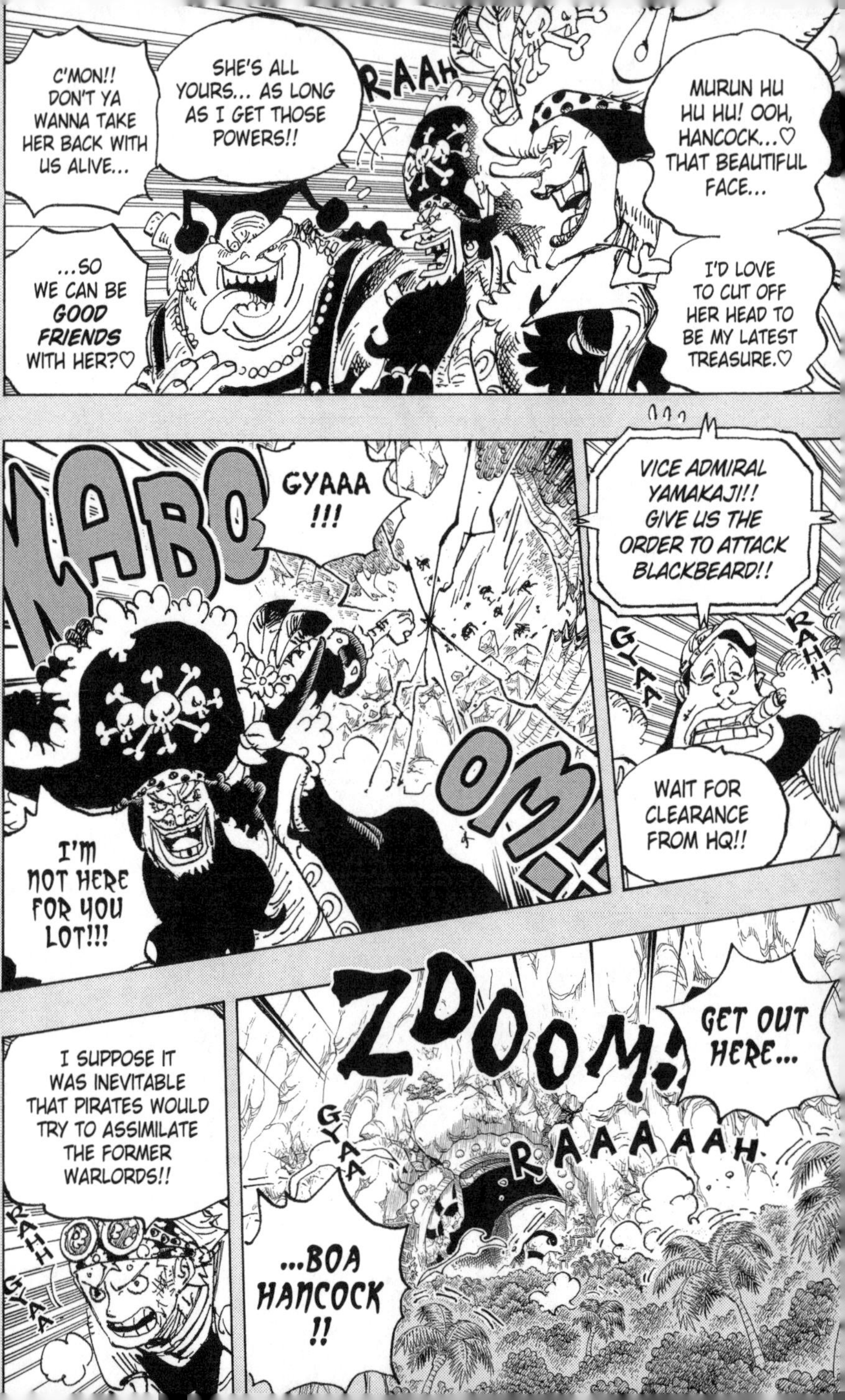
MURUN HU HU HU! OOH, HANCOCK...♡ THAT BEAUTIFUL FACE...
I'D LOVE TO CUT OFF HER HEAD TO BE MY LATEST TREASURE.♡
RAAH
SHE'S ALL YOURS... AS LONG AS I GET THOSE POWERS!!
C'MON!! DON'T YA WANNA TAKE HER BACK WITH US ALIVE...
...SO WE CAN BE GOOD FRIENDS WITH HER?♡
VICE ADMIRAL YAMAKAJI!! GIVE US THE ORDER TO ATTACK BLACKBEARD!!
GYAA
RAHH
WAIT FOR CLEARANCE FROM HQ!!
GYAAA !!!
I'M NOT HERE FOR YOU LOT!!!
ZDOOM
GET OUT HERE...
GYAA
RAAAAAAH
...BOA HANCOCK !!
I SUPPOSE IT WAS INEVITABLE THAT PIRATES WOULD TRY TO ASSIMILATE THE FORMER WARLORDS!!
RAHH
GYAA

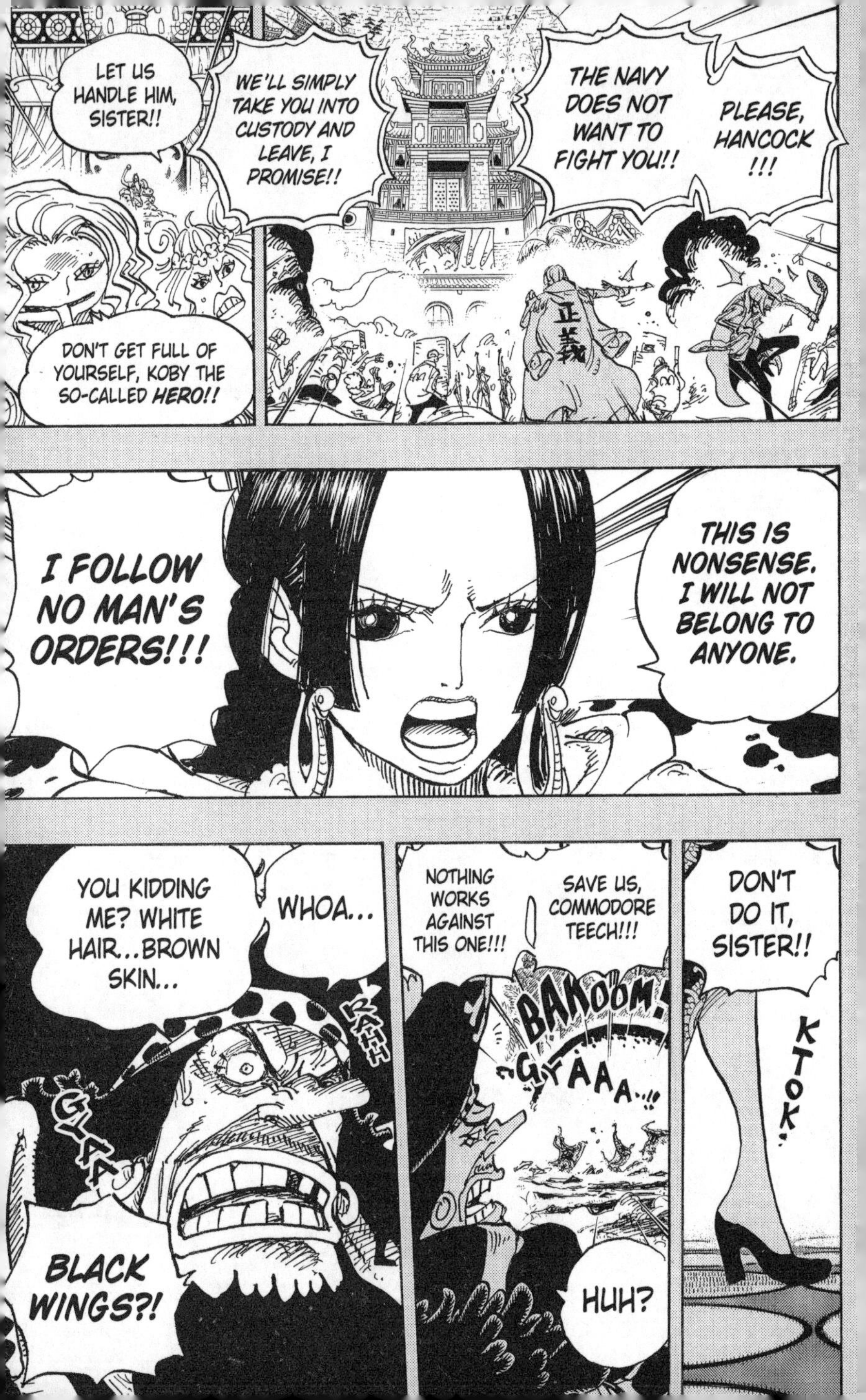
PLEASE, HANCOCK!!!
THE NAVY DOES NOT WANT TO FIGHT YOU!!
WE'LL SIMPLY TAKE YOU INTO CUSTODY AND LEAVE, I PROMISE!!
LET US HANDLE HIM, SISTER!!
DON'T GET FULL OF YOURSELF, KOBY THE SO-CALLED HERO!!
THIS IS NONSENSE. I WILL NOT BELONG TO ANYONE.
I FOLLOW NO MAN'S ORDERS!!!
DON'T DO IT, SISTER!!
KTOK
SAVE US, COMMODORE TEECH!!!
!
NOTHING WORKS AGAINST THIS ONE!!!
BAKOOM
GYAAA..!!
HUH?
WHOA...
YOU KIDDING ME? WHITE HAIR...BROWN SKIN...
GYAA
BLACK WINGS?!

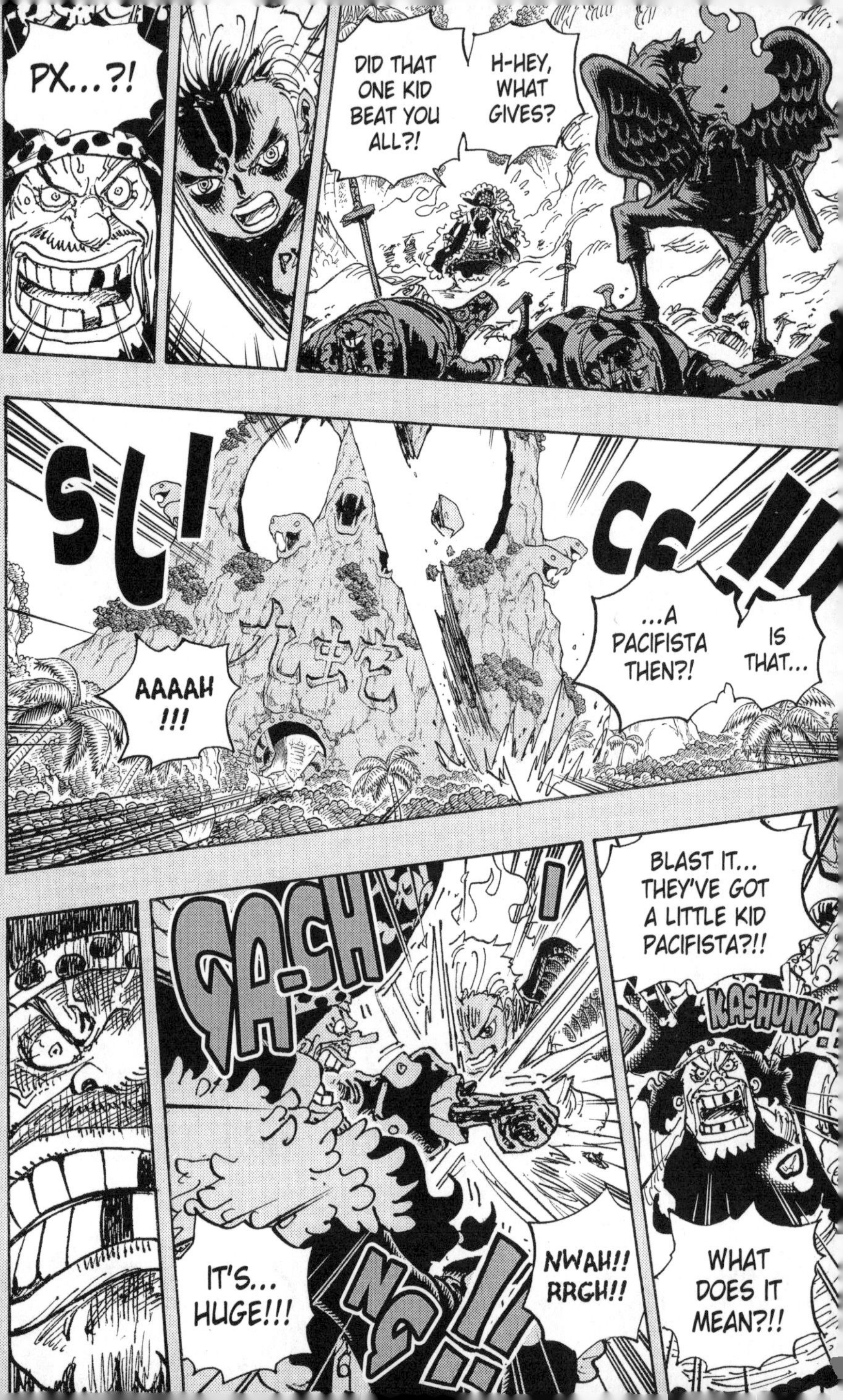
H-HEY, WHAT GIVES?
DID THAT ONE KID BEAT YOU ALL?!
PX...?!
CA
IS THAT...
...A PACIFISTA THEN?!
AAAAH!!!
SLI
BLAST IT... THEY'VE GOT A LITTLE KID PACIFISTA?!!
KASHUNK!!
WHAT DOES IT MEAN?!!
GA-CH
NWAH!! RRGH!!
NG!!
IT'S... HUGE!!!

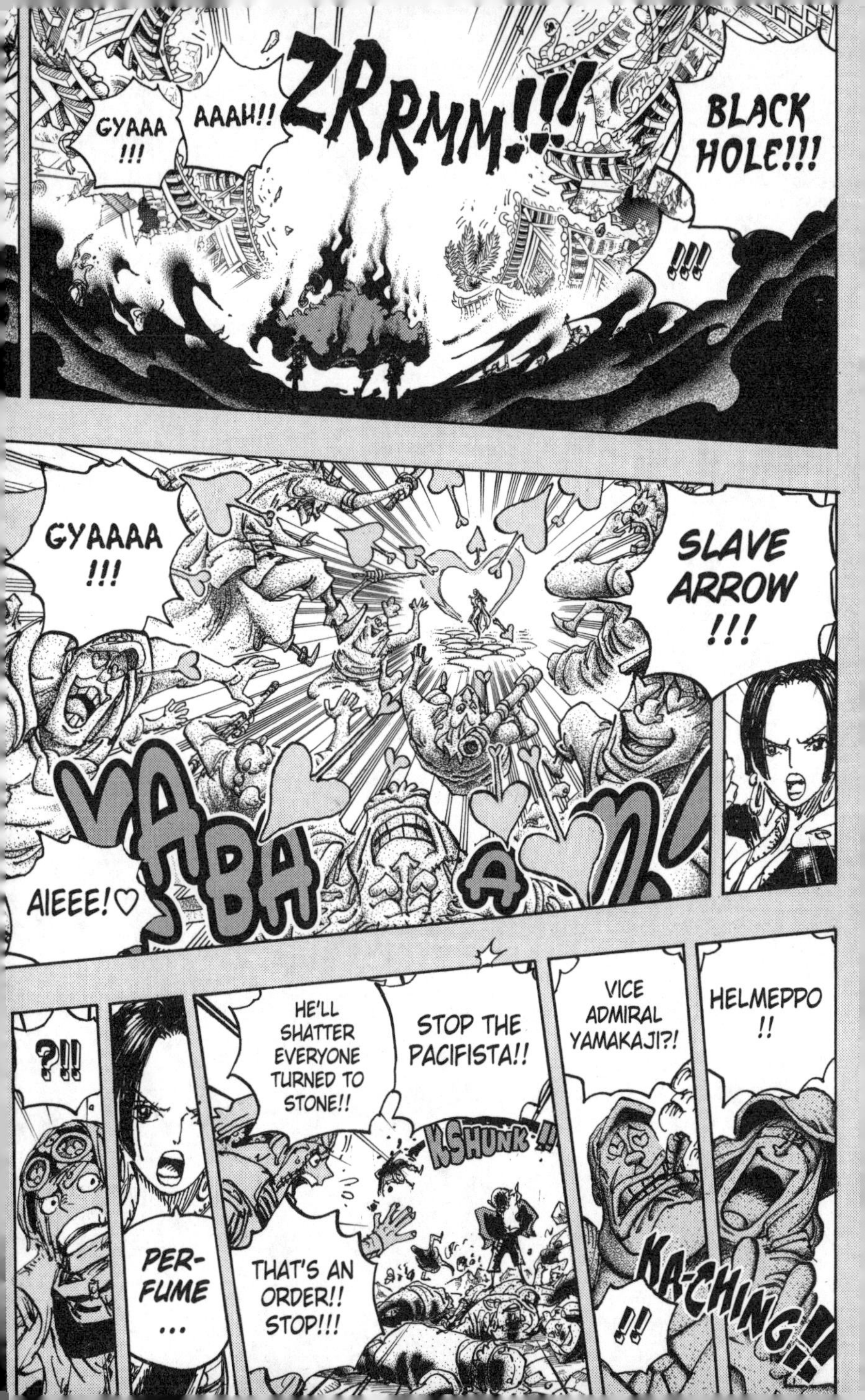
BLACK HOLE!!!
ZRRMM!!!
AAAH!!
GYAAA !!!
!!!
SLAVE ARROW !!!
GYAAAA !!!
VA BA A N
AIEEE!♡
HELMEPPO !!
VICE ADMIRAL YAMAKAJI?!
!!
KA-CHING!!
STOP THE PACIFISTA!!
HE'LL SHATTER EVERYONE TURNED TO STONE!!
KSHUNK!!
THAT'S AN ORDER!! STOP!!!
PER-FUME ...
?!!

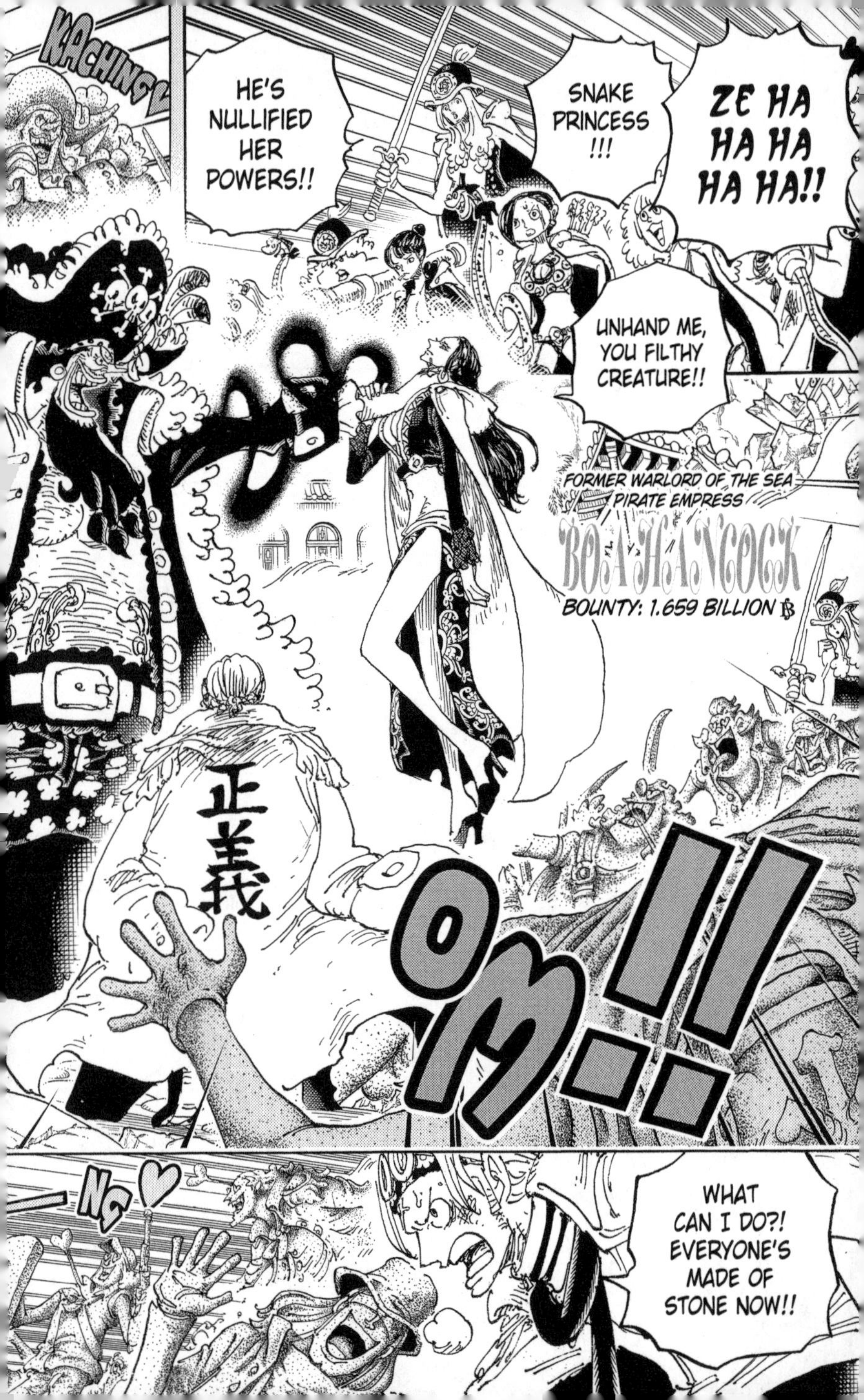
ZE HA HA HA HA HA!!
SNAKE PRINCESS!!!
HE'S NULLIFIED HER POWERS!!
KACHING
UNHAND ME, YOU FILTHY CREATURE!!
FORMER WARLORD OF THE SEA
PIRATE EMPRESS
BOA HANCOCK
BOUNTY: 1.659 BILLION ฿
正義
WHAT CAN I DO?! EVERYONE'S MADE OF STONE NOW!!
NG ♥

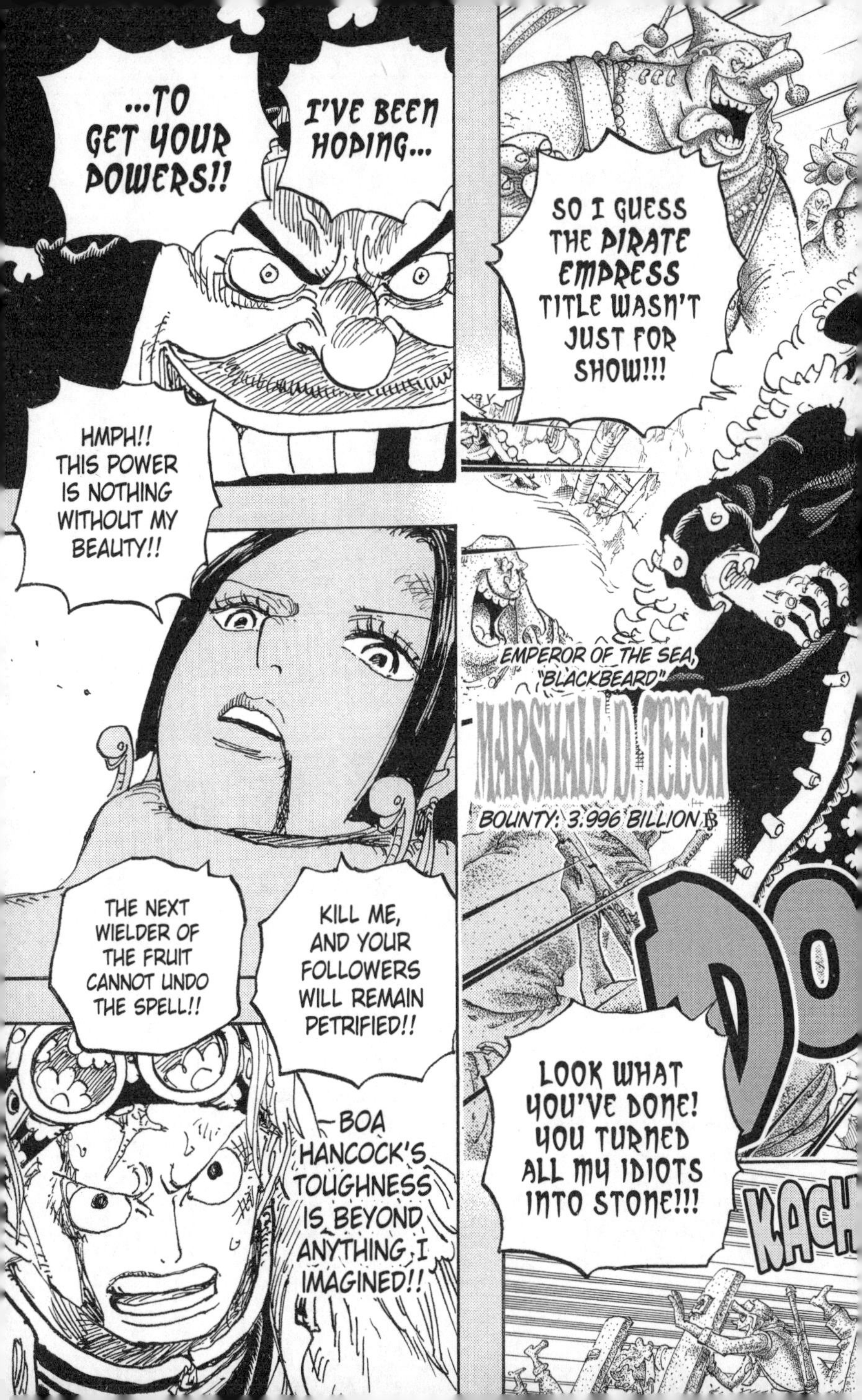
SO I GUESS THE PIRATE EMPRESS TITLE WASN'T JUST FOR SHOW!!!
EMPEROR OF THE SEA, "BLACKBEARD"
MARSHALL D. TEECH
BOUNTY: 3.996 BILLION ฿
DO
LOOK WHAT YOU'VE DONE! YOU TURNED ALL MY IDIOTS INTO STONE!!!
KACH
I'VE BEEN HOPING...
...TO GET YOUR POWERS!!
HMPH!! THIS POWER IS NOTHING WITHOUT MY BEAUTY!!
KILL ME, AND YOUR FOLLOWERS WILL REMAIN PETRIFIED!!
THE NEXT WIELDER OF THE FRUIT CANNOT UNDO THE SPELL!!
BOA HANCOCK'S TOUGHNESS IS BEYOND ANYTHING I IMAGINED!!

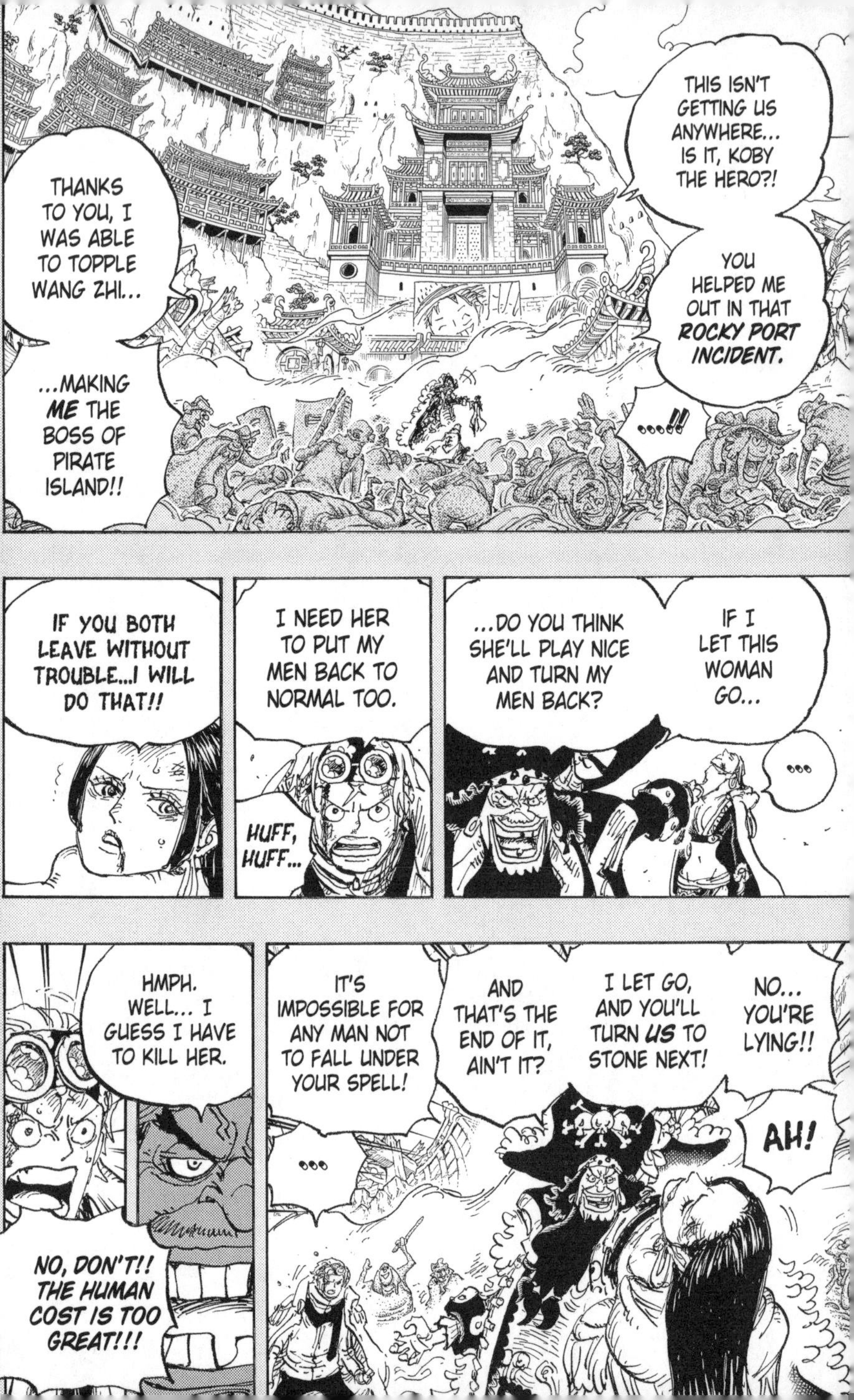
THIS ISN'T GETTING US ANYWHERE... IS IT, KOBY THE HERO?!
YOU HELPED ME OUT IN THAT ROCKY PORT INCIDENT.
...!!
THANKS TO YOU, I WAS ABLE TO TOPPLE WANG ZHI...
...MAKING ME THE BOSS OF PIRATE ISLAND!!
IF I LET THIS WOMAN GO...
...DO YOU THINK SHE'LL PLAY NICE AND TURN MY MEN BACK?
...
I NEED HER TO PUT MY MEN BACK TO NORMAL TOO.
HUFF, HUFF...
IF YOU BOTH LEAVE WITHOUT TROUBLE...I WILL DO THAT!!
NO... YOU'RE LYING!!
I LET GO, AND YOU'LL TURN US TO STONE NEXT!
AND THAT'S THE END OF IT, AIN'T IT?
IT'S IMPOSSIBLE FOR ANY MAN NOT TO FALL UNDER YOUR SPELL!
AH!
...
HMPH. WELL... I GUESS I HAVE TO KILL HER.
NO, DON'T!! THE HUMAN COST IS TOO GREAT!!!

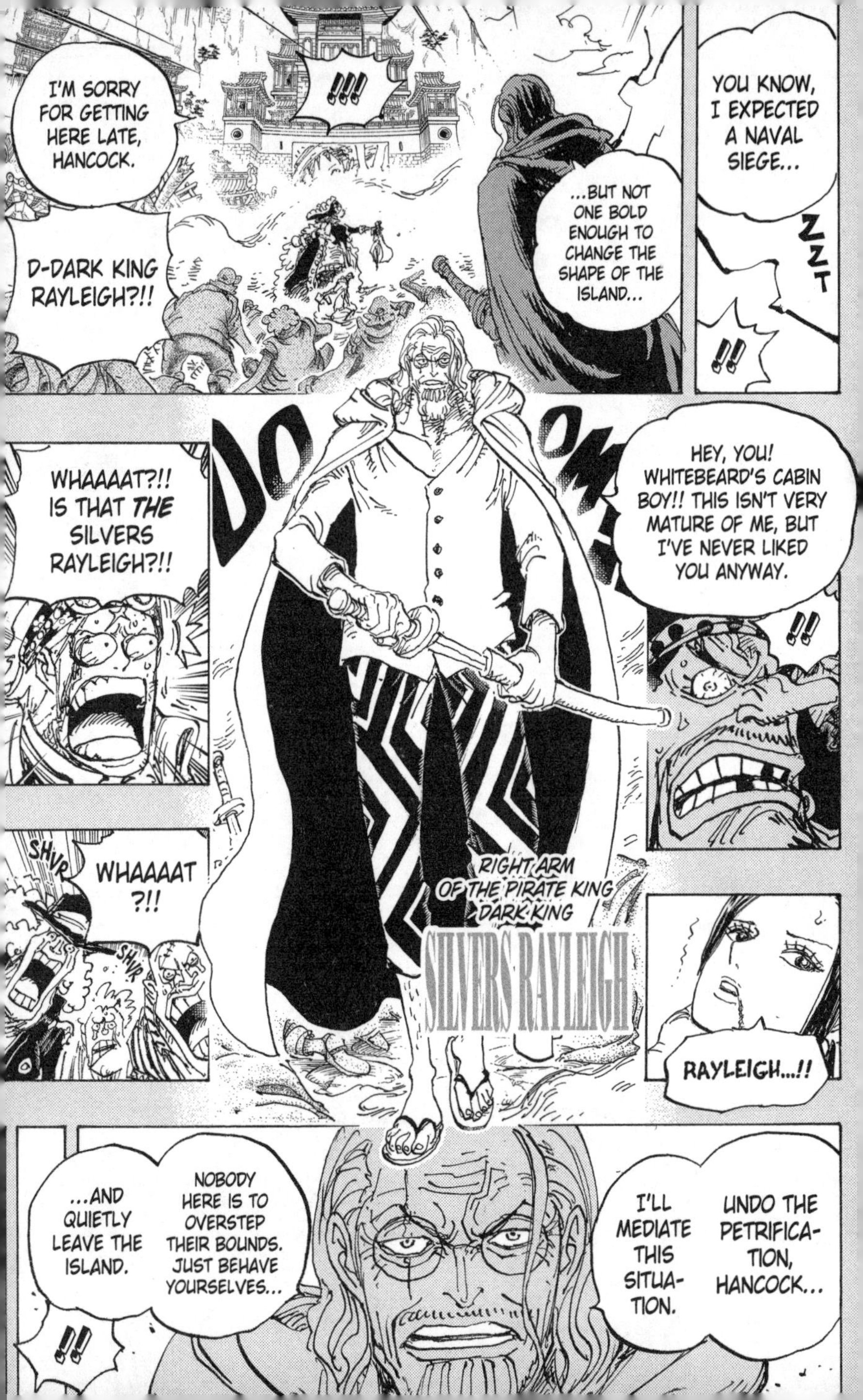
YOU KNOW, I EXPECTED A NAVAL SIEGE...
ZZZT
!!
...BUT NOT ONE BOLD ENOUGH TO CHANGE THE SHAPE OF THE ISLAND...
!!!
I'M SORRY FOR GETTING HERE LATE, HANCOCK.
D-DARK KING RAYLEIGH?!!
HEY, YOU! WHITEBEARD'S CABIN BOY!! THIS ISN'T VERY MATURE OF ME, BUT I'VE NEVER LIKED YOU ANYWAY.
!!
DOOM
WHAAAAT?!! IS THAT *THE* SILVERS RAYLEIGH?!!
RAYLEIGH...!!
RIGHT ARM OF THE PIRATE KING
DARK KING
SILVERS RAYLEIGH
WHAAAAT ?!!
SHIVR
SHIVR
UNDO THE PETRIFICATION, HANCOCK...
I'LL MEDIATE THIS SITUATION.
NOBODY HERE IS TO OVERSTEP THEIR BOUNDS. JUST BEHAVE YOURSELVES...
...AND QUIETLY LEAVE THE ISLAND.
!!

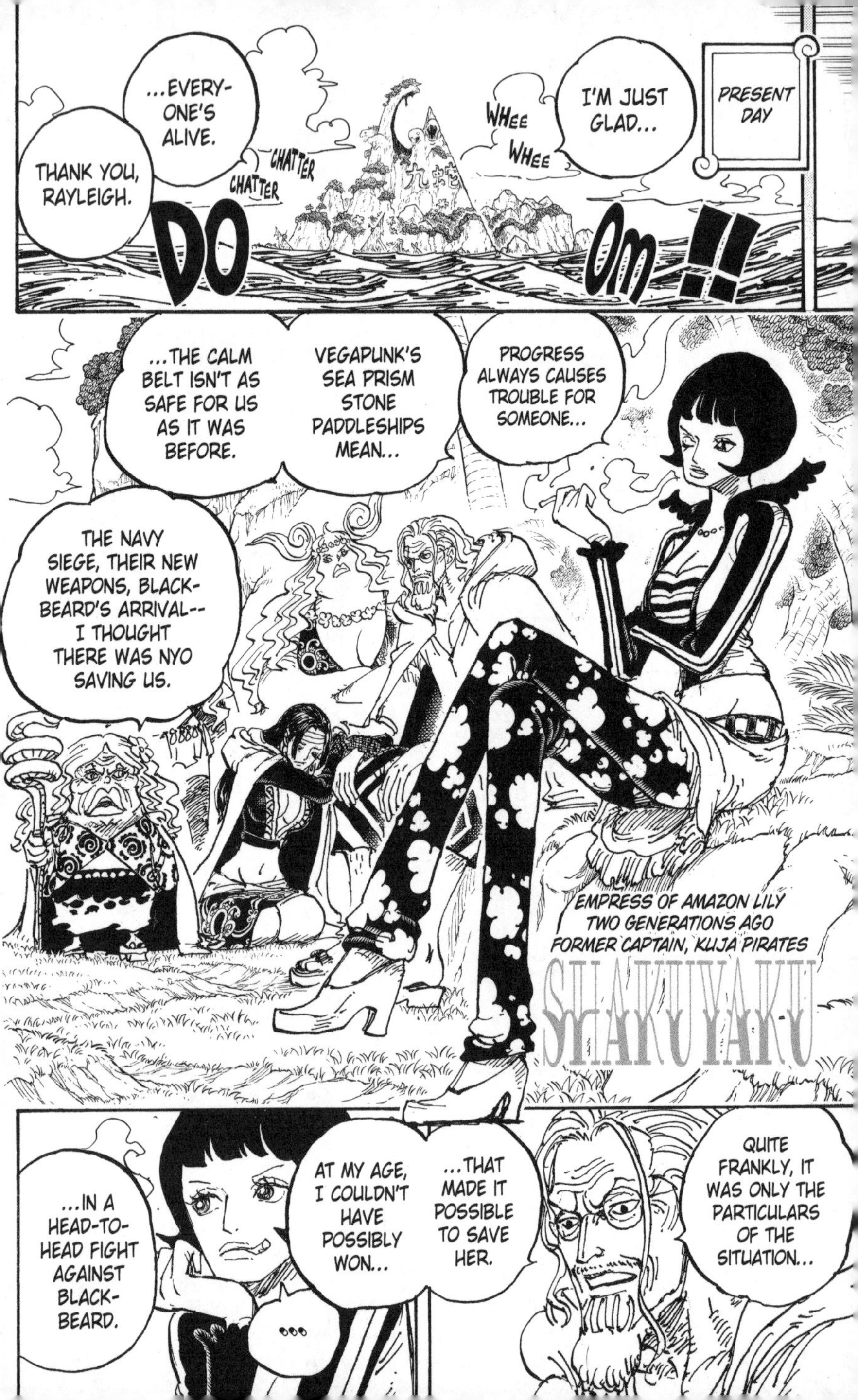
PRESENT DAY
I'M JUST GLAD...
WHEE WHEE
...EVERYONE'S ALIVE.
CHATTER CHATTER
THANK YOU, RAYLEIGH.
九蛇
DOOM!!
PROGRESS ALWAYS CAUSES TROUBLE FOR SOMEONE...
VEGAPUNK'S SEA PRISM STONE PADDLESHIPS MEAN...
...THE CALM BELT ISN'T AS SAFE FOR US AS IT WAS BEFORE.
THE NAVY SIEGE, THEIR NEW WEAPONS, BLACKBEARD'S ARRIVAL-- I THOUGHT THERE WAS NYO SAVING US.
EMPRESS OF AMAZON LILY TWO GENERATIONS AGO FORMER CAPTAIN, KUJA PIRATES
SHAKUYAKU
QUITE FRANKLY, IT WAS ONLY THE PARTICULARS OF THE SITUATION...
...THAT MADE IT POSSIBLE TO SAVE HER.
AT MY AGE, I COULDN'T HAVE POSSIBLY WON...
...IN A HEAD-TO-HEAD FIGHT AGAINST BLACKBEARD.
...

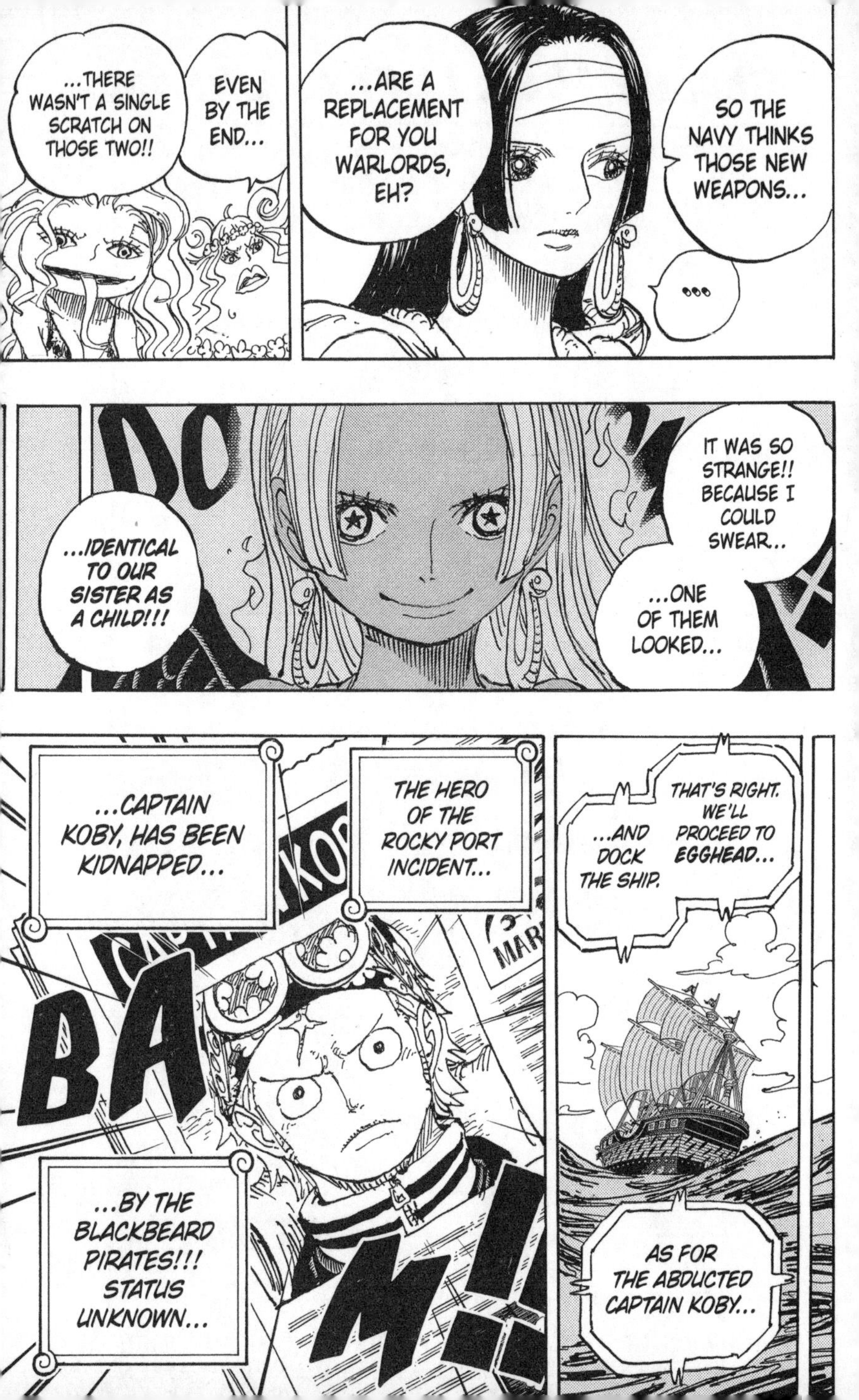
SO THE NAVY THINKS THOSE NEW WEAPONS...
...ARE A REPLACEMENT FOR YOU WARLORDS, EH?
...
EVEN BY THE END...
...THERE WASN'T A SINGLE SCRATCH ON THOSE TWO!!
IT WAS SO STRANGE!! BECAUSE I COULD SWEAR...
...ONE OF THEM LOOKED...
...IDENTICAL TO OUR SISTER AS A CHILD!!!
THAT'S RIGHT. WE'LL PROCEED TO EGGHEAD...
...AND DOCK THE SHIP.
AS FOR THE ABDUCTED CAPTAIN KOBY...
THE HERO OF THE ROCKY PORT INCIDENT...
...CAPTAIN KOBY, HAS BEEN KIDNAPPED...
BAM!!
...BY THE BLACKBEARD PIRATES!!! STATUS UNKNOWN...

Chapter 1060: LUFFY'S DREAM

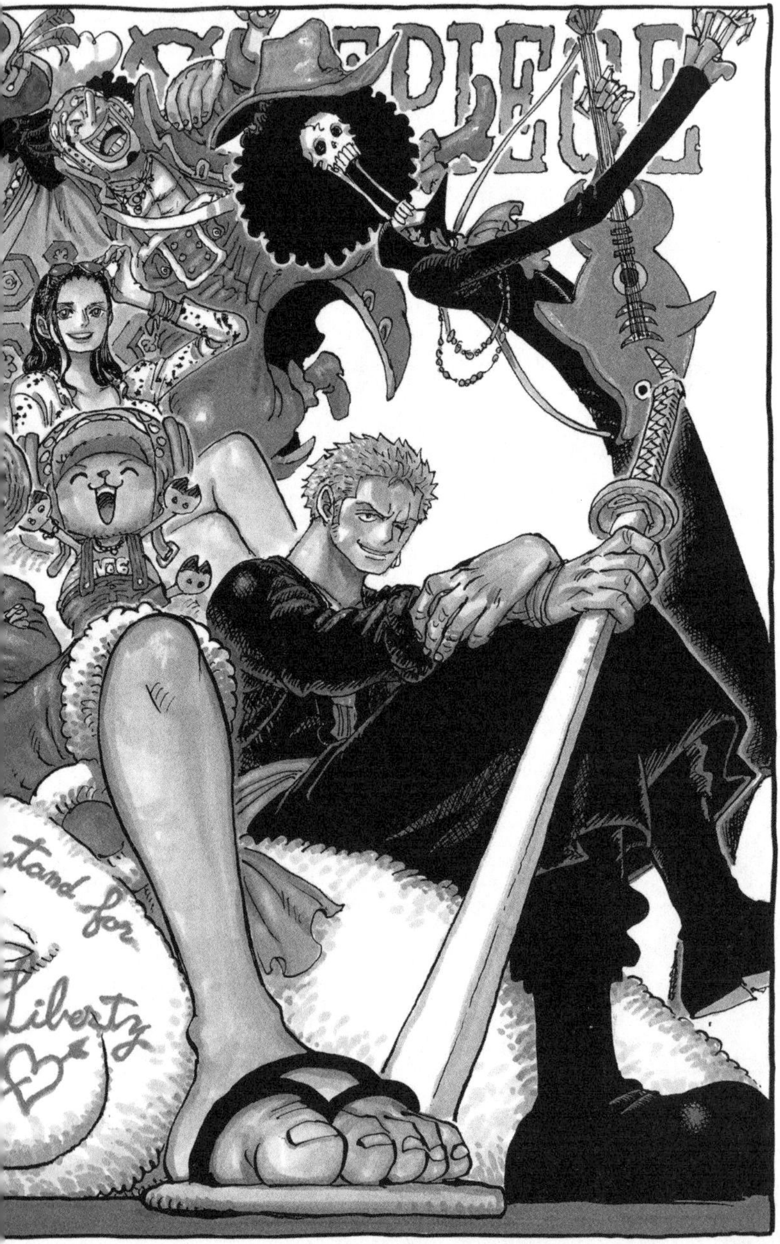

stand for
Liberty

READER REQUEST: "REDRAW THE COLORING CORNER PAGE FROM VOLUME 8 BUT WITH ALL 10 CREWMATES!" BY IWASAKKI

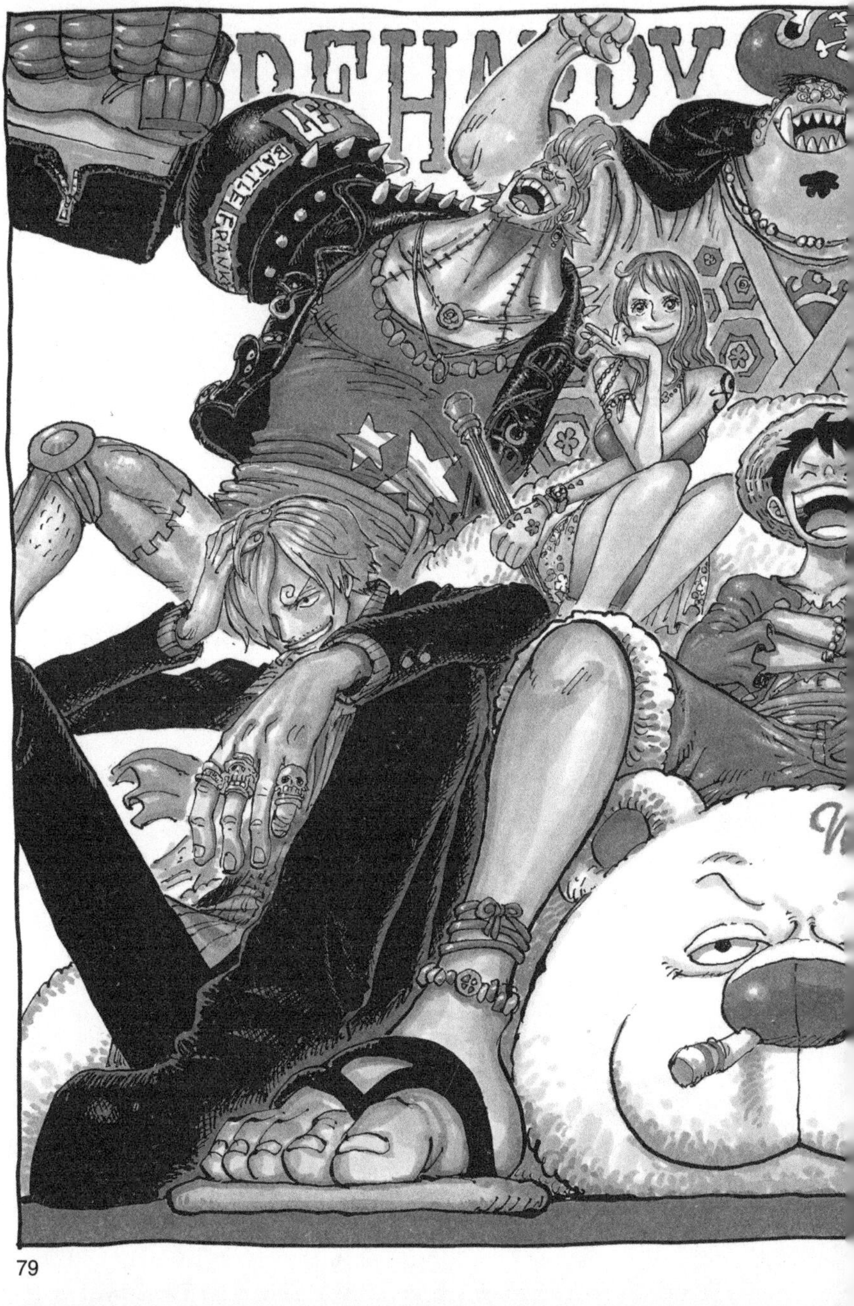

vol.105
ONE PIECE

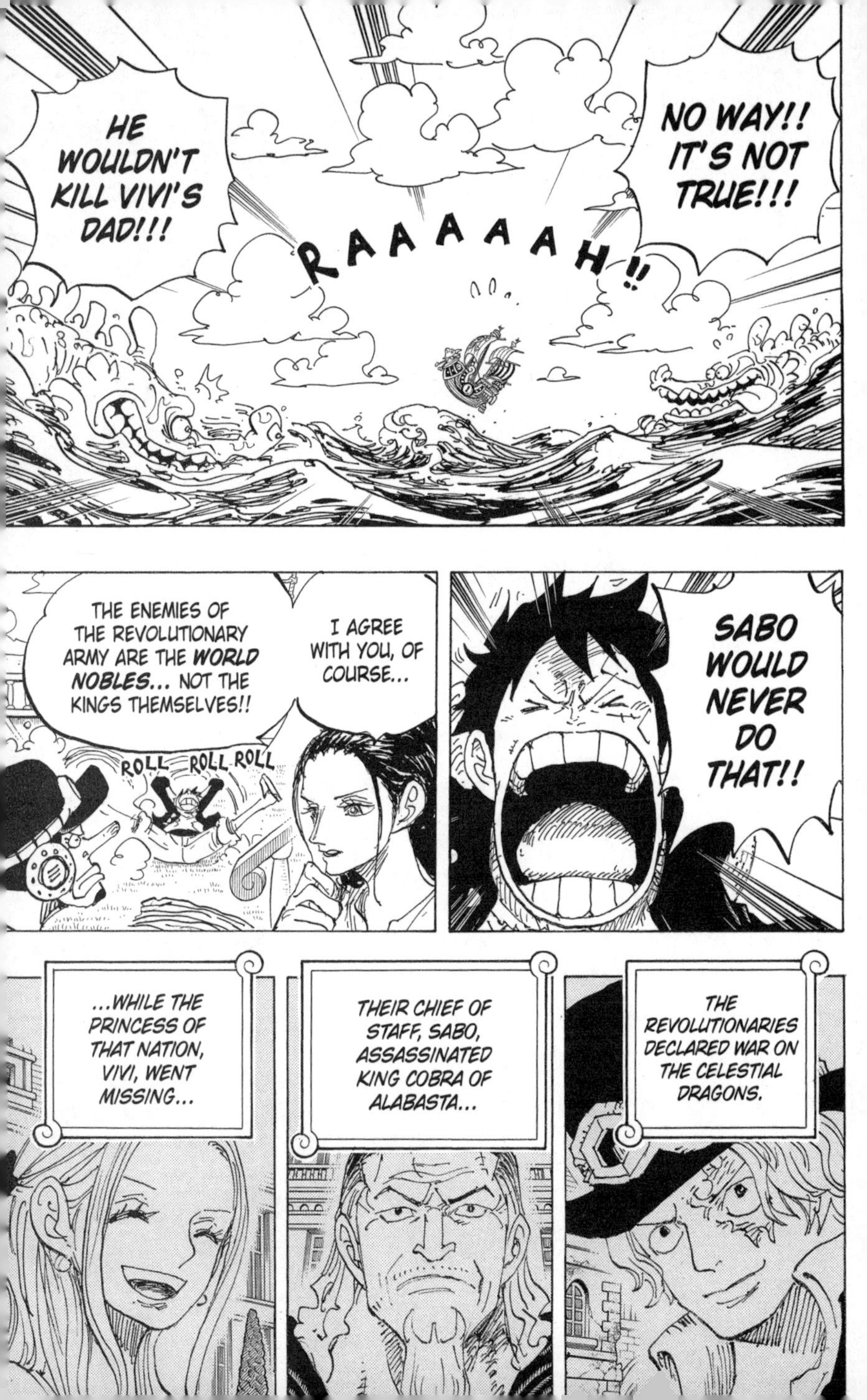
NO WAY!! IT'S NOT TRUE!!!
HE WOULDN'T KILL VIVI'S DAD!!!
RAAAAAH!!
SABO WOULD NEVER DO THAT!!
I AGREE WITH YOU, OF COURSE...
THE ENEMIES OF THE REVOLUTIONARY ARMY ARE THE WORLD NOBLES... NOT THE KINGS THEMSELVES!!
ROLL ROLL ROLL
THE REVOLUTIONARIES DECLARED WAR ON THE CELESTIAL DRAGONS.
THEIR CHIEF OF STAFF, SABO, ASSASSINATED KING COBRA OF ALABASTA...
...WHILE THE PRINCESS OF THAT NATION, VIVI, WENT MISSING...

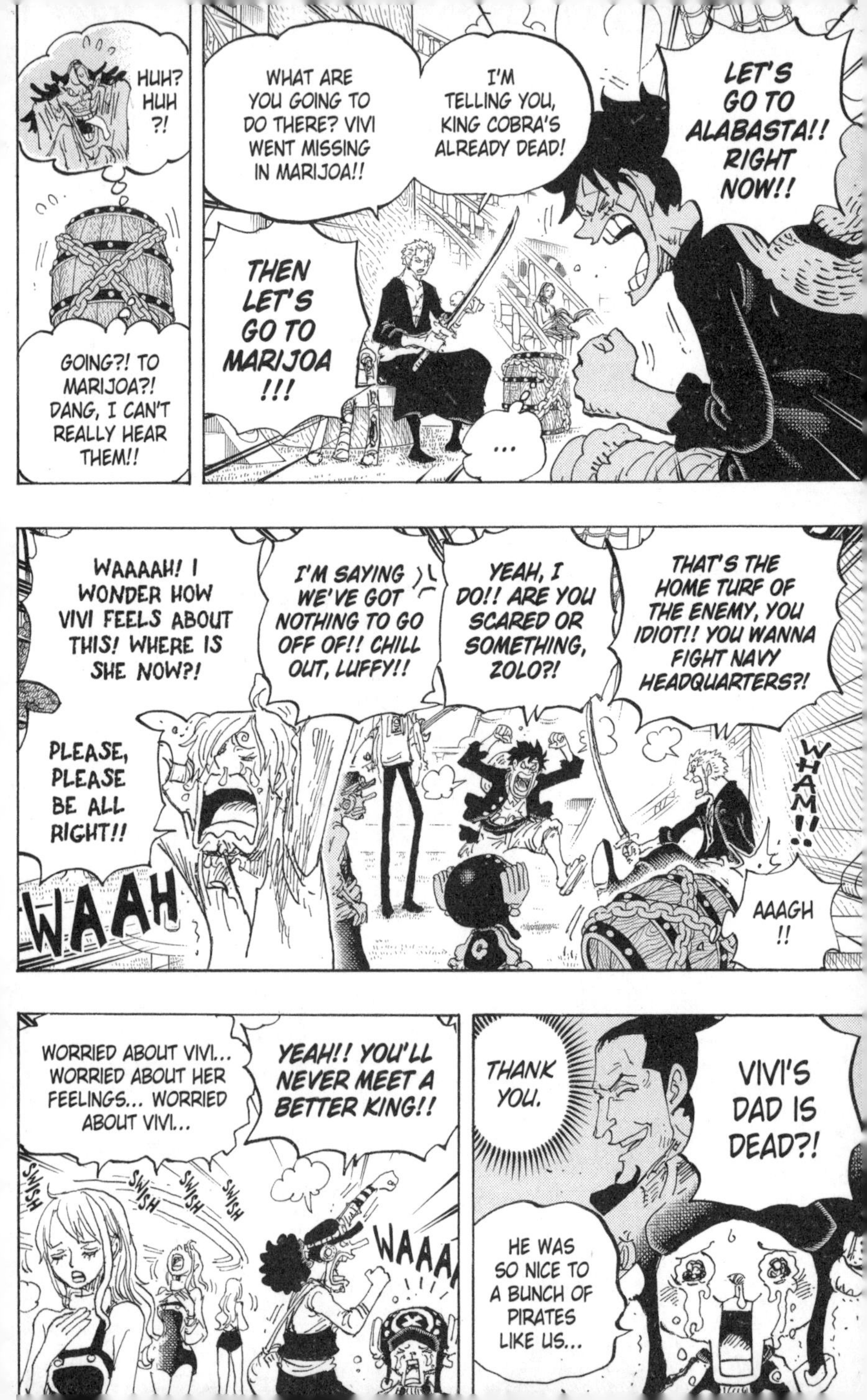
LET'S GO TO ALABASTA!! RIGHT NOW!!
I'M TELLING YOU, KING COBRA'S ALREADY DEAD!
WHAT ARE YOU GOING TO DO THERE? VIVI WENT MISSING IN MARIJOA!!
THEN LET'S GO TO MARIJOA!!!
...
HUH? HUH ?!
GOING?! TO MARIJOA?! DANG, I CAN'T REALLY HEAR THEM!!
THAT'S THE HOME TURF OF THE ENEMY, YOU IDIOT!! YOU WANNA FIGHT NAVY HEADQUARTERS?!
YEAH, I DO!! ARE YOU SCARED OR SOMETHING, ZOLO?!
I'M SAYING WE'VE GOT NOTHING TO GO OFF OF!! CHILL OUT, LUFFY!!
WAAAAH! I WONDER HOW VIVI FEELS ABOUT THIS! WHERE IS SHE NOW?!
WHAM!!
AAAGH !!
PLEASE, PLEASE BE ALL RIGHT!!
WAAH
VIVI'S DAD IS DEAD?!
THANK YOU.
HE WAS SO NICE TO A BUNCH OF PIRATES LIKE US...
YEAH!! YOU'LL NEVER MEET A BETTER KING!!
WORRIED ABOUT VIVI... WORRIED ABOUT HER FEELINGS... WORRIED ABOUT VIVI...
WAAA
SWISH
SWISH
SWISH
SWISH

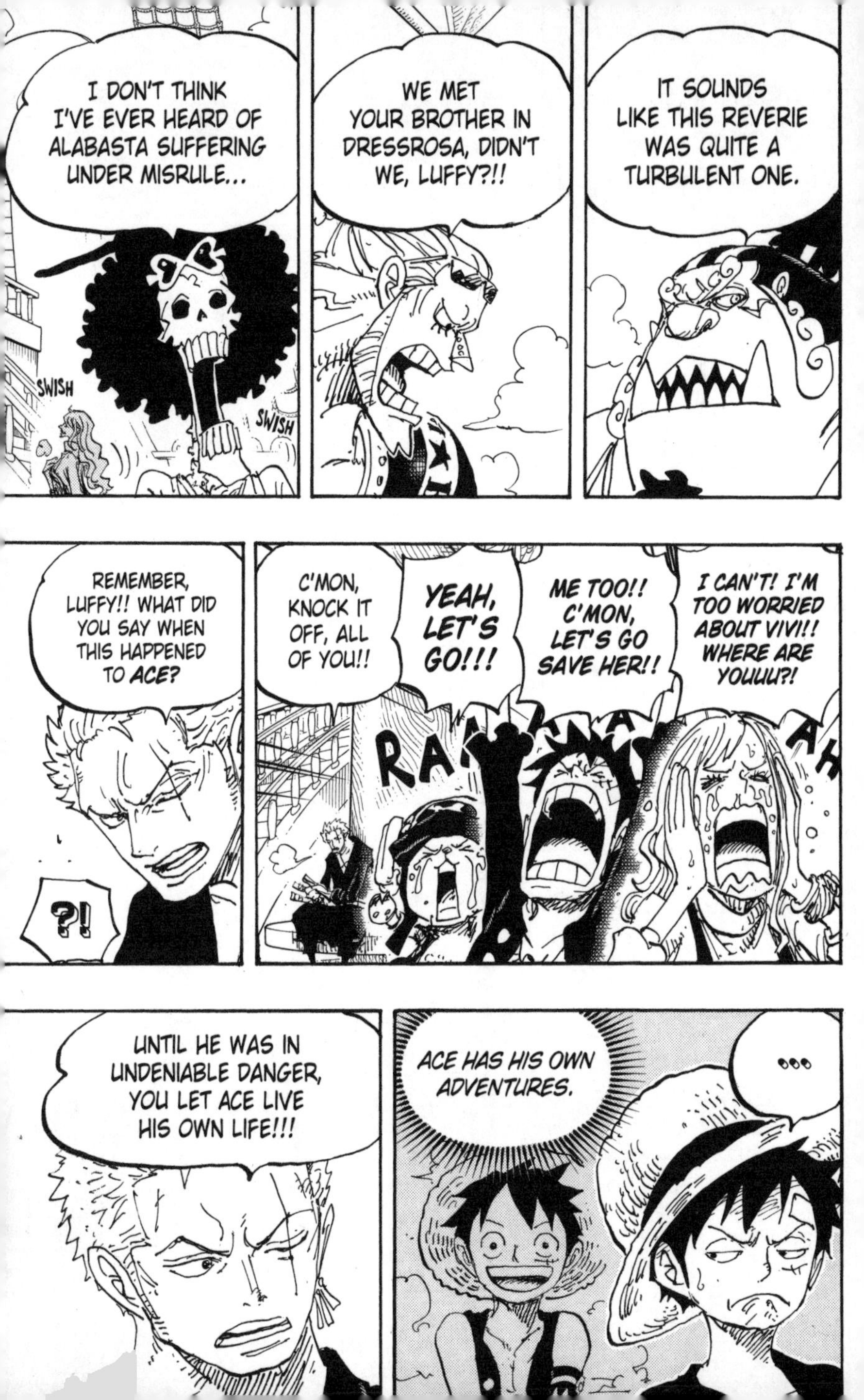
IT SOUNDS LIKE THIS REVERIE WAS QUITE A TURBULENT ONE.
WE MET YOUR BROTHER IN DRESSROSA, DIDN'T WE, LUFFY?!!
I DON'T THINK I'VE EVER HEARD OF ALABASTA SUFFERING UNDER MISRULE...
SWISH
SWISH
I CAN'T! I'M TOO WORRIED ABOUT VIVI!! WHERE ARE YOUUU?!
ME TOO!! C'MON, LET'S GO SAVE HER!!
YEAH, LET'S GO!!!
C'MON, KNOCK IT OFF, ALL OF YOU!!
REMEMBER, LUFFY!! WHAT DID YOU SAY WHEN THIS HAPPENED TO ACE?
?!
...
ACE HAS HIS OWN ADVENTURES.
UNTIL HE WAS IN UNDENIABLE DANGER, YOU LET ACE LIVE HIS OWN LIFE!!!

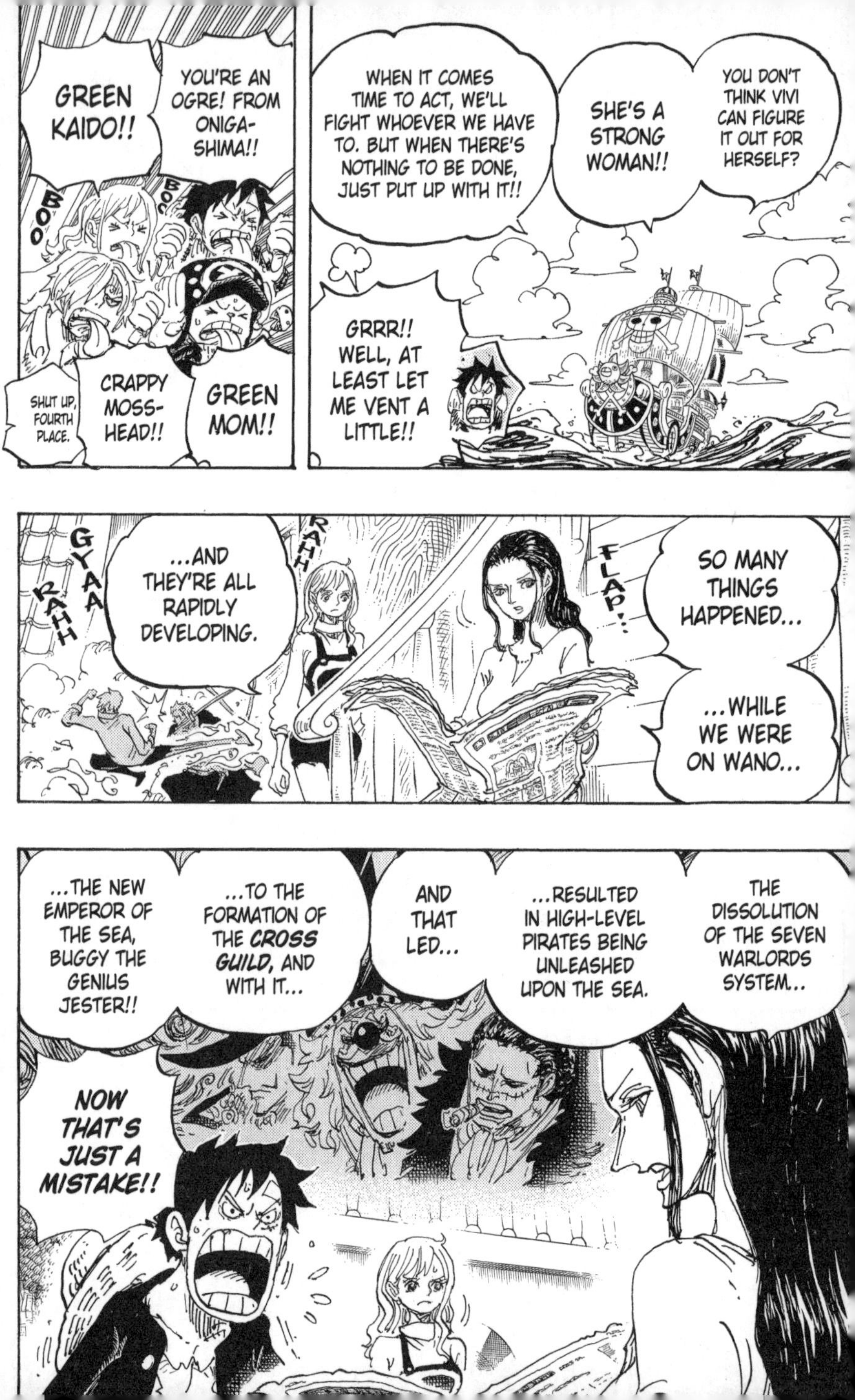
YOU DON'T THINK VIVI CAN FIGURE IT OUT FOR HERSELF?
SHE'S A STRONG WOMAN!!
WHEN IT COMES TIME TO ACT, WE'LL FIGHT WHOEVER WE HAVE TO. BUT WHEN THERE'S NOTHING TO BE DONE, JUST PUT UP WITH IT!!
GRRR!! WELL, AT LEAST LET ME VENT A LITTLE!!
YOU'RE AN OGRE! FROM ONIGA-SHIMA!!
GREEN KAIDO!!
BOO
BOO
GREEN MOM!!
CRAPPY MOSS-HEAD!!
SHUT UP, FOURTH PLACE.
SO MANY THINGS HAPPENED...
...WHILE WE WERE ON WANO...
FLAP..
RAHH
...AND THEY'RE ALL RAPIDLY DEVELOPING.
GYAA
RAHH
THE DISSOLUTION OF THE SEVEN WARLORDS SYSTEM...
...RESULTED IN HIGH-LEVEL PIRATES BEING UNLEASHED UPON THE SEA.
AND THAT LED...
...TO THE FORMATION OF THE *CROSS GUILD*, AND WITH IT...
...THE NEW EMPEROR OF THE SEA, BUGGY THE GENIUS JESTER!!
NOW THAT'S JUST A MISTAKE!!

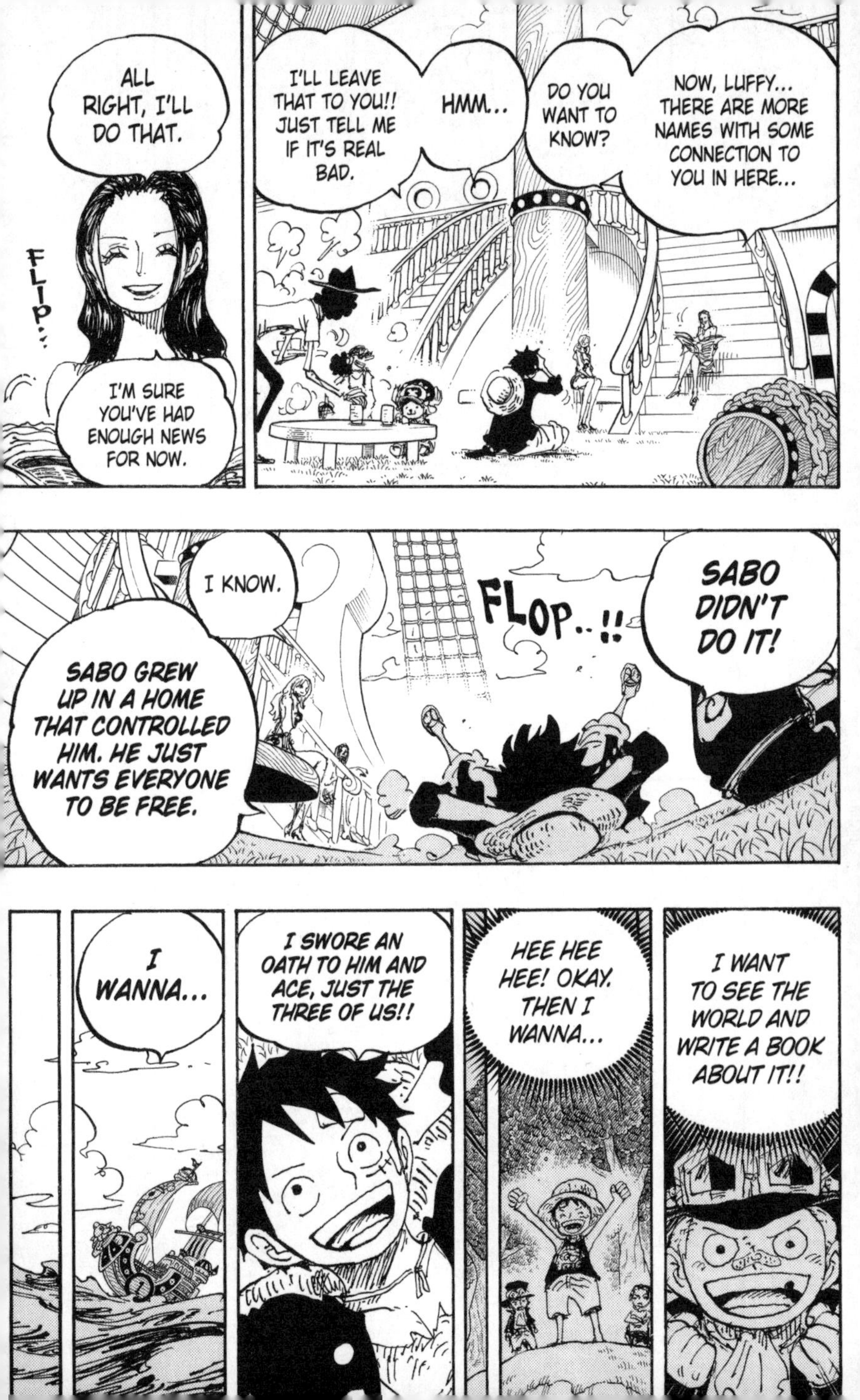
NOW, LUFFY... THERE ARE MORE NAMES WITH SOME CONNECTION TO YOU IN HERE...
DO YOU WANT TO KNOW?
HMM...
I'LL LEAVE THAT TO YOU!! JUST TELL ME IF IT'S REAL BAD.
ALL RIGHT, I'LL DO THAT.
FLIP...
I'M SURE YOU'VE HAD ENOUGH NEWS FOR NOW.
SABO DIDN'T DO IT!
FLOP..!!
I KNOW.
SABO GREW UP IN A HOME THAT CONTROLLED HIM. HE JUST WANTS EVERYONE TO BE FREE.
I WANT TO SEE THE WORLD AND WRITE A BOOK ABOUT IT!!
HEE HEE HEE! OKAY. THEN I WANNA...
I SWORE AN OATH TO HIM AND ACE, JUST THE THREE OF US!!
I WANNA...

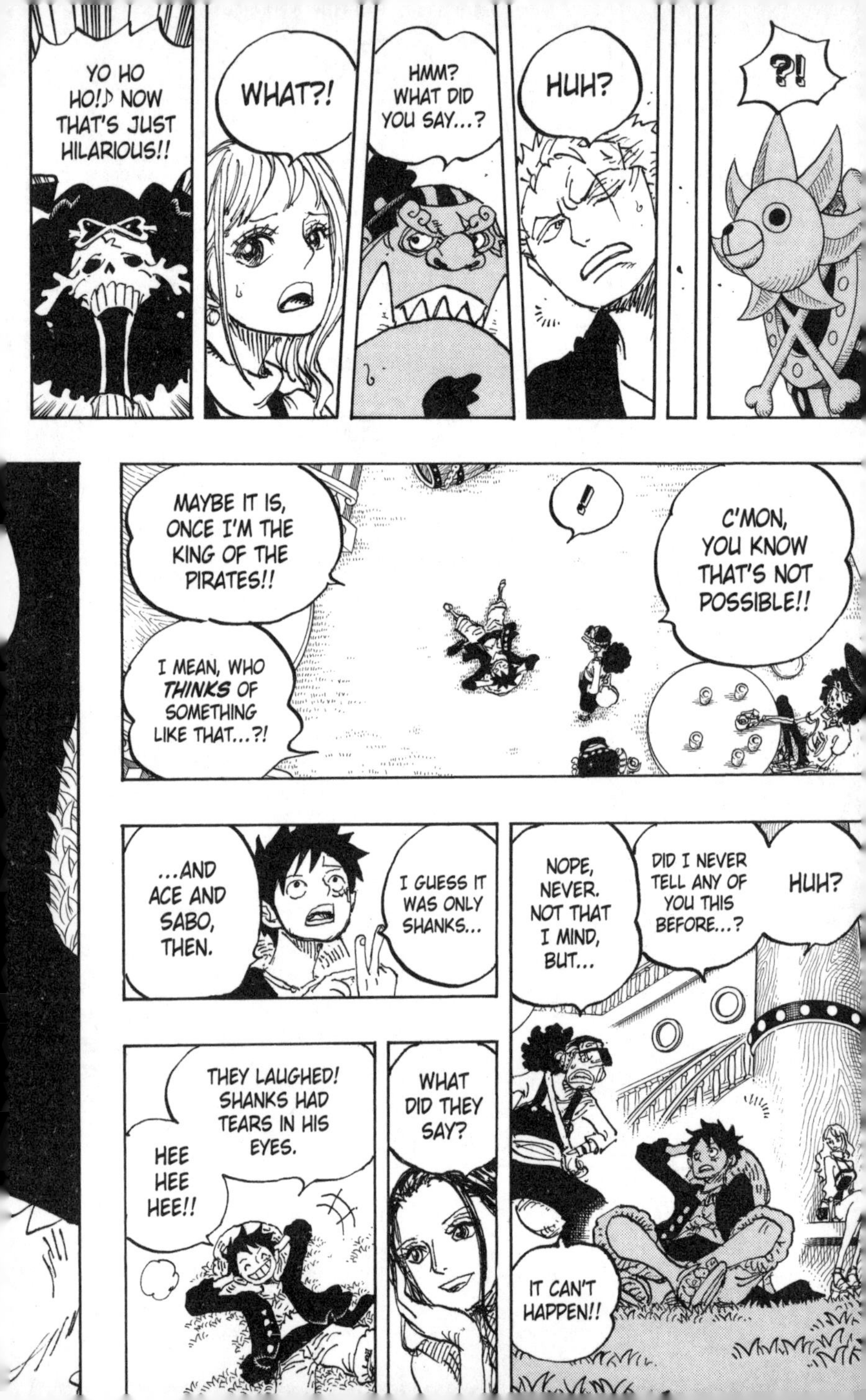
?!
HUH?
HMM? WHAT DID YOU SAY...?
WHAT?!
YO HO HO!♪ NOW THAT'S JUST HILARIOUS!!
C'MON, YOU KNOW THAT'S NOT POSSIBLE!!
!
MAYBE IT IS, ONCE I'M THE KING OF THE PIRATES!!
I MEAN, WHO *THINKS* OF SOMETHING LIKE THAT...?!
HUH?
DID I NEVER TELL ANY OF YOU THIS BEFORE...?
NOPE, NEVER. NOT THAT I MIND, BUT...
IT CAN'T HAPPEN!!
I GUESS IT WAS ONLY SHANKS...
...AND ACE AND SABO, THEN.
WHAT DID THEY SAY?
THEY LAUGHED! SHANKS HAD TEARS IN HIS EYES.
HEE HEE HEE!!

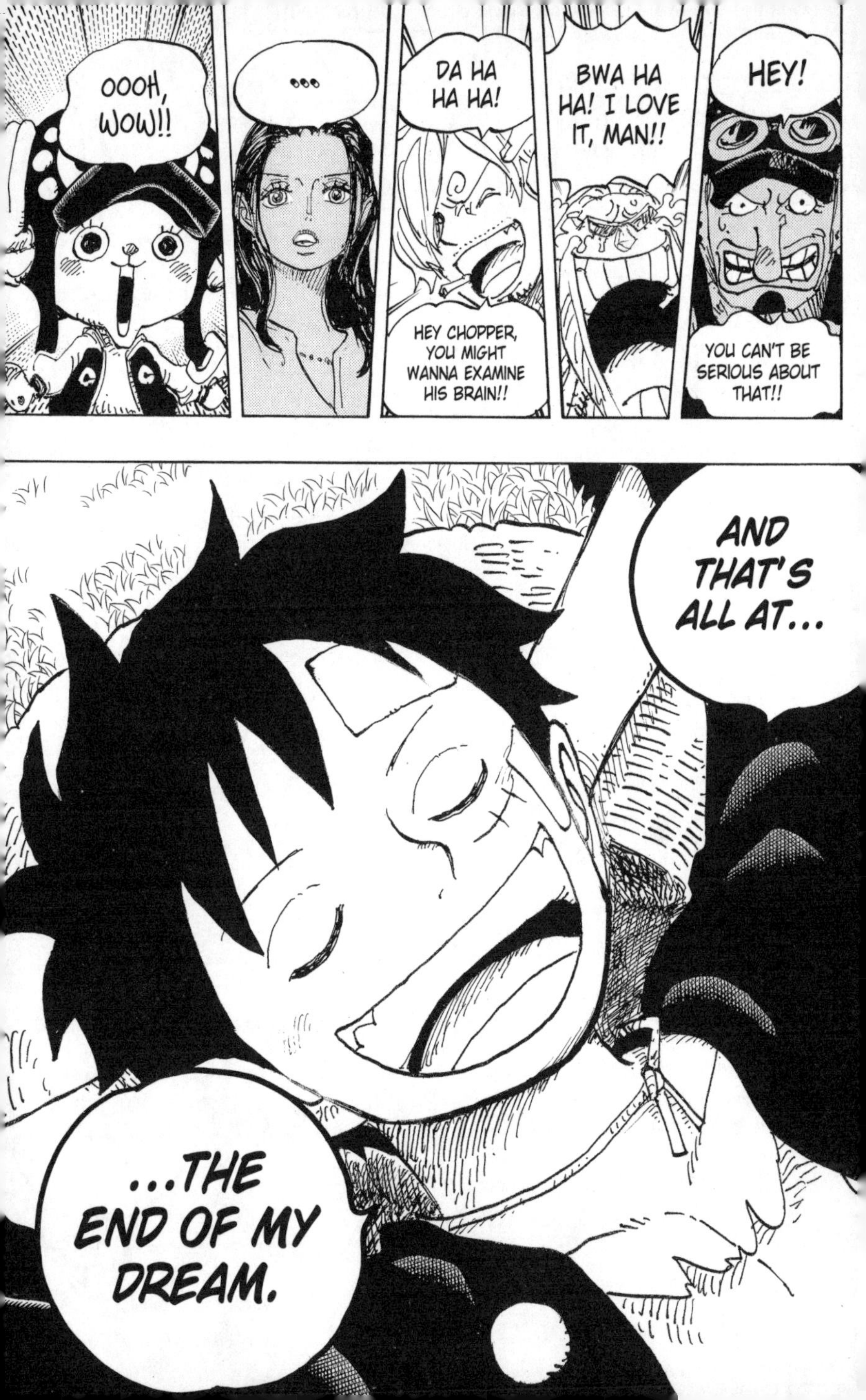
HEY!
YOU CAN'T BE SERIOUS ABOUT THAT!!
BWA HA HA! I LOVE IT, MAN!!
DA HA HA HA!
HEY CHOPPER, YOU MIGHT WANNA EXAMINE HIS BRAIN!!
...
OOOH, WOW!!
AND THAT'S ALL AT...
...THE END OF MY DREAM.

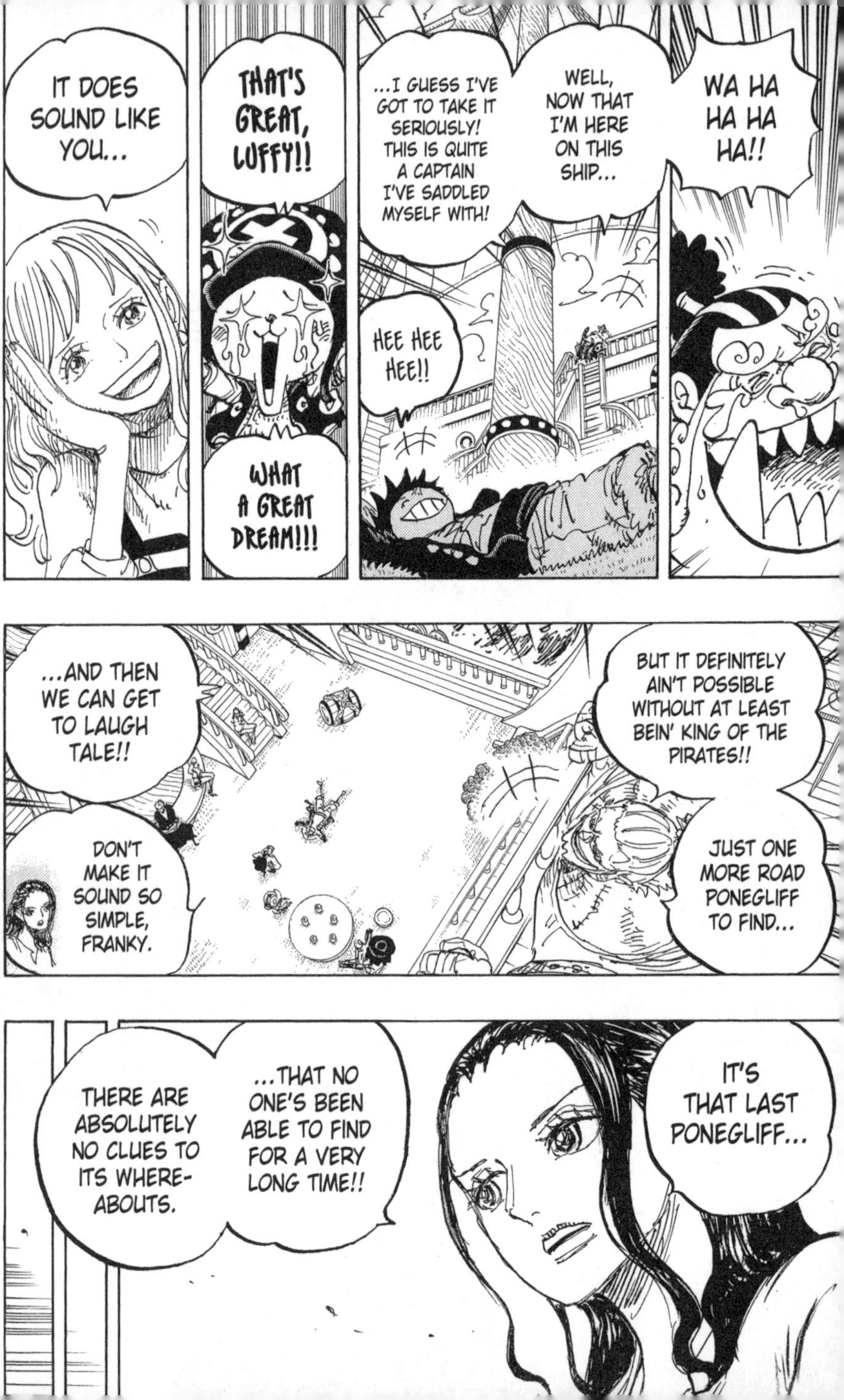
WA HA HA HA HA!!
WELL, NOW THAT I'M HERE ON THIS SHIP...
...I GUESS I'VE GOT TO TAKE IT SERIOUSLY! THIS IS QUITE A CAPTAIN I'VE SADDLED MYSELF WITH!
HEE HEE HEE!!
THAT'S GREAT, LUFFY!!
WHAT A GREAT DREAM!!!
IT DOES SOUND LIKE YOU...
BUT IT DEFINITELY AIN'T POSSIBLE WITHOUT AT LEAST BEIN' KING OF THE PIRATES!!
JUST ONE MORE ROAD PONEGLIFF TO FIND...
...AND THEN WE CAN GET TO LAUGH TALE!!
DON'T MAKE IT SOUND SO SIMPLE, FRANKY.
IT'S THAT LAST PONEGLIFF...
...THAT NO ONE'S BEEN ABLE TO FIND FOR A VERY LONG TIME!!
THERE ARE ABSOLUTELY NO CLUES TO ITS WHERE-ABOUTS.

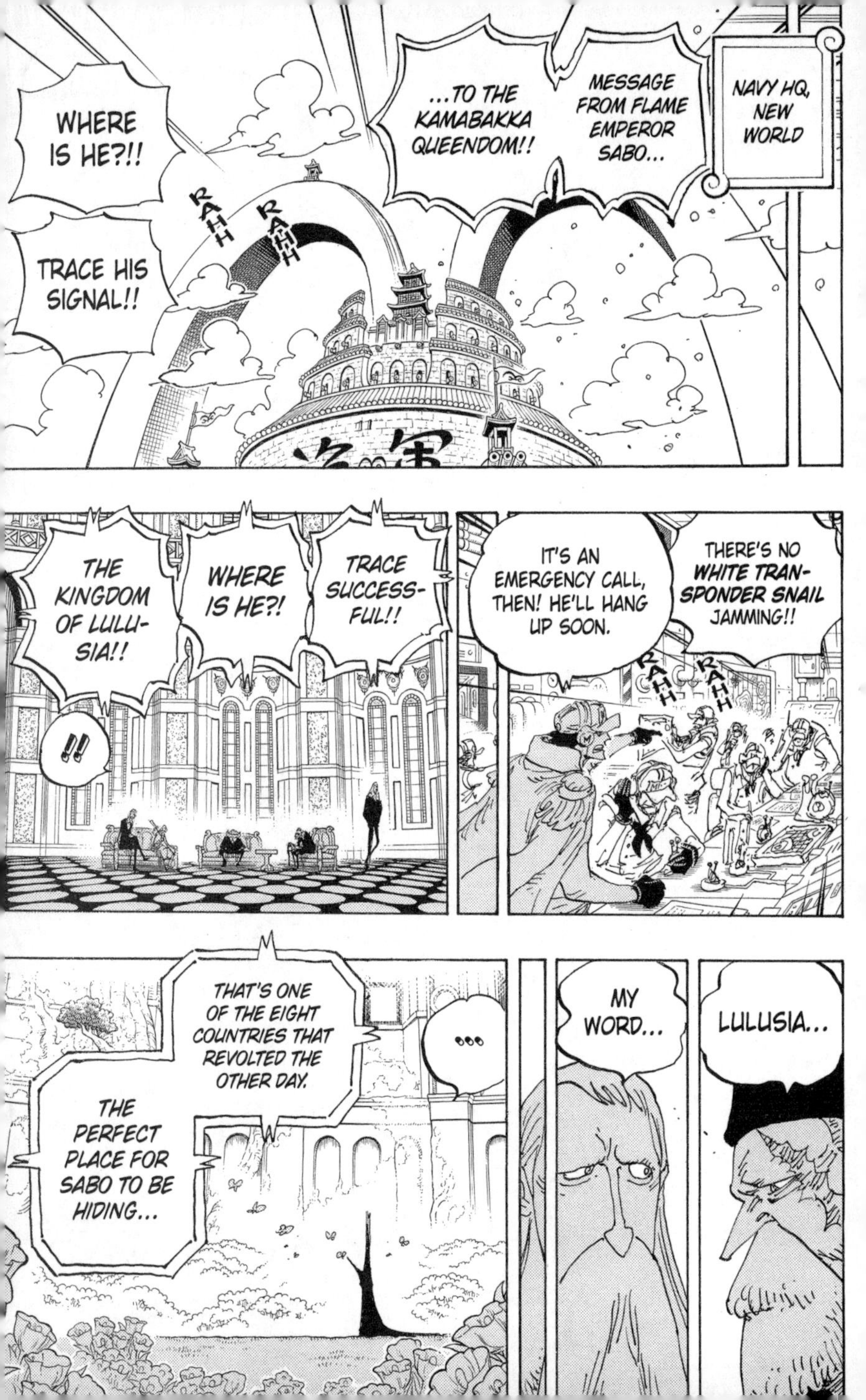
NAVY HQ, NEW WORLD
MESSAGE FROM FLAME EMPEROR SABO...
...TO THE KAMABAKKA QUEENDOM!!
RAHH
RAHH
WHERE IS HE?!!
TRACE HIS SIGNAL!!
THERE'S NO WHITE TRANSPONDER SNAIL JAMMING!!
IT'S AN EMERGENCY CALL, THEN! HE'LL HANG UP SOON.
RAHH
RAHH
TRACE SUCCESSFUL!!
WHERE IS HE?!
THE KINGDOM OF LULUSIA!!
!!
LULUSIA...
MY WORD...
...
THAT'S ONE OF THE EIGHT COUNTRIES THAT REVOLTED THE OTHER DAY.
THE PERFECT PLACE FOR SABO TO BE HIDING...

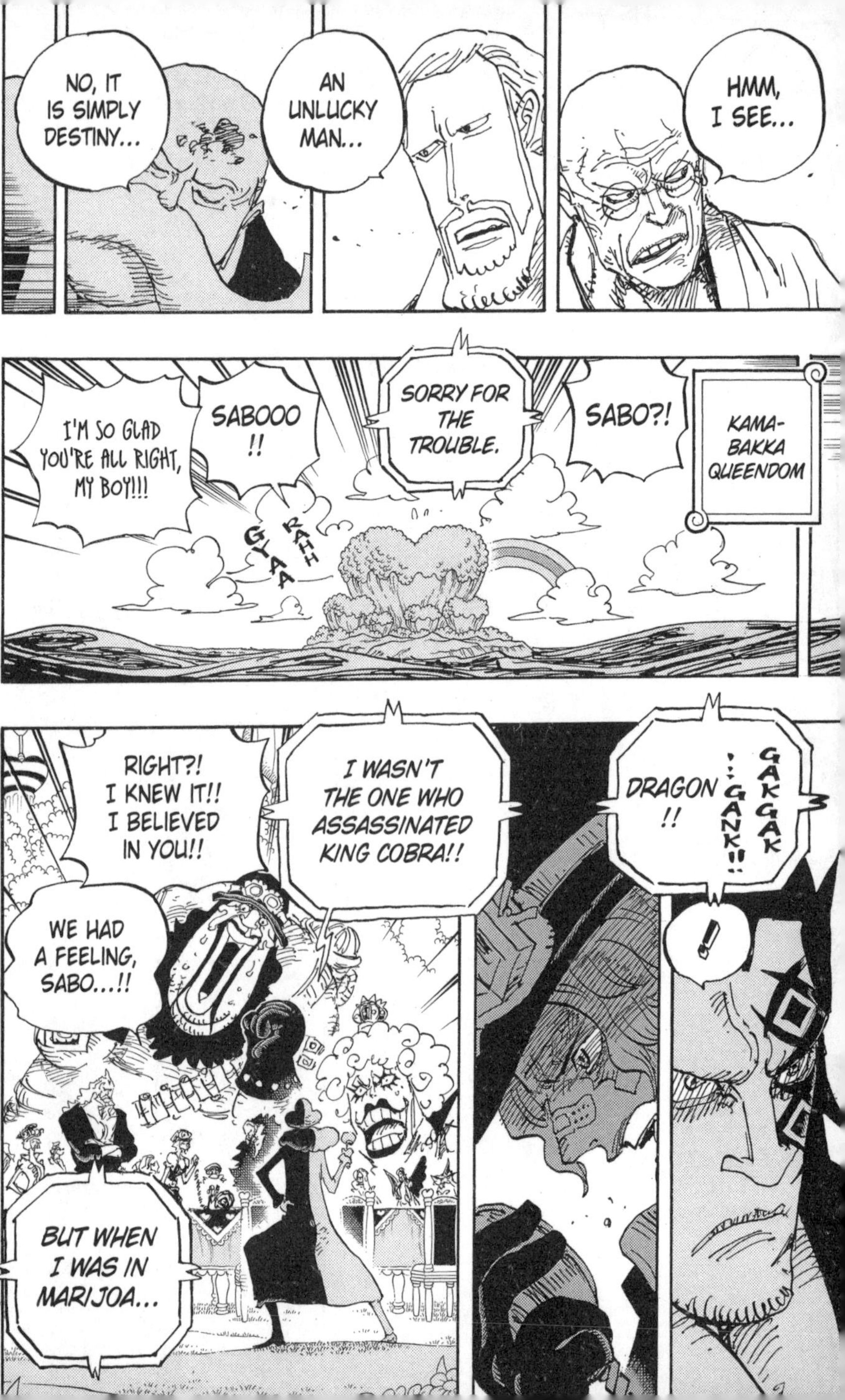
HMM, I SEE...
AN UNLUCKY MAN...
NO, IT IS SIMPLY DESTINY...
KAMABAKKA QUEENDOM
SABO?!
SORRY FOR THE TROUBLE.
SABOOO!!
I'M SO GLAD YOU'RE ALL RIGHT, MY BOY!!!
GYAA RAHH
GAKGAK
GANK!!
DRAGON!!
!
I WASN'T THE ONE WHO ASSASSINATED KING COBRA!!
RIGHT?! I KNEW IT!! I BELIEVED IN YOU!!
WE HAD A FEELING, SABO...!!
BUT WHEN I WAS IN MARIJOA...

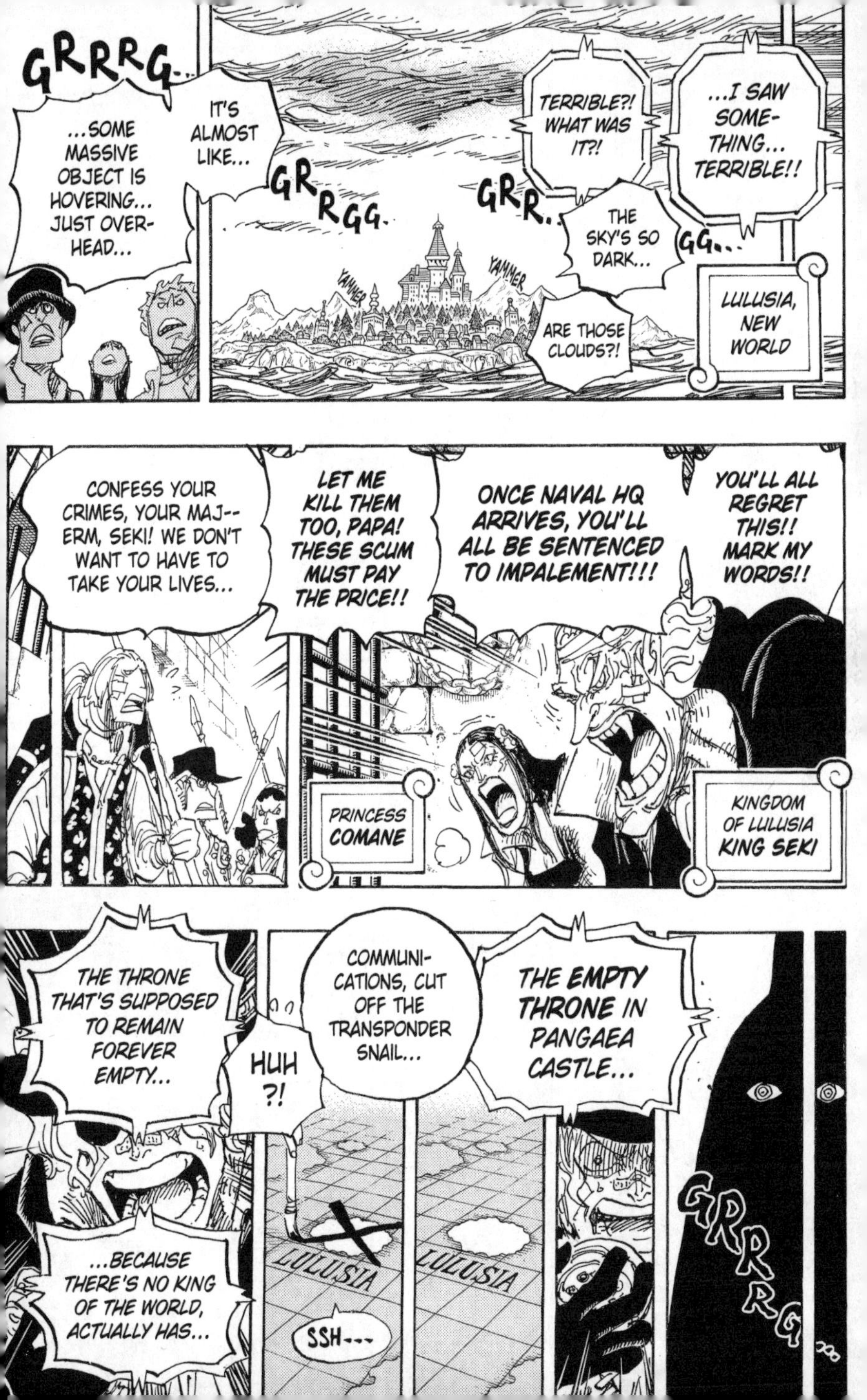
LULUSIA, NEW WORLD
...I SAW SOME-THING... TERRIBLE!!
TERRIBLE?! WHAT WAS IT?!
GRR...GG...
THE SKY'S SO DARK...
ARE THOSE CLOUDS?!
YAMMER
YAMMER
GRRGG..
GRRRG..
IT'S ALMOST LIKE...
...SOME MASSIVE OBJECT IS HOVERING... JUST OVER-HEAD...
KINGDOM OF LULUSIA KING SEKI
YOU'LL ALL REGRET THIS!! MARK MY WORDS!!
ONCE NAVAL HQ ARRIVES, YOU'LL ALL BE SENTENCED TO IMPALEMENT!!!
PRINCESS COMANE
LET ME KILL THEM TOO, PAPA! THESE SCUM MUST PAY THE PRICE!!
CONFESS YOUR CRIMES, YOUR MAJ-- ERM, SEKI! WE DON'T WANT TO HAVE TO TAKE YOUR LIVES...
THE EMPTY THRONE IN PANGAEA CASTLE...
GRRRG
COMMUNI-CATIONS, CUT OFF THE TRANSPONDER SNAIL...
LULUSIA
LULUSIA
SSH---
HUH ?!
THE THRONE THAT'S SUPPOSED TO REMAIN FOREVER EMPTY...
...BECAUSE THERE'S NO KING OF THE WORLD, ACTUALLY HAS...

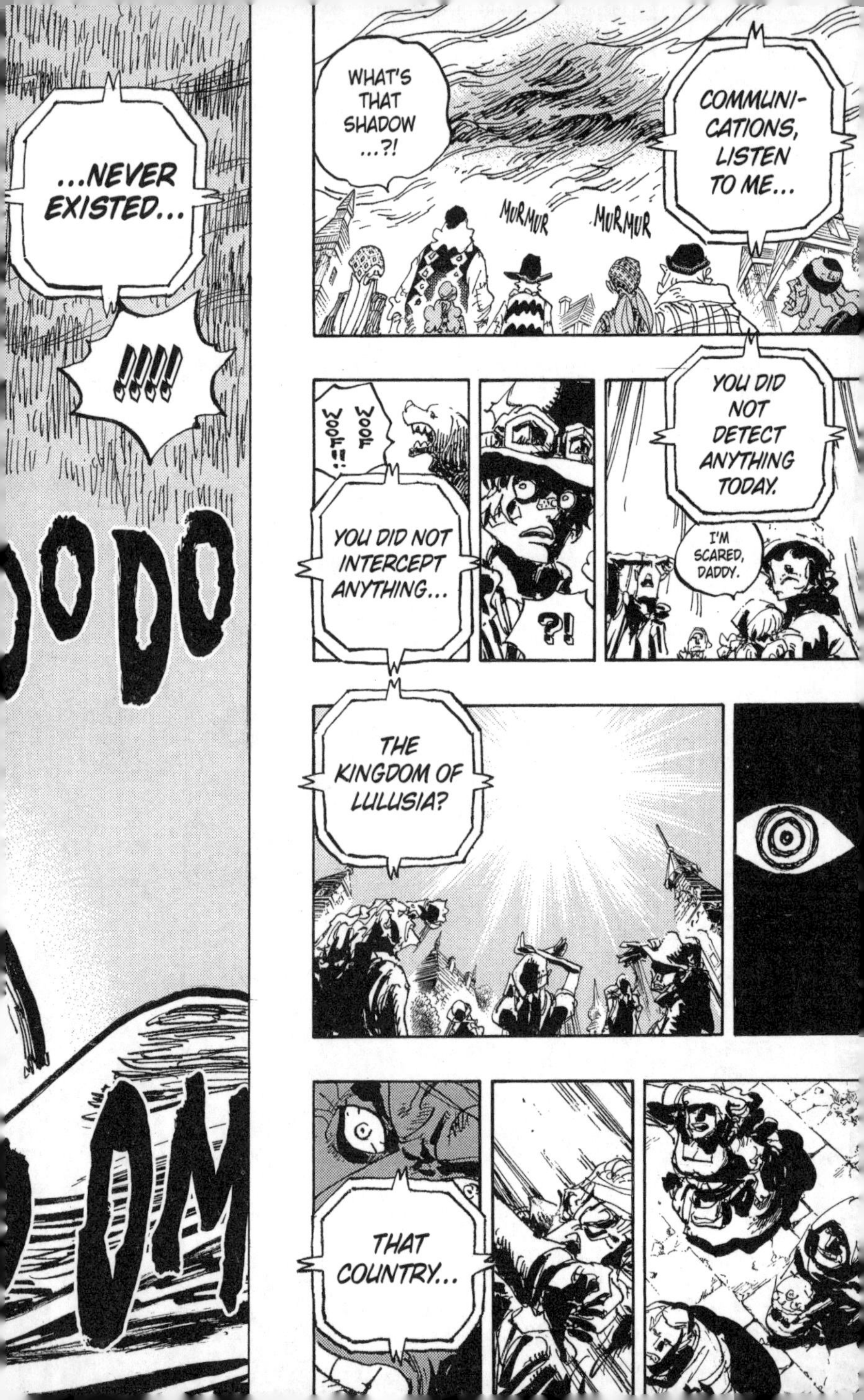
COMMUNICATIONS, LISTEN TO ME...
WHAT'S THAT SHADOW ...?!
MURMUR
MURMUR
YOU DID NOT DETECT ANYTHING TODAY.
I'M SCARED, DADDY.
?!
WOOF WOOF!!
YOU DID NOT INTERCEPT ANYTHING...
THE KINGDOM OF LULUSIA?
THAT COUNTRY...
...NEVER EXISTED...
!!!!
DO DO
OM

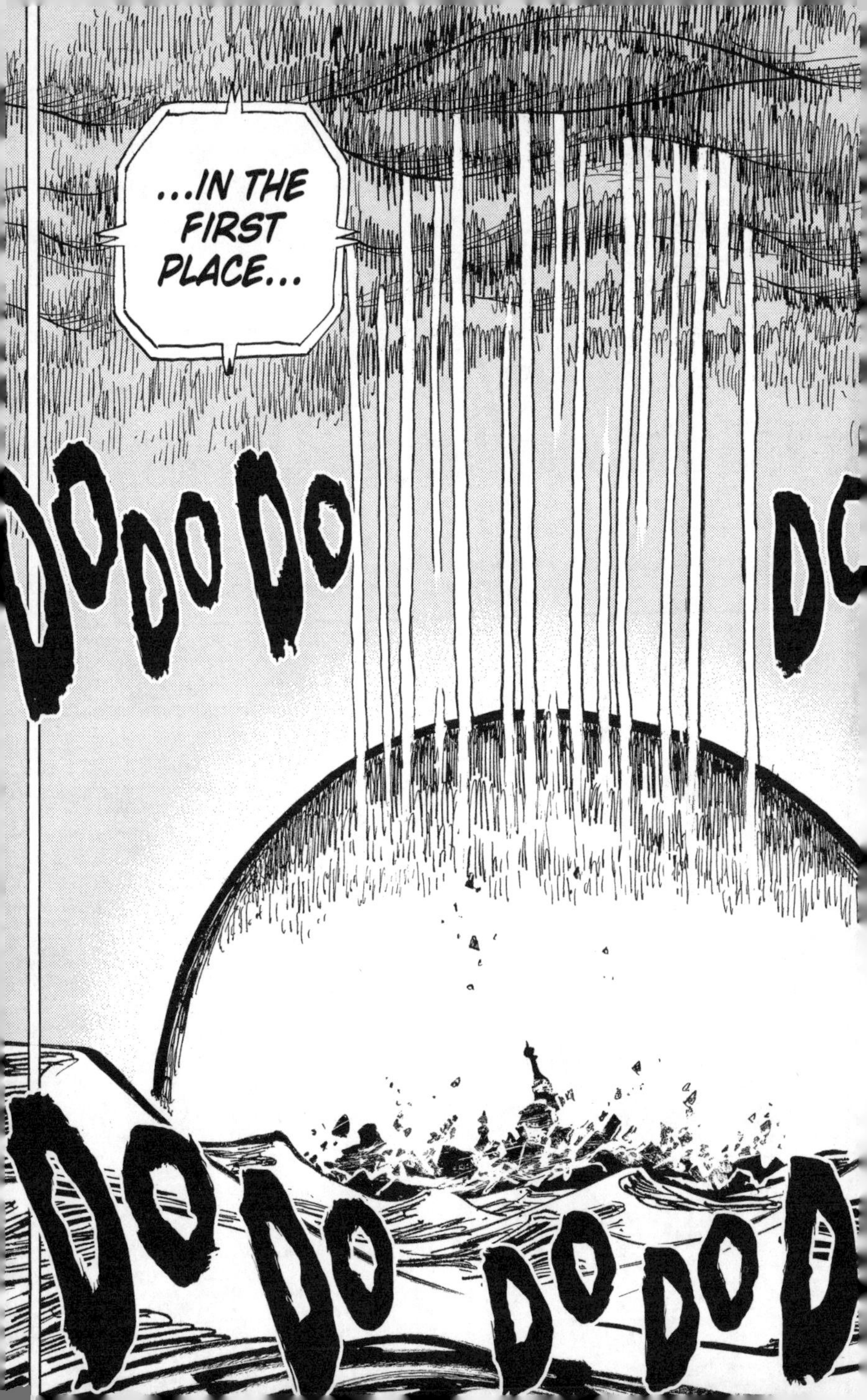
...IN THE FIRST PLACE...
DODODO
DO
DODODODODOD

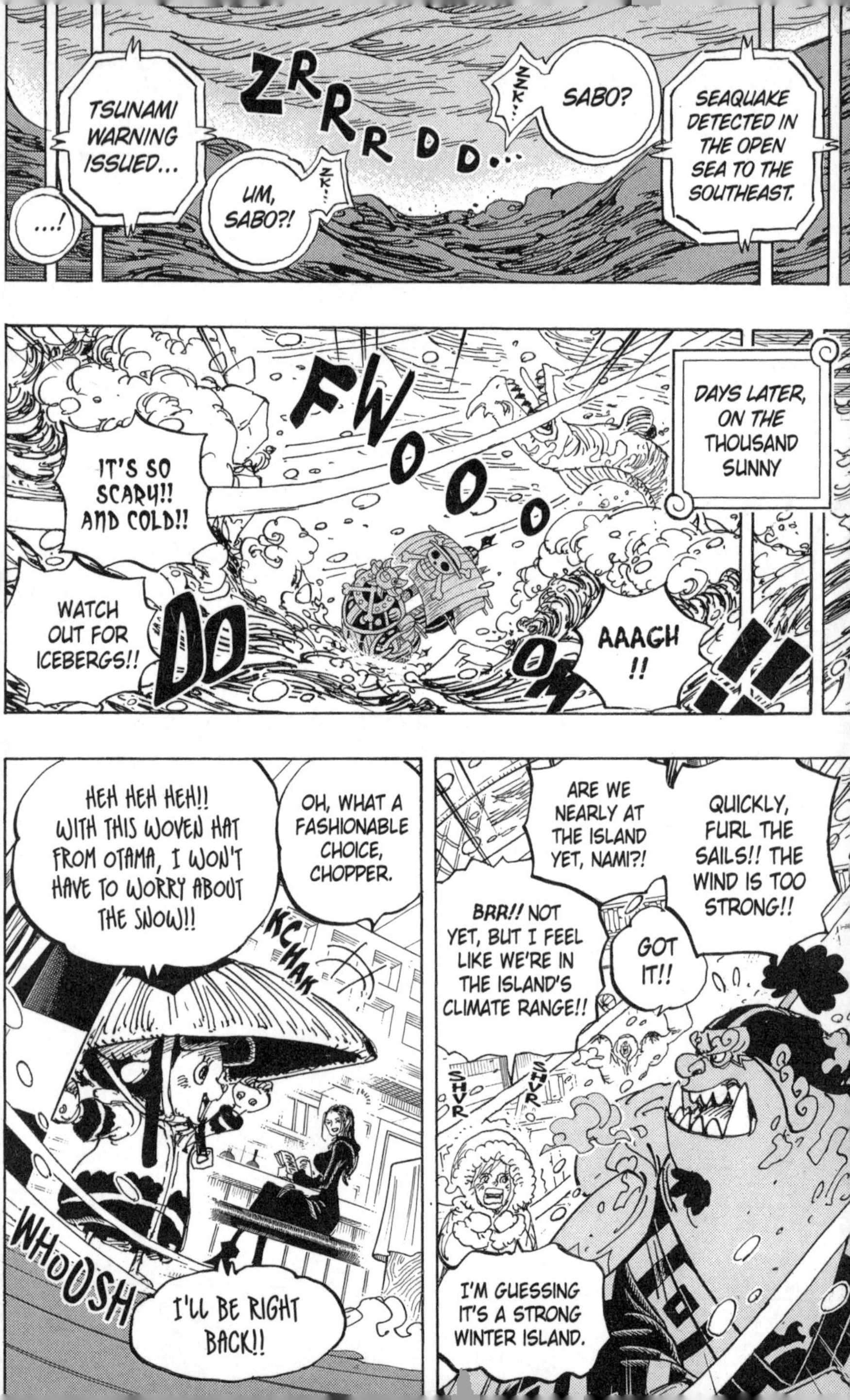
SEAQUAKE DETECTED IN THE OPEN SEA TO THE SOUTHEAST.
ZZK...
SABO?
ZRRRRDD...
ZK...
UM, SABO?!
TSUNAMI WARNING ISSUED...
...!
DAYS LATER, ON THE THOUSAND SUNNY
FWOOOO
AAAGH!!
IT'S SO SCARY!! AND COLD!!
DOOM
!!
WATCH OUT FOR ICEBERGS!!
QUICKLY, FURL THE SAILS!! THE WIND IS TOO STRONG!!
GOT IT!!
ARE WE NEARLY AT THE ISLAND YET, NAMI?!
BRR!! NOT YET, BUT I FEEL LIKE WE'RE IN THE ISLAND'S CLIMATE RANGE!!
SHVR
SHVR
I'M GUESSING IT'S A STRONG WINTER ISLAND.
OH, WHAT A FASHIONABLE CHOICE, CHOPPER.
HEH HEH HEH!! WITH THIS WOVEN HAT FROM OTAMA, I WON'T HAVE TO WORRY ABOUT THE SNOW!!
KCHAK
WHOOSH
I'LL BE RIGHT BACK!!

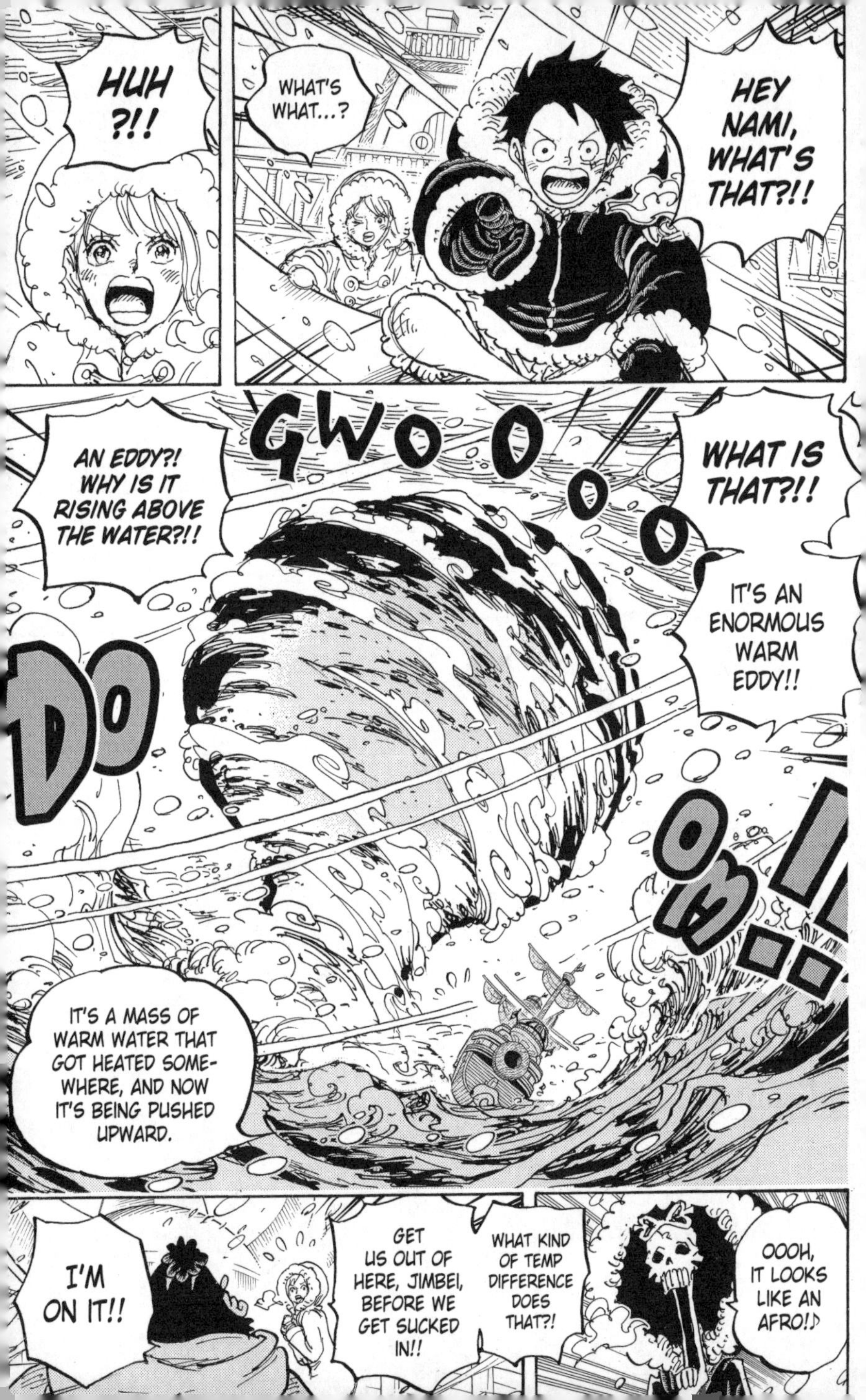

HEY NAMI, WHAT'S THAT?!!
WHAT'S WHAT...?
HUH ?!!
WHAT IS THAT?!!
GWOOOOO
AN EDDY?! WHY IS IT RISING ABOVE THE WATER?!!
IT'S AN ENORMOUS WARM EDDY!!
DOOM!!
IT'S A MASS OF WARM WATER THAT GOT HEATED SOME-WHERE, AND NOW IT'S BEING PUSHED UPWARD.
OOOH, IT LOOKS LIKE AN AFRO!♪
WHAT KIND OF TEMP DIFFERENCE DOES THAT?!
GET US OUT OF HERE, JIMBEI, BEFORE WE GET SUCKED IN!!
I'M ON IT!!

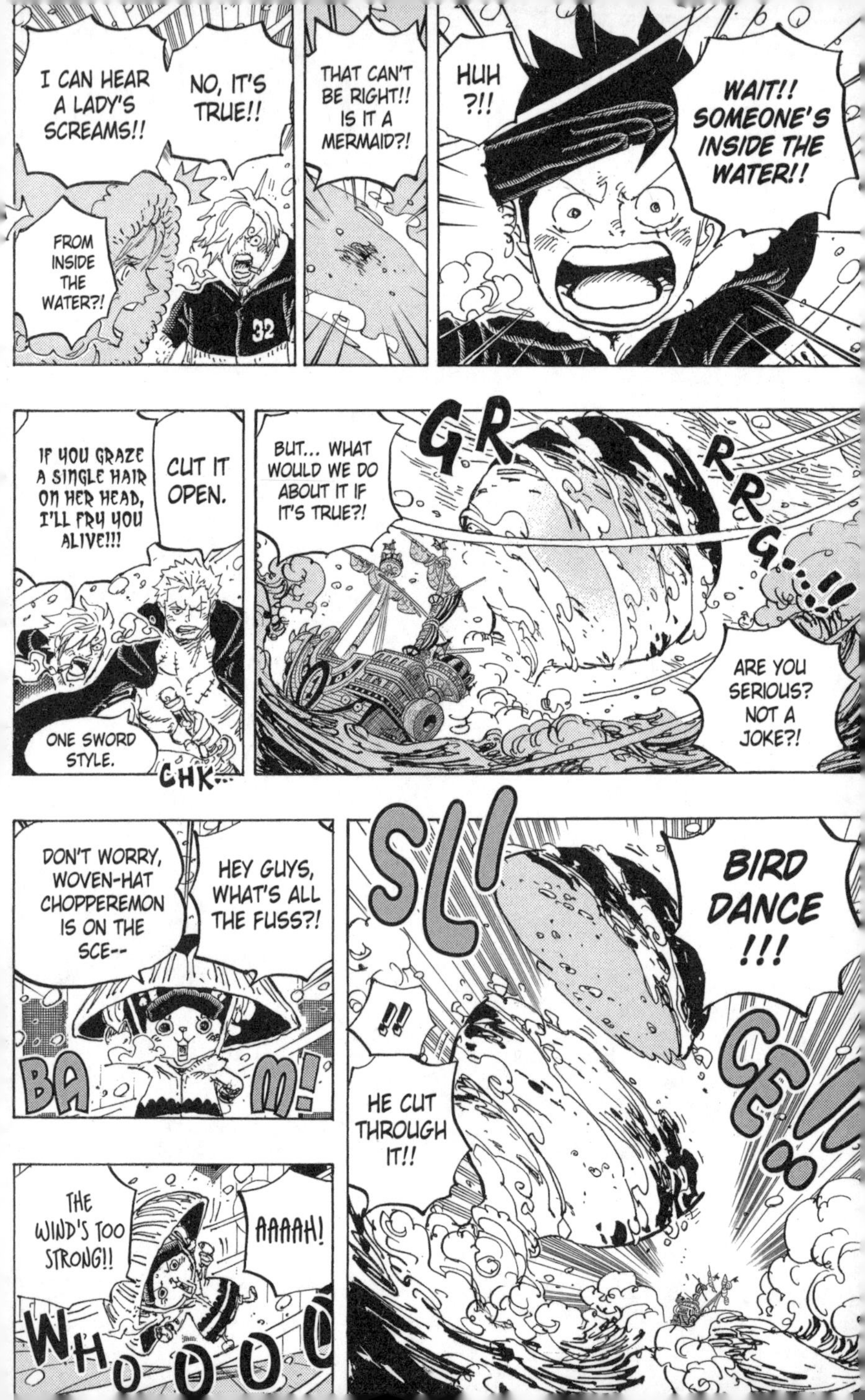
WAIT!! SOMEONE'S INSIDE THE WATER!!
HUH ?!!
THAT CAN'T BE RIGHT!! IS IT A MERMAID?!
NO, IT'S TRUE!!
I CAN HEAR A LADY'S SCREAMS!!
FROM INSIDE THE WATER?!
GRRRRG...!!
BUT... WHAT WOULD WE DO ABOUT IT IF IT'S TRUE?!
ARE YOU SERIOUS? NOT A JOKE?!
CUT IT OPEN.
IF YOU GRAZE A SINGLE HAIR ON HER HEAD, I'LL FRY YOU ALIVE!!!
ONE SWORD STYLE.
CHK...
BIRD DANCE!!!
SLI
CE..!!
!!
HE CUT THROUGH IT!!
HEY GUYS, WHAT'S ALL THE FUSS?!
DON'T WORRY, WOVEN-HAT CHOPPEREMON IS ON THE SCE--
BAM!
AAAAH!
THE WIND'S TOO STRONG!!
WHOOOO

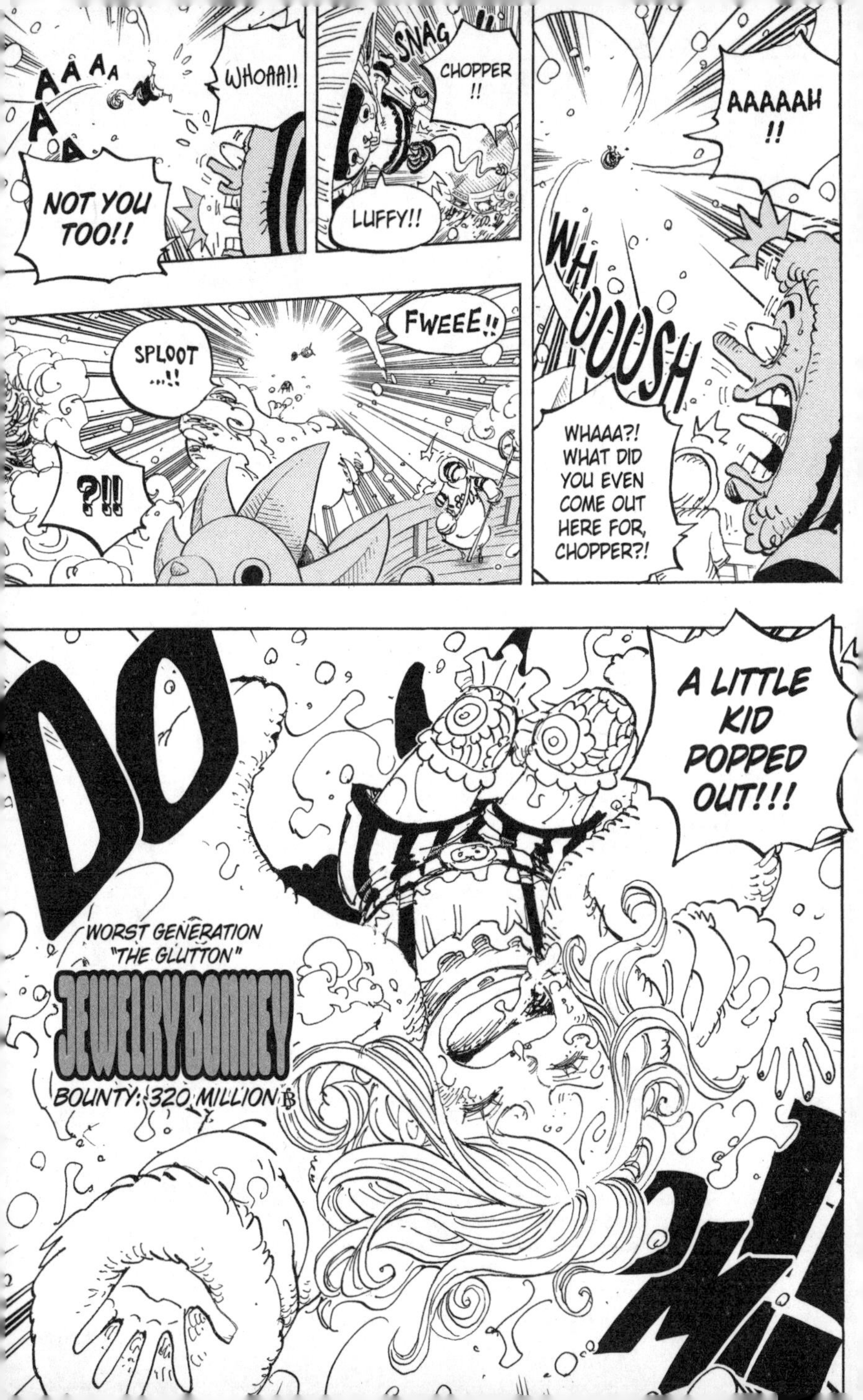
AAAAAH!!
WHOOOSH
WHAAA?! WHAT DID YOU EVEN COME OUT HERE FOR, CHOPPER?!
SNAG
CHOPPER!!
LUFFY!!
AAAAA
WHOAA!!
NOT YOU TOO!!
FWEEE!!
SPLOOT...!!
?!!
A LITTLE KID POPPED OUT!!!
DO
WORST GENERATION "THE GLUTTON"
JEWELRY BONNEY
BOUNTY: 320 MILLION ฿

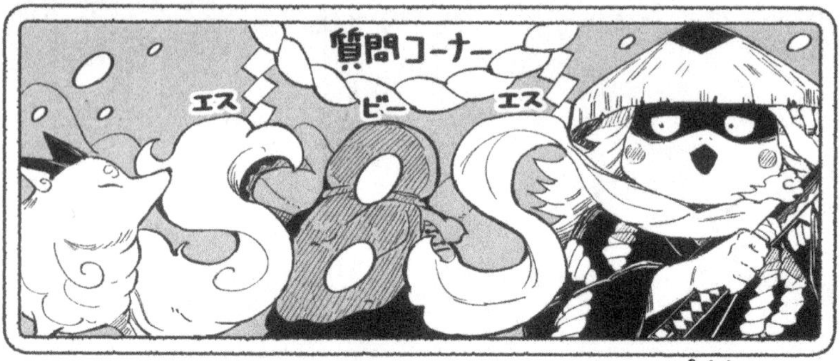
質問コーナー
エス
ビー
エス
SBS

(Tsuke-bo, Saitama)

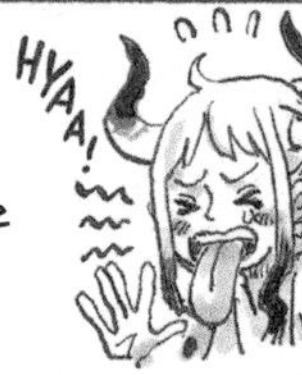
HYAAA!

Q: Does Yamato have a least favorite food?

--Gum-Flame Fruit

A: Anything spicy. Over-stimulating foods like chiles and wasabi make Yamato go, "Hyaa!"

Q: If you look really closely at the grave markers for Otama's parents, you can make out the kanji for Kurozumi! Does this mean that despite coming from the same background as Orochi, who responded to the persecution of the Kurozumis with revenge, Otama is meant to be a symbol of hope for the future of the new Wano, much like Koala was with Hody?

--Rimika

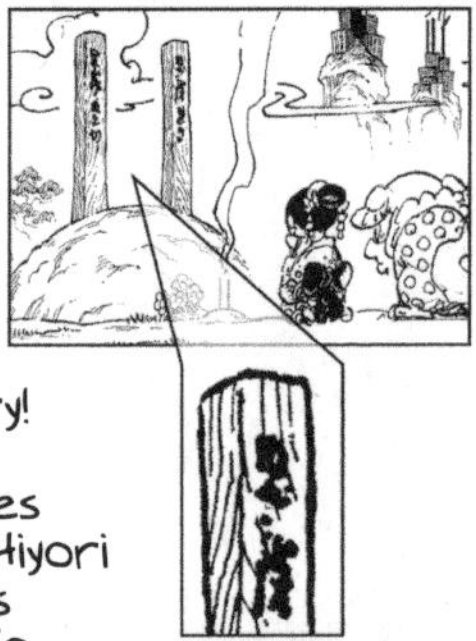

A: You've really gotten very deep into this story! I'll confirm it for you: Otama's birth name is Kurozumi Tama. Does that mean she deserves to be hated? In the final scenes of the arc, Hiyori proclaims, "Kurozumi was born to burn." Does that mean she's talking about Otama too? No, of course not. It's clear from the story that Hiyori is referring specifically to Orochi. But how would everyone react if they found out that Otama is from the Kurozumi bloodline? I ask you to use your imagination. It's a major problem throughout human history that continues to this day.

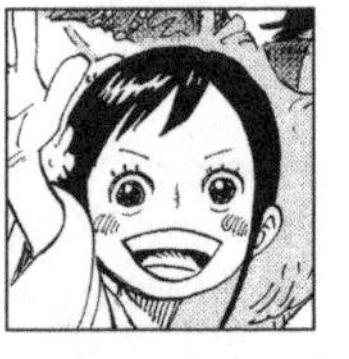

Q: Where do they make Navy crackers? Where do they sell them? I want to try them!

--Tomari Shinonome

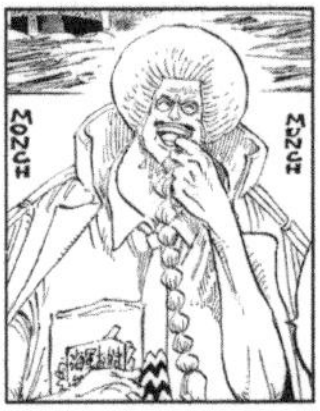
MUNCH
MUNCH

A: I believe you're all familiar with the cantankerous old cracker craftsman in the western part of the South Blue named Eiyess Emmar. His famous catchphrase is "Crackers are rock'n'roll!" Sengoku loves his crackers, so the Navy buys a supply from him. They sell them at the store in Navy HQ.

Chapter 1061:

FUTURE ISLAND EGGHEAD

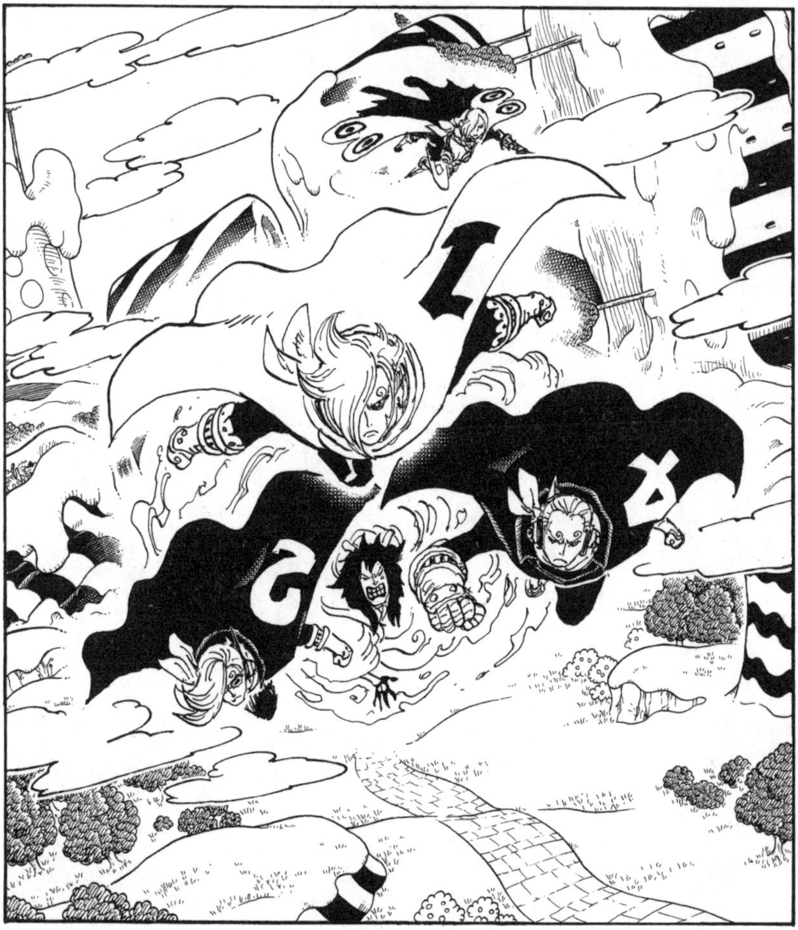

GERMA 66'S AHH… AN EMOTIONLESS EXCURSION, VOL. 19:
"ESCAPE!! A SUCCESSFUL RESCUE OF NIJI AND YONJI!!"

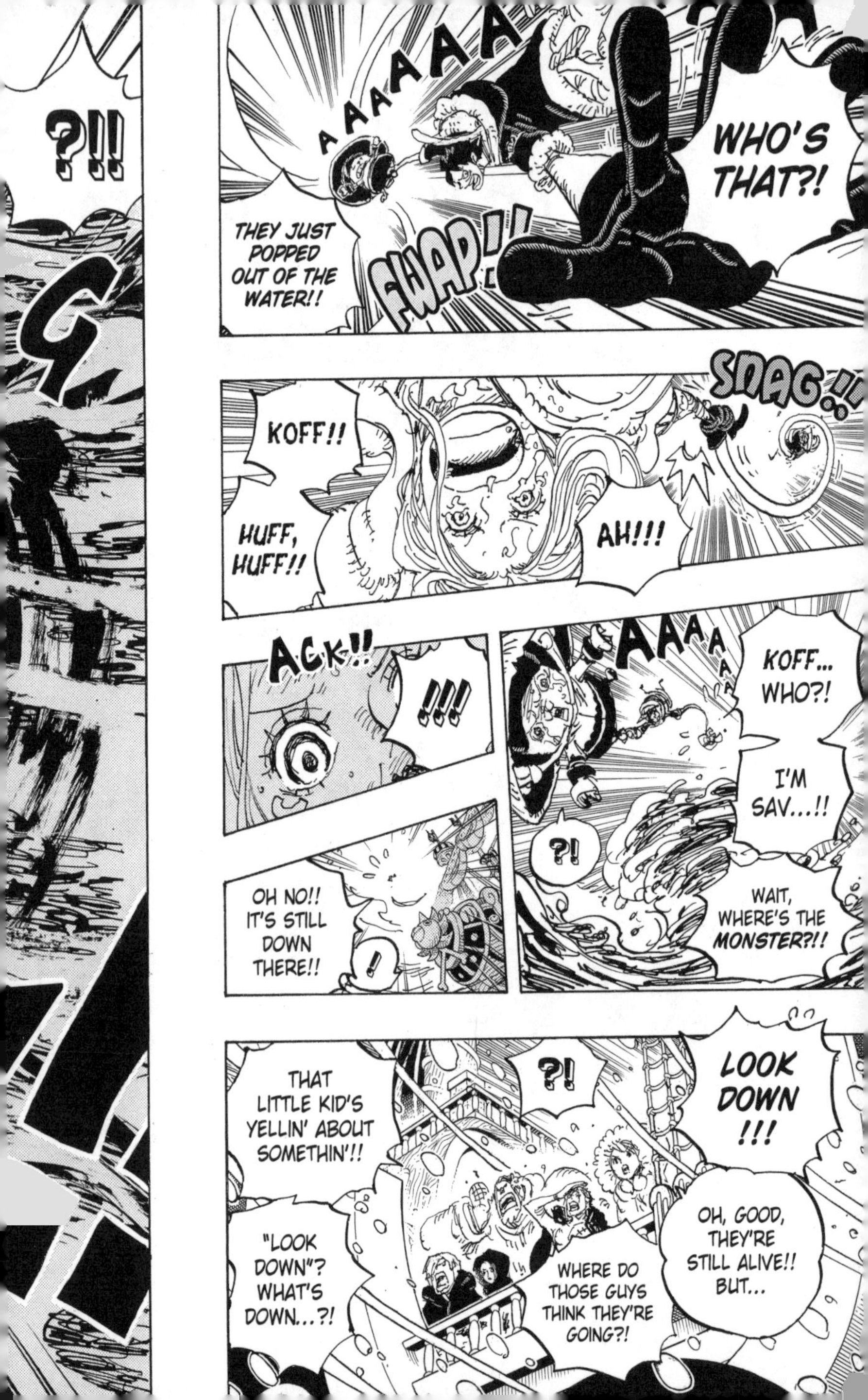
AAAAAAA
WHO'S THAT?!
THEY JUST POPPED OUT OF THE WATER!!
FWAP!!
SNAG!!
AH!!!
KOFF!!
HUFF, HUFF!!
AAAAAA
KOFF... WHO?!
I'M SAV...!!
?!
WAIT, WHERE'S THE MONSTER?!!
ACK!!
!!!
OH NO!! IT'S STILL DOWN THERE!!
!
LOOK DOWN!!!
?!
THAT LITTLE KID'S YELLIN' ABOUT SOMETHIN'!!
OH, GOOD, THEY'RE STILL ALIVE!! BUT...
WHERE DO THOSE GUYS THINK THEY'RE GOING?!
"LOOK DOWN"? WHAT'S DOWN...?!
?!!

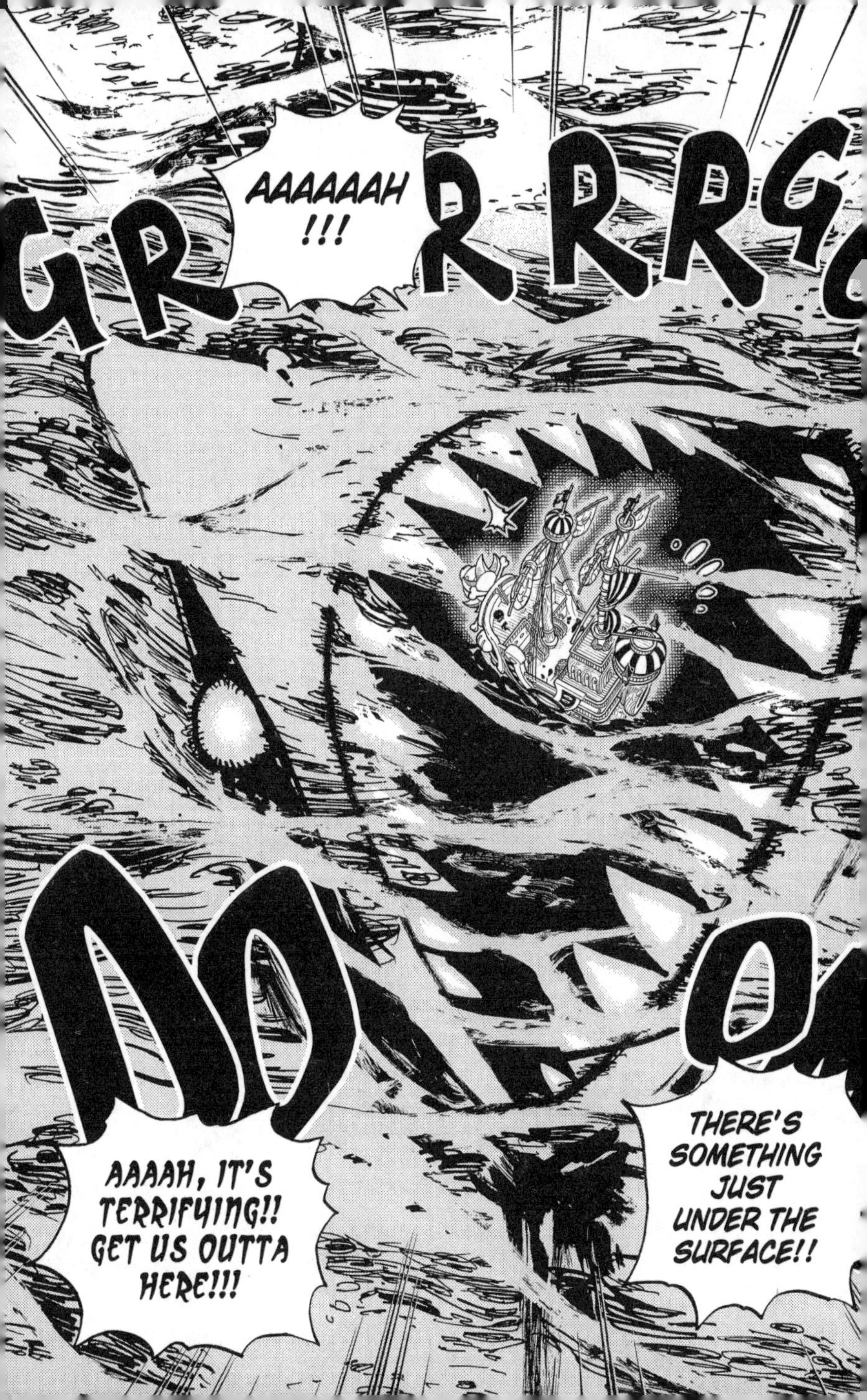
GRRRRG
AAAAAAH!!!
OO
THERE'S SOMETHING JUST UNDER THE SURFACE!!
AAAAH, IT'S TERRIFYING!! GET US OUTTA HERE!!!

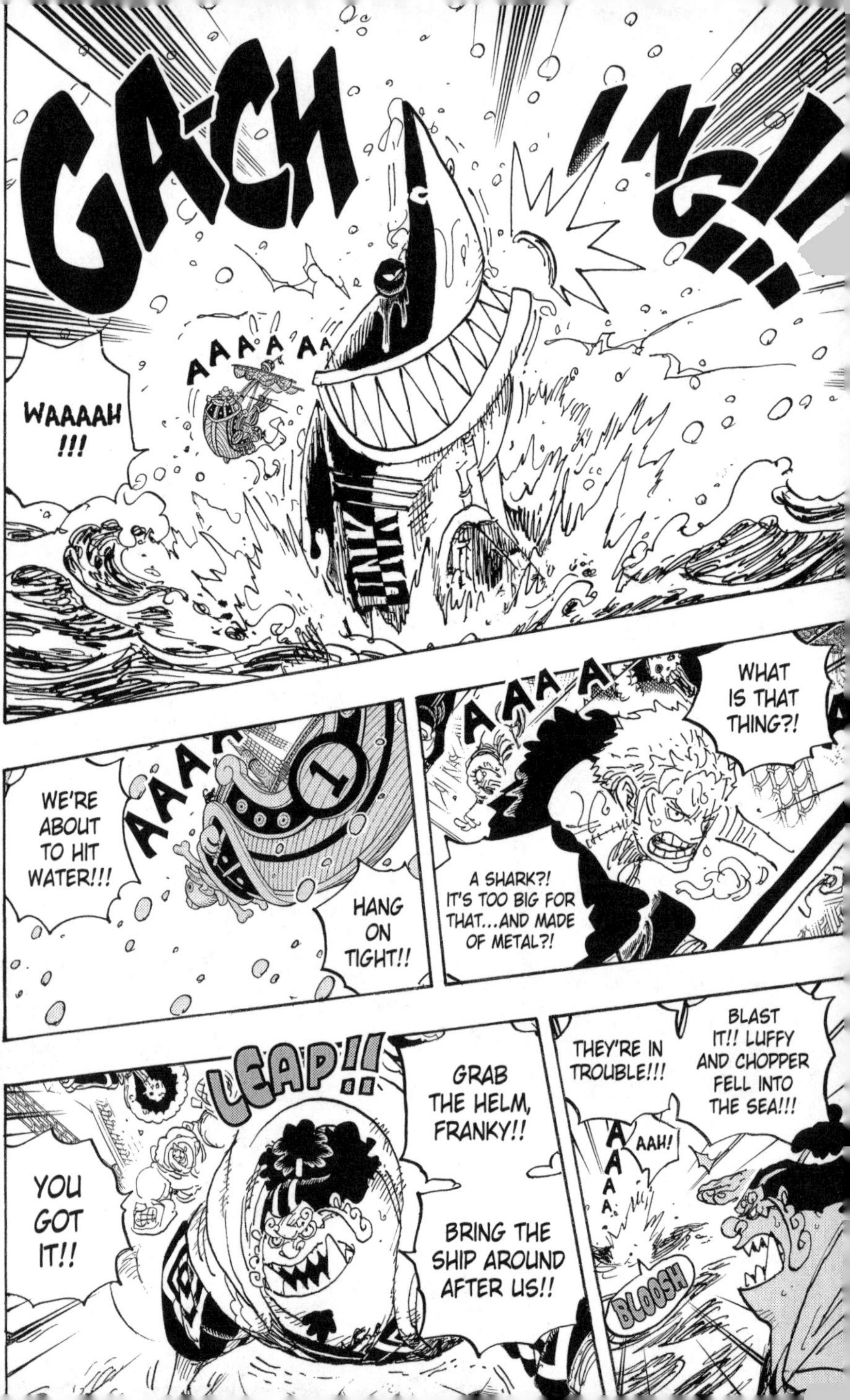
GACH ING!!
AAAAAA
WAAAAH!!!
AAAA
WHAT IS THAT THING?!
A SHARK?! IT'S TOO BIG FOR THAT...AND MADE OF METAL?!
GAAA
WE'RE ABOUT TO HIT WATER!!!
HANG ON TIGHT!!
BLAST IT!! LUFFY AND CHOPPER FELL INTO THE SEA!!!
THEY'RE IN TROUBLE!!!
AAH!
AAAAA
BLOOSH
GRAB THE HELM, FRANKY!!
LEAP!!
BRING THE SHIP AROUND AFTER US!!
YOU GOT IT!!

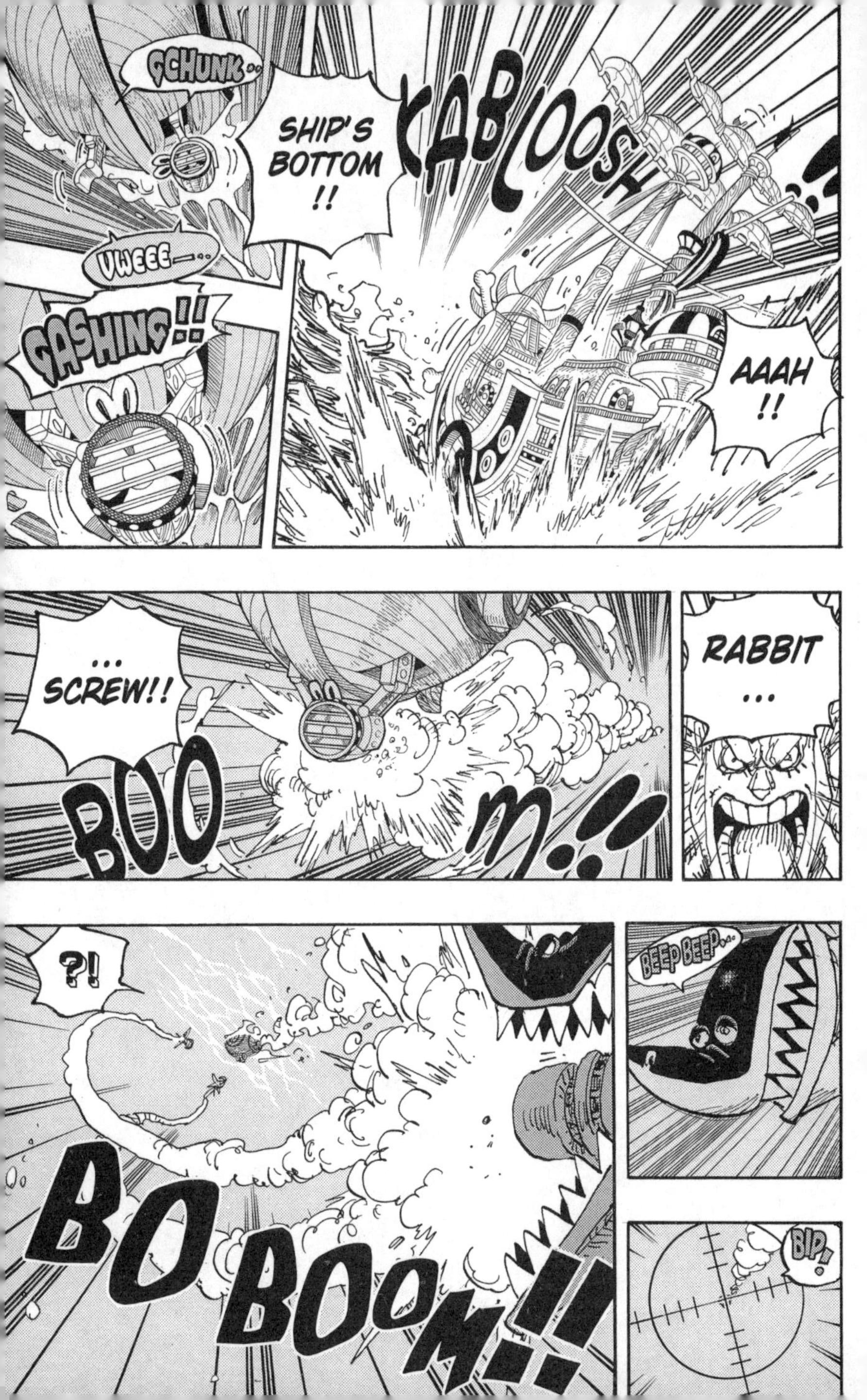
KABLOOSH
AAAH!!
GCHUNK..
SHIP'S BOTTOM!!
UWEEE—..
GASHING!!
RABBIT...
...SCREW!!
BOOM!!
BEEP BEEP..
BIP.
?!
BOBOOM!!

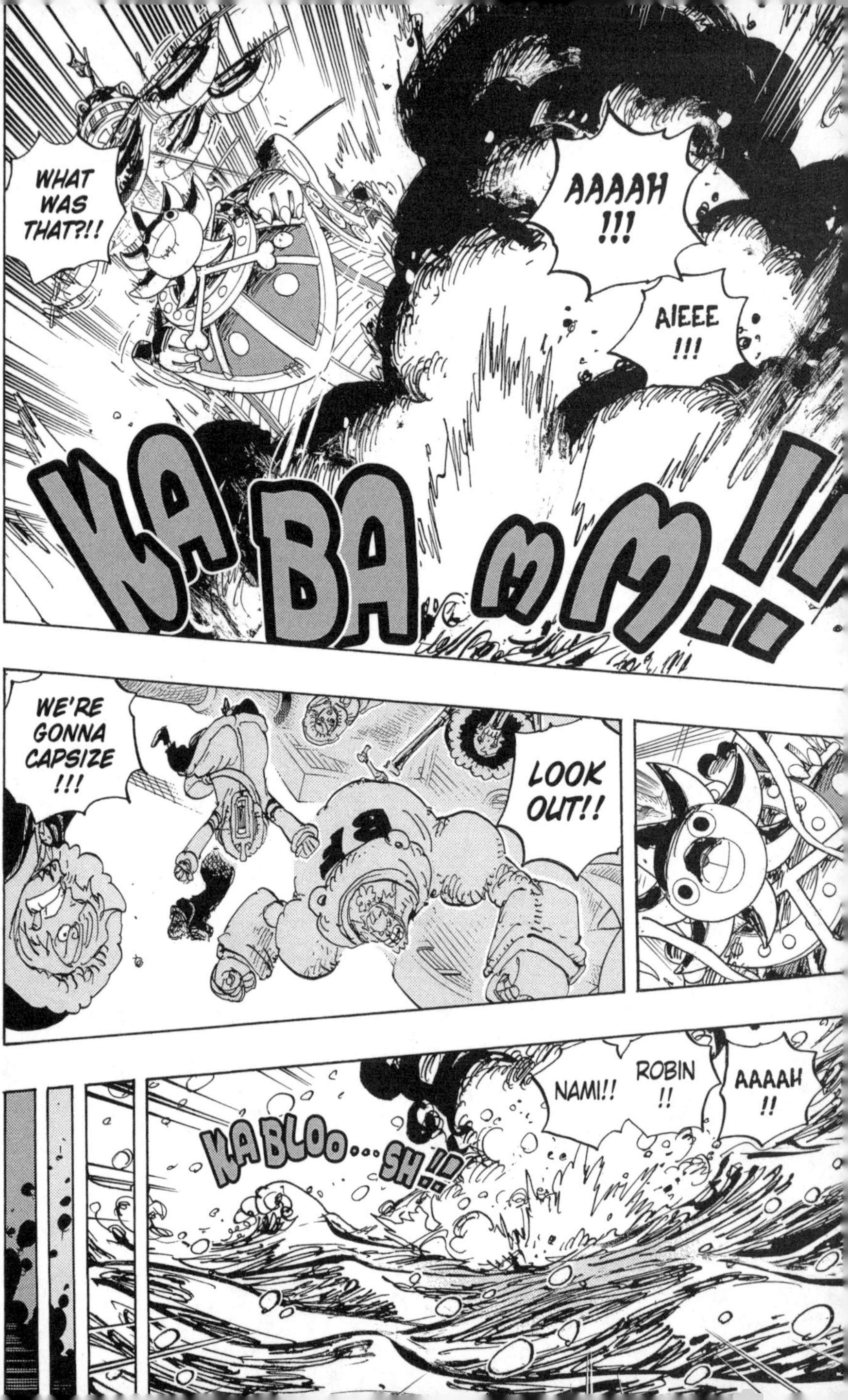
AAAAH!!!
AIEEE!!!
WHAT WAS THAT?!!
KABAMM!!
LOOK OUT!!
WE'RE GONNA CAPSIZE!!!
AAAAH!!
ROBIN!!
NAMI!!
KABLOO...SH!!

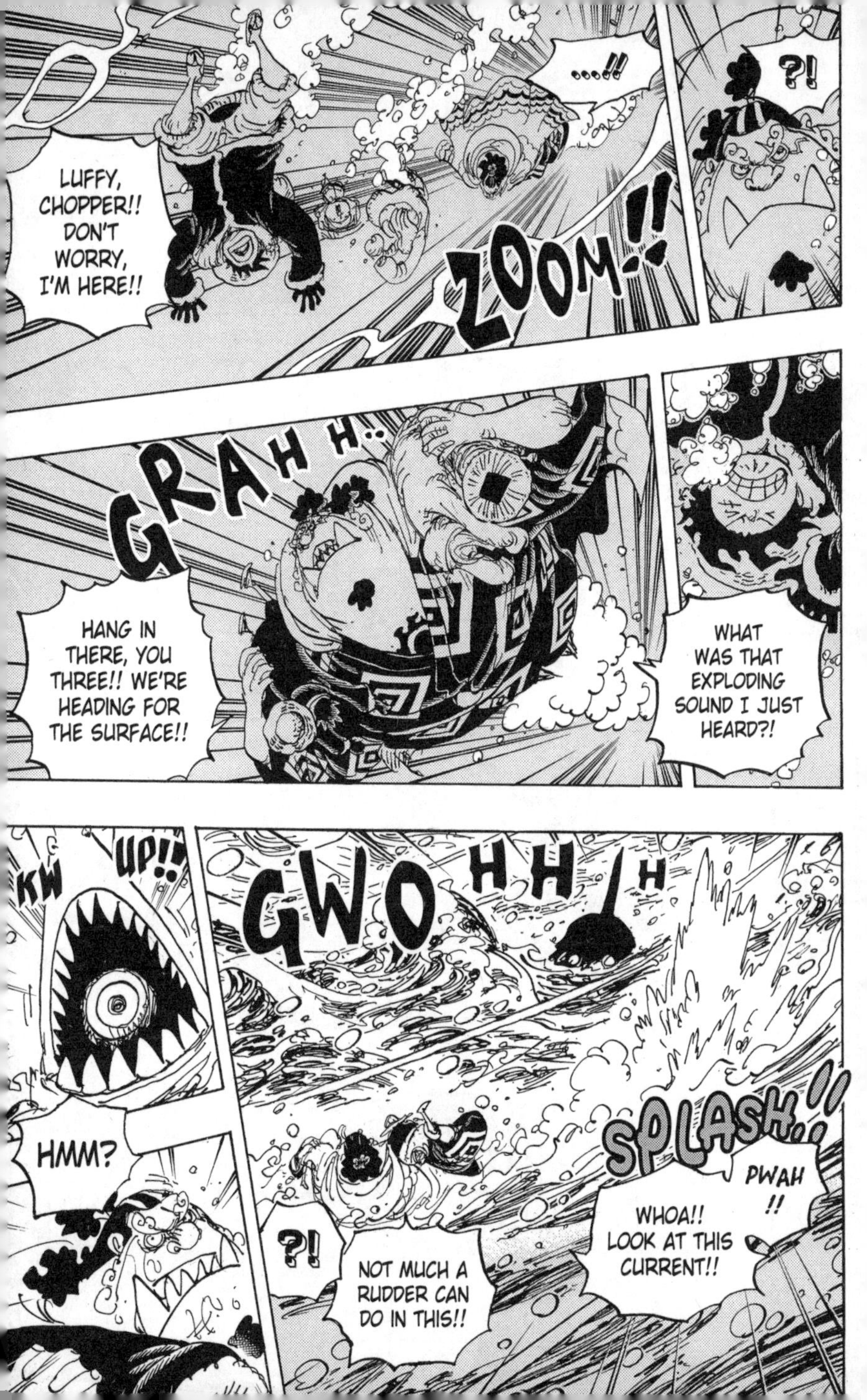
?!
....!!
ZOOM!!
LUFFY, CHOPPER!! DON'T WORRY, I'M HERE!!
WHAT WAS THAT EXPLODING SOUND I JUST HEARD?!
GRAHH..
HANG IN THERE, YOU THREE!! WE'RE HEADING FOR THE SURFACE!!
GWOHHH
SPLASH!!
PWAH!!
WHOA!! LOOK AT THIS CURRENT!!
?!
NOT MUCH A RUDDER CAN DO IN THIS!!
KWUP!!
HMM?

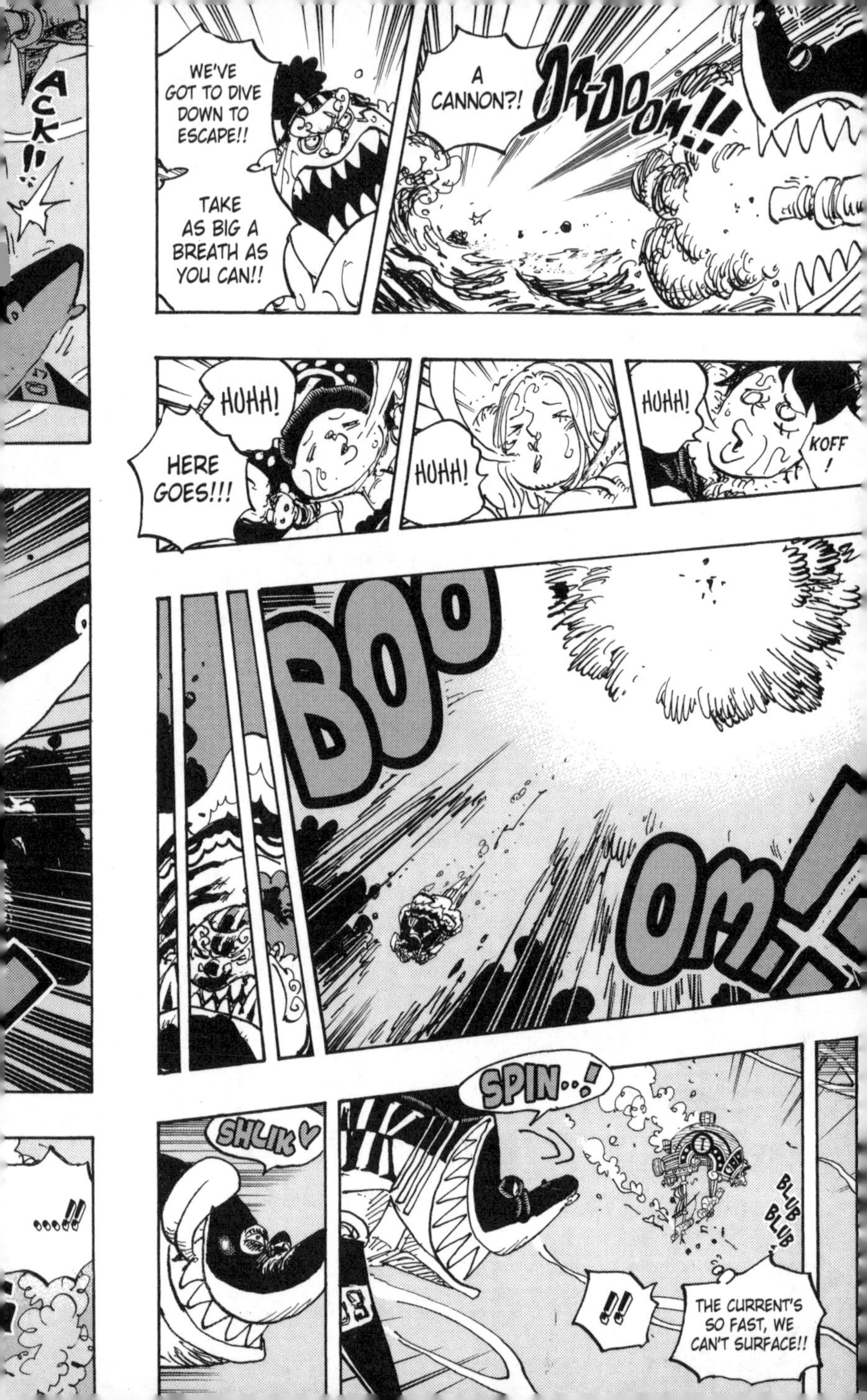
DR-DOOM!!
A CANNON?!
WE'VE GOT TO DIVE DOWN TO ESCAPE!!
TAKE AS BIG A BREATH AS YOU CAN!!
HUHH!
KOFF!
HUHH!
HUHH!
HERE GOES!!!
BOOOM!!
BLUB BLUB
!!
THE CURRENT'S SO FAST, WE CAN'T SURFACE!!
SPIN..!
SHLIK♥
ACK!!
....!!

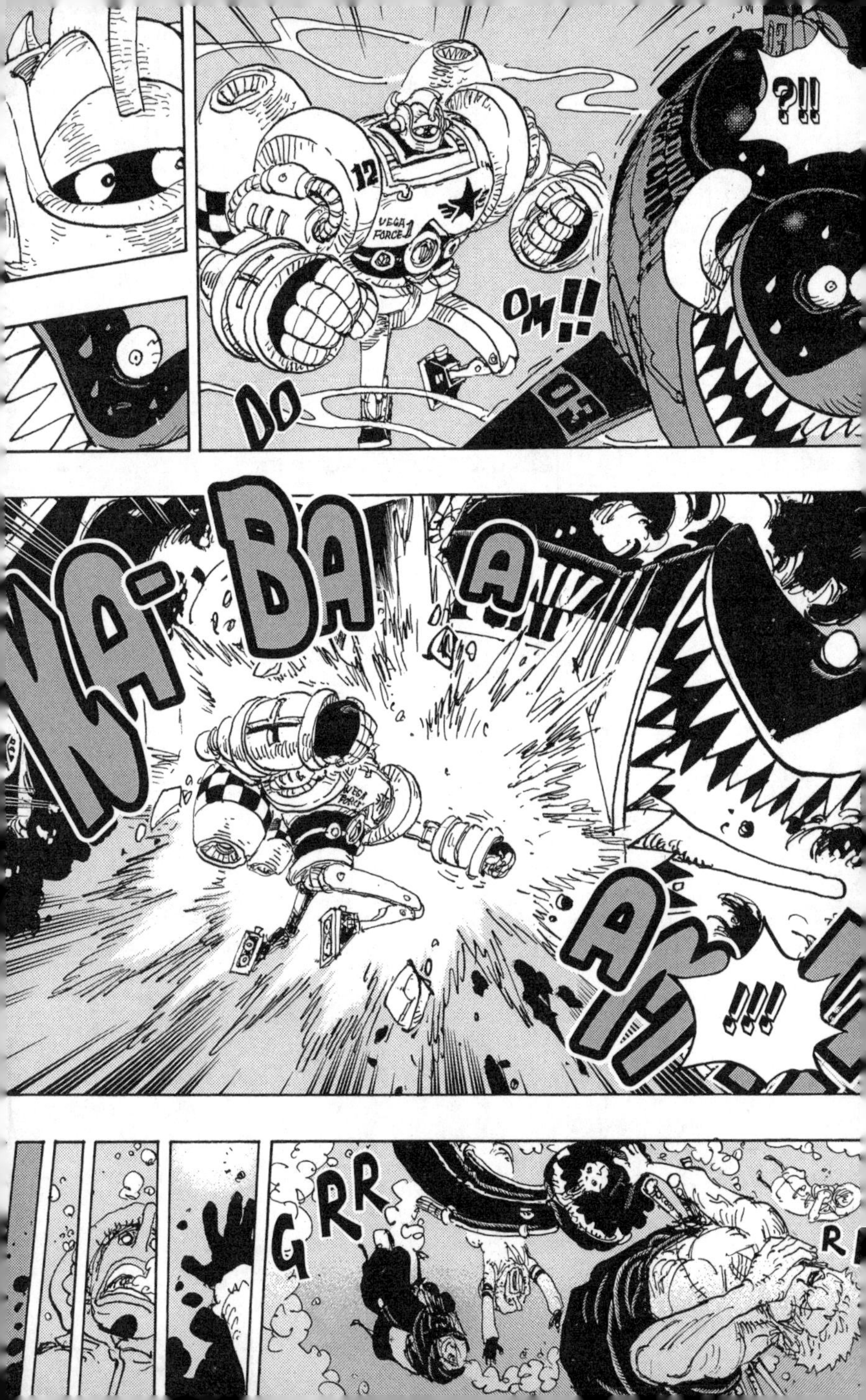
?!!
OM!!
DO
KA-BA
A
A
AM
!!!
R
GRR

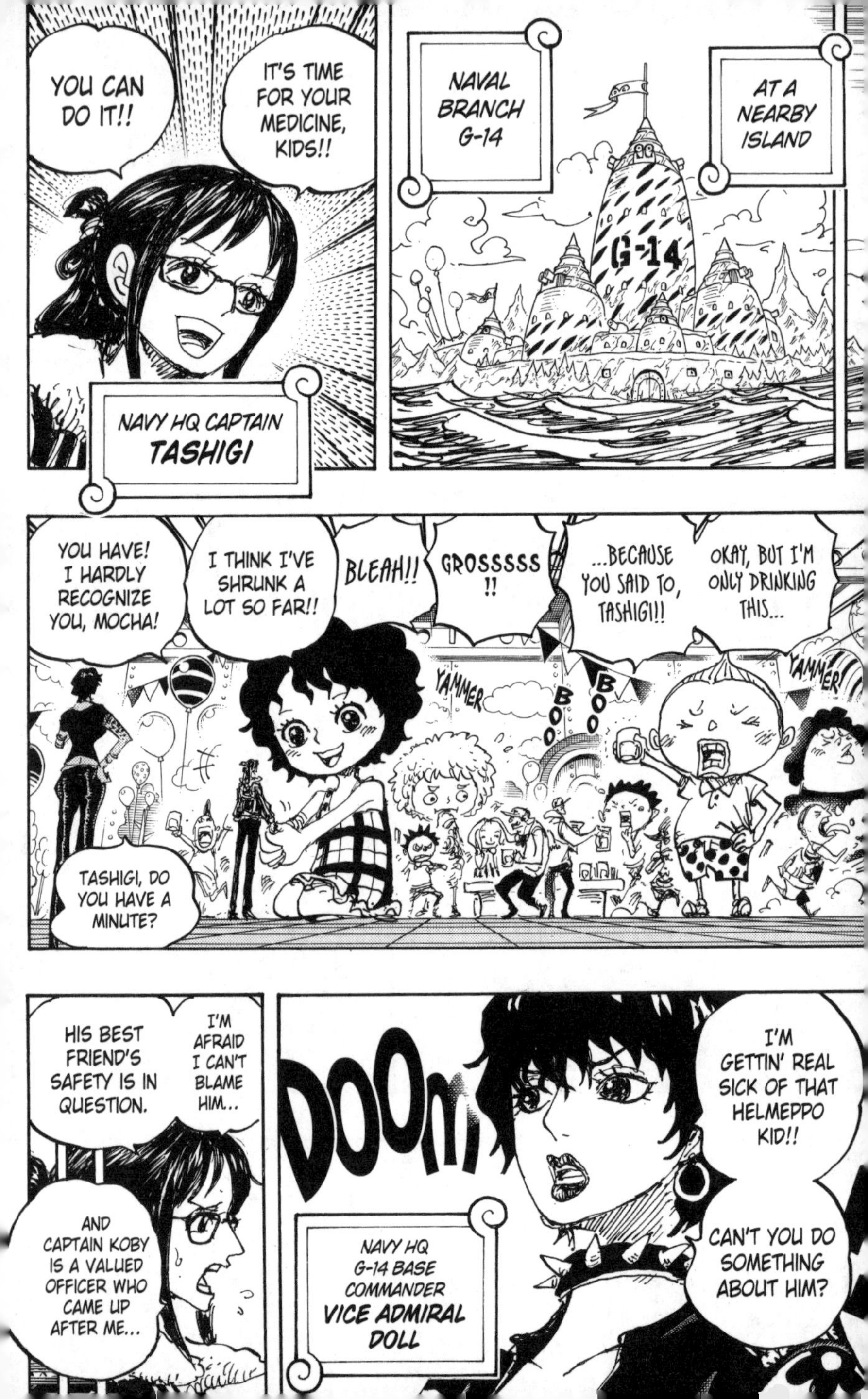
AT A NEARBY ISLAND
NAVAL BRANCH G-14
G-14
IT'S TIME FOR YOUR MEDICINE, KIDS!!
YOU CAN DO IT!!
NAVY HQ CAPTAIN TASHIGI
OKAY, BUT I'M ONLY DRINKING THIS...
...BECAUSE YOU SAID TO, TASHIGI!!
YAMMER
GROSSSSS !!
BLEAH!!
BOO
BOO
YAMMER
I THINK I'VE SHRUNK A LOT SO FAR!!
YOU HAVE! I HARDLY RECOGNIZE YOU, MOCHA!
TASHIGI, DO YOU HAVE A MINUTE?
I'M GETTIN' REAL SICK OF THAT HELMEPPO KID!!
CAN'T YOU DO SOMETHING ABOUT HIM?
DOOM
NAVY HQ G-14 BASE COMMANDER VICE ADMIRAL DOLL
I'M AFRAID I CAN'T BLAME HIM...
HIS BEST FRIEND'S SAFETY IS IN QUESTION.
AND CAPTAIN KOBY IS A VALUED OFFICER WHO CAME UP AFTER ME...

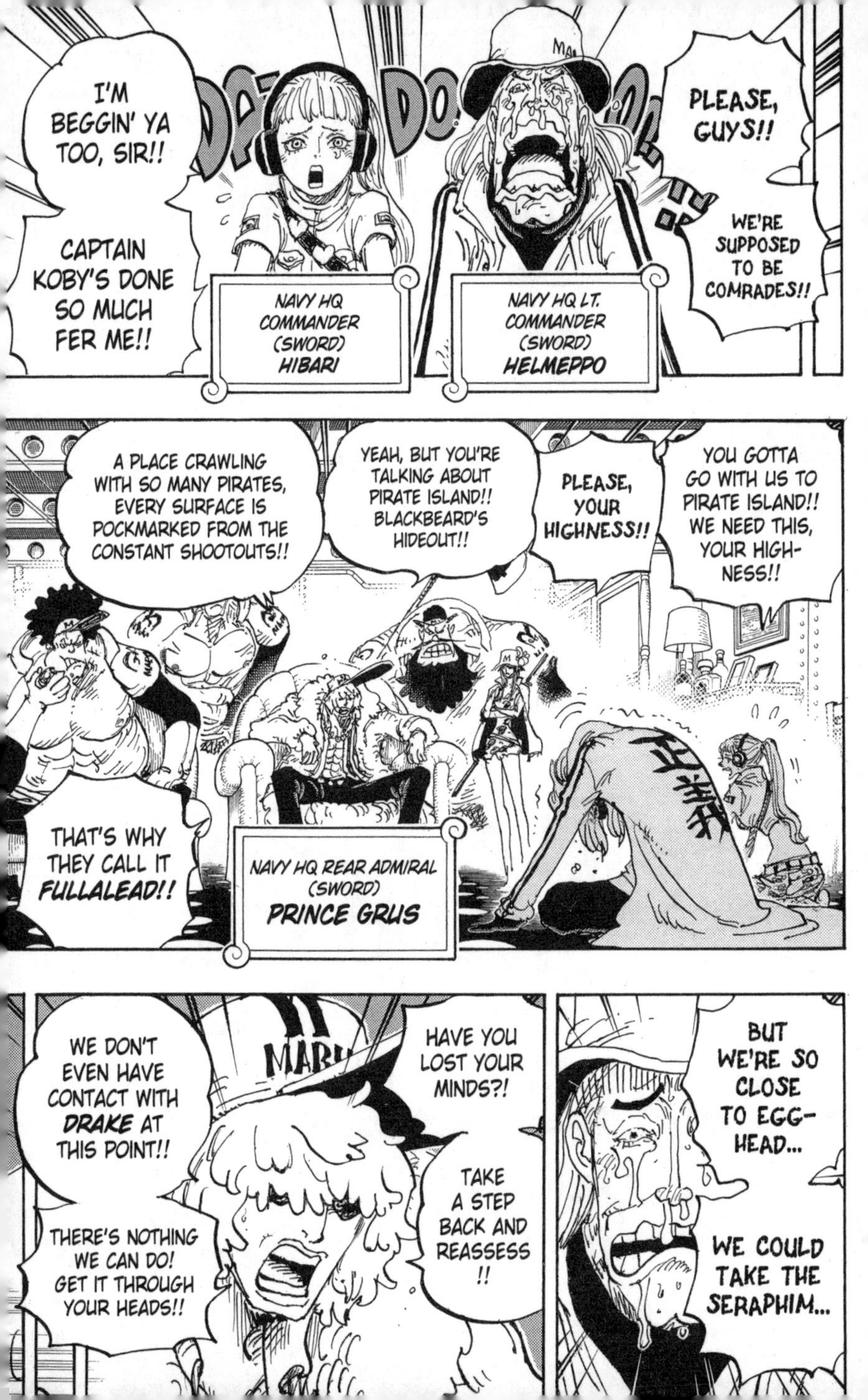
PLEASE, GUYS!!
WE'RE SUPPOSED TO BE COMRADES!!
NAVY HQ LT. COMMANDER (SWORD) HELMEPPO
NAVY HQ COMMANDER (SWORD) HIBARI
I'M BEGGIN' YA TOO, SIR!!
CAPTAIN KOBY'S DONE SO MUCH FER ME!!
YOU GOTTA GO WITH US TO PIRATE ISLAND!! WE NEED THIS, YOUR HIGH-NESS!!
PLEASE, YOUR HIGHNESS!!
YEAH, BUT YOU'RE TALKING ABOUT PIRATE ISLAND!! BLACKBEARD'S HIDEOUT!!
A PLACE CRAWLING WITH SO MANY PIRATES, EVERY SURFACE IS POCKMARKED FROM THE CONSTANT SHOOTOUTS!!
NAVY HQ REAR ADMIRAL (SWORD) PRINCE GRUS
THAT'S WHY THEY CALL IT FULLALEAD!!
BUT WE'RE SO CLOSE TO EGG-HEAD...
WE COULD TAKE THE SERAPHIM...
HAVE YOU LOST YOUR MINDS?!
TAKE A STEP BACK AND REASSESS!!
WE DON'T EVEN HAVE CONTACT WITH DRAKE AT THIS POINT!!
THERE'S NOTHING WE CAN DO! GET IT THROUGH YOUR HEADS!!

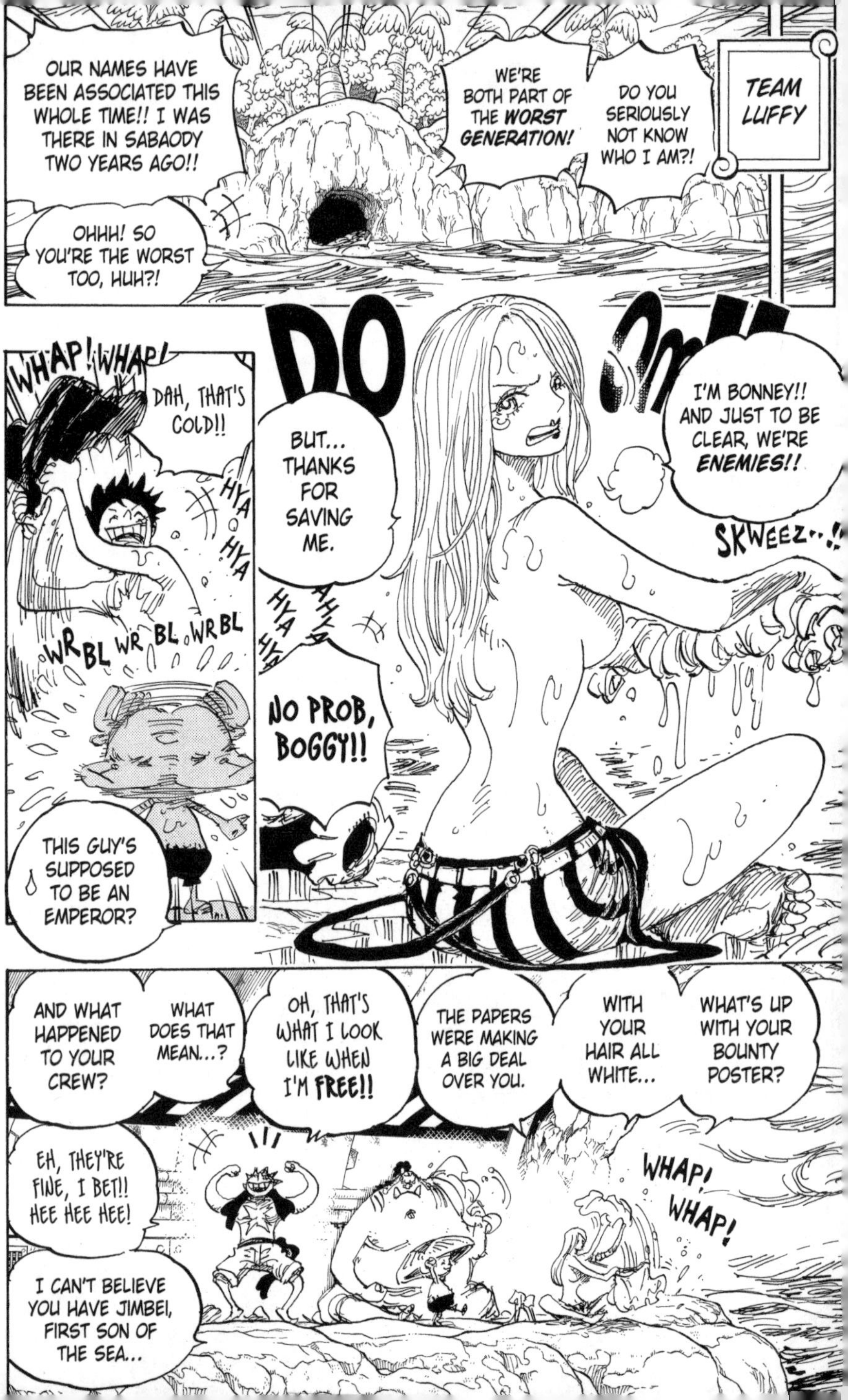
TEAM LUFFY
DO YOU SERIOUSLY NOT KNOW WHO I AM?!
WE'RE BOTH PART OF THE **WORST GENERATION!**
OUR NAMES HAVE BEEN ASSOCIATED THIS WHOLE TIME!! I WAS THERE IN SABAODY TWO YEARS AGO!!
OHHH! SO YOU'RE THE WORST TOO, HUH?!
DO
I'M BONNEY!! AND JUST TO BE CLEAR, WE'RE **ENEMIES!!**
SKWEEZ..!!
BUT... THANKS FOR SAVING ME.
HYA HYA HYA HYA
NO PROB, BOGGY!!
WHAP! WHAP!
DAH, THAT'S COLD!!
HYA HYA HYA
WR BL WR BL WR BL
THIS GUY'S SUPPOSED TO BE AN EMPEROR?
WHAT'S UP WITH YOUR BOUNTY POSTER?
WITH YOUR HAIR ALL WHITE...
THE PAPERS WERE MAKING A BIG DEAL OVER YOU.
OH, THAT'S WHAT I LOOK LIKE WHEN I'M **FREE!!**
WHAT DOES THAT MEAN...?
AND WHAT HAPPENED TO YOUR CREW?
WHAP! WHAP!
EH, THEY'RE FINE, I BET!! HEE HEE HEE!
I CAN'T BELIEVE YOU HAVE JIMBEI, FIRST SON OF THE SEA...

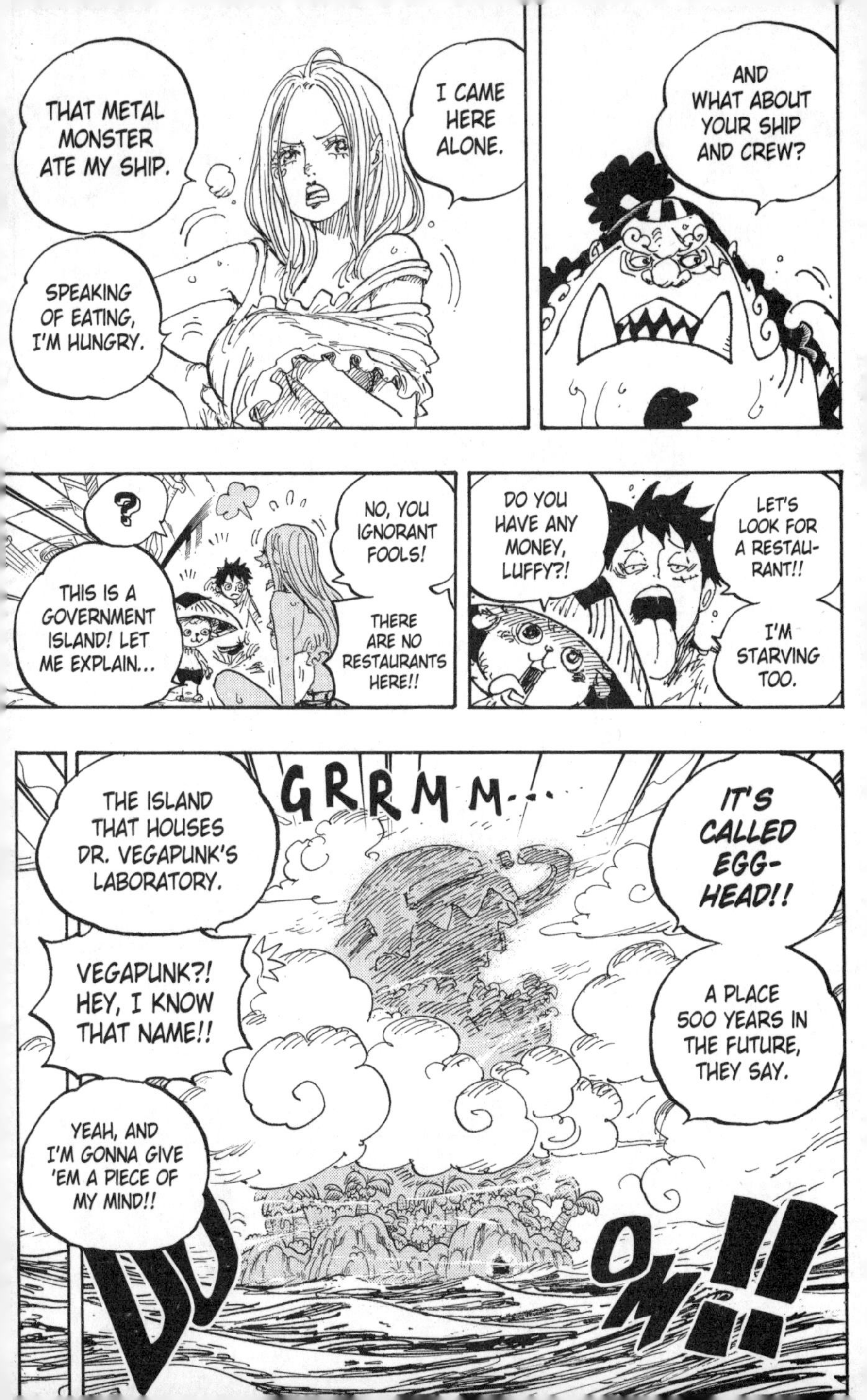
AND WHAT ABOUT YOUR SHIP AND CREW?
I CAME HERE ALONE.
THAT METAL MONSTER ATE MY SHIP.
SPEAKING OF EATING, I'M HUNGRY.
LET'S LOOK FOR A RESTAURANT!!
DO YOU HAVE ANY MONEY, LUFFY?!
I'M STARVING TOO.
NO, YOU IGNORANT FOOLS!
THERE ARE NO RESTAURANTS HERE!!
?
THIS IS A GOVERNMENT ISLAND! LET ME EXPLAIN...
IT'S CALLED EGG-HEAD!!
THE ISLAND THAT HOUSES DR. VEGAPUNK'S LABORATORY.
GRRMM...
A PLACE 500 YEARS IN THE FUTURE, THEY SAY.
VEGAPUNK?! HEY, I KNOW THAT NAME!!
YEAH, AND I'M GONNA GIVE 'EM A PIECE OF MY MIND!!
DOOM!!

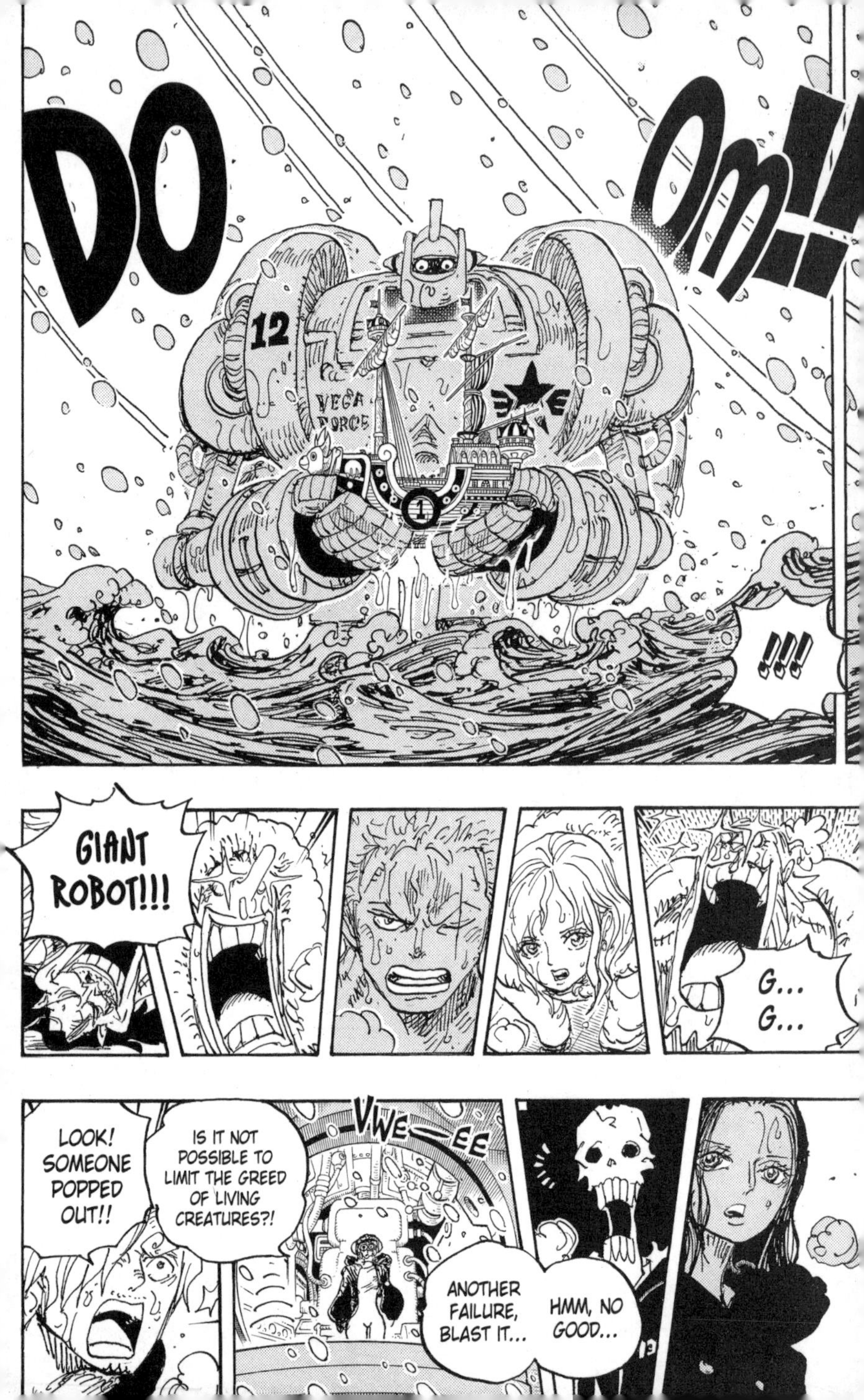
DO
OM!!
12
VEGA FORCE
1
!!!
G... G...
GIANT ROBOT!!!
HMM, NO GOOD...
ANOTHER FAILURE, BLAST IT...
VWE—EE
IS IT NOT POSSIBLE TO LIMIT THE GREED OF LIVING CREATURES?!
LOOK! SOMEONE POPPED OUT!!

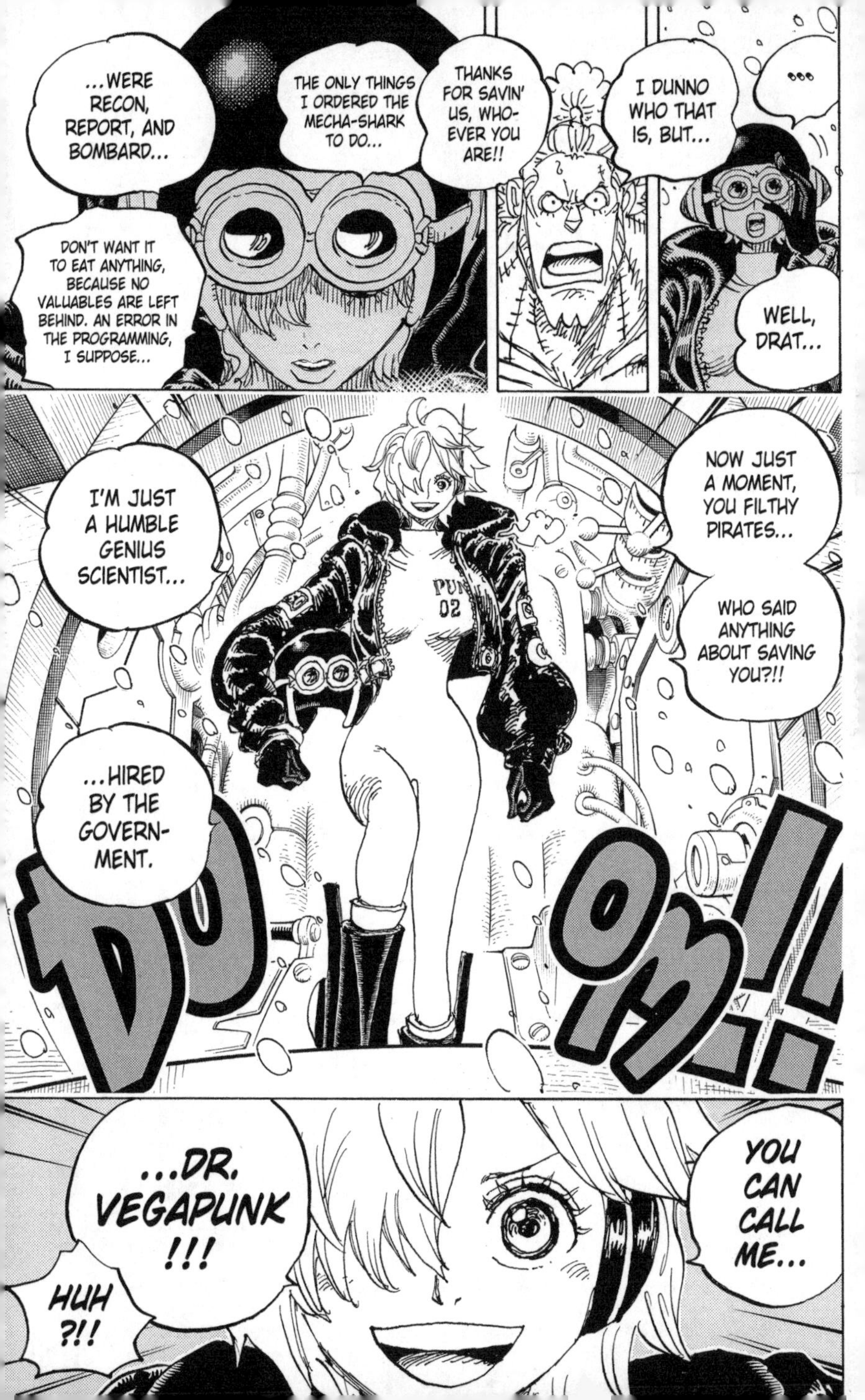
...
WELL, DRAT...
I DUNNO WHO THAT IS, BUT...
THANKS FOR SAVIN' US, WHOEVER YOU ARE!!
THE ONLY THINGS I ORDERED THE MECHA-SHARK TO DO...
...WERE RECON, REPORT, AND BOMBARD...
DON'T WANT IT TO EAT ANYTHING, BECAUSE NO VALUABLES ARE LEFT BEHIND. AN ERROR IN THE PROGRAMMING, I SUPPOSE...
NOW JUST A MOMENT, YOU FILTHY PIRATES...
WHO SAID ANYTHING ABOUT SAVING YOU?!!
I'M JUST A HUMBLE GENIUS SCIENTIST...
...HIRED BY THE GOVERNMENT.
PUNK 02
DOOM!!
YOU CAN CALL ME...
...DR. VEGAPUNK!!!
HUH?!!

(Hippo Iron, Saitama)

A: A female reader has sent me a message addressed to Sanada. You tell him off for me!

Q: I've got a comment I need to get off my chest regarding Sanadacchi.
"I too want to worship and drool and get very very aroused over the altar of my beloved Shanks's chest!"
And that desire is every bit as strong as your perverted passionate feelings for Nami! That's all. Ahh, I feel so much better now!♡
--Munecchicchi

A: Wait a second! ⚡ You're trying to compete with him?!

Q: I want to take a big chomp out of Nami's enormous millet dumplings!
--Sanadacchi

A: Not you too!! ⚡ You're both banned! Get out of here!!
And what about your PTA job?

Q: I have a question. Is Killer eating takoyaki in this scene?! He's only supposed to be able to eat very thin noodles.
--Occhi

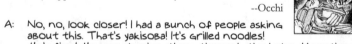

A: No, no, look closer! I had a bunch of people asking about this. That's yakisoba! It's grilled noodles!
He's fine! He was slurping them through the holes. My astigmatism has gotten worse lately, so I could have made that clearer. Sorry about that!

Q: Hi, Oda Sensei! In chapter 1052, what kind of book is Nami reading to Toko? I'm curious, but I can already tell one thing--it's not something Sanji's interested in!
--Yuu-kun

A: Ah, you noticed them? It's a heartwarming scene, isn't it? Nami loves to pore over the books she finds wherever they go. She must have found that in the castle's library. I believe it's a fashion book about kimonos. But Sanji's looking the other way.

Chapter 1062:
ADVENTURE IN THE LAND OF SCIENCE

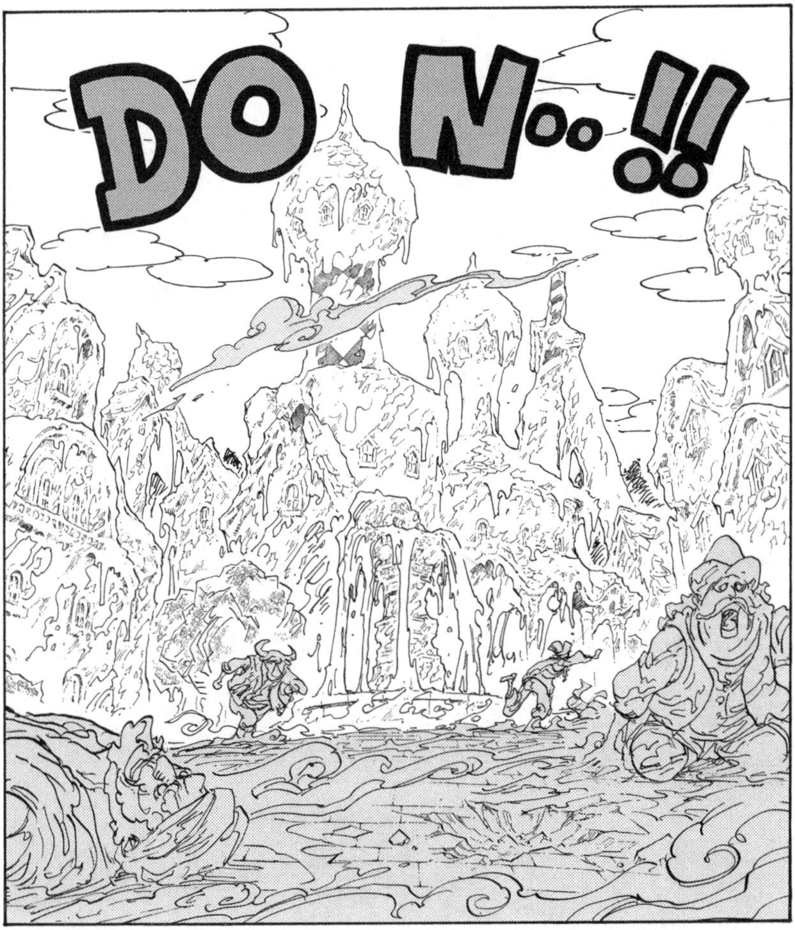
DO N..!!

GERMA 66'S AHH… AN EMOTIONLESS EXCURSION, VOL. 20:
"MEANWHILE, IN CHOCOLAT TOWN, CACAO ISLAND"

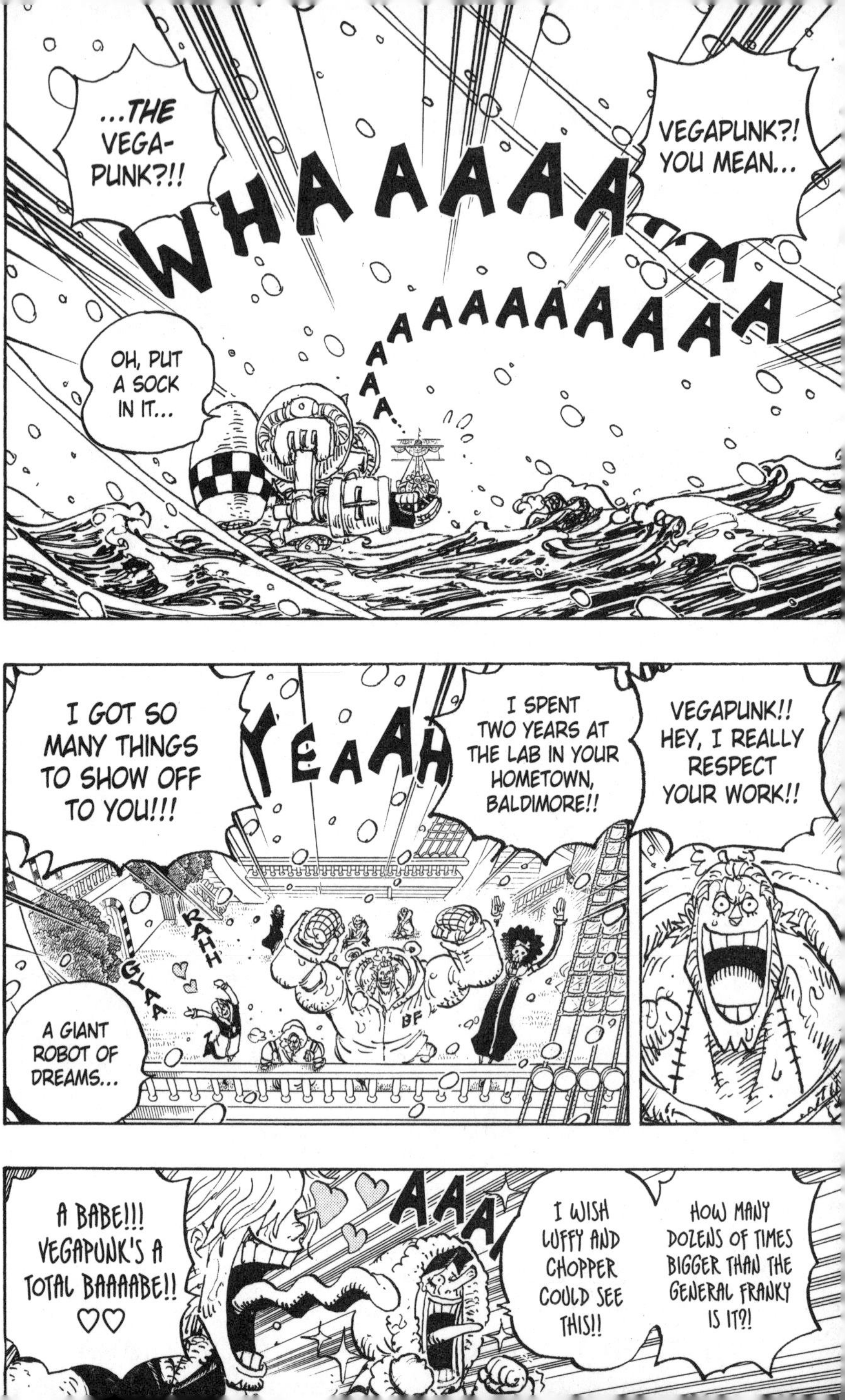
VEGAPUNK?! YOU MEAN...
...THE VEGA-PUNK?!!
WHAAAAAAAAAAAAAAAAAA...
OH, PUT A SOCK IN IT...
VEGAPUNK!! HEY, I REALLY RESPECT YOUR WORK!!
I SPENT TWO YEARS AT THE LAB IN YOUR HOMETOWN, BALDIMORE!!
YEAAH
I GOT SO MANY THINGS TO SHOW OFF TO YOU!!!
RAHH
GYAA
A GIANT ROBOT OF DREAMS...
HOW MANY DOZENS OF TIMES BIGGER THAN THE GENERAL FRANKY IS IT?!
I WISH LUFFY AND CHOPPER COULD SEE THIS!!
AAA
A BABE!!! VEGAPUNK'S A TOTAL BAAAABE!! ♡♡

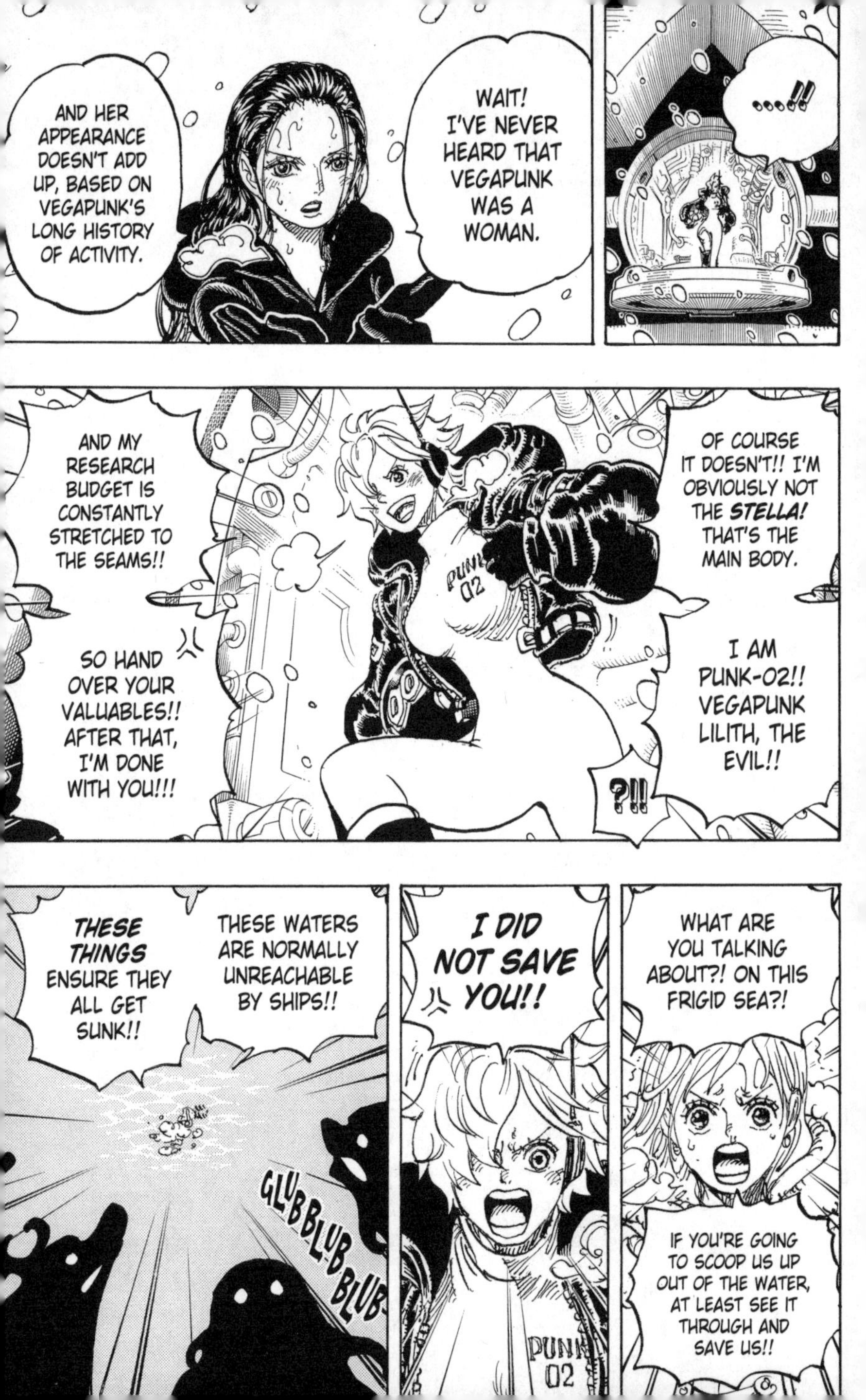
....!!
WAIT! I'VE NEVER HEARD THAT VEGAPUNK WAS A WOMAN.
AND HER APPEARANCE DOESN'T ADD UP, BASED ON VEGAPUNK'S LONG HISTORY OF ACTIVITY.
OF COURSE IT DOESN'T!! I'M OBVIOUSLY NOT THE *STELLA!* THAT'S THE MAIN BODY.
I AM PUNK-02!! VEGAPUNK LILITH, THE EVIL!!
?!!
AND MY RESEARCH BUDGET IS CONSTANTLY STRETCHED TO THE SEAMS!!
SO HAND OVER YOUR VALUABLES!! AFTER THAT, I'M DONE WITH YOU!!!
PUNK 02
WHAT ARE YOU TALKING ABOUT?! ON THIS FRIGID SEA?!
IF YOU'RE GOING TO SCOOP US UP OUT OF THE WATER, AT LEAST SEE IT THROUGH AND SAVE US!!
I DID NOT SAVE YOU!!
PUNK 02
THESE WATERS ARE NORMALLY UNREACHABLE BY SHIPS!!
THESE THINGS ENSURE THEY ALL GET SUNK!!
GLUB BLUB BLUB

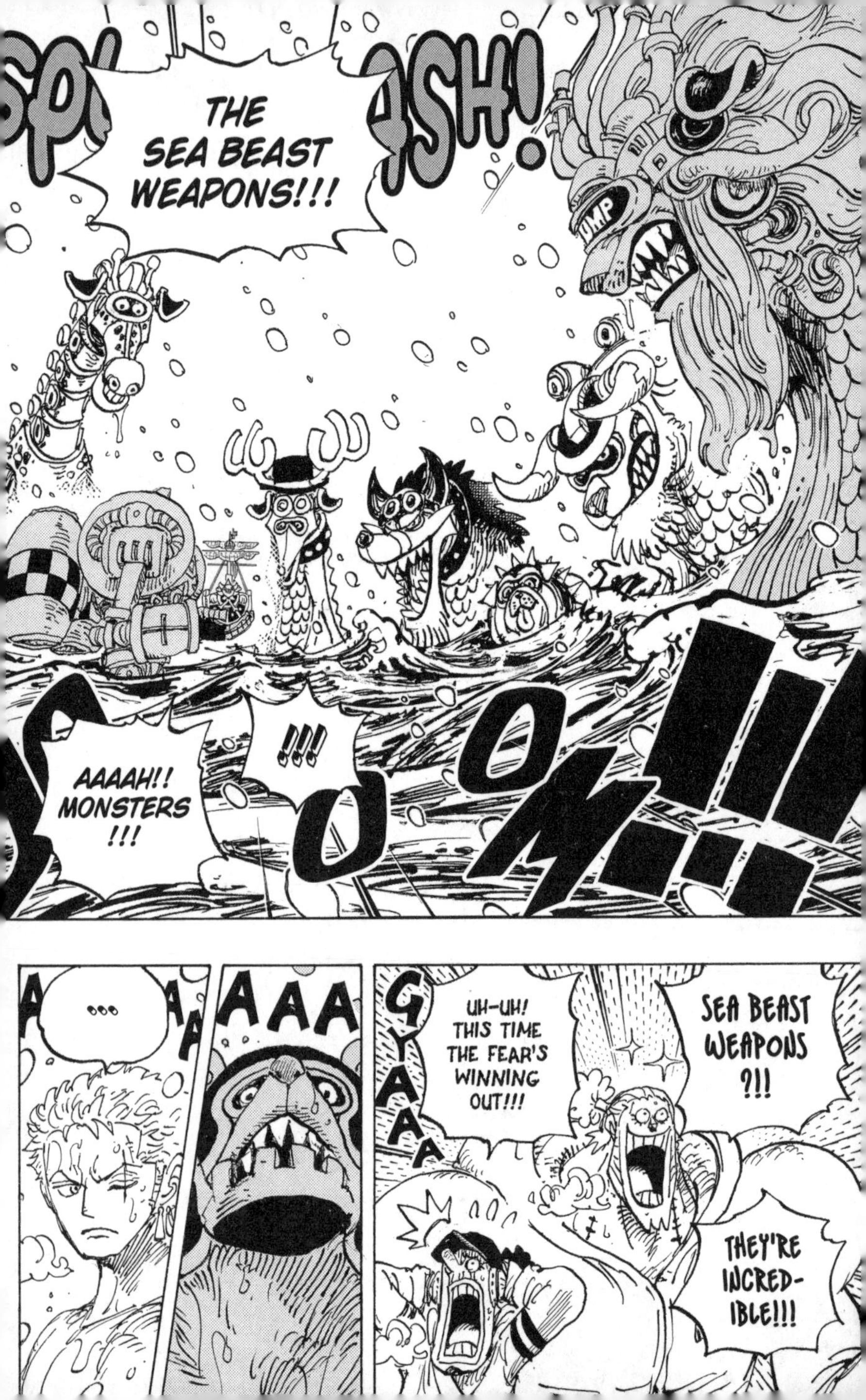
THE SEA BEAST WEAPONS!!!
!!!
AAAAH!! MONSTERS !!!
SEA BEAST WEAPONS ?!!
THEY'RE INCRED-IBLE!!!
UH-UH! THIS TIME THE FEAR'S WINNING OUT!!!
GYAAAA
AAA
...

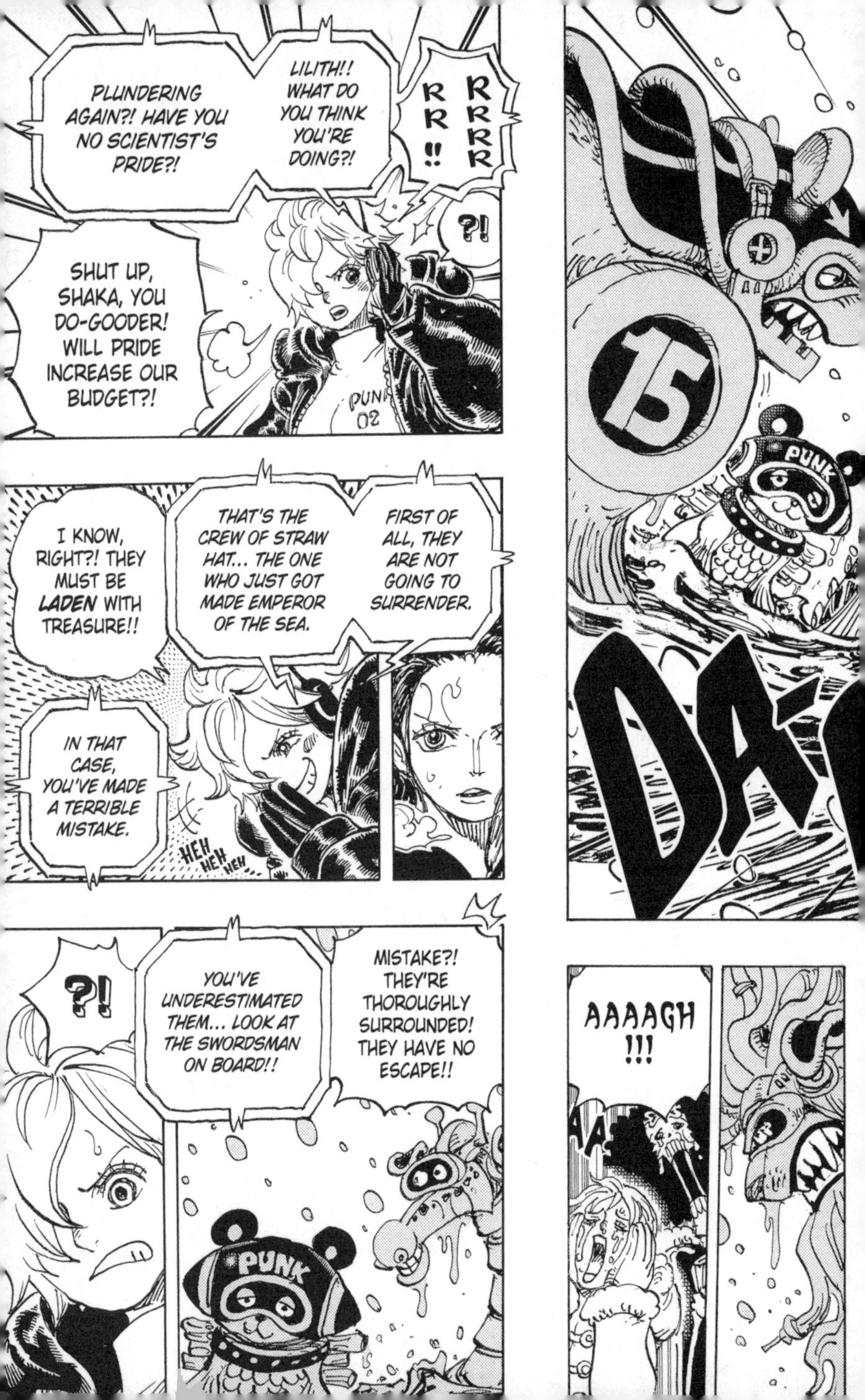
DA
AAAAGH!!!
AA
RRRRRR!!
LILITH!! WHAT DO YOU THINK YOU'RE DOING?!
PLUNDERING AGAIN?! HAVE YOU NO SCIENTIST'S PRIDE?!
?!
SHUT UP, SHAKA, YOU DO-GOODER! WILL PRIDE INCREASE OUR BUDGET?!
PUNK 02
FIRST OF ALL, THEY ARE NOT GOING TO SURRENDER.
THAT'S THE CREW OF STRAW HAT... THE ONE WHO JUST GOT MADE EMPEROR OF THE SEA.
I KNOW, RIGHT?! THEY MUST BE **LADEN** WITH TREASURE!!
IN THAT CASE, YOU'VE MADE A TERRIBLE MISTAKE.
HEH HEH HEH
MISTAKE?! THEY'RE THOROUGHLY SURROUNDED! THEY HAVE NO ESCAPE!!
YOU'VE UNDERESTIMATED THEM... LOOK AT THE SWORDSMAN ON BOARD!!
?!
PUNK

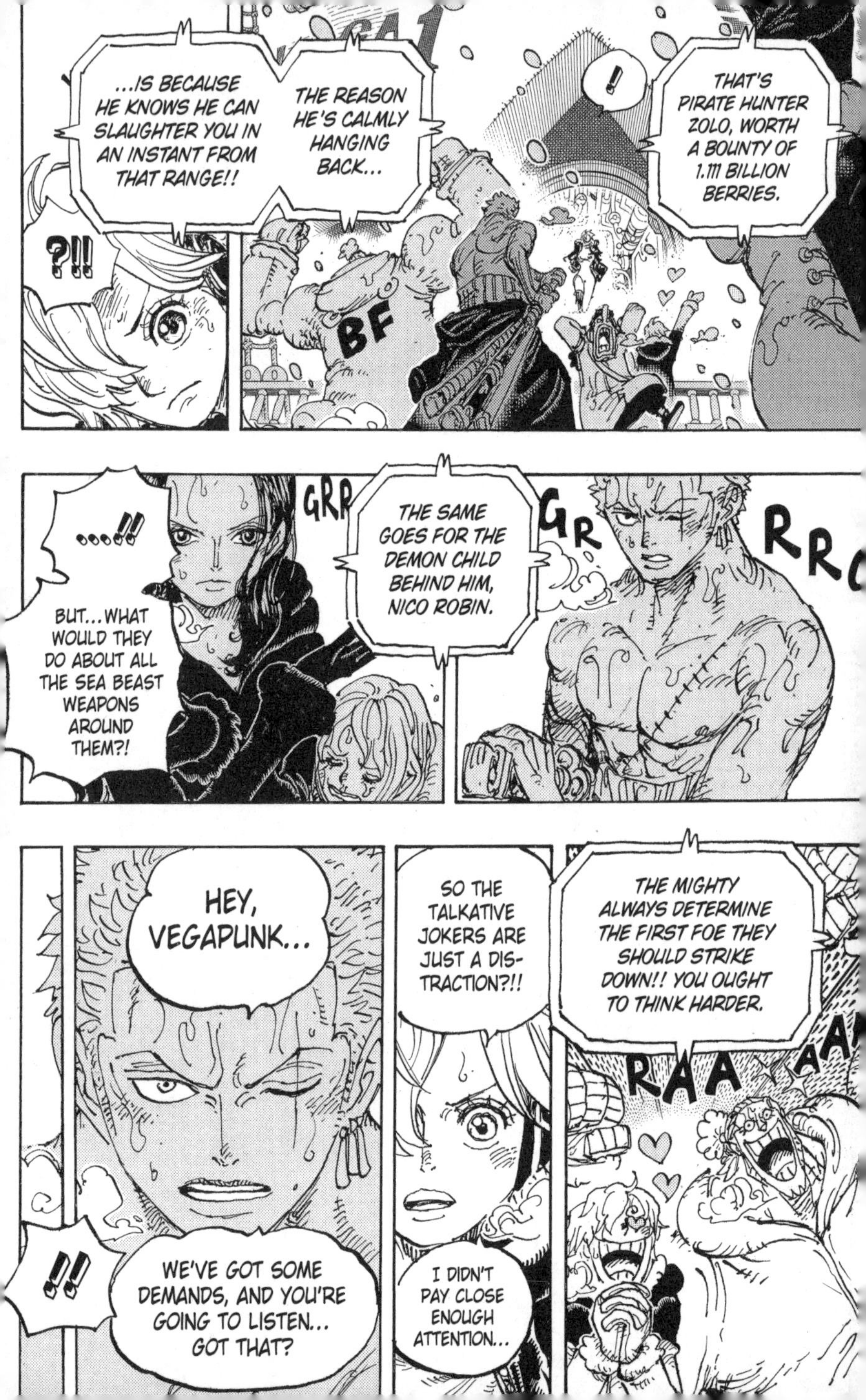
THAT'S PIRATE HUNTER ZOLO, WORTH A BOUNTY OF 1.111 BILLION BERRIES.
!
THE REASON HE'S CALMLY HANGING BACK...
...IS BECAUSE HE KNOWS HE CAN SLAUGHTER YOU IN AN INSTANT FROM THAT RANGE!!
BF
?!!
GR
RRR
THE SAME GOES FOR THE DEMON CHILD BEHIND HIM, NICO ROBIN.
GRR
...!!
BUT...WHAT WOULD THEY DO ABOUT ALL THE SEA BEAST WEAPONS AROUND THEM?!
THE MIGHTY ALWAYS DETERMINE THE FIRST FOE THEY SHOULD STRIKE DOWN!! YOU OUGHT TO THINK HARDER.
RAA
AA
SO THE TALKATIVE JOKERS ARE JUST A DISTRACTION?!!
I DIDN'T PAY CLOSE ENOUGH ATTENTION...
HEY, VEGAPUNK...
!!
WE'VE GOT SOME DEMANDS, AND YOU'RE GOING TO LISTEN... GOT THAT?

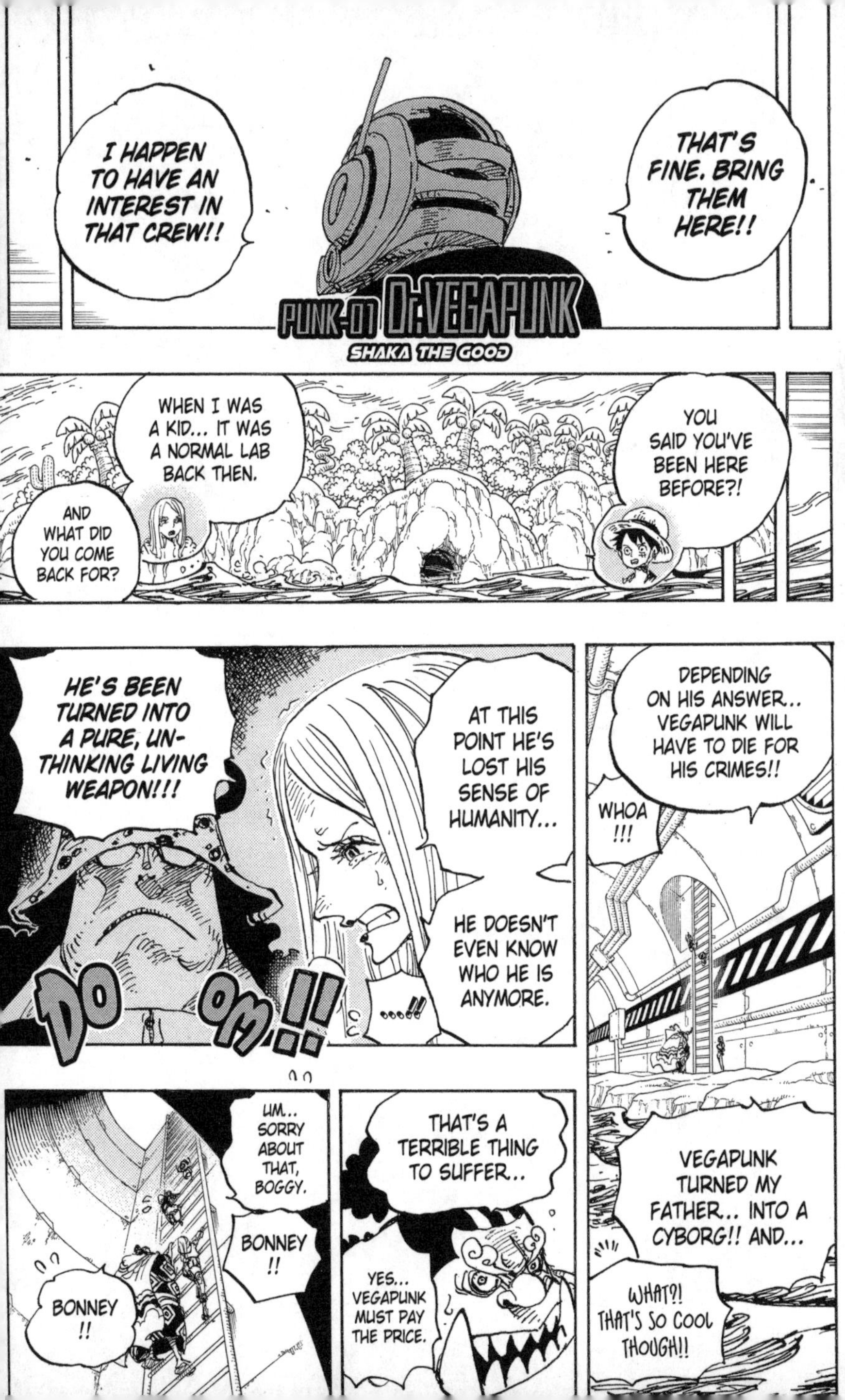
THAT'S FINE. BRING THEM HERE!!
I HAPPEN TO HAVE AN INTEREST IN THAT CREW!!
PUNK-01 Dr. VEGAPUNK
SHAKA THE GOOD
YOU SAID YOU'VE BEEN HERE BEFORE?!
WHEN I WAS A KID... IT WAS A NORMAL LAB BACK THEN.
AND WHAT DID YOU COME BACK FOR?
DEPENDING ON HIS ANSWER... VEGAPUNK WILL HAVE TO DIE FOR HIS CRIMES!!
WHOA !!!
VEGAPUNK TURNED MY FATHER... INTO A CYBORG!! AND...
WHAT?! THAT'S SO COOL THOUGH!!
AT THIS POINT HE'S LOST HIS SENSE OF HUMANITY...
HE'S BEEN TURNED INTO A PURE, UNTHINKING LIVING WEAPON!!!
HE DOESN'T EVEN KNOW WHO HE IS ANYMORE.
....!!
DO OM!!
THAT'S A TERRIBLE THING TO SUFFER...
YES... VEGAPUNK MUST PAY THE PRICE.
UM... SORRY ABOUT THAT, BOGGY.
BONNEY !!
BONNEY !!

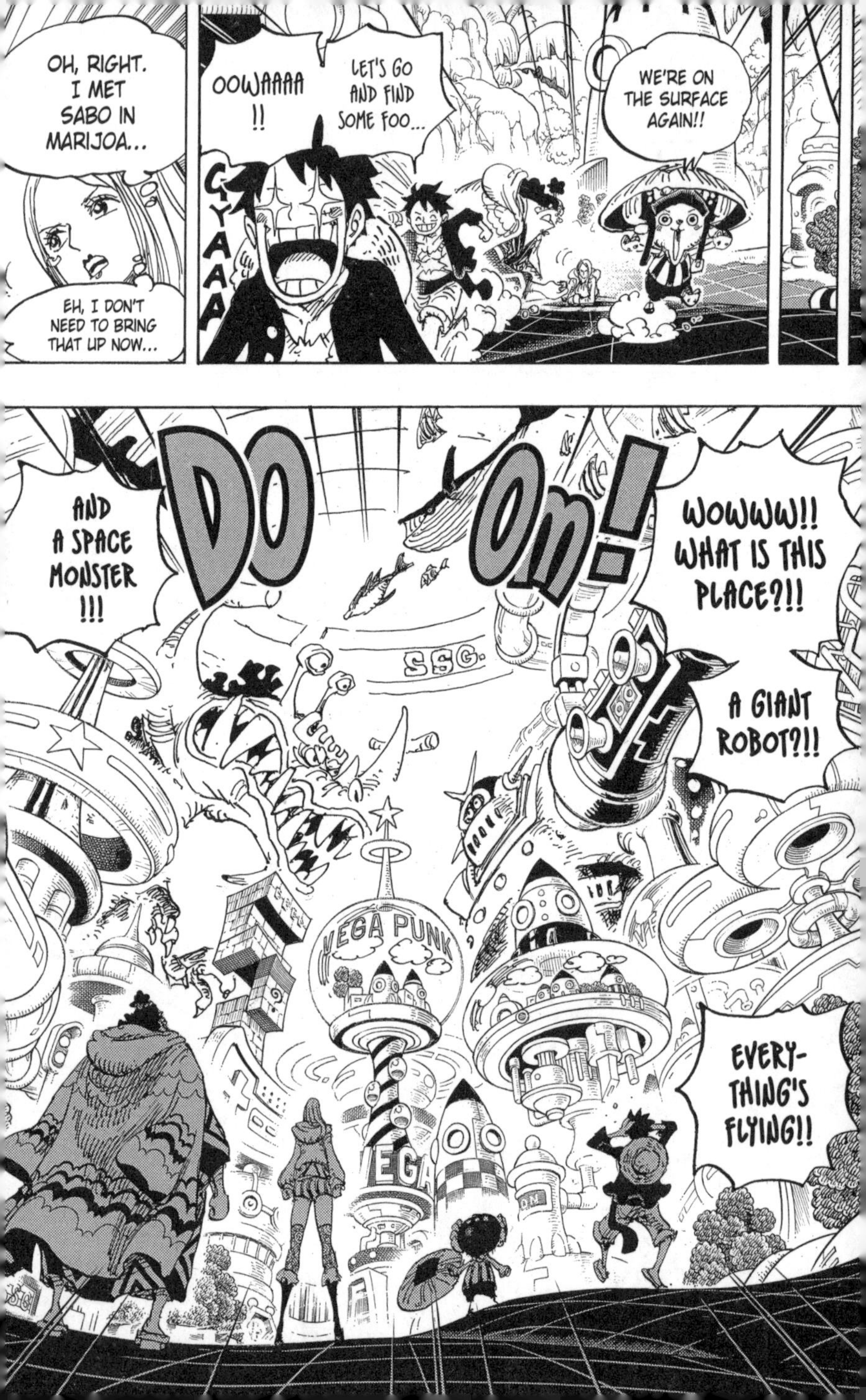
WE'RE ON THE SURFACE AGAIN!!
LET'S GO AND FIND SOME FOO...
OOWAAAA !!
GYAAAA
OH, RIGHT. I MET SABO IN MARIJOA...
EH, I DON'T NEED TO BRING THAT UP NOW...
WOWWW!! WHAT IS THIS PLACE?!!
A GIANT ROBOT?!!
DOOM!
AND A SPACE MONSTER !!!
SSG
VEGA PUNK
VEGA
EVERY-THING'S FLYING!!

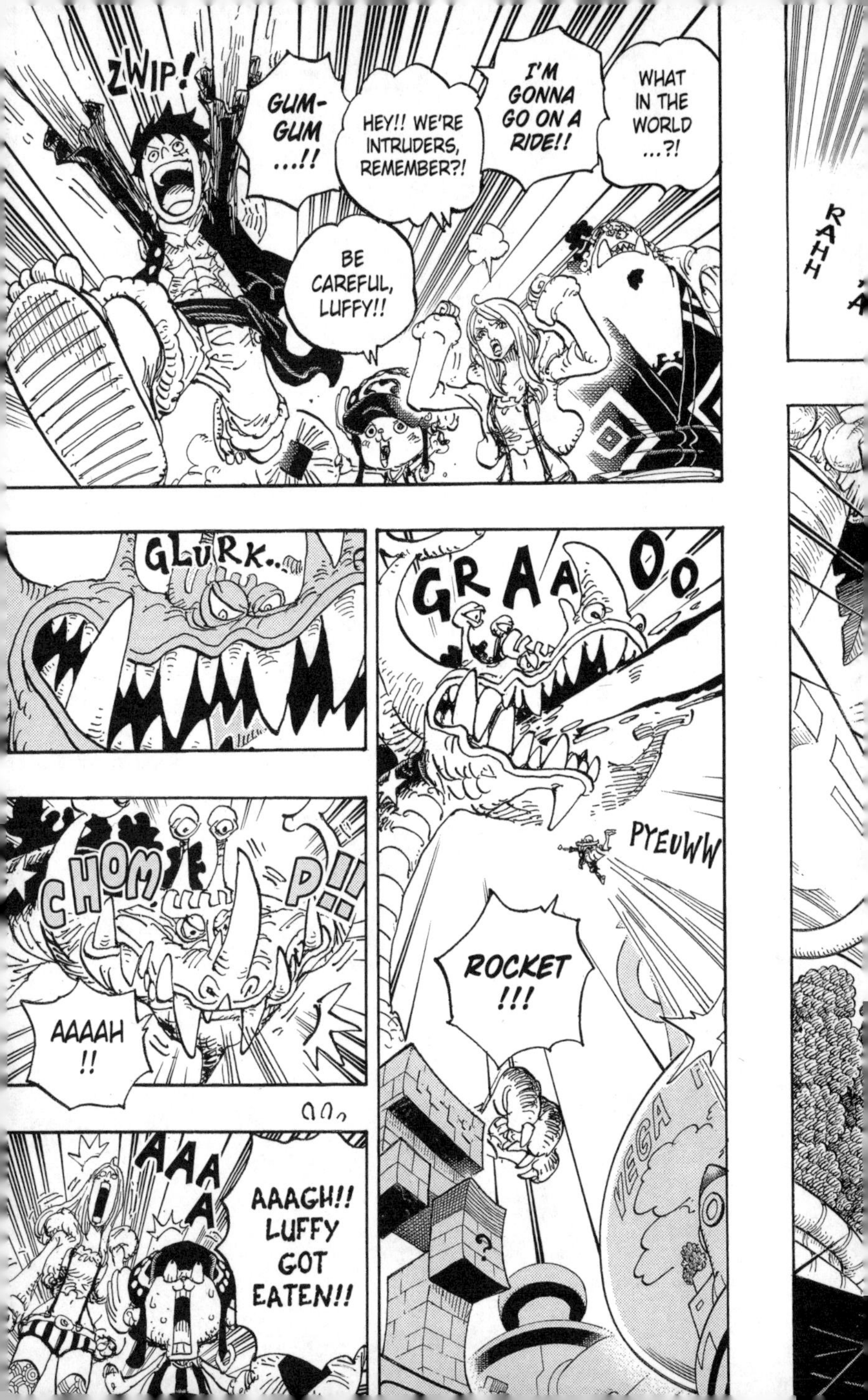
RAHH
WHAT IN THE WORLD ...?!
I'M GONNA GO ON A RIDE!!
HEY!! WE'RE INTRUDERS, REMEMBER?!
GUM-GUM ...!!
ZWIP!
BE CAREFUL, LUFFY!!
GRAAOO
PYEUWW
ROCKET !!!
VEGA
GLURK...
CHOMP!!
AAAAH !!
AAAA
AAAGH!! LUFFY GOT EATEN!!

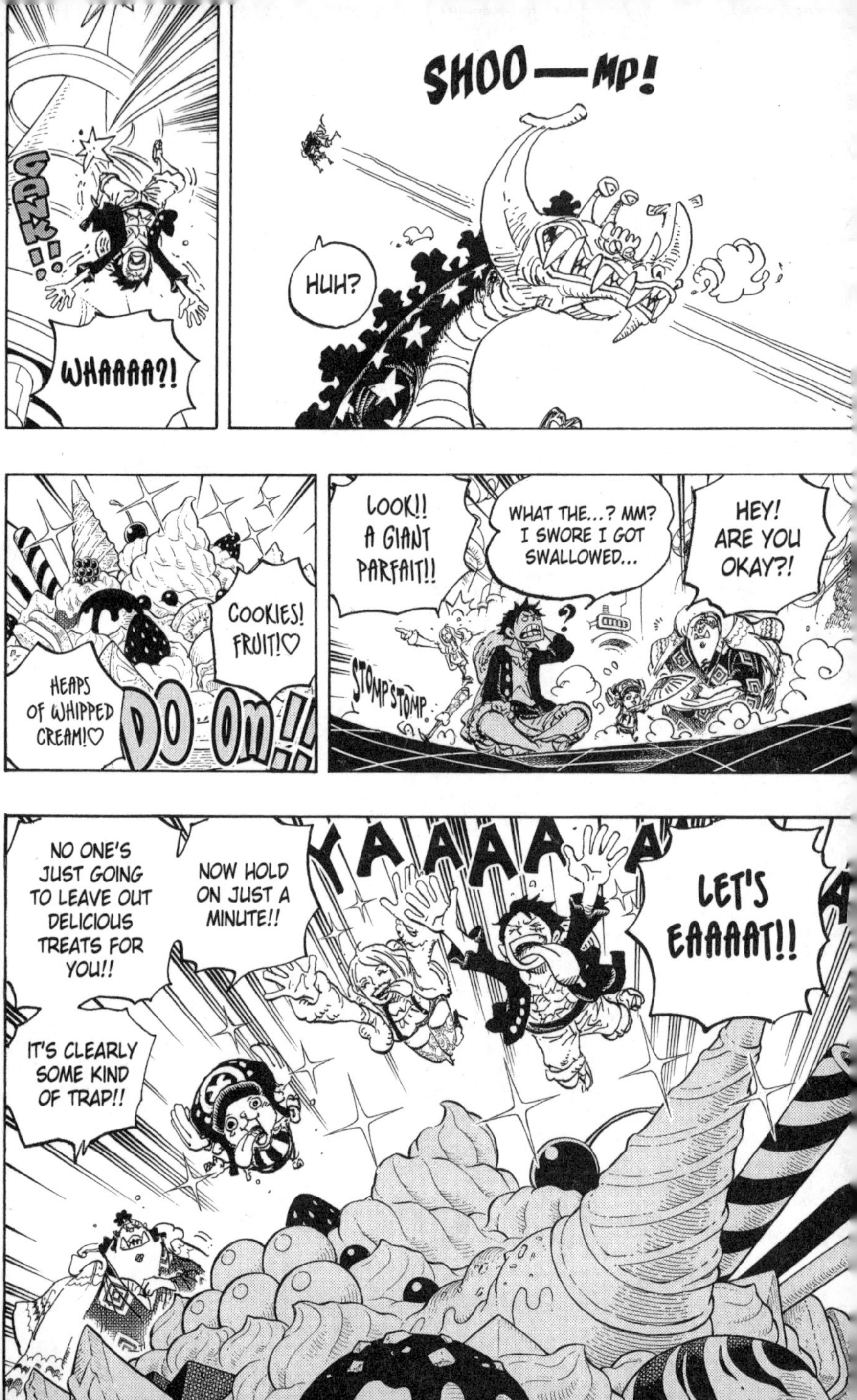
SHOO—MP!
HUH?
GANK!!
WHAAAA?!
HEY! ARE YOU OKAY?!
WHAT THE...? MM? I SWORE I GOT SWALLOWED...
LOOK!! A GIANT PARFAIT!!
STOMP STOMP
COOKIES! FRUIT!♡
HEAPS OF WHIPPED CREAM!♡
DO-OM!!
LET'S EAAAAT!!
NOW HOLD ON JUST A MINUTE!!
NO ONE'S JUST GOING TO LEAVE OUT DELICIOUS TREATS FOR YOU!!
IT'S CLEARLY SOME KIND OF TRAP!!

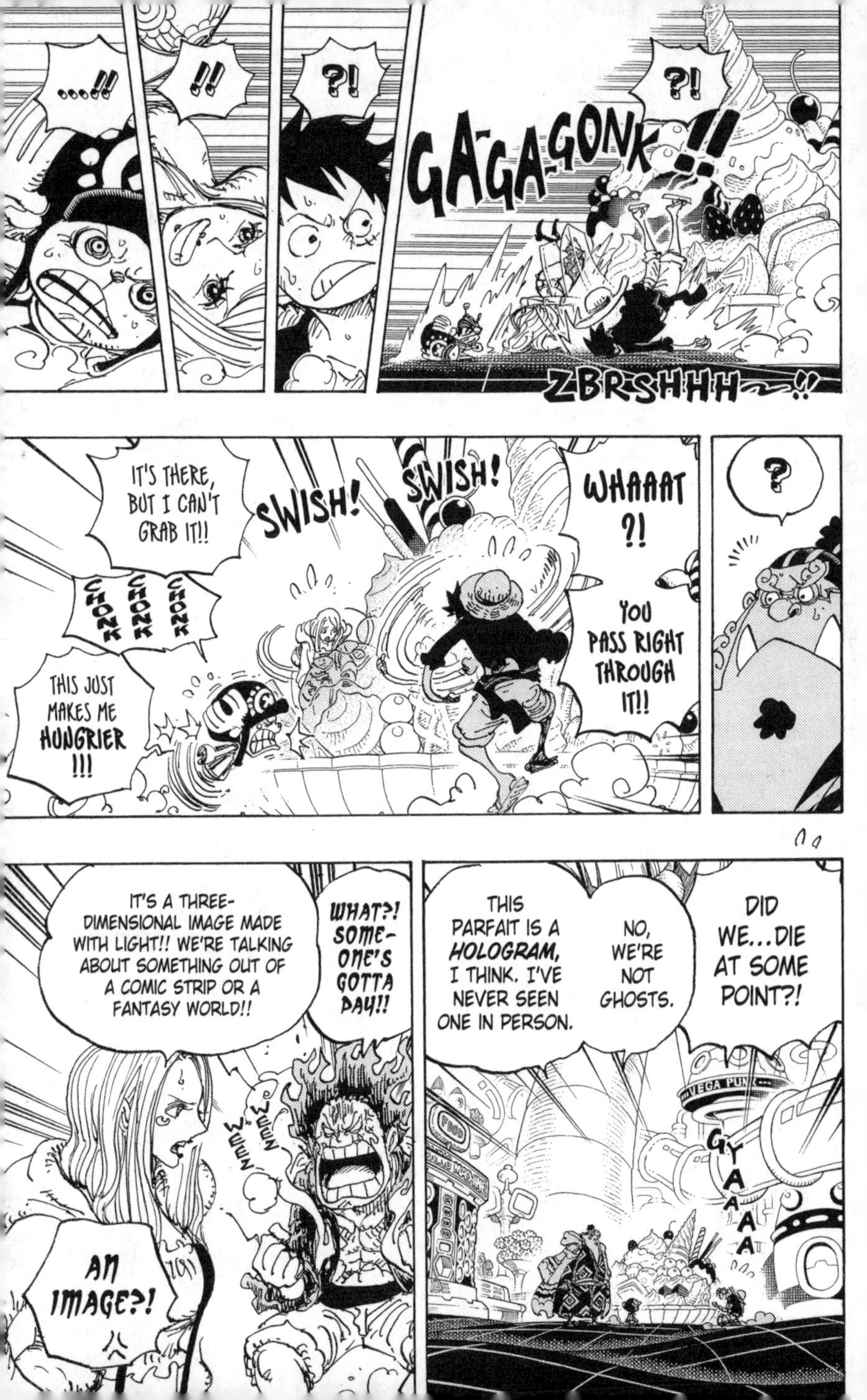
?!
GAGAGONK!!
?!
!!
...!!
ZBRSHHH!!
?
WHAAAT?!
YOU PASS RIGHT THROUGH IT!!
SWISH!
SWISH!
IT'S THERE, BUT I CAN'T GRAB IT!!
CHONK CHONK CHONK
THIS JUST MAKES ME HUNGRIER!!!
DID WE...DIE AT SOME POINT?!
NO, WE'RE NOT GHOSTS.
THIS PARFAIT IS A HOLOGRAM, I THINK. I'VE NEVER SEEN ONE IN PERSON.
VEGA PUNK
FOOD
GYAAAAA
WHAT?! SOME-ONE'S GOTTA PAY!!
WEEN WEEN
IT'S A THREE-DIMENSIONAL IMAGE MADE WITH LIGHT!! WE'RE TALKING ABOUT SOMETHING OUT OF A COMIC STRIP OR A FANTASY WORLD!!
AN IMAGE?!

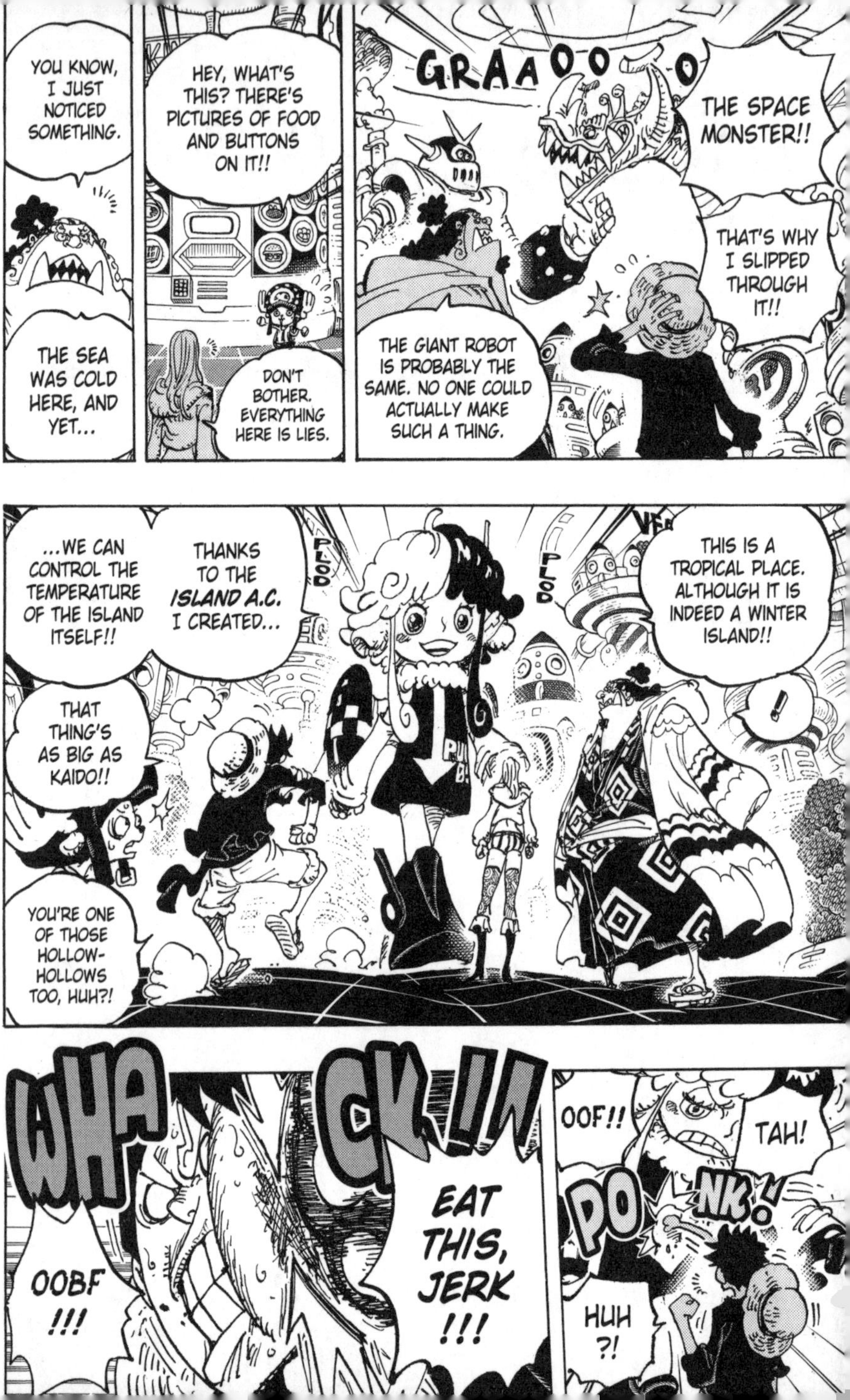
GRAAOO-O
THE SPACE MONSTER!!
THAT'S WHY I SLIPPED THROUGH IT!!
THE GIANT ROBOT IS PROBABLY THE SAME. NO ONE COULD ACTUALLY MAKE SUCH A THING.
HEY, WHAT'S THIS? THERE'S PICTURES OF FOOD AND BUTTONS ON IT!!
DON'T BOTHER. EVERYTHING HERE IS LIES.
YOU KNOW, I JUST NOTICED SOMETHING.
THE SEA WAS COLD HERE, AND YET...
THIS IS A TROPICAL PLACE. ALTHOUGH IT IS INDEED A WINTER ISLAND!!
!
PLOD
PLOD
THANKS TO THE *ISLAND A.C.* I CREATED...
...WE CAN CONTROL THE TEMPERATURE OF THE ISLAND ITSELF!!
THAT THING'S AS BIG AS KAIDO!!
YOU'RE ONE OF THOSE HOLLOW-HOLLOWS TOO, HUH?!
OOF!!
TAH!
PONK!
HUH ?!
WHACK!!
EAT THIS, JERK !!!
OOBF !!!

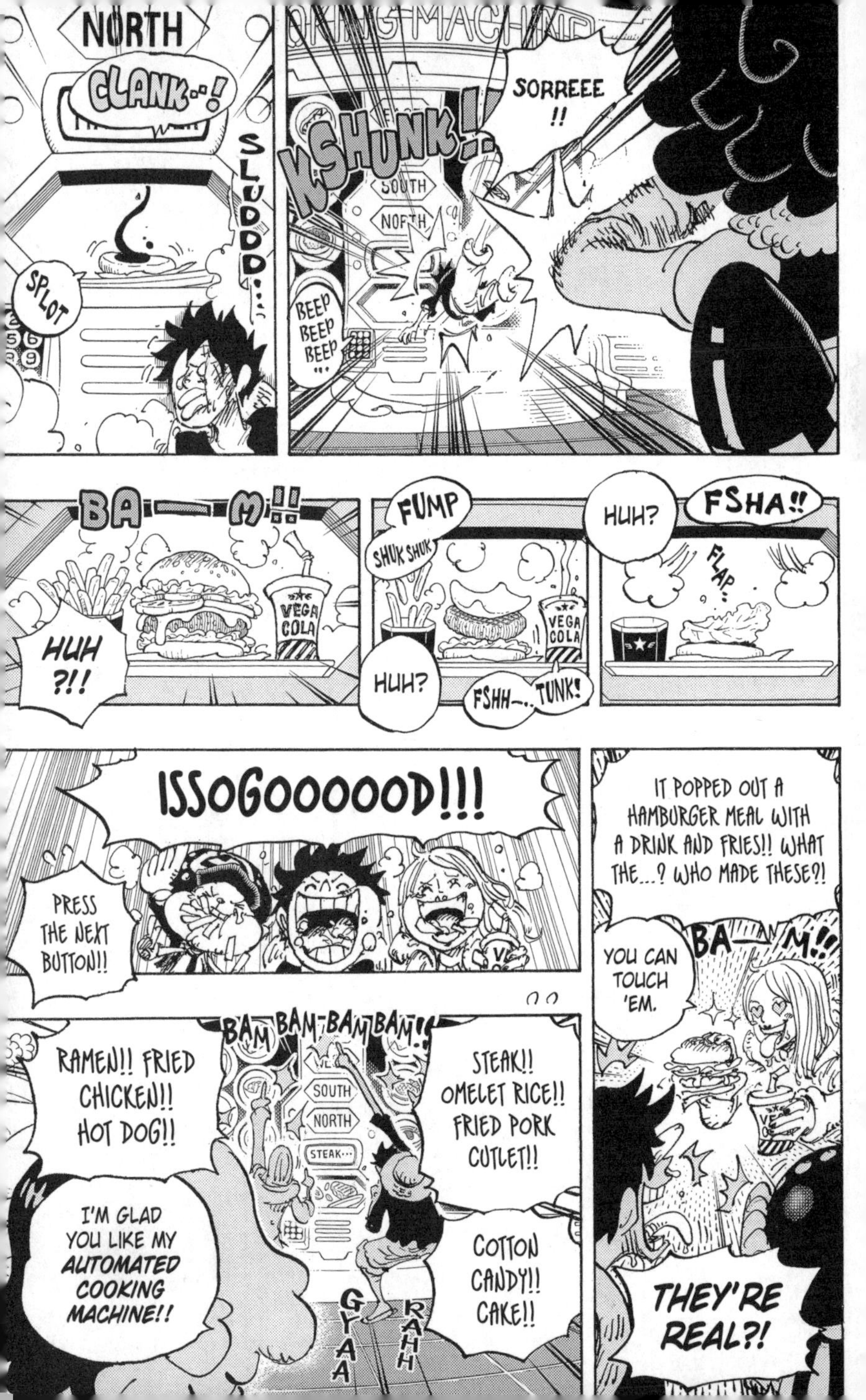
SORREEE !!
KSHUNK!!
SOUTH
NORTH
BEEP BEEP BEEP...
NORTH
CLANK..!
SLUDDD...
SPLOT
FSHA!!
HUH?
FLAP..
FUMP
SHUK SHUK
VEGA COLA
HUH?
FSHH—..TUNK!
BA——M!!
VEGA COLA
HUH ?!!
IT POPPED OUT A HAMBURGER MEAL WITH A DRINK AND FRIES!! WHAT THE...? WHO MADE THESE?!
BA—M!!
YOU CAN TOUCH 'EM.
THEY'RE REAL?!
ISSOGOOOOOD!!!
PRESS THE NEXT BUTTON!!
BAM BAM-BAM BAM!!
STEAK!! OMELET RICE!! FRIED PORK CUTLET!!
SOUTH
NORTH
STEAK...
RAMEN!! FRIED CHICKEN!! HOT DOG!!
COTTON CANDY!! CAKE!!
RAHH
GYAA
I'M GLAD YOU LIKE MY *AUTOMATED COOKING MACHINE!!*

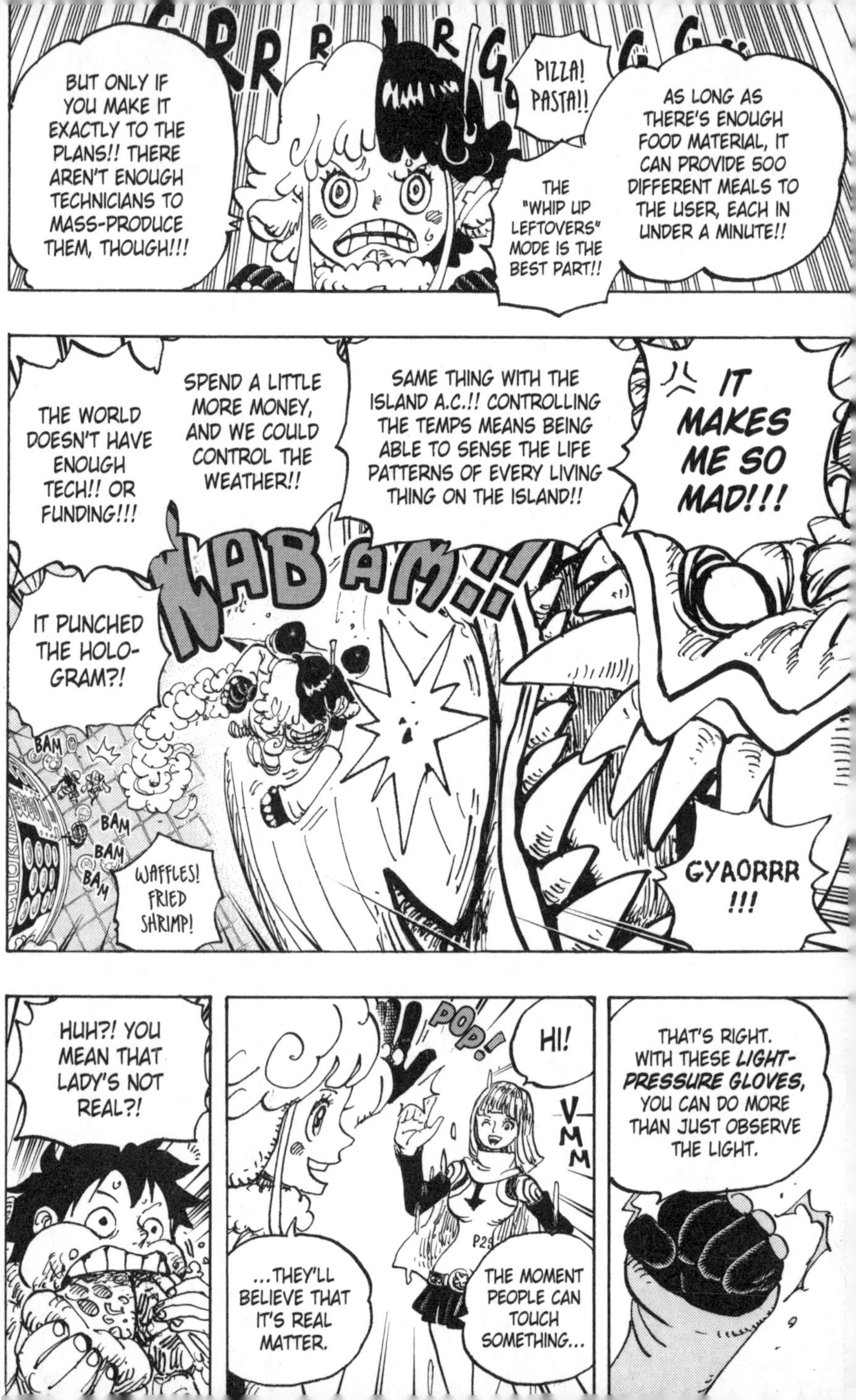
AS LONG AS THERE'S ENOUGH FOOD MATERIAL, IT CAN PROVIDE 500 DIFFERENT MEALS TO THE USER, EACH IN UNDER A MINUTE!!
PIZZA! PASTA!!
THE "WHIP UP LEFTOVERS" MODE IS THE BEST PART!!
BUT ONLY IF YOU MAKE IT EXACTLY TO THE PLANS!! THERE AREN'T ENOUGH TECHNICIANS TO MASS-PRODUCE THEM, THOUGH!!!
IT MAKES ME SO MAD!!!
SAME THING WITH THE ISLAND A.C.!! CONTROLLING THE TEMPS MEANS BEING ABLE TO SENSE THE LIFE PATTERNS OF EVERY LIVING THING ON THE ISLAND!!
SPEND A LITTLE MORE MONEY, AND WE COULD CONTROL THE WEATHER!!
THE WORLD DOESN'T HAVE ENOUGH TECH!! OR FUNDING!!!
KABAM!!
IT PUNCHED THE HOLOGRAM?!
GYAORRR!!!
BAM
BAM
BAM
BAM
WAFFLES! FRIED SHRIMP!
THAT'S RIGHT. WITH THESE LIGHT-PRESSURE GLOVES, YOU CAN DO MORE THAN JUST OBSERVE THE LIGHT.
HI!
POP!
VMM
THE MOMENT PEOPLE CAN TOUCH SOMETHING...
...THEY'LL BELIEVE THAT IT'S REAL MATTER.
HUH?! YOU MEAN THAT LADY'S NOT REAL?!

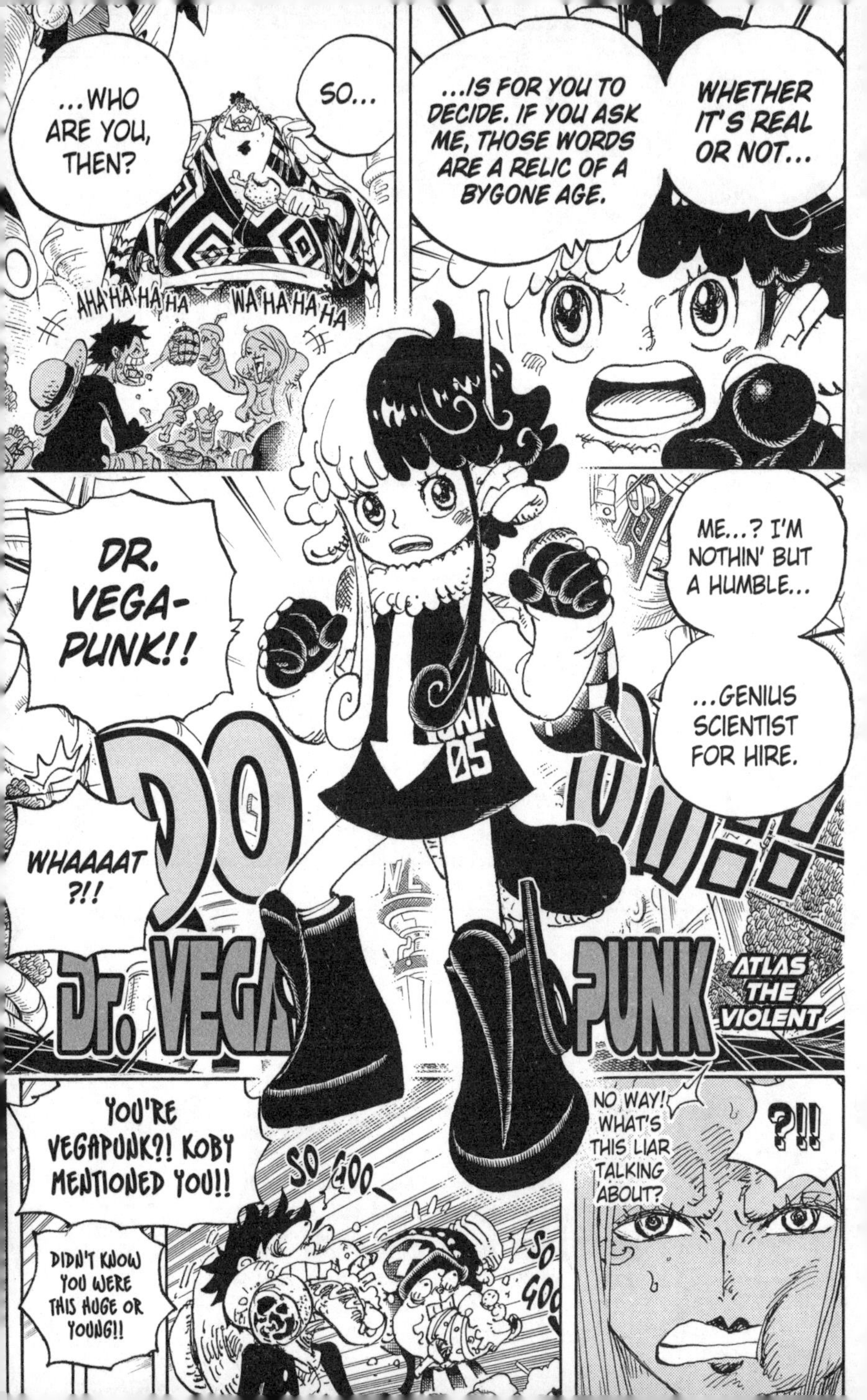
WHETHER IT'S REAL OR NOT...
...IS FOR YOU TO DECIDE. IF YOU ASK ME, THOSE WORDS ARE A RELIC OF A BYGONE AGE.
SO...
...WHO ARE YOU, THEN?
WA HA HA HA HA
AHA HA HA HA
ME...? I'M NOTHIN' BUT A HUMBLE...
...GENIUS SCIENTIST FOR HIRE.
DR. VEGA-PUNK!!
WHAAAAT ?!!
DO
Dr. VEGAPUNK
ATLAS THE VIOLENT
?!!
NO WAY! WHAT'S THIS LIAR TALKING ABOUT?
YOU'RE VEGAPUNK?! KOBY MENTIONED YOU!!
DIDN'T KNOW YOU WERE THIS HUGE OR YOUNG!!
SO GOO
SO GOO

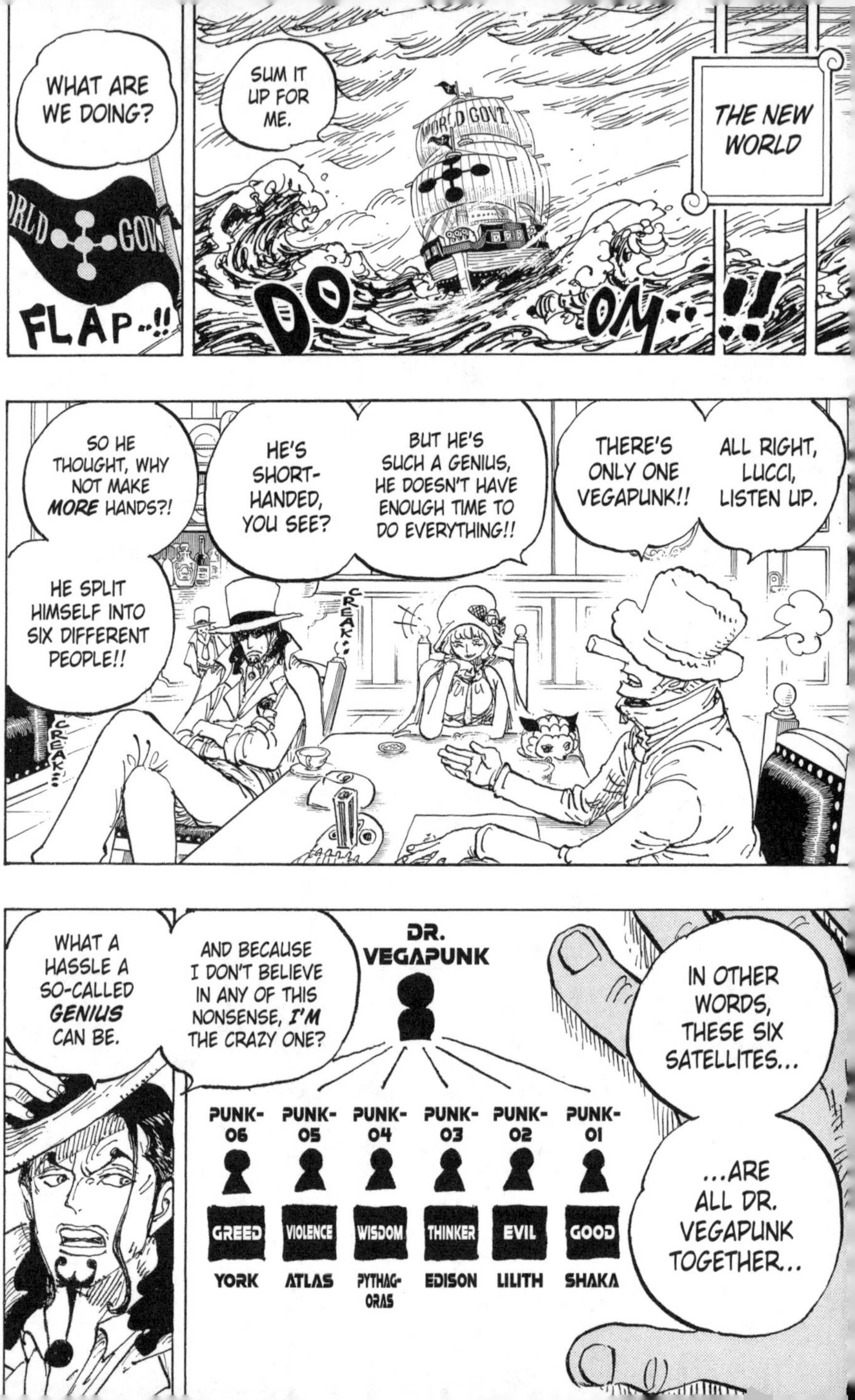
THE NEW WORLD
SUM IT UP FOR ME.
DO-OM..!!
WHAT ARE WE DOING?
WORLD GOVT
FLAP..!!
ALL RIGHT, LUCCI, LISTEN UP.
THERE'S ONLY ONE VEGAPUNK!!
BUT HE'S SUCH A GENIUS, HE DOESN'T HAVE ENOUGH TIME TO DO EVERYTHING!!
HE'S SHORT-HANDED, YOU SEE?
SO HE THOUGHT, WHY NOT MAKE *MORE* HANDS?!
CREAK...
HE SPLIT HIMSELF INTO SIX DIFFERENT PEOPLE!!
CREAK...
IN OTHER WORDS, THESE SIX SATELLITES...
...ARE ALL DR. VEGAPUNK TOGETHER...
DR. VEGAPUNK
PUNK-06 GREED YORK
PUNK-05 VIOLENCE ATLAS
PUNK-04 WISDOM PYTHAG-ORAS
PUNK-03 THINKER EDISON
PUNK-02 EVIL LILITH
PUNK-01 GOOD SHAKA
AND BECAUSE I DON'T BELIEVE IN ANY OF THIS NONSENSE, *I'M* THE CRAZY ONE?
WHAT A HASSLE A SO-CALLED *GENIUS* CAN BE.

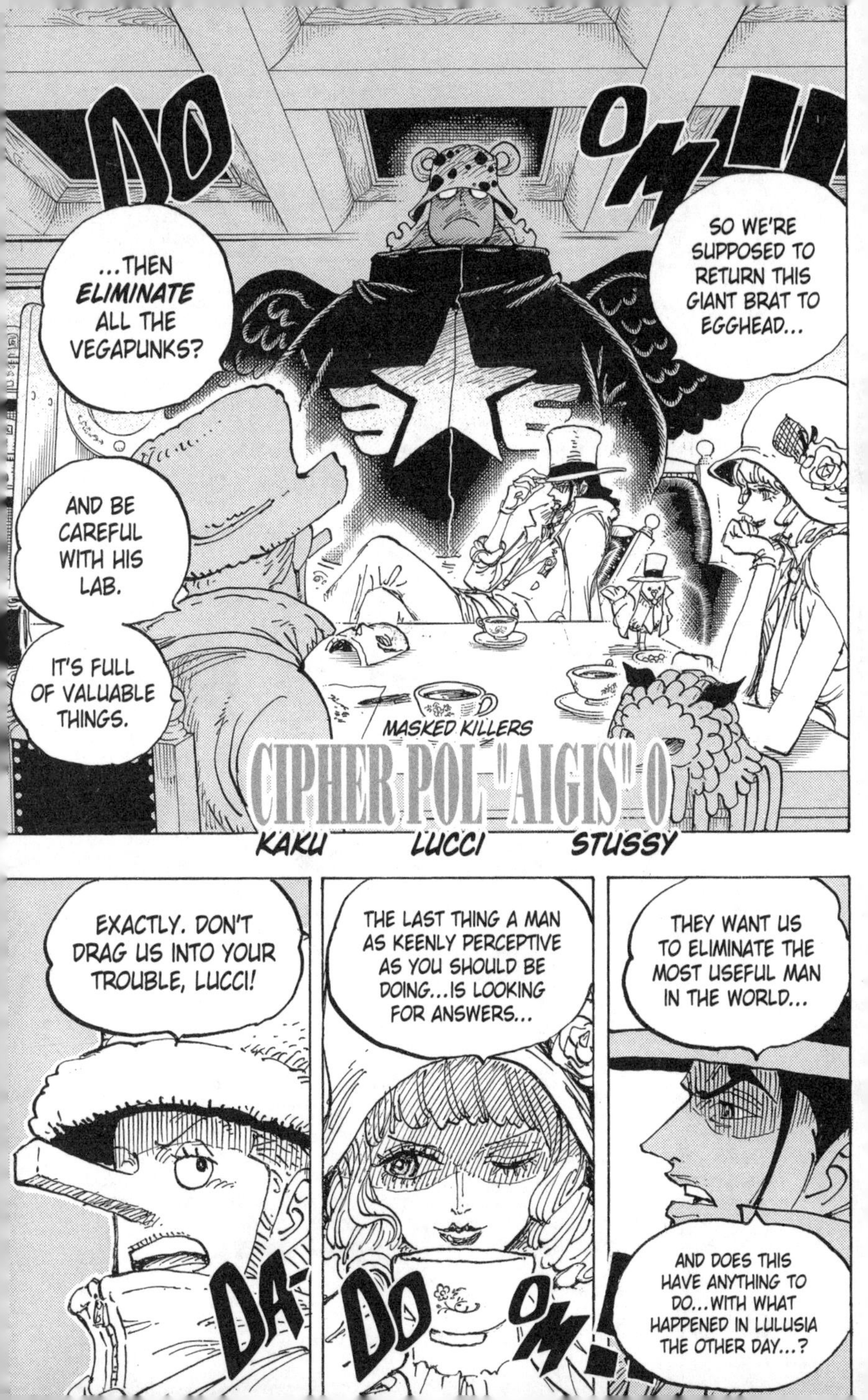
DO
OM
SO WE'RE SUPPOSED TO RETURN THIS GIANT BRAT TO EGGHEAD...
...THEN ELIMINATE ALL THE VEGAPUNKS?
AND BE CAREFUL WITH HIS LAB.
IT'S FULL OF VALUABLE THINGS.
MASKED KILLERS
CIPHER POL "AIGIS" 0
KAKU
LUCCI
STUSSY
THEY WANT US TO ELIMINATE THE MOST USEFUL MAN IN THE WORLD...
AND DOES THIS HAVE ANYTHING TO DO...WITH WHAT HAPPENED IN LULUSIA THE OTHER DAY...?
THE LAST THING A MAN AS KEENLY PERCEPTIVE AS YOU SHOULD BE DOING...IS LOOKING FOR ANSWERS...
EXACTLY. DON'T DRAG US INTO YOUR TROUBLE, LUCCI!
DA-
DO
OM!!

A: I had a lot of questions about Zolo's bloodline. Since I don't think I'll be showing it in the story itself, I'll announce it here.

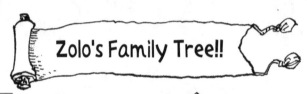

Zolo's Family Tree!!

55 Years Ago	**Shimotsuki Kozaburo**

• Made Wado Ichmonji and Enma (gifted for Oden's fourth birthday)
• Left Wano with a group of 25 (including Ushimaru's sister Furiko and Minatomo the carpenter)

52 Years Ago

• Wins a battle against bandits attacking a village in the East Blue.
• Ten members of the crew stay and settle down, creating Shimotsuki (Frost-Moon) Village.

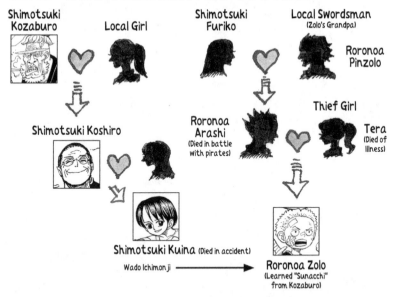

Shimotsuki Kozaburo ♥ Local Girl

Shimotsuki Furiko ♥ Local Swordsman (Zolo's Grandpa) Roronoa Pinzolo

⬇ Shimotsuki Koshiro ♥

Roronoa Arashi (Died in battle with pirates) ♥ Thief Girl Tera (Died of illness)

Shimotsuki Kuina (Died in accident)

Wado Ichimonji ⟶ Roronoa Zolo (Learned "Sunacchi" from Kozaburo)

A: The younger brother of Shimotsuki Furiko, one of the members who sailed away from Wano, was none other than the "So-and-So" Yamato met as a child in the cave, also known as Shimotsuki Ushimaru, former daimyo of Ringo, and descendant of Shimotsuki Ryuma, the legendary samurai Zolo met on Thriller Bark. Does that mean what I think it does...? Yes! It's a story of a very strange, twisted fate that even Zolo is unaware of.

Chapter 1063:
MY ONLY FAMILY

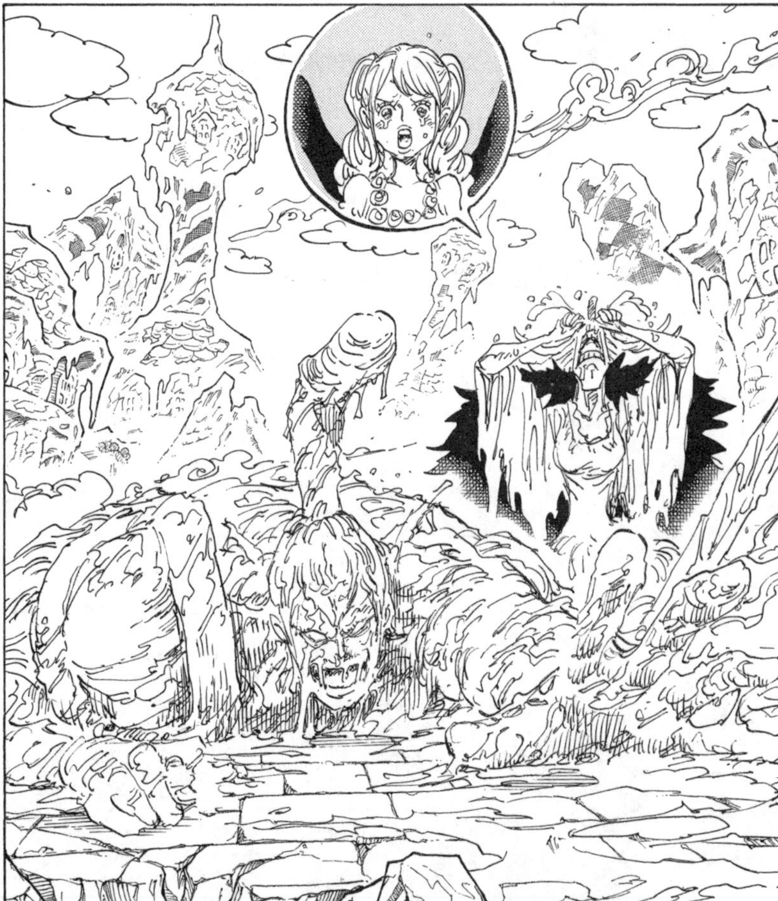

GERMA 66'S AHH... AN EMOTIONLESS EXCURSION, VOL. 21: "PUDDING'S BEEN ABDUCTED!!"

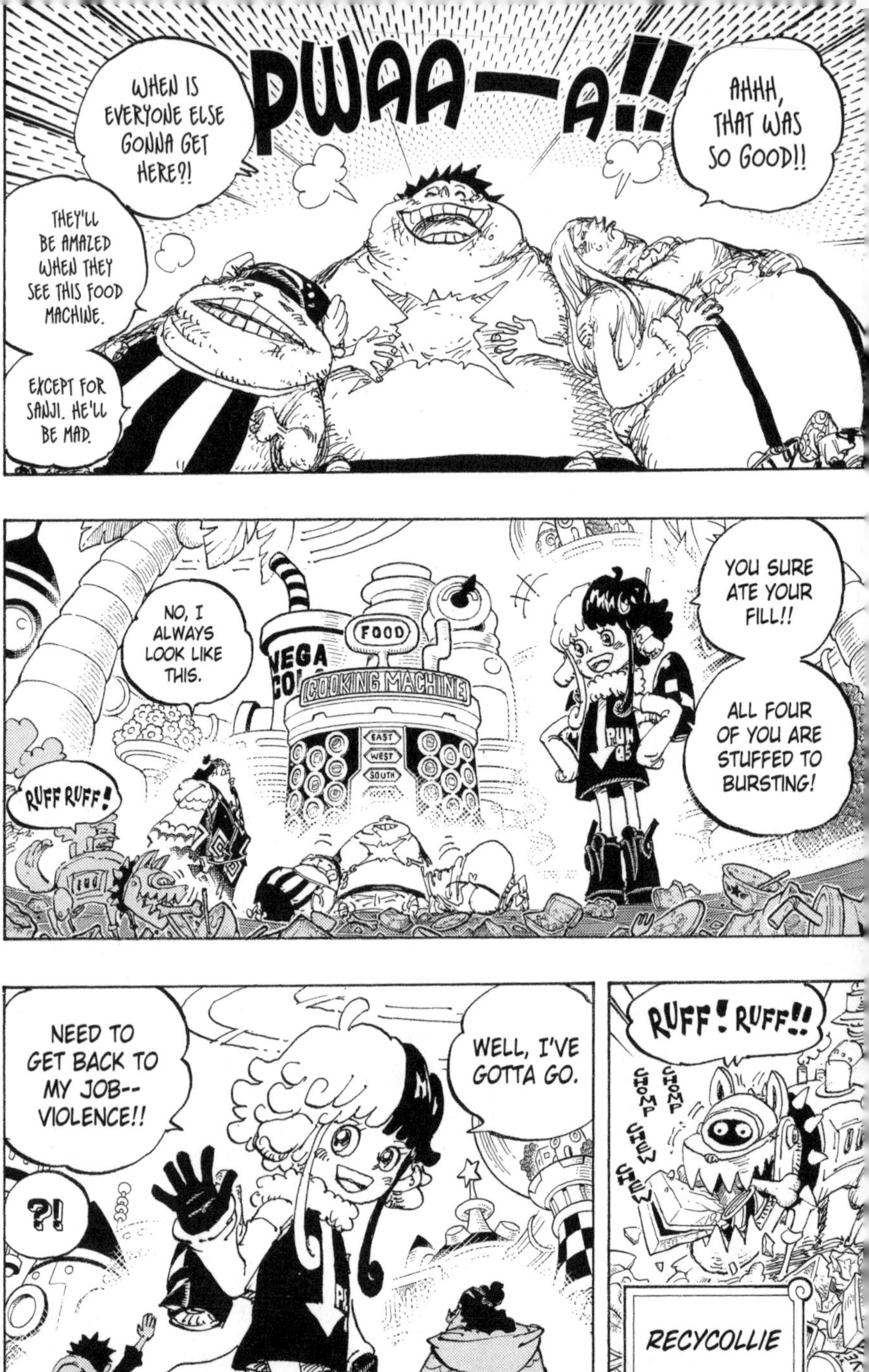
AHHH, THAT WAS SO GOOD!!
PWAA—A!!
WHEN IS EVERYONE ELSE GONNA GET HERE?!
THEY'LL BE AMAZED WHEN THEY SEE THIS FOOD MACHINE.
EXCEPT FOR SANJI. HE'LL BE MAD.
YOU SURE ATE YOUR FILL!!
ALL FOUR OF YOU ARE STUFFED TO BURSTING!
FOOD
COOKING MACHINE
EAST
WEST
SOUTH
NO, I ALWAYS LOOK LIKE THIS.
RUFF RUFF!
RUFF! RUFF!!
CHOMP CHOMP
CHEW CHEW
RECYCOLLIE
WELL, I'VE GOTTA GO.
NEED TO GET BACK TO MY JOB-- VIOLENCE!!
?!

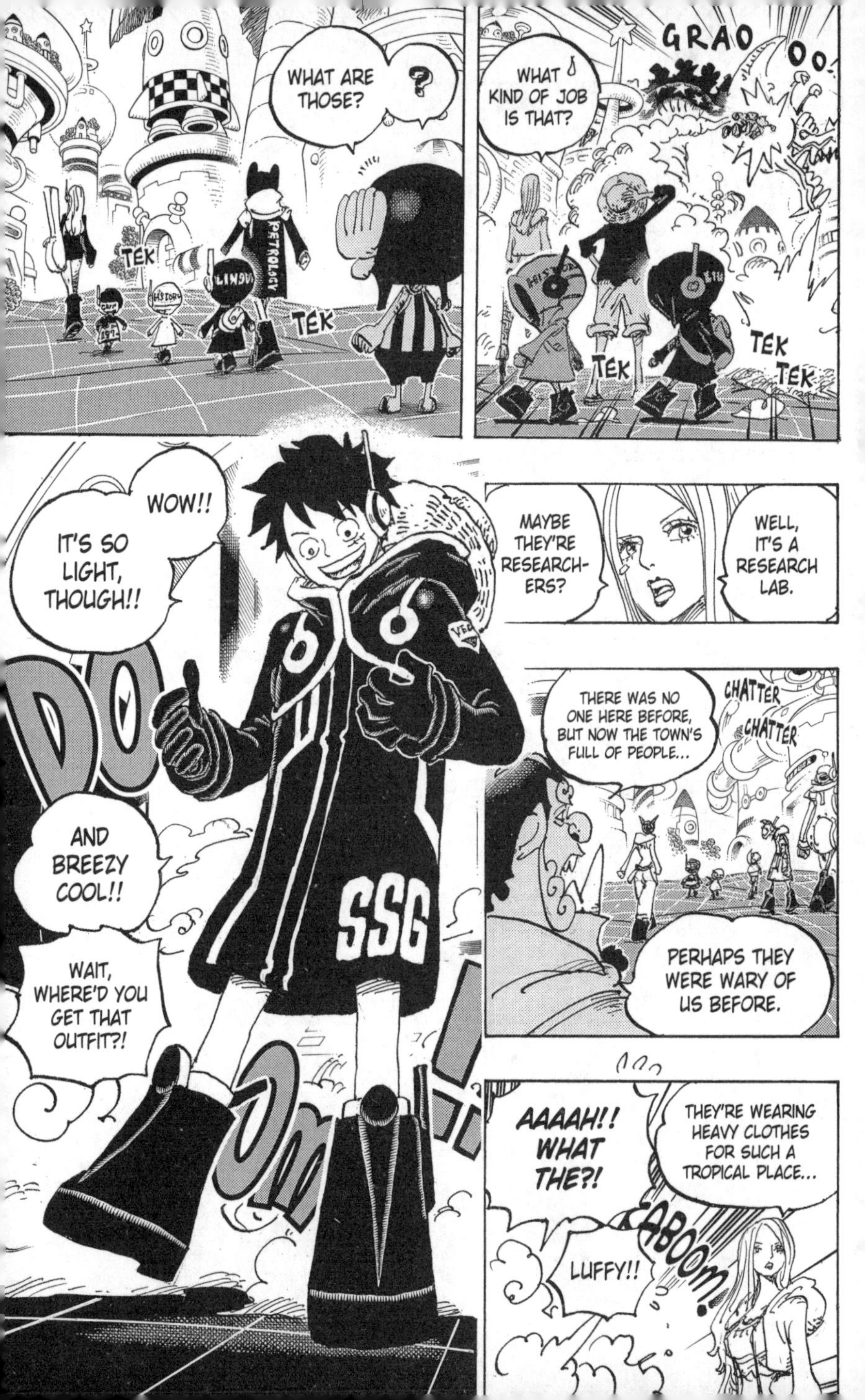
GRAO
OO
WHAT KIND OF JOB IS THAT?
TEK
TEK
TEK
WHAT ARE THOSE?
?
PETROLOGY
TEK
TEK
WELL, IT'S A RESEARCH LAB.
MAYBE THEY'RE RESEARCH-ERS?
CHATTER
CHATTER
THERE WAS NO ONE HERE BEFORE, BUT NOW THE TOWN'S FULL OF PEOPLE...
PERHAPS THEY WERE WARY OF US BEFORE.
THEY'RE WEARING HEAVY CLOTHES FOR SUCH A TROPICAL PLACE...
AAAAH!! WHAT THE?!
KABOOM!
LUFFY!!
WOW!!
IT'S SO LIGHT, THOUGH!!
AND BREEZY COOL!!
WAIT, WHERE'D YOU GET THAT OUTFIT?!
SSG

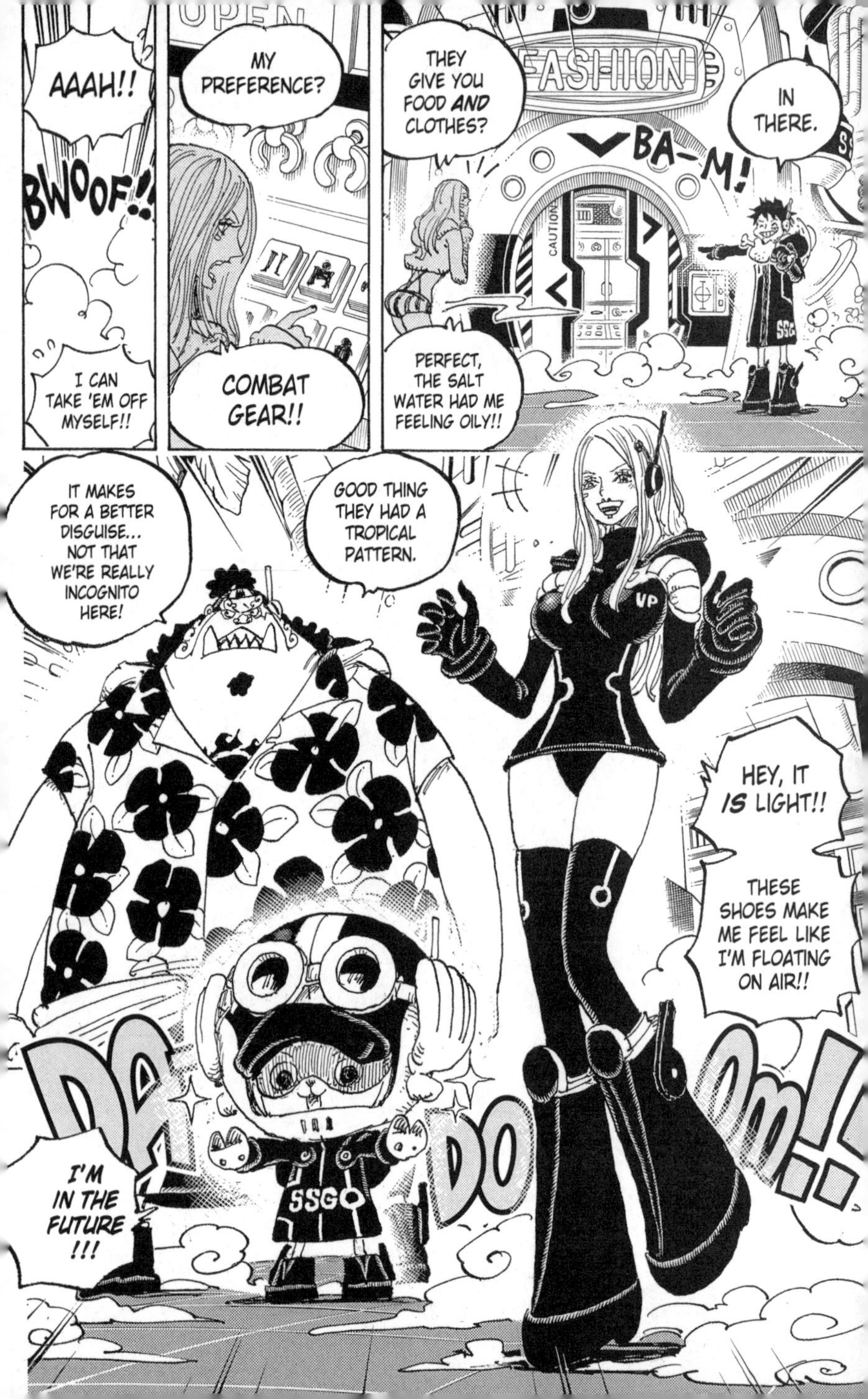
FASHION
IN THERE.
THEY GIVE YOU FOOD AND CLOTHES?
BA-M!
CAUTION
SSG
PERFECT, THE SALT WATER HAD ME FEELING OILY!!
MY PREFERENCE?
COMBAT GEAR!!
AAAH!!
BWOOF!!
I CAN TAKE 'EM OFF MYSELF!!
HEY, IT IS LIGHT!!
THESE SHOES MAKE ME FEEL LIKE I'M FLOATING ON AIR!!
VP
GOOD THING THEY HAD A TROPICAL PATTERN.
IT MAKES FOR A BETTER DISGUISE... NOT THAT WE'RE REALLY INCOGNITO HERE!
DA DO OM!!
SSGO
I'M IN THE FUTURE!!!

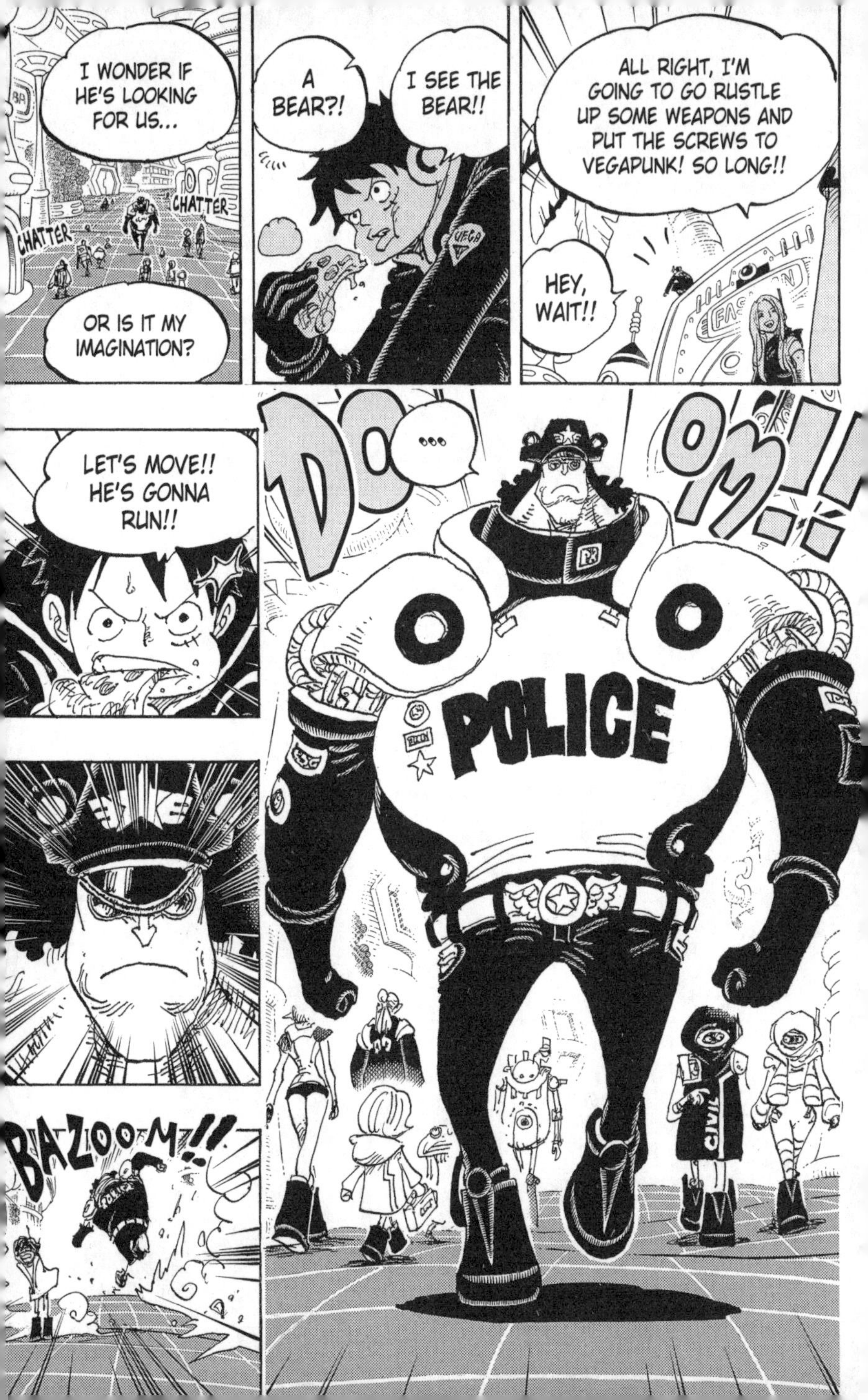
ALL RIGHT, I'M GOING TO GO RUSTLE UP SOME WEAPONS AND PUT THE SCREWS TO VEGAPUNK! SO LONG!!
HEY, WAIT!!
I SEE THE BEAR!!
A BEAR?!
I WONDER IF HE'S LOOKING FOR US...
CHATTER
CHATTER
OR IS IT MY IMAGINATION?
DOOM!!
...
POLICE
CIVIL
LET'S MOVE!! HE'S GONNA RUN!!
BAZOOM!!

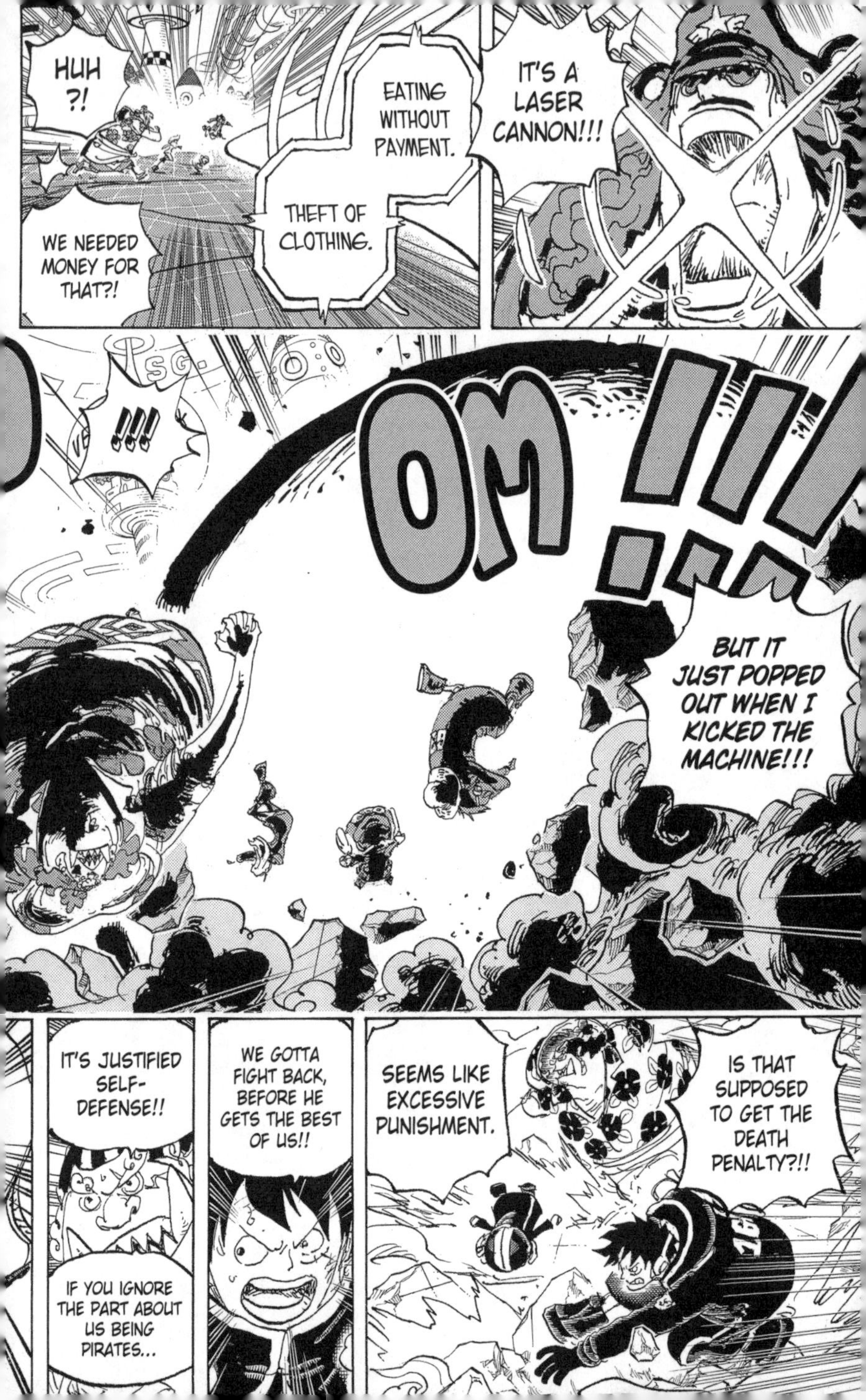

IT'S A LASER CANNON!!!
EATING WITHOUT PAYMENT.
THEFT OF CLOTHING.
HUH ?!
WE NEEDED MONEY FOR THAT?!
OM !!!
BUT IT JUST POPPED OUT WHEN I KICKED THE MACHINE!!!
!!!
IS THAT SUPPOSED TO GET THE DEATH PENALTY?!!
SEEMS LIKE EXCESSIVE PUNISHMENT.
WE GOTTA FIGHT BACK, BEFORE HE GETS THE BEST OF US!!
IT'S JUSTIFIED SELF-DEFENSE!!
IF YOU IGNORE THE PART ABOUT US BEING PIRATES...

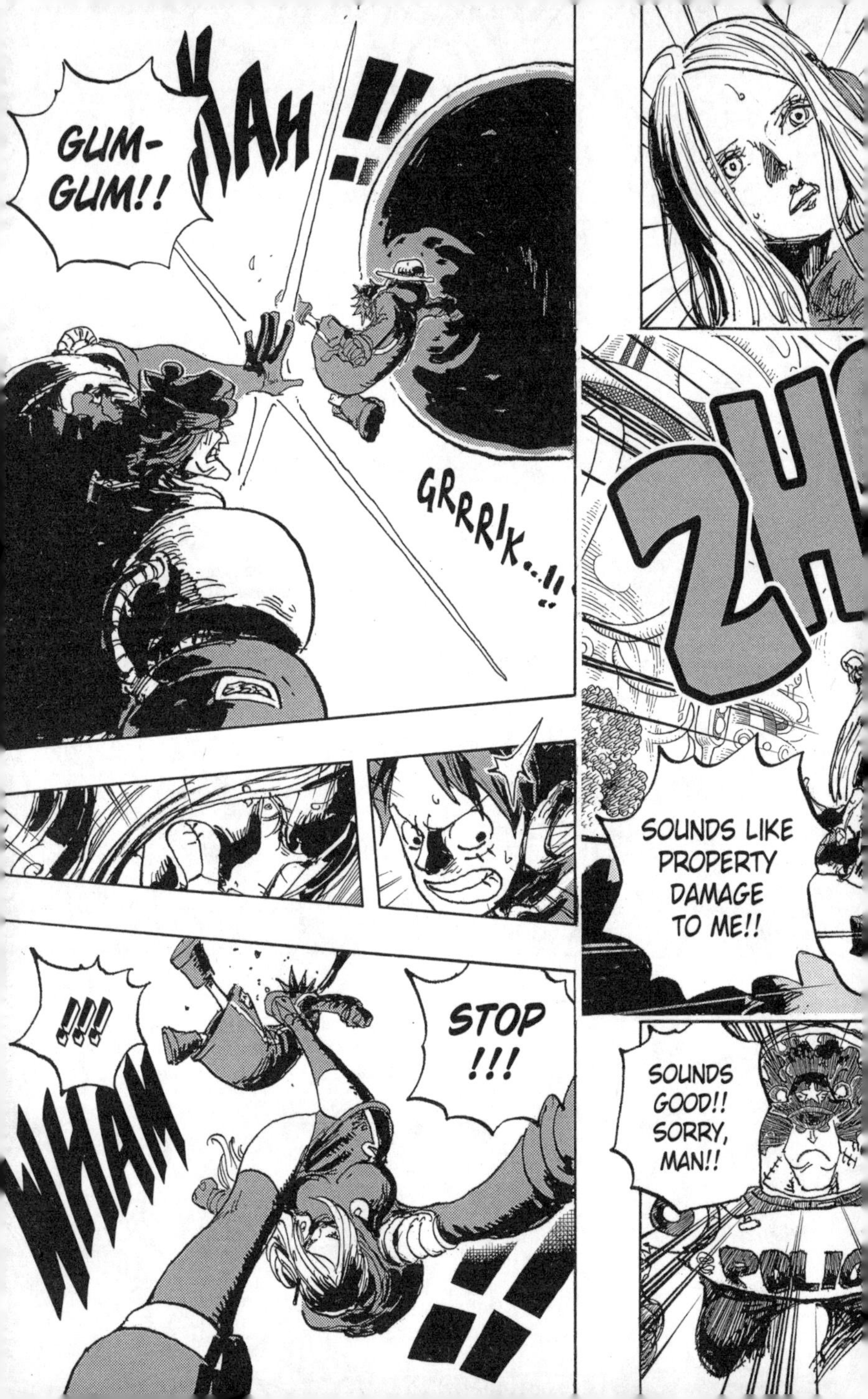
ZH
SOUNDS LIKE PROPERTY DAMAGE TO ME!!
SOUNDS GOOD!! SORRY, MAN!!
GUM-GUM!!
AH!!
GRRRIK...!!
STOP!!!
!!!
WHAM!!

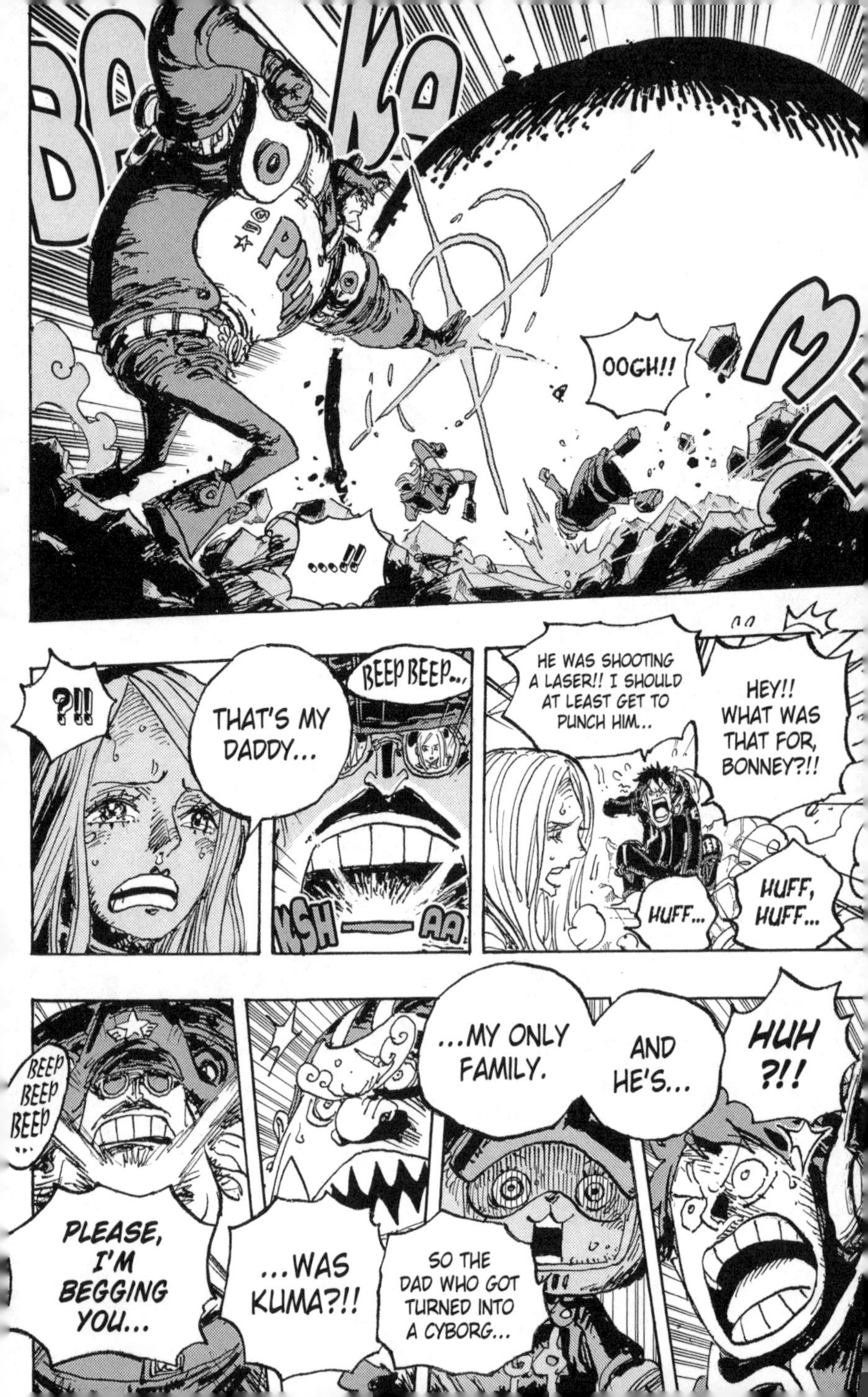
OOGH!!
....!!
HEY!! WHAT WAS THAT FOR, BONNEY?!!
HE WAS SHOOTING A LASER!! I SHOULD AT LEAST GET TO PUNCH HIM...
HUFF, HUFF...
HUFF...
BEEP BEEP...
KSH—AA
THAT'S MY DADDY...
?!!
HUH ?!!
AND HE'S...
...MY ONLY FAMILY.
SO THE DAD WHO GOT TURNED INTO A CYBORG...
...WAS KUMA?!!
BEEP BEEP BEEP...
PLEASE, I'M BEGGING YOU...

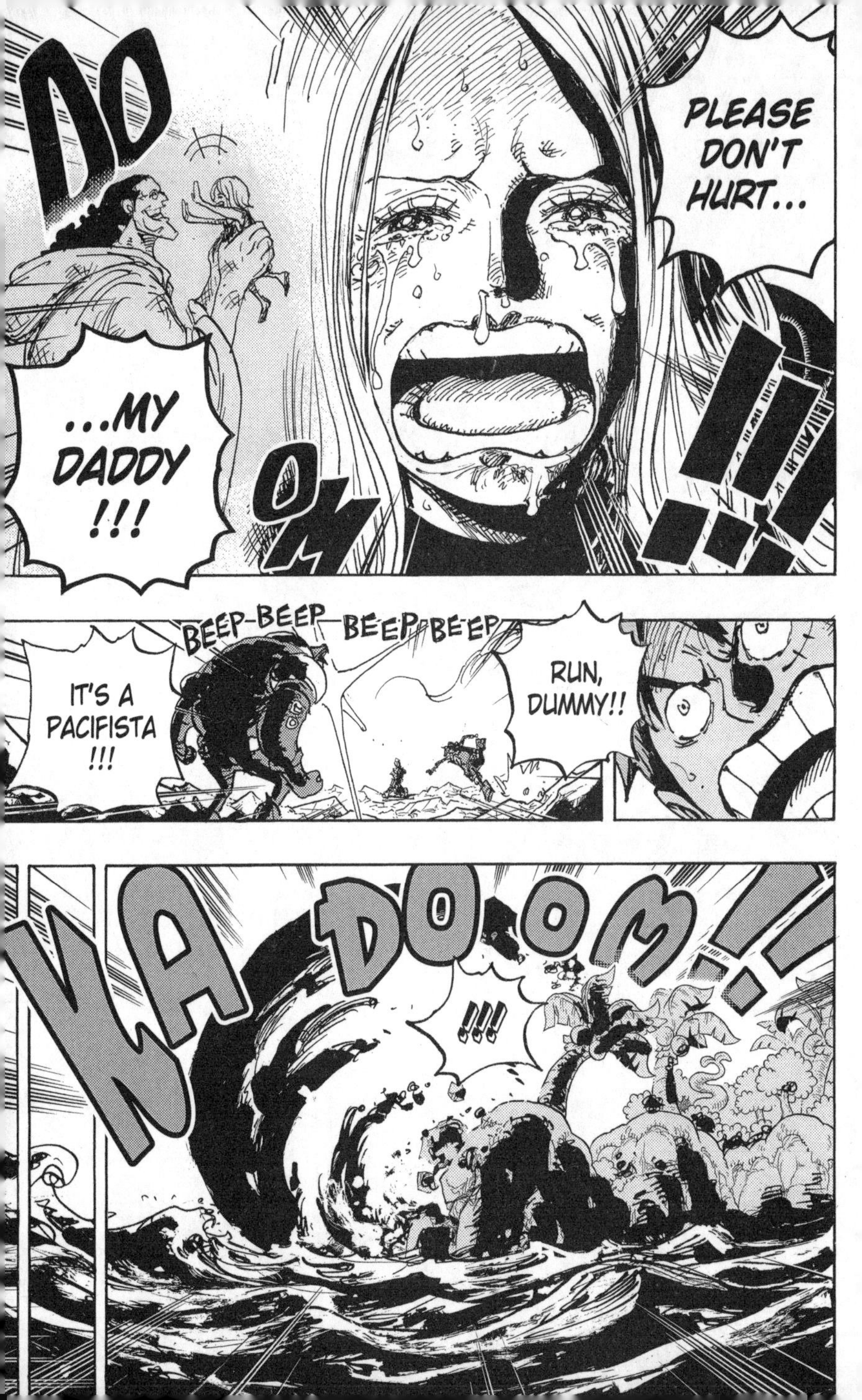
PLEASE DON'T HURT...
...MY DADDY!!!
DO
OM
!!
RUN, DUMMY!!
BEEP-BEEP
BEEP-BEEP
IT'S A PACIFISTA!!!
KA-DOOM!!
!!!

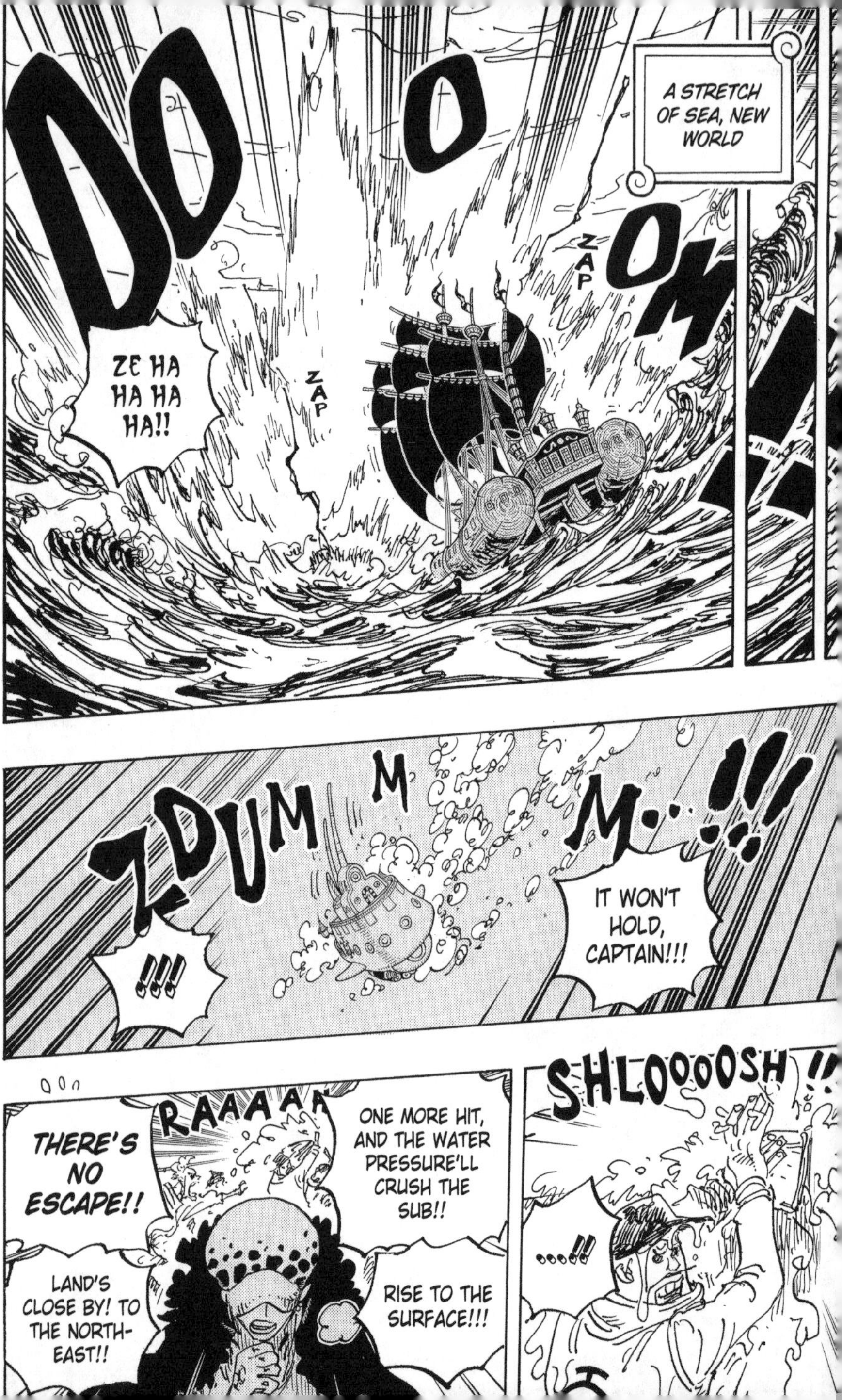
A STRETCH OF SEA, NEW WORLD
DOOOM!!
ZAP
ZAP
ZE HA HA HA HA!!
ZDUMMM...!!
IT WON'T HOLD, CAPTAIN!!!
!!!
SHLOOOOSH!!
....!!
RAAAAA
ONE MORE HIT, AND THE WATER PRESSURE'LL CRUSH THE SUB!!
THERE'S NO ESCAPE!!
RISE TO THE SURFACE!!!
LAND'S CLOSE BY! TO THE NORTH-EAST!!

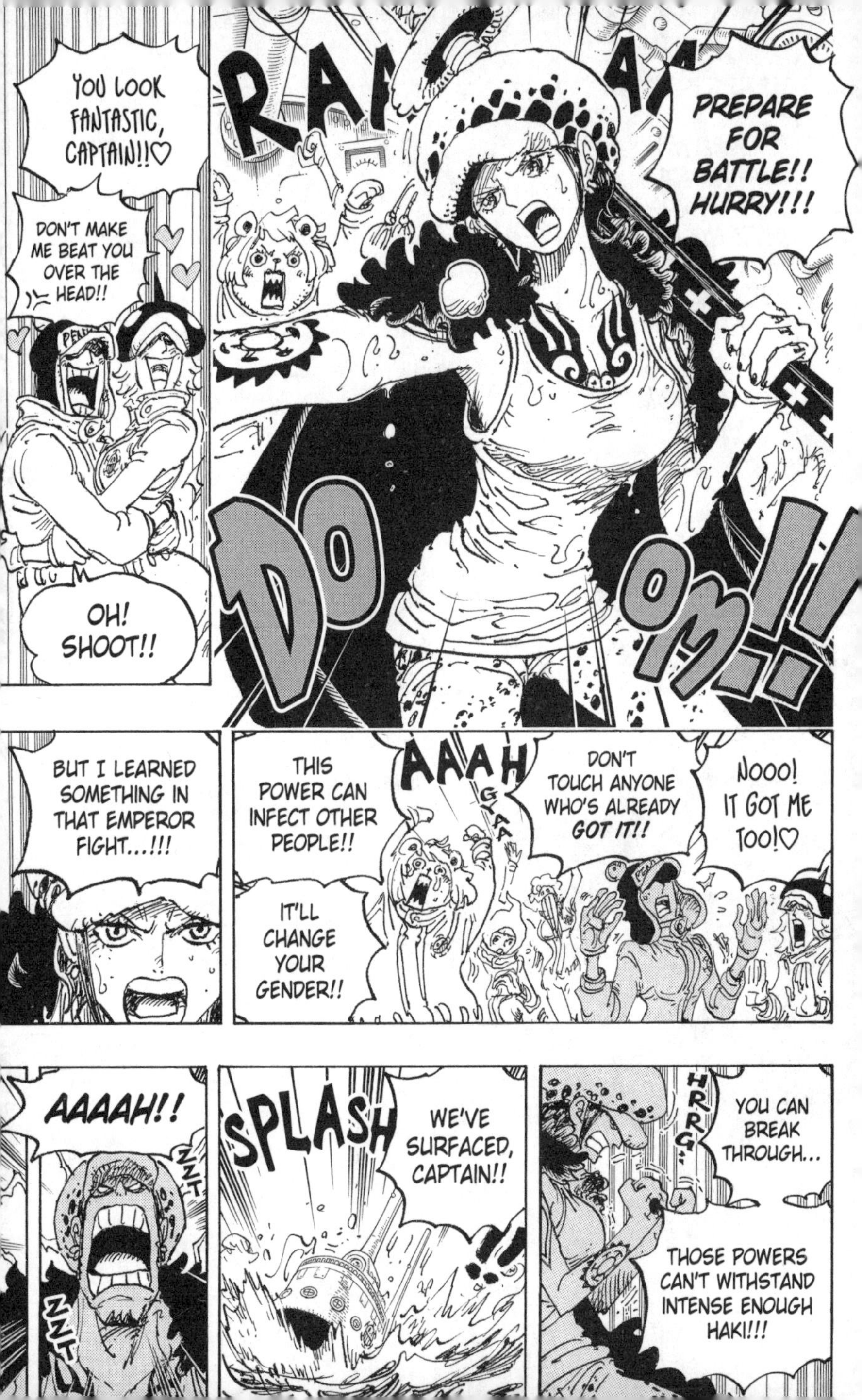

RAA
AA
PREPARE FOR BATTLE!! HURRY!!!
DOOM!!
YOU LOOK FANTASTIC, CAPTAIN!!♡
DON'T MAKE ME BEAT YOU OVER THE HEAD!!
OH! SHOOT!!
NOOO! IT GOT ME TOO!♡
DON'T TOUCH ANYONE WHO'S ALREADY GOT IT!!
AAAH
GYAA
THIS POWER CAN INFECT OTHER PEOPLE!!
IT'LL CHANGE YOUR GENDER!!
BUT I LEARNED SOMETHING IN THAT EMPEROR FIGHT...!!!
HRRG
YOU CAN BREAK THROUGH...
THOSE POWERS CAN'T WITHSTAND INTENSE ENOUGH HAKI!!!
SPLASH
WE'VE SURFACED, CAPTAIN!!
AAAAH!!
ZZT
ZZT

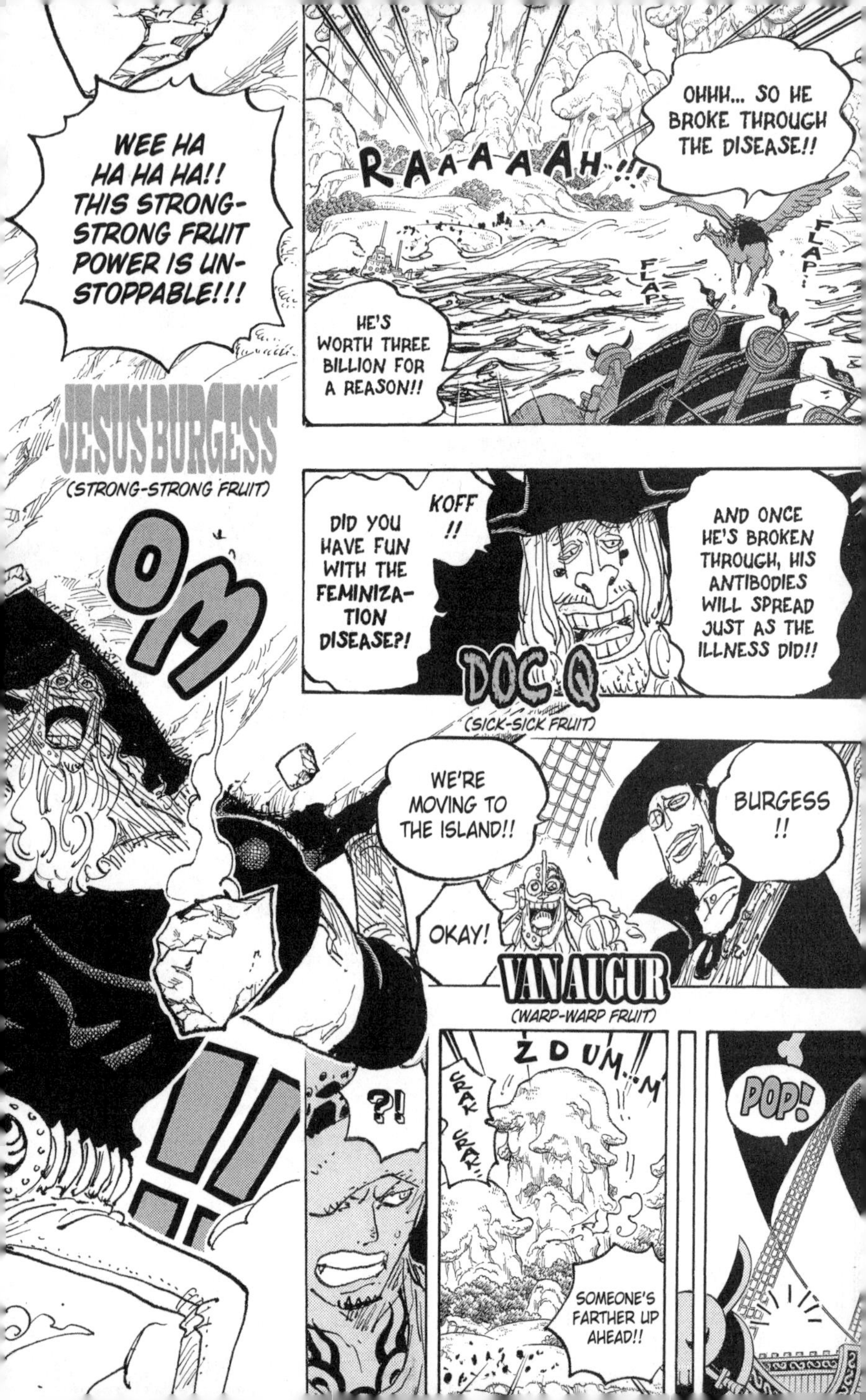

OHHH... SO HE BROKE THROUGH THE DISEASE!!
RAAAAAH!!!
FLAP
FLAP
HE'S WORTH THREE BILLION FOR A REASON!!
WEE HA HA HA HA!! THIS STRONG-STRONG FRUIT POWER IS UN-STOPPABLE!!!
JESUS BURGESS
(STRONG-STRONG FRUIT)
OM
AND ONCE HE'S BROKEN THROUGH, HIS ANTIBODIES WILL SPREAD JUST AS THE ILLNESS DID!!
KOFF !!
DID YOU HAVE FUN WITH THE FEMINIZA-TION DISEASE?!
DOC Q
(SICK-SICK FRUIT)
BURGESS !!
WE'RE MOVING TO THE ISLAND!!
OKAY!
VAN AUGUR
(WARP-WARP FRUIT)
POP!
ZDUM...M
CRAK
CRAK
SOMEONE'S FARTHER UP AHEAD!!
?!

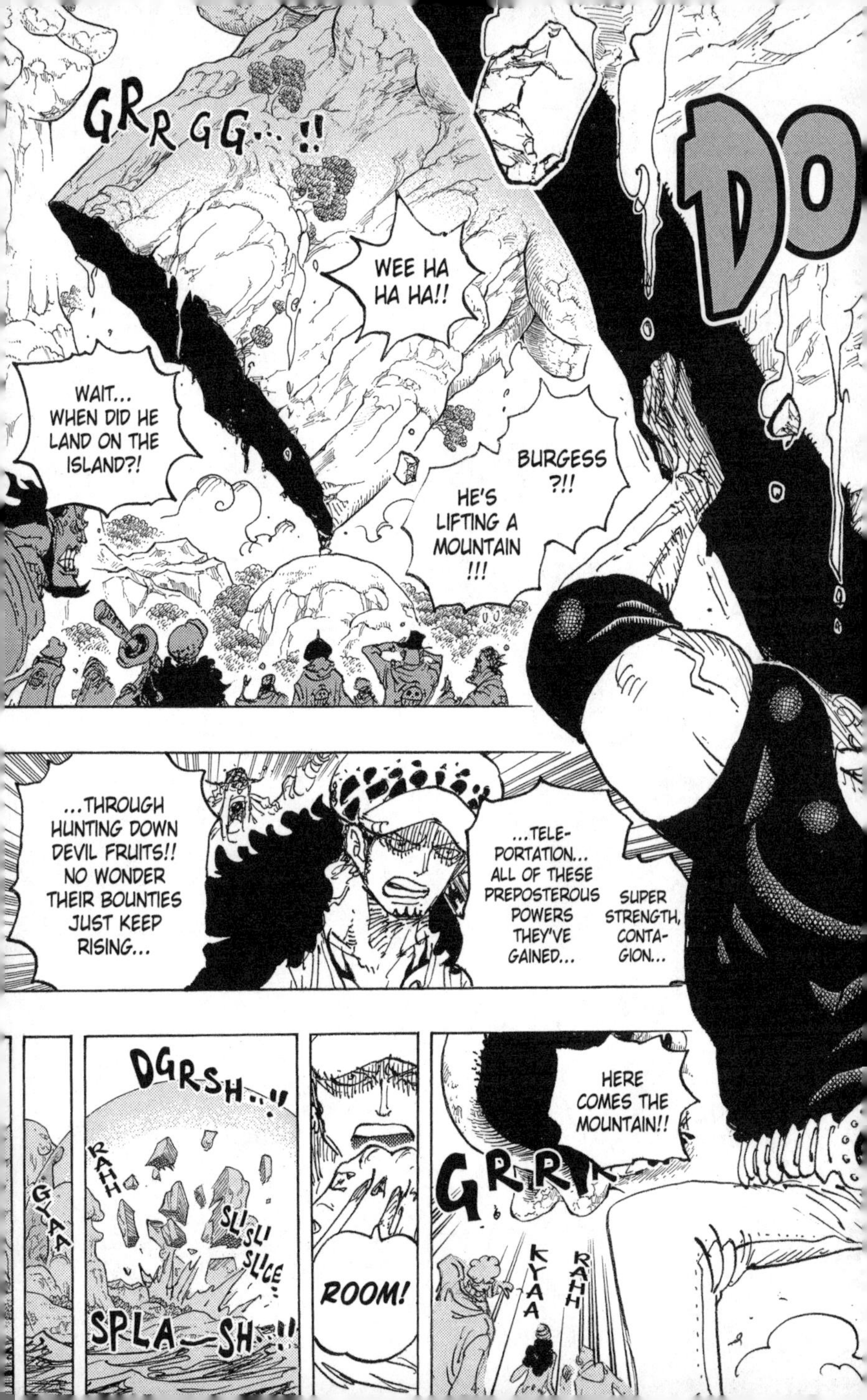
DO
BURGESS?!!
HE'S LIFTING A MOUNTAIN!!!
WEE HA HA HA!!
GRRGG...!!
WAIT... WHEN DID HE LAND ON THE ISLAND?!
SUPER STRENGTH, CONTAGION...
...TELEPORTATION... ALL OF THESE PREPOSTEROUS POWERS THEY'VE GAINED...
...THROUGH HUNTING DOWN DEVIL FRUITS!! NO WONDER THEIR BOUNTIES JUST KEEP RISING...
HERE COMES THE MOUNTAIN!!
GRRR
RAHH
KYAA
ROOM!
DGRSH..!!
RAHH
SLI SLI SLICE
SPLA—SH..!!
GYAA

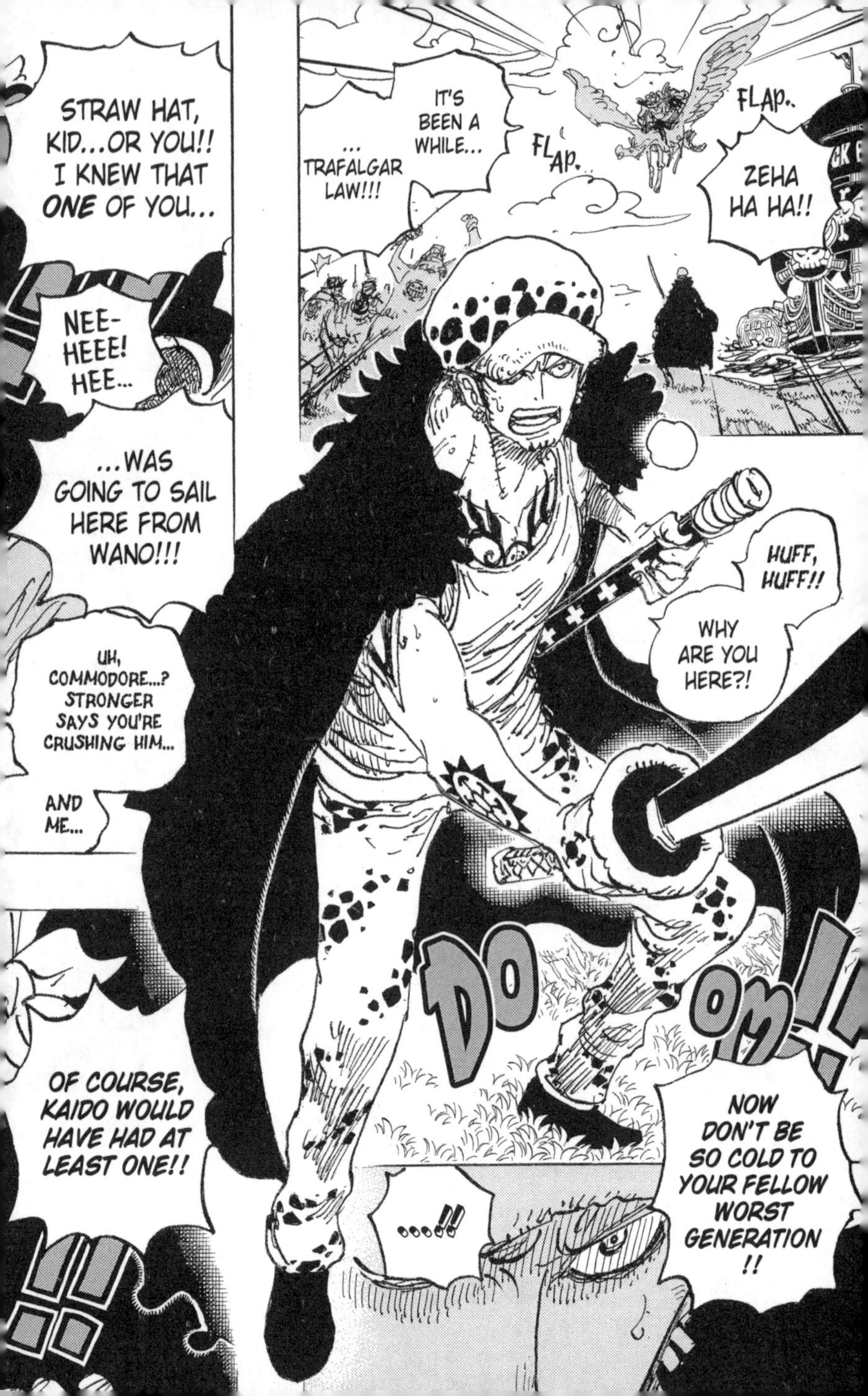
ZEHA HA HA!!
FLAP..
FLAP..
IT'S BEEN A WHILE...
...TRAFALGAR LAW!!!
HUFF, HUFF!!
WHY ARE YOU HERE?!
DOOM!!
NOW DON'T BE SO COLD TO YOUR FELLOW WORST GENERATION!!
...!!
STRAW HAT, KID...OR YOU!! I KNEW THAT ONE OF YOU...
NEE-HEEE! HEE...
...WAS GOING TO SAIL HERE FROM WANO!!!
UH, COMMODORE...? STRONGER SAYS YOU'RE CRUSHING HIM...
AND ME...
OF COURSE, KAIDO WOULD HAVE HAD AT LEAST ONE!!

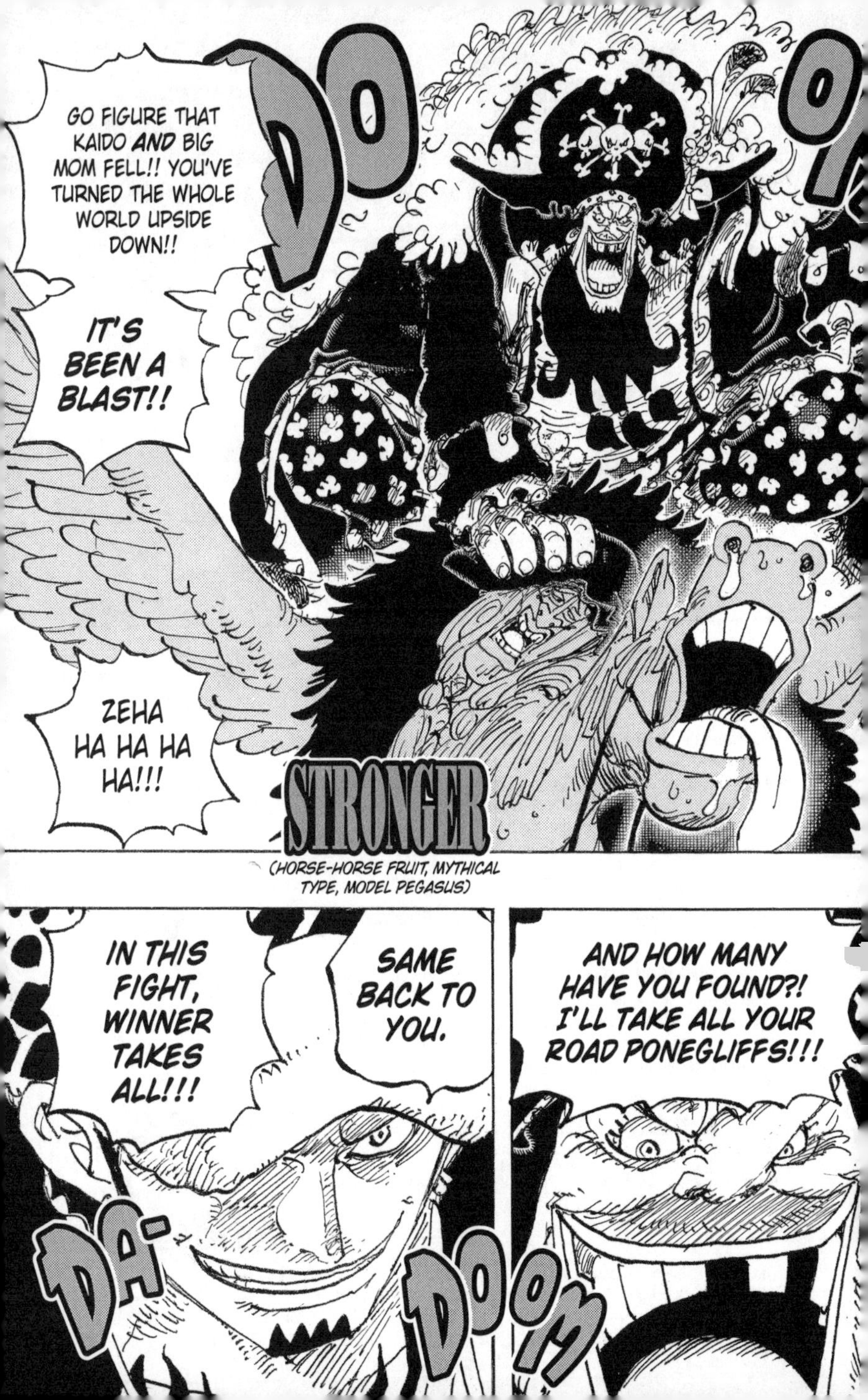
DOO
GO FIGURE THAT KAIDO AND BIG MOM FELL!! YOU'VE TURNED THE WHOLE WORLD UPSIDE DOWN!!
IT'S BEEN A BLAST!!
ZEHA HA HA HA HA!!!
STRONGER
(HORSE-HORSE FRUIT, MYTHICAL TYPE, MODEL PEGASUS)
AND HOW MANY HAVE YOU FOUND?! I'LL TAKE ALL YOUR ROAD PONEGLIFFS!!!
SAME BACK TO YOU.
IN THIS FIGHT, WINNER TAKES ALL!!!
DA-DOOM

SBS Question Corner

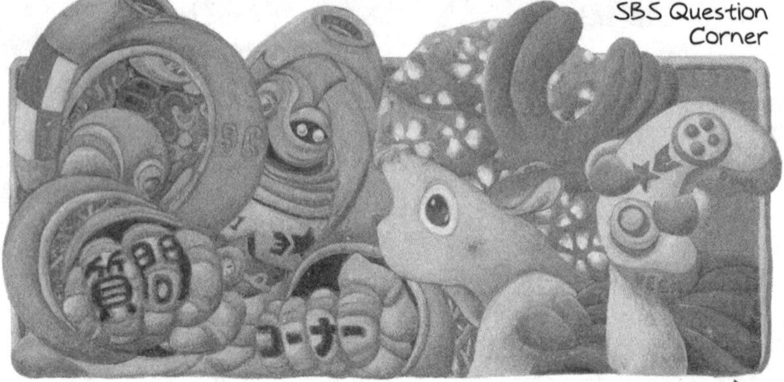
コーナー

(Takahisa Fujimoto, Nara)

Q: What does Kaido look like when he eats an *umeboshi* (sour pickled plum)?

--Junya

A: Like this. ➡

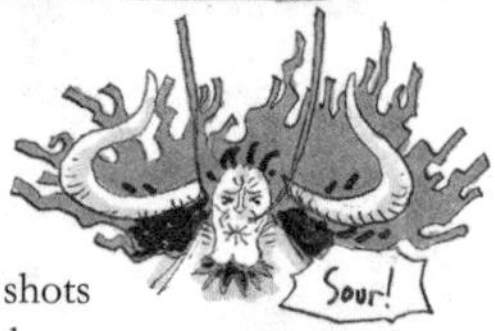
Sour!

Q: This is a serious question. I've noticed that there are cleavage shots in *One Piece,* but no panty shots. Is there a personal policy you have that informs that decision?

--Panty Shot God

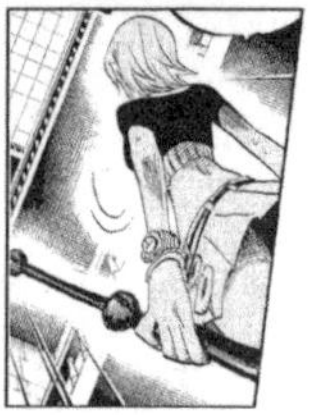

A: Well... I'm just not interested in them. (LOL)
All my life, I've seen panty shots used in manga as a fan service thing, but it's always something that passively happens to the female characters... Which is why I thought it was a revolutionary move for Nami to take an active role instead when she did "Happiness Punch."

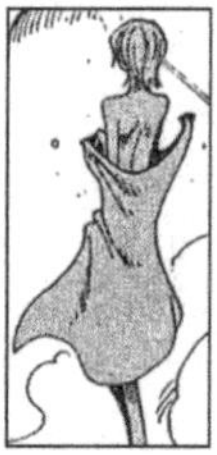

Q: Odacchi, was the move "Flame Dragon Torch" in chapter 1048 based on the classic rakugo story, "The Flaming Drum"?

--Shinnosuke

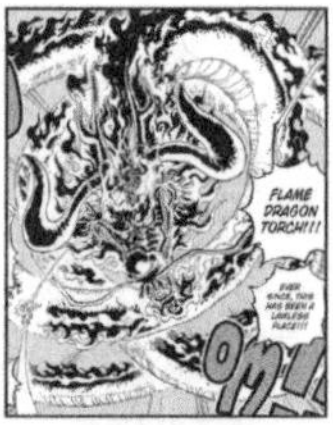
FLAME DRAGON TORCH!!!

A: That's right! In Japanese they're both pronounced the same way, but with different kanji. Not that I think anyone cares! *(laughs)*. By the way, there's a hit new manga in *Shonen Jump* about rakugo called *Akane-banashi*. You should check it out, it's really good.

Q: Mr. Oda! In chapter 1052, is that storytelling gentleman perhaps based on the classical singer and actor Torazo Hirosawa? I believe you said on a radio interview a long time ago that you were a fan…

--Negixile

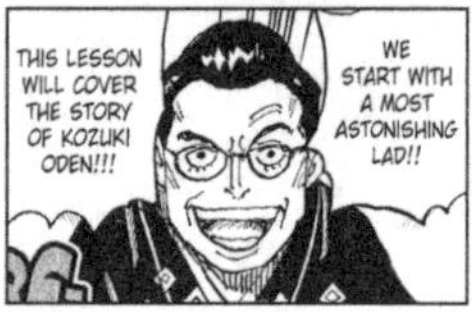
WE START WITH A MOST ASTONISHING LAD!!
THIS LESSON WILL COVER THE STORY OF KOZUKI ODEN!!!

A: That's right! Now you're getting into even more hardcore territory than just rakugo, but that's correct! Rakugo, shamisen, historical lectures, and samurai dramas! The Wano arc has been packed with all of my favorite traditional arts! *Be-beng!!*
That's all for this SBS! See you next volume!!

Chapter 1064:
EGGHEAD LABOPHASE

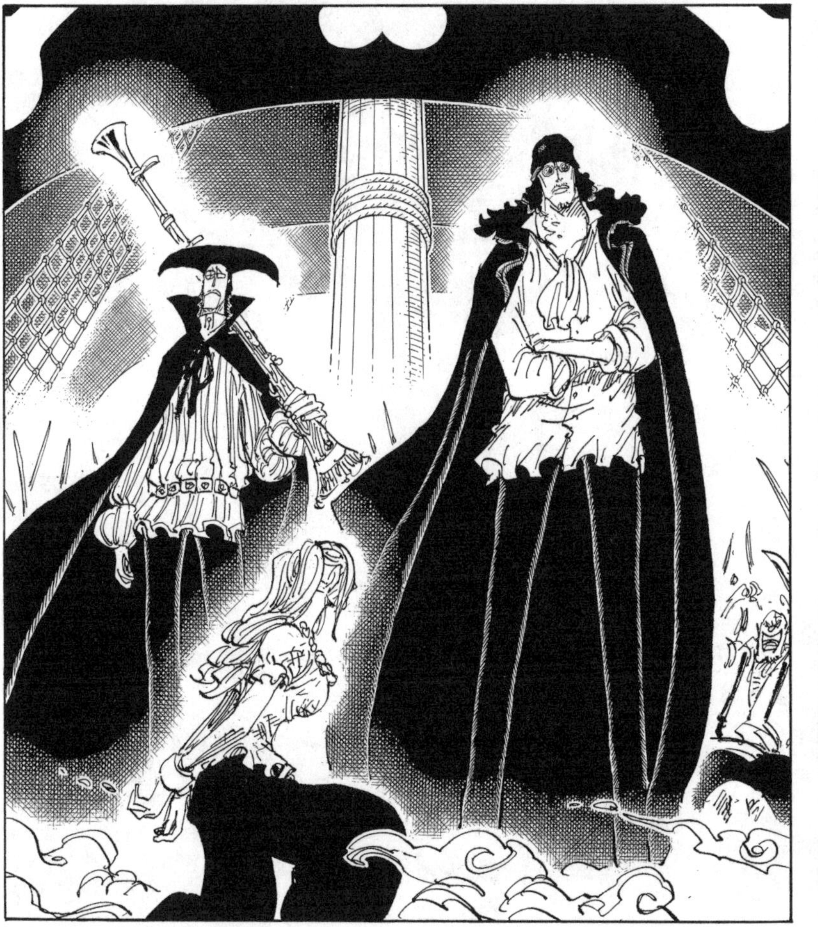

GERMA 66'S AHH... AN EMOTIONLESS EXCURSION,
VOL. 22: "BLACKBEARD PIRATES, KUZAN AND AUGUR"

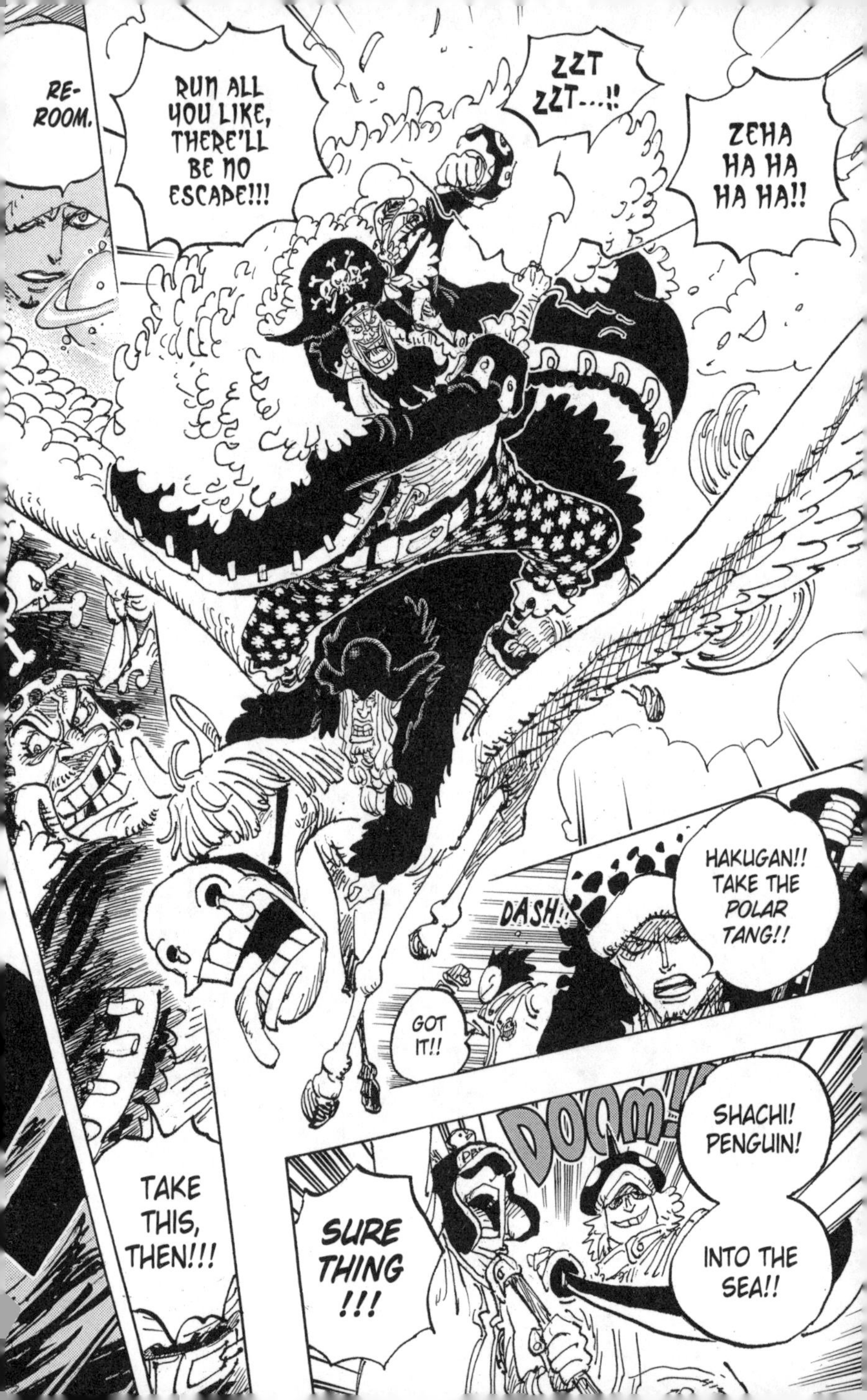

ZEHA HA HA HA HA!!
ZZT ZZT...!!
RUN ALL YOU LIKE, THERE'LL BE NO ESCAPE!!!
RE-ROOM.
HAKUGAN!! TAKE THE POLAR TANG!!
DASH!!
GOT IT!!
SHACHI! PENGUIN!
INTO THE SEA!!
DOOM!!
SURE THING!!!
TAKE THIS, THEN!!!

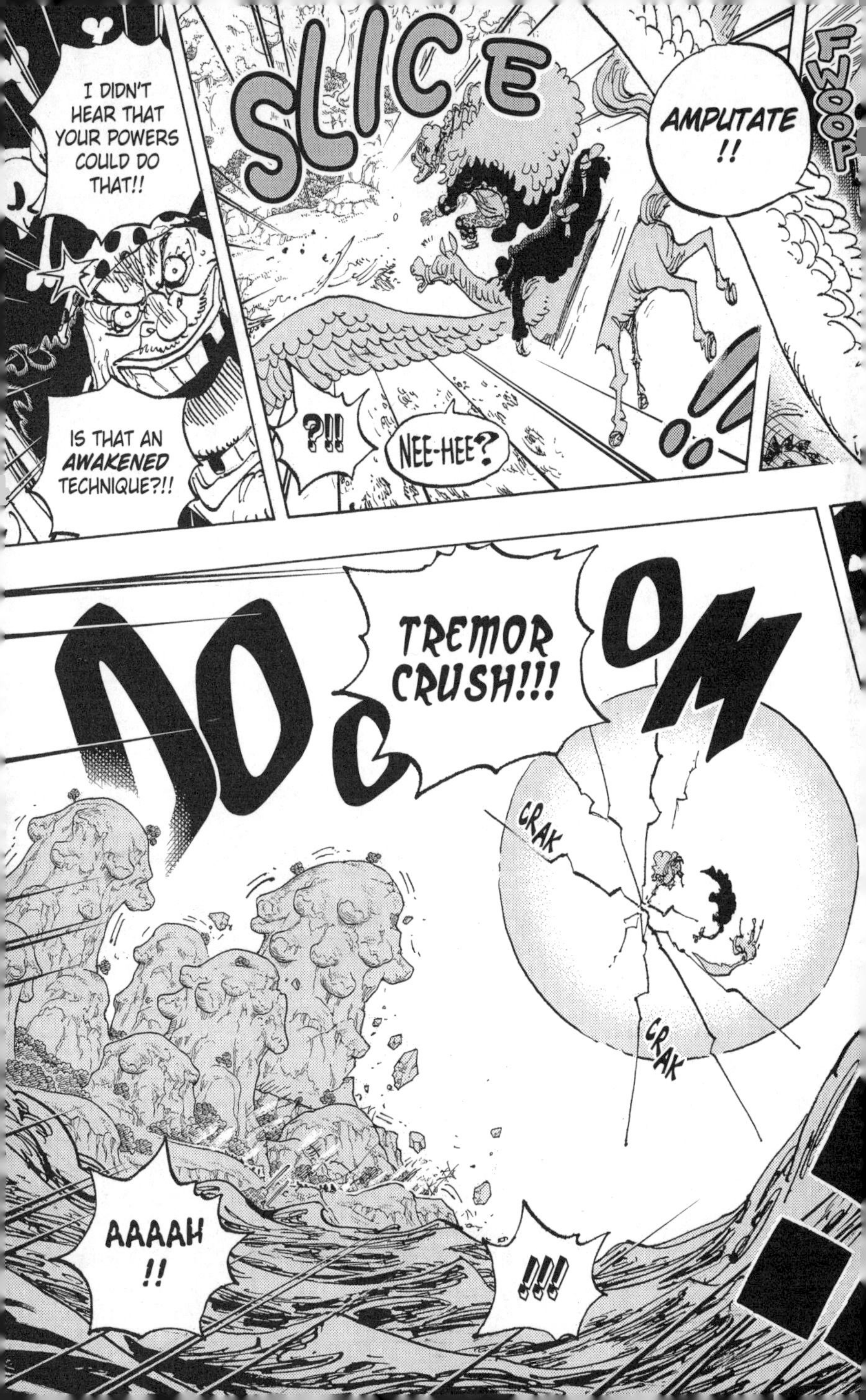
FWOOP
AMPUTATE!!
SLICE
NEE-HEE?
?!!
I DIDN'T HEAR THAT YOUR POWERS COULD DO THAT!!
IS THAT AN AWAKENED TECHNIQUE?!!
DOOOM
TREMOR CRUSH!!!
CRAK
CRAK
!!!
AAAAH!!

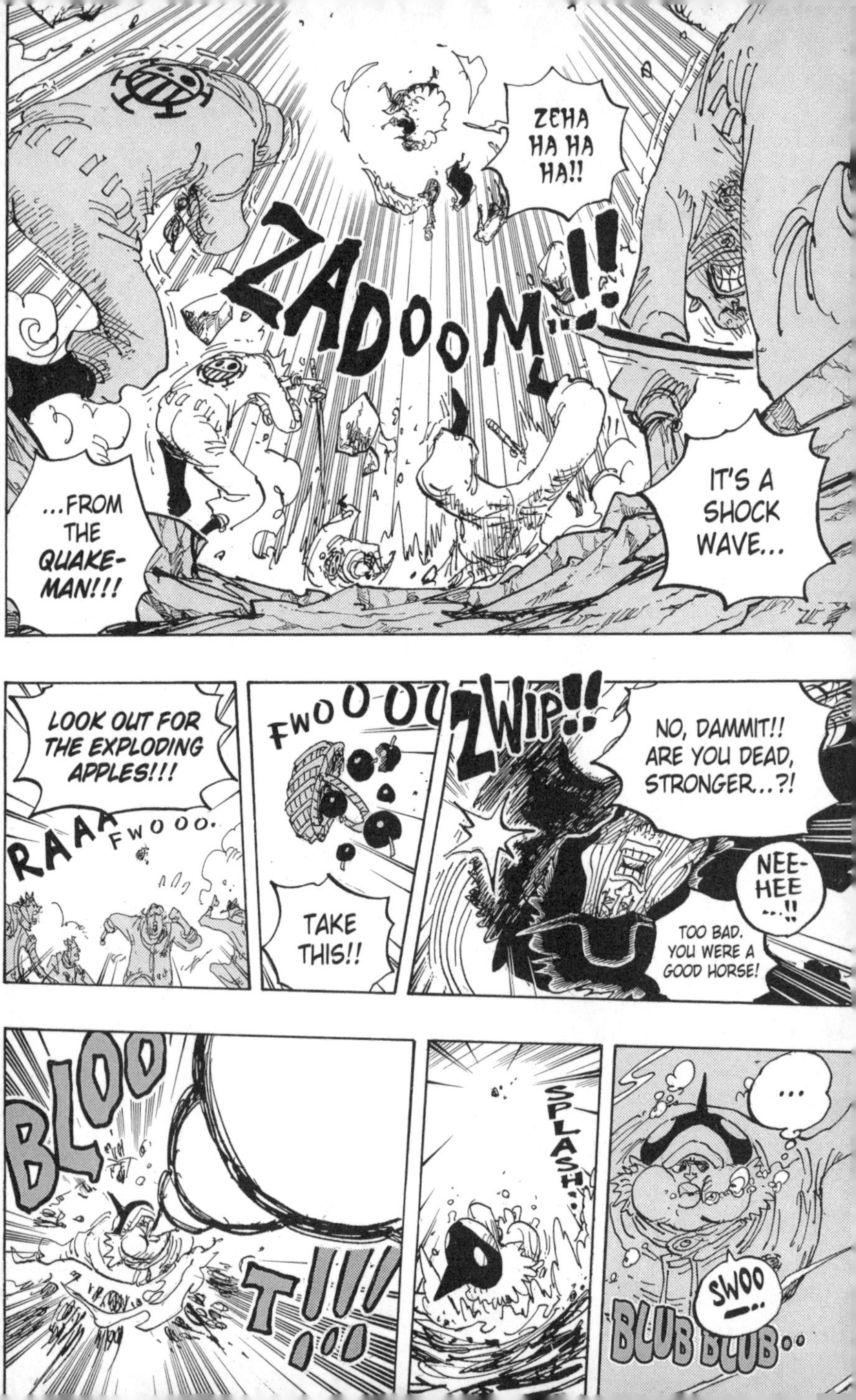
ZEHA HA HA HA!!
IT'S A SHOCK WAVE...
ZADOOM!!
...FROM THE QUAKE-MAN!!!
ZWIP!!
NO, DAMMIT!! ARE YOU DEAD, STRONGER...?!
NEE-HEE...!!
TOO BAD. YOU WERE A GOOD HORSE!
FWOOOO
TAKE THIS!!
LOOK OUT FOR THE EXPLODING APPLES!!!
RAAA
FWOOO.
...
SWOO...
BLUB BLUB..
SPLASH...
BLOOT!!!

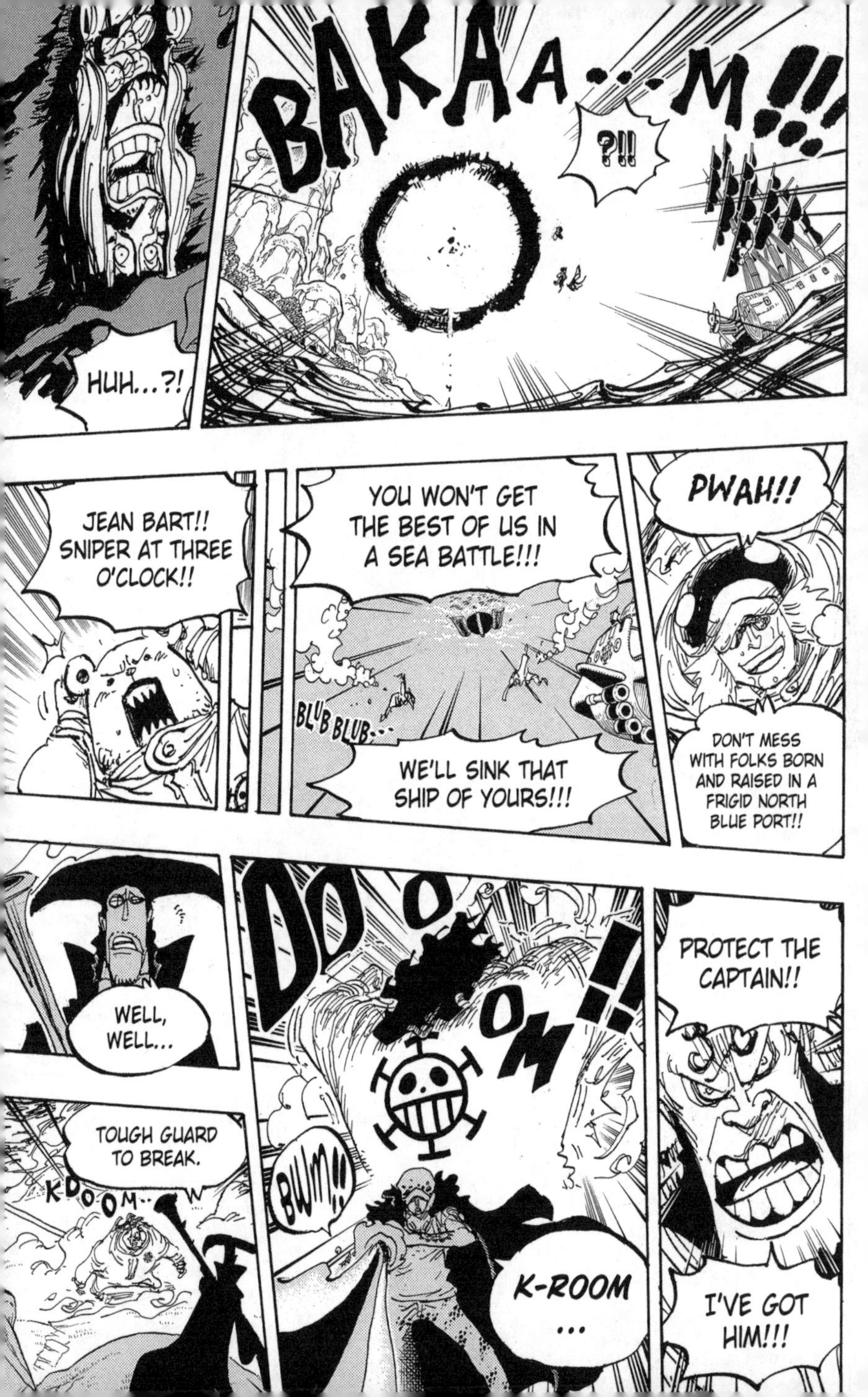
BAKAA...M!!
?!!
HUH...?!
PWAH!!
DON'T MESS WITH FOLKS BORN AND RAISED IN A FRIGID NORTH BLUE PORT!!
YOU WON'T GET THE BEST OF US IN A SEA BATTLE!!!
BLUB BLUB...
WE'LL SINK THAT SHIP OF YOURS!!!
JEAN BART!! SNIPER AT THREE O'CLOCK!!
PROTECT THE CAPTAIN!!
I'VE GOT HIM!!!
DOOOM!!
BWM!!
K-ROOM...
WELL, WELL...
TOUGH GUARD TO BREAK.
KDOOM...

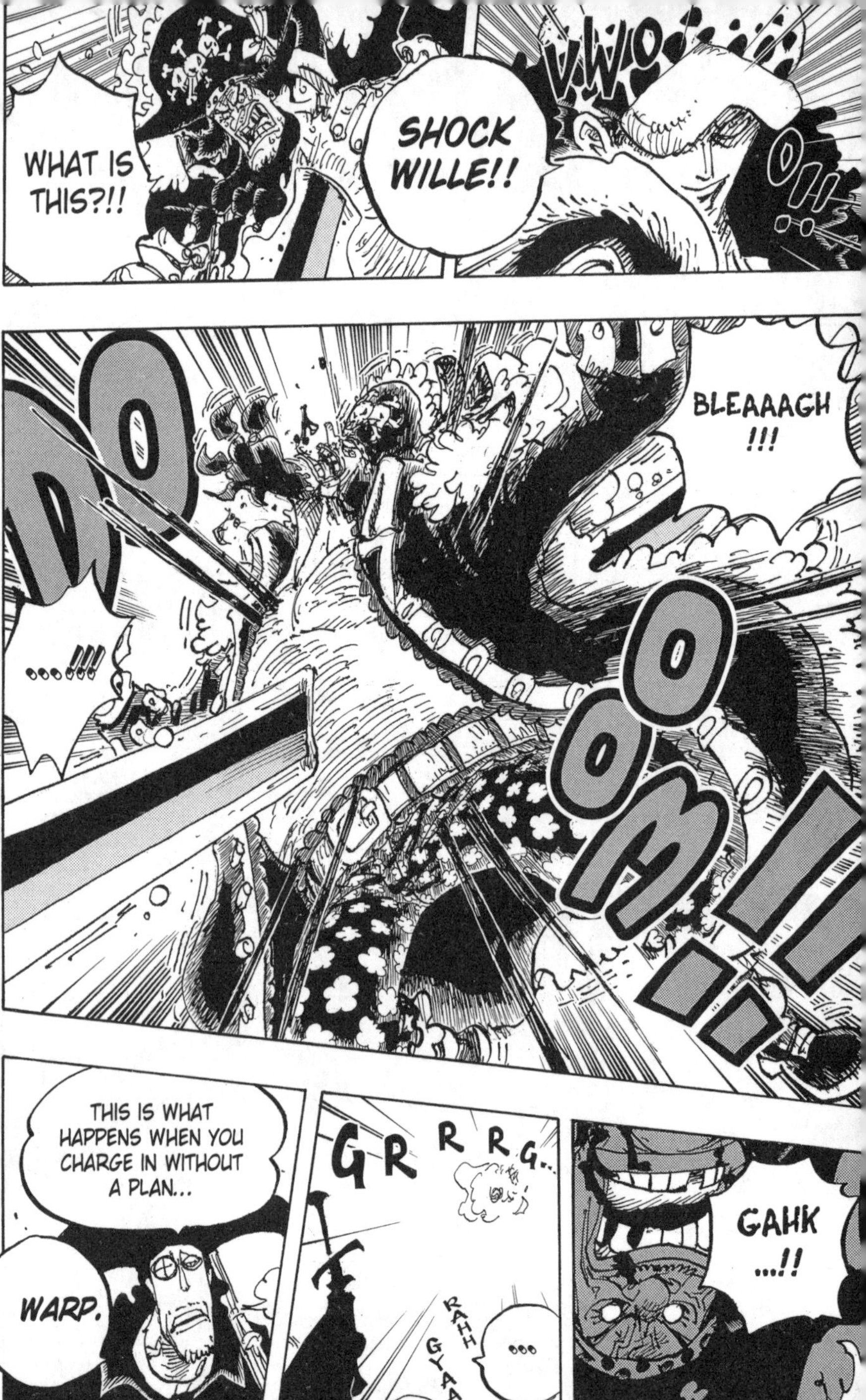
VWO
O!!
SHOCK WILLE!!
WHAT IS THIS?!!
BLEAAAGH !!!
DOOOM!!
...!!!
GAHK ...!!
GRRRG...
RAHH GYAA...
...
THIS IS WHAT HAPPENS WHEN YOU CHARGE IN WITHOUT A PLAN...
WARP.

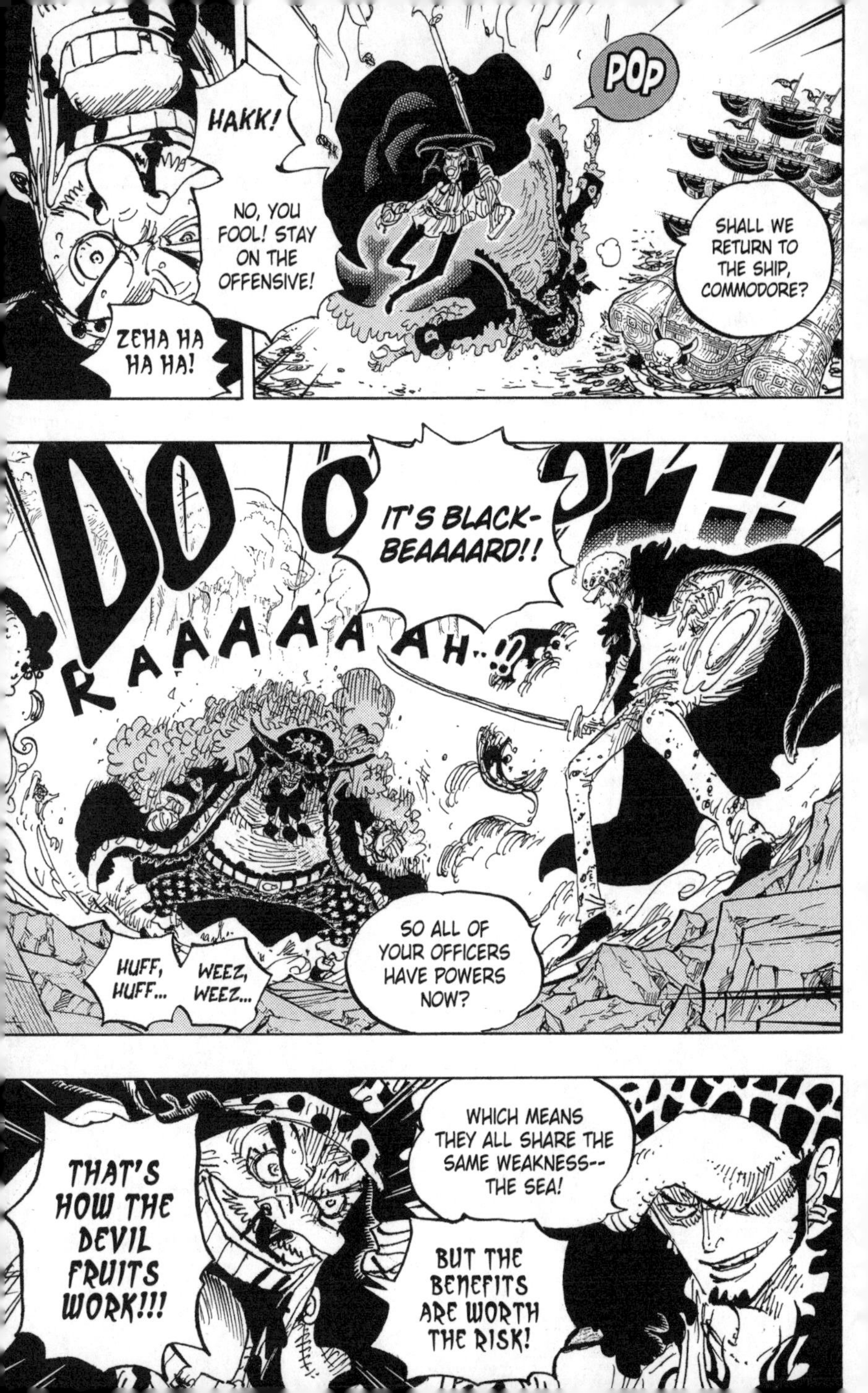
POP
SHALL WE RETURN TO THE SHIP, COMMODORE?
HAKK!
NO, YOU FOOL! STAY ON THE OFFENSIVE!
ZEHA HA HA HA!
DOOOM!!
IT'S BLACK-BEAAAARD!!
RAAAAAAAH..!!
SO ALL OF YOUR OFFICERS HAVE POWERS NOW?
WEEZ, WEEZ...
HUFF, HUFF...
WHICH MEANS THEY ALL SHARE THE SAME WEAKNESS-- THE SEA!
BUT THE BENEFITS ARE WORTH THE RISK!
THAT'S HOW THE DEVIL FRUITS WORK!!!

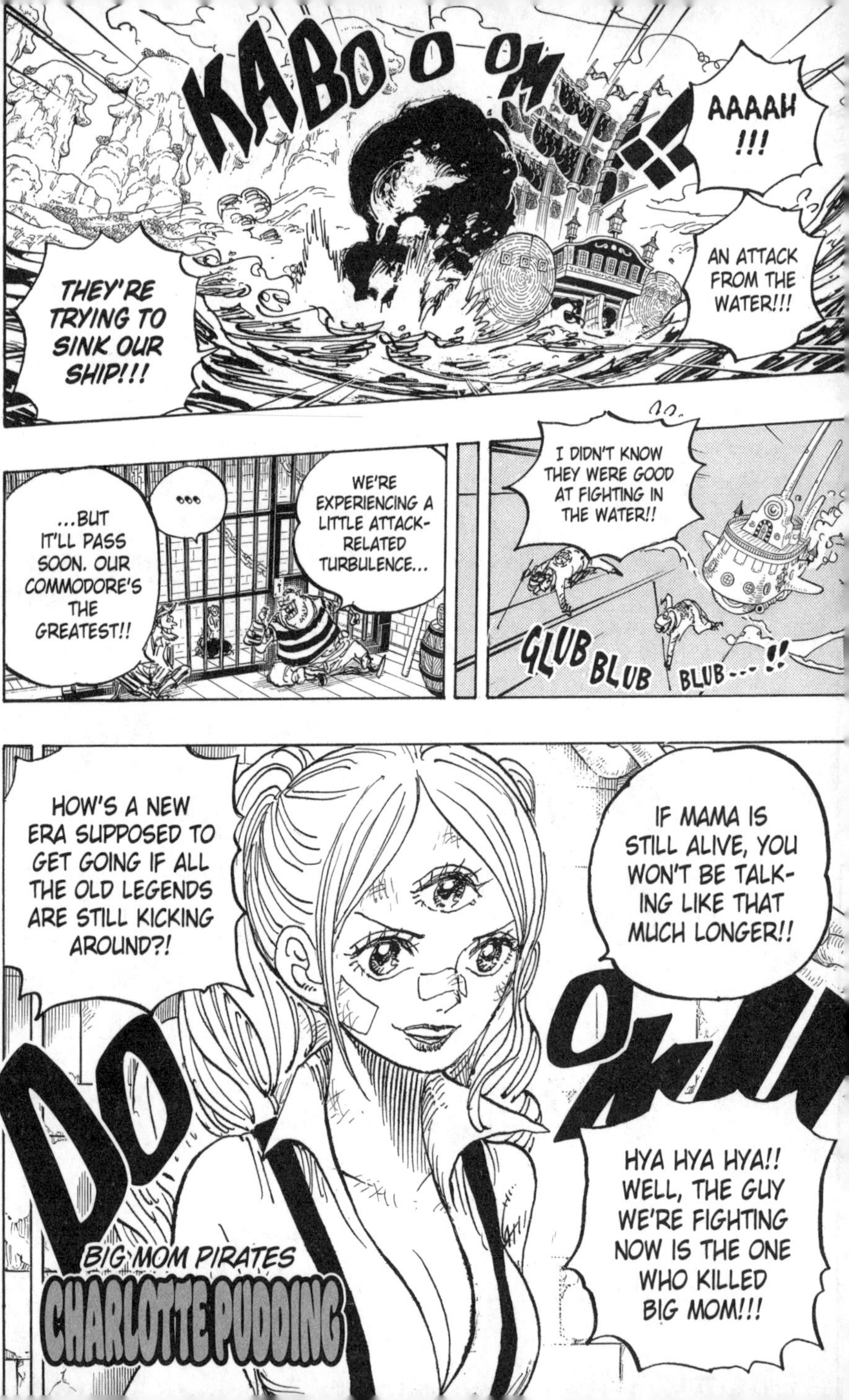
KABOOOM...!!
AAAAH!!!
AN ATTACK FROM THE WATER!!!
THEY'RE TRYING TO SINK OUR SHIP!!!
I DIDN'T KNOW THEY WERE GOOD AT FIGHTING IN THE WATER!!
GLUB BLUB BLUB...!!
WE'RE EXPERIENCING A LITTLE ATTACK-RELATED TURBULENCE...
...
...BUT IT'LL PASS SOON. OUR COMMODORE'S THE GREATEST!!
IF MAMA IS STILL ALIVE, YOU WON'T BE TALKING LIKE THAT MUCH LONGER!!
HOW'S A NEW ERA SUPPOSED TO GET GOING IF ALL THE OLD LEGENDS ARE STILL KICKING AROUND?!
HYA HYA HYA!! WELL, THE GUY WE'RE FIGHTING NOW IS THE ONE WHO KILLED BIG MOM!!!
BIG MOM PIRATES
CHARLOTTE PUDDING

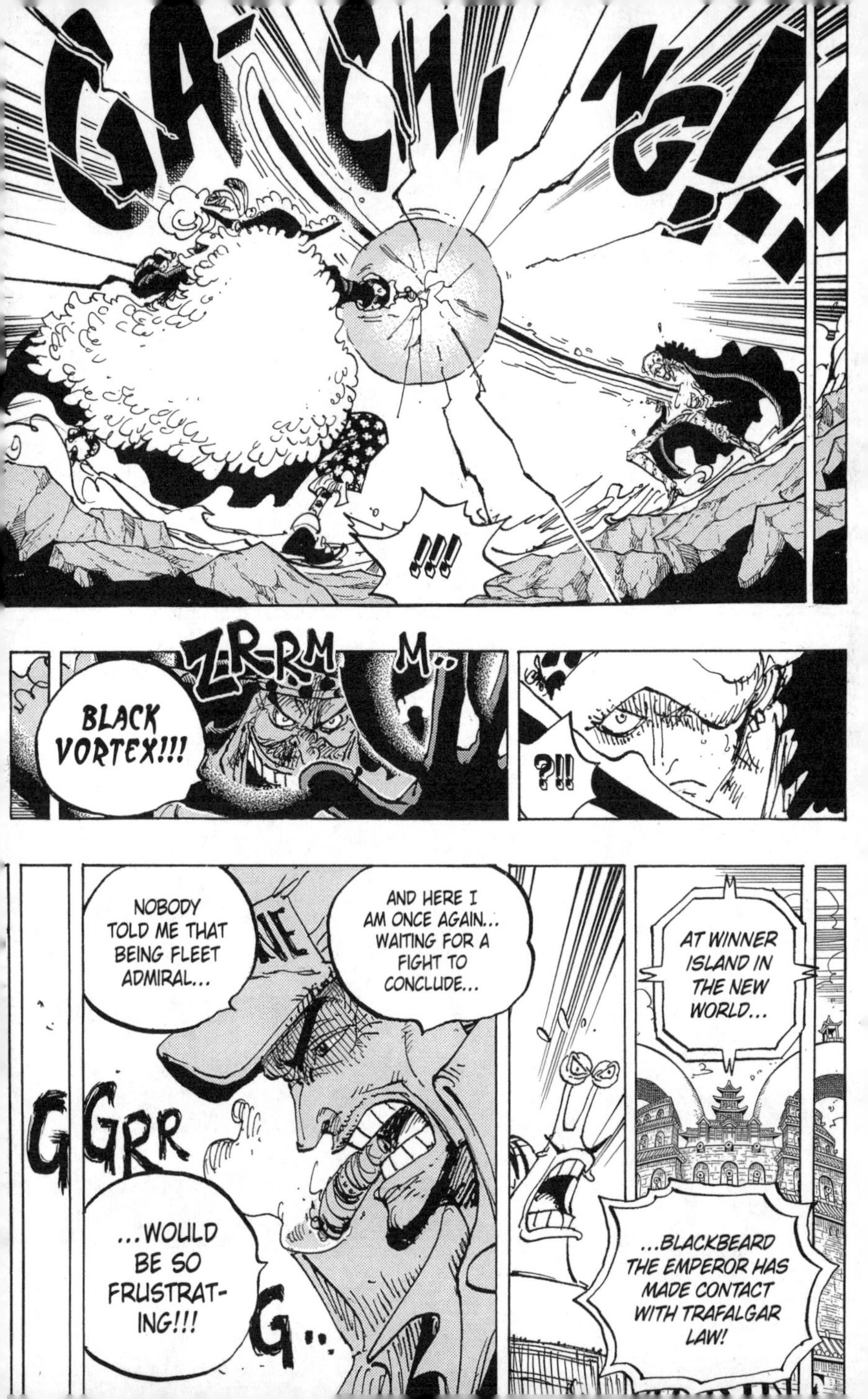
GA-CHI-N-G!!!
!!!
?!!
ZR-R-M M..
BLACK VORTEX!!!
AT WINNER ISLAND IN THE NEW WORLD...
...BLACKBEARD THE EMPEROR HAS MADE CONTACT WITH TRAFALGAR LAW!
AND HERE I AM ONCE AGAIN... WAITING FOR A FIGHT TO CONCLUDE...
NOBODY TOLD ME THAT BEING FLEET ADMIRAL...
GGRR
...WOULD BE SO FRUSTRAT-ING!!!
G..

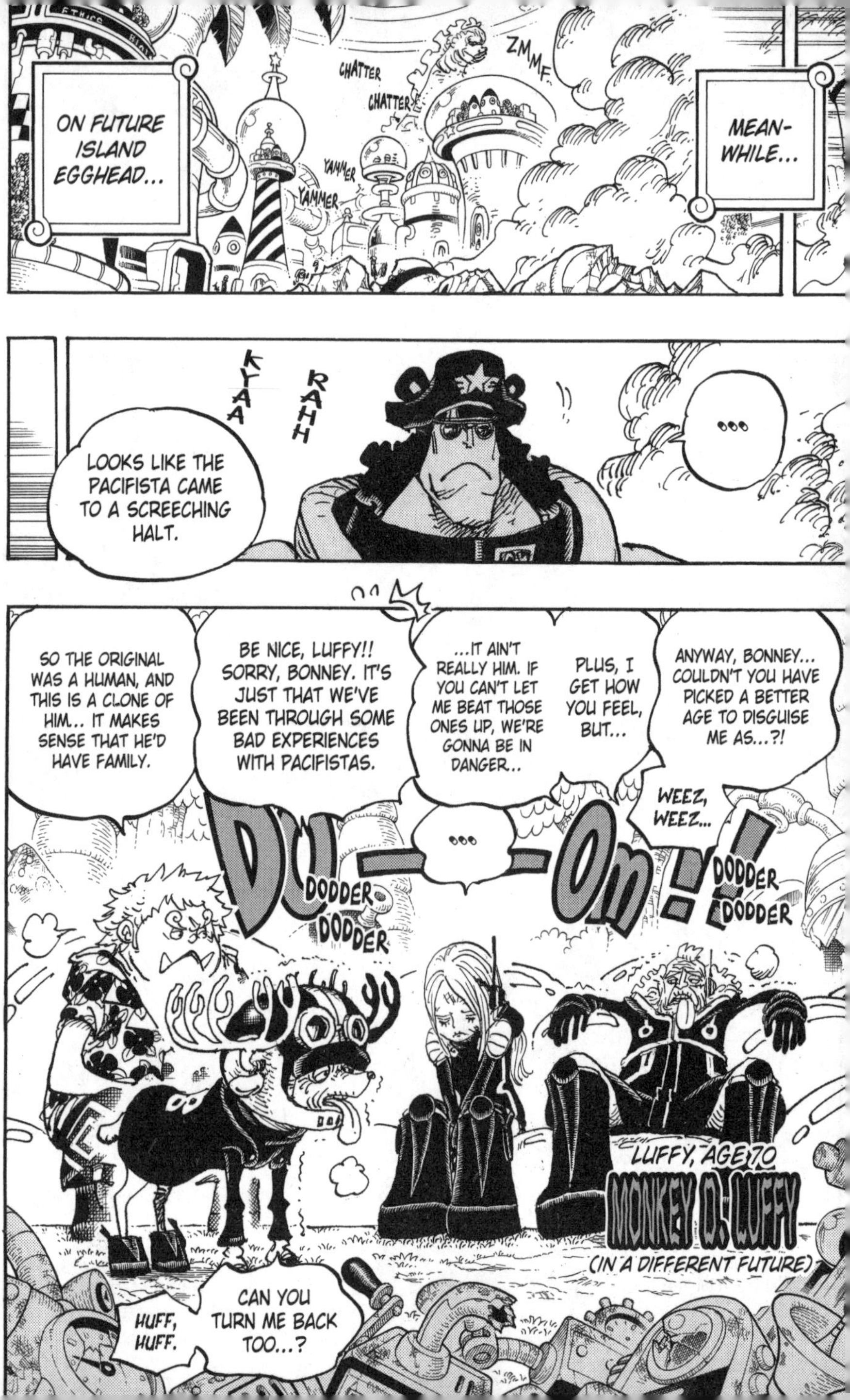
MEAN-WHILE...
ZMMF
CHATTER
CHATTER
YAMMER
YAMMER
ON FUTURE ISLAND EGGHEAD...
...
RAHH
KYAA
LOOKS LIKE THE PACIFISTA CAME TO A SCREECHING HALT.
ANYWAY, BONNEY... COULDN'T YOU HAVE PICKED A BETTER AGE TO DISGUISE ME AS...?!
PLUS, I GET HOW YOU FEEL, BUT...
...IT AIN'T REALLY HIM. IF YOU CAN'T LET ME BEAT THOSE ONES UP, WE'RE GONNA BE IN DANGER..
BE NICE, LUFFY!! SORRY, BONNEY. IT'S JUST THAT WE'VE BEEN THROUGH SOME BAD EXPERIENCES WITH PACIFISTAS.
SO THE ORIGINAL WAS A HUMAN, AND THIS IS A CLONE OF HIM... IT MAKES SENSE THAT HE'D HAVE FAMILY.
WEEZ, WEEZ...
DODDER DODDER
DU—OM!!
...
DODDER DODDER
LUFFY, AGE 70
MONKEY D. LUFFY
(IN A DIFFERENT FUTURE)
CAN YOU TURN ME BACK TOO...?
HUFF, HUFF.

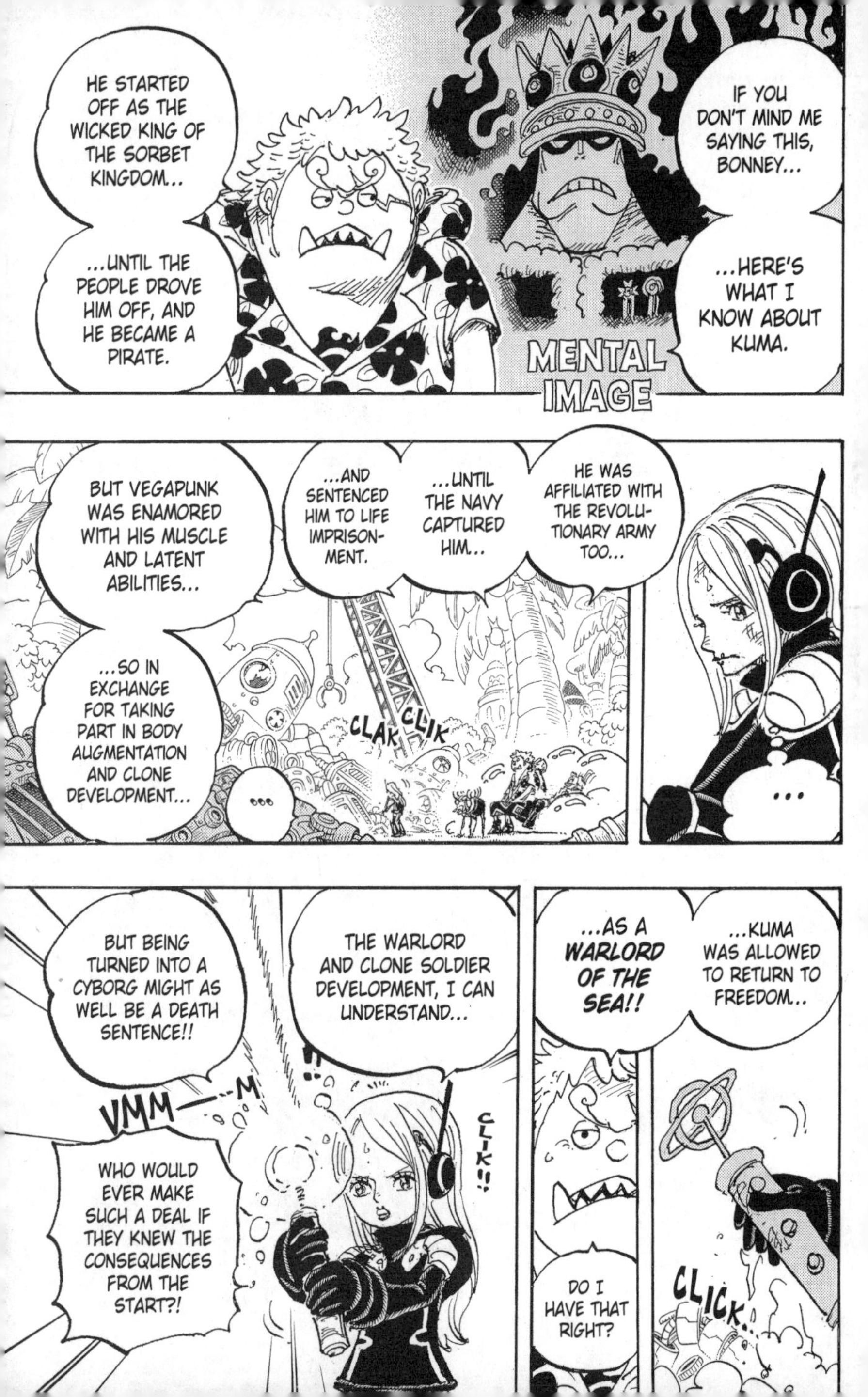
IF YOU DON'T MIND ME SAYING THIS, BONNEY...
...HERE'S WHAT I KNOW ABOUT KUMA.
MENTAL IMAGE
HE STARTED OFF AS THE WICKED KING OF THE SORBET KINGDOM...
...UNTIL THE PEOPLE DROVE HIM OFF, AND HE BECAME A PIRATE.
...
HE WAS AFFILIATED WITH THE REVOLUTIONARY ARMY TOO...
...UNTIL THE NAVY CAPTURED HIM...
...AND SENTENCED HIM TO LIFE IMPRISONMENT.
BUT VEGAPUNK WAS ENAMORED WITH HIS MUSCLE AND LATENT ABILITIES...
CLIK
CLAK
...SO IN EXCHANGE FOR TAKING PART IN BODY AUGMENTATION AND CLONE DEVELOPMENT...
...
...KUMA WAS ALLOWED TO RETURN TO FREEDOM...
...AS A WARLORD OF THE SEA!!
DO I HAVE THAT RIGHT?
CLICK...
CLIK!!
THE WARLORD AND CLONE SOLDIER DEVELOPMENT, I CAN UNDERSTAND...
BUT BEING TURNED INTO A CYBORG MIGHT AS WELL BE A DEATH SENTENCE!!
VMM—M
WHO WOULD EVER MAKE SUCH A DEAL IF THEY KNEW THE CONSEQUENCES FROM THE START?!

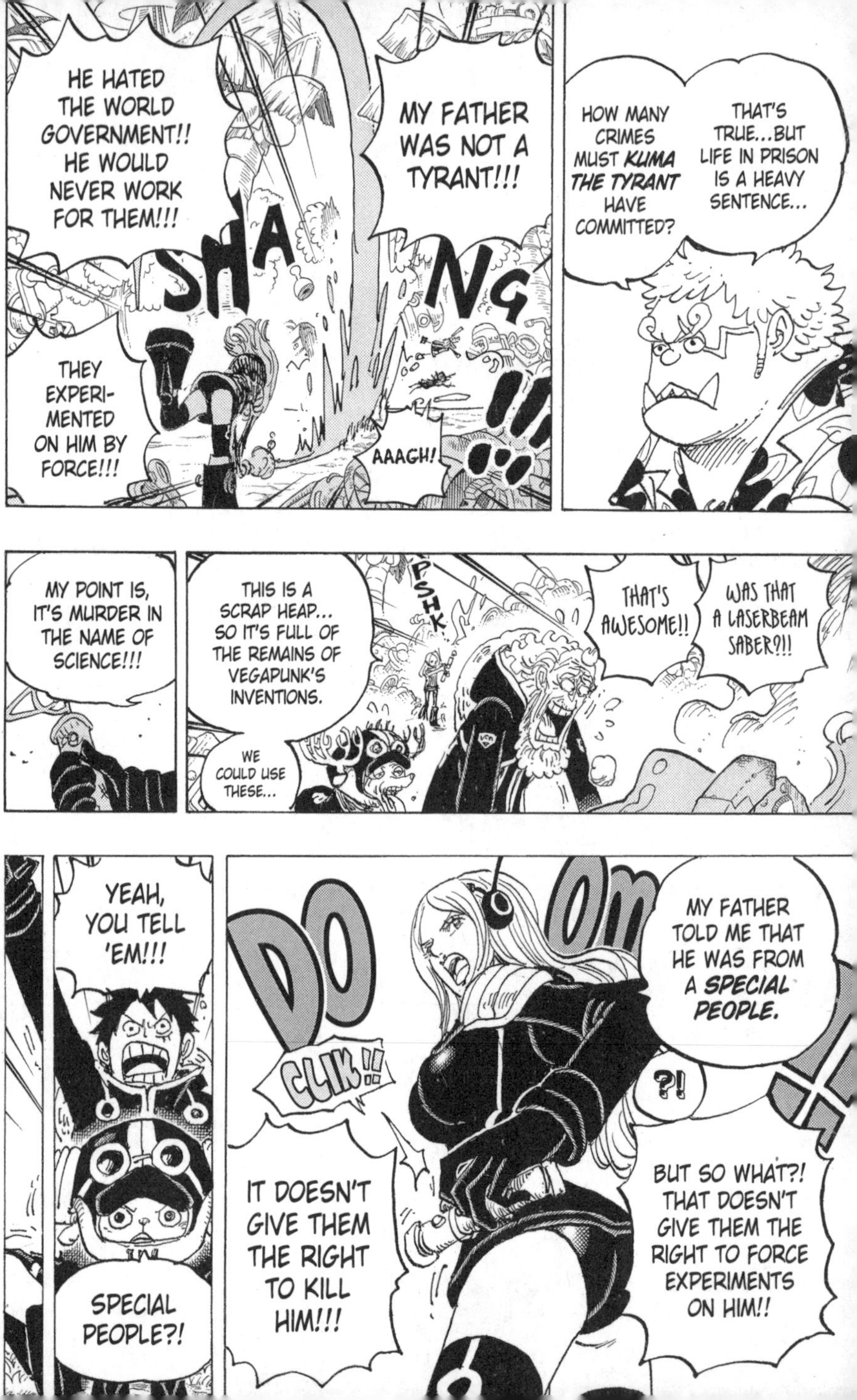
THAT'S TRUE...BUT LIFE IN PRISON IS A HEAVY SENTENCE...
HOW MANY CRIMES MUST KUMA THE TYRANT HAVE COMMITTED?
MY FATHER WAS NOT A TYRANT!!!
HE HATED THE WORLD GOVERNMENT!! HE WOULD NEVER WORK FOR THEM!!!
SHANG
AAAGH!
THEY EXPERI-MENTED ON HIM BY FORCE!!!
WAS THAT A LASERBEAM SABER?!!
THAT'S AWESOME!!
PSHK
THIS IS A SCRAP HEAP... SO IT'S FULL OF THE REMAINS OF VEGAPUNK'S INVENTIONS.
WE COULD USE THESE...
MY POINT IS, IT'S MURDER IN THE NAME OF SCIENCE!!!
MY FATHER TOLD ME THAT HE WAS FROM A SPECIAL PEOPLE.
DOOOM
?!
CLIK!!
BUT SO WHAT?! THAT DOESN'T GIVE THEM THE RIGHT TO FORCE EXPERIMENTS ON HIM!!
IT DOESN'T GIVE THEM THE RIGHT TO KILL HIM!!!
YEAH, YOU TELL 'EM!!!
SPECIAL PEOPLE?!

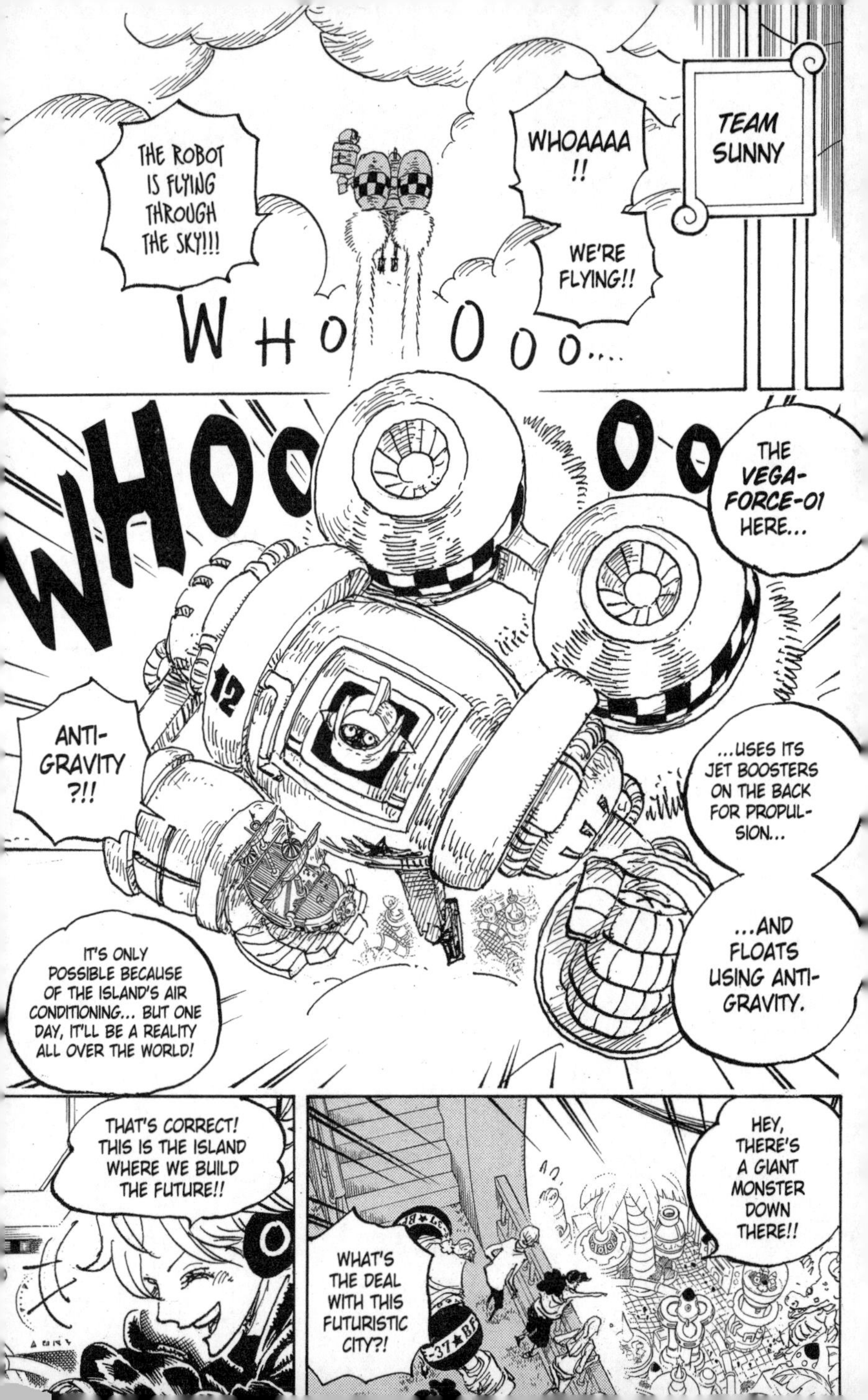
TEAM SUNNY
WHOAAAA!!
WE'RE FLYING!!
THE ROBOT IS FLYING THROUGH THE SKY!!!
WHOOOO...
WHOOOO
THE VEGA-FORCE-01 HERE...
...USES ITS JET BOOSTERS ON THE BACK FOR PROPULSION...
...AND FLOATS USING ANTI-GRAVITY.
ANTI-GRAVITY?!!
IT'S ONLY POSSIBLE BECAUSE OF THE ISLAND'S AIR CONDITIONING... BUT ONE DAY, IT'LL BE A REALITY ALL OVER THE WORLD!
HEY, THERE'S A GIANT MONSTER DOWN THERE!!
WHAT'S THE DEAL WITH THIS FUTURISTIC CITY?!
THAT'S CORRECT! THIS IS THE ISLAND WHERE WE BUILD THE FUTURE!!

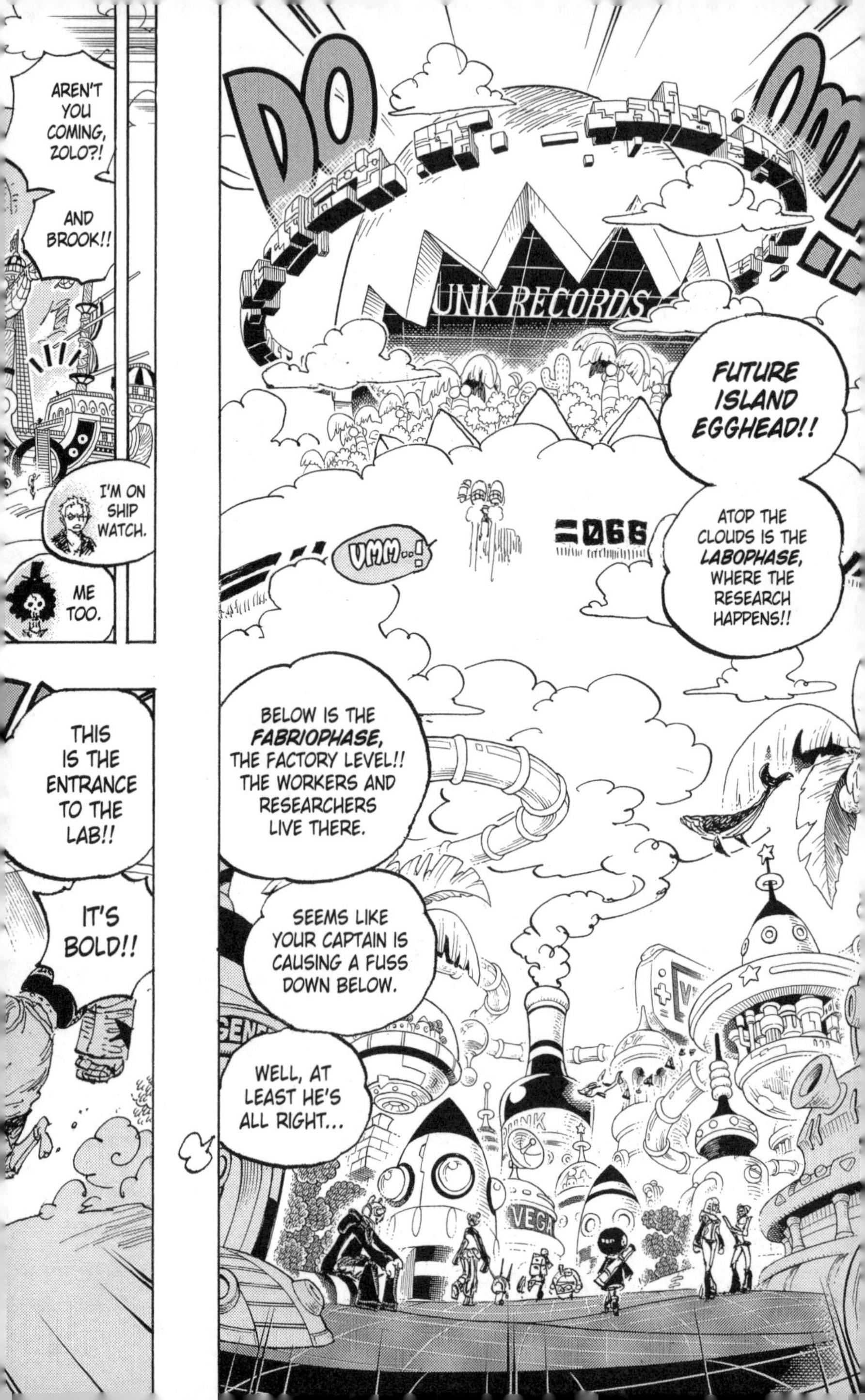
DO
OM
UNK RECORDS
FUTURE ISLAND EGGHEAD!!
ATOP THE CLOUDS IS THE LABOPHASE, WHERE THE RESEARCH HAPPENS!!
=066
UMM..!
BELOW IS THE FABRIOPHASE, THE FACTORY LEVEL!! THE WORKERS AND RESEARCHERS LIVE THERE.
SEEMS LIKE YOUR CAPTAIN IS CAUSING A FUSS DOWN BELOW.
WELL, AT LEAST HE'S ALL RIGHT...
VEGA
AREN'T YOU COMING, ZOLO?!
AND BROOK!!
I'M ON SHIP WATCH.
ME TOO.
THIS IS THE ENTRANCE TO THE LAB!!
IT'S BOLD!!

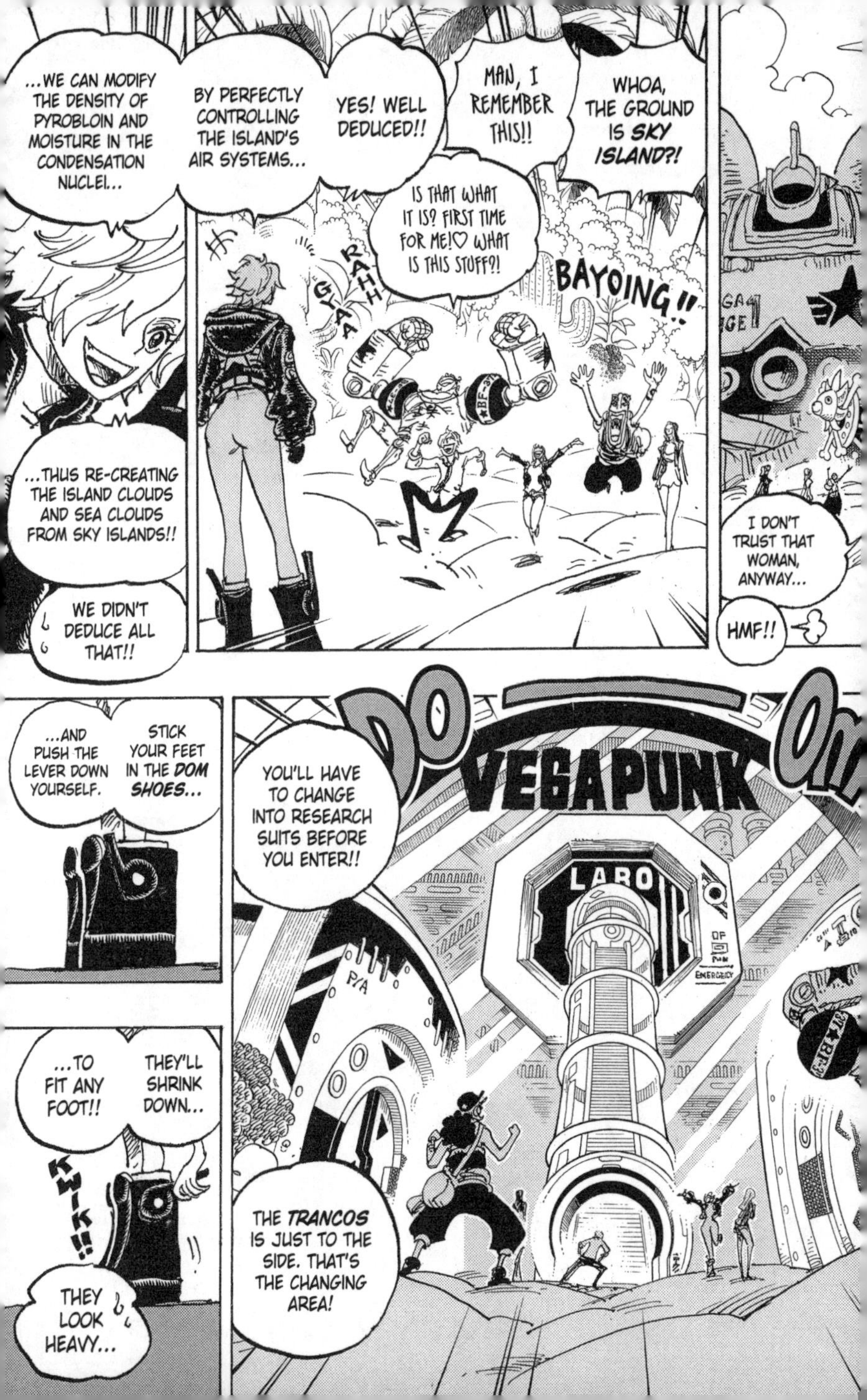
I DON'T TRUST THAT WOMAN, ANYWAY...
HMF!!
WHOA, THE GROUND IS *SKY ISLAND?!*
MAN, I REMEMBER THIS!!
IS THAT WHAT IT IS? FIRST TIME FOR ME!♡ WHAT IS THIS STUFF?!
YES! WELL DEDUCED!!
BAYOING!!
RAHH
GYAA
BY PERFECTLY CONTROLLING THE ISLAND'S AIR SYSTEMS...
...WE CAN MODIFY THE DENSITY OF PYROBLOIN AND MOISTURE IN THE CONDENSATION NUCLEI...
...THUS RE-CREATING THE ISLAND CLOUDS AND SEA CLOUDS FROM SKY ISLANDS!!
WE DIDN'T DEDUCE ALL THAT!!
DO—OM
VEGAPUNK
LABO
YOU'LL HAVE TO CHANGE INTO RESEARCH SUITS BEFORE YOU ENTER!!
THE *TRANCOS* IS JUST TO THE SIDE. THAT'S THE CHANGING AREA!
STICK YOUR FEET IN THE *DOM SHOES...*
...AND PUSH THE LEVER DOWN YOURSELF.
THEY'LL SHRINK DOWN...
...TO FIT ANY FOOT!!
KWIK!!
THEY LOOK HEAVY...

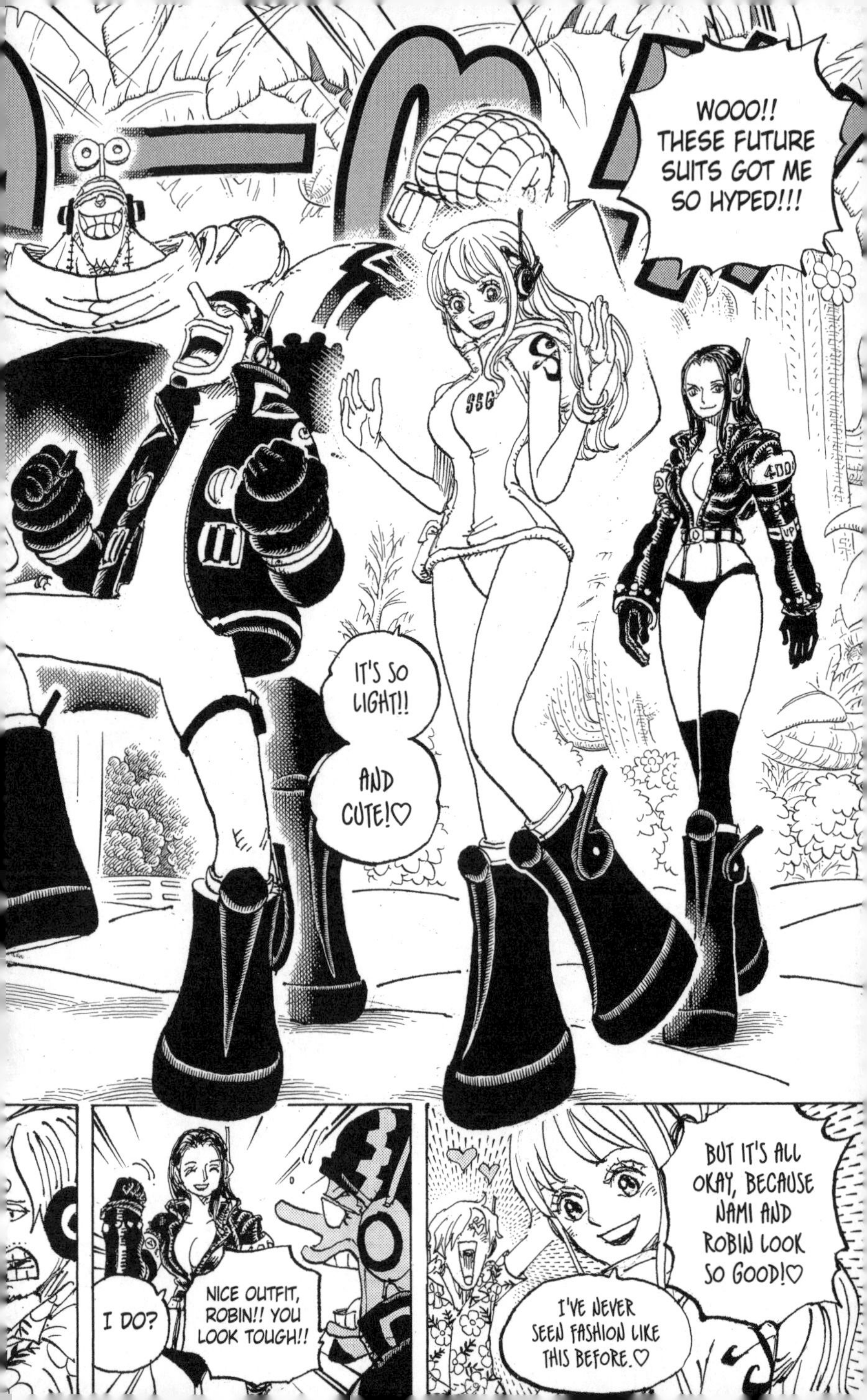
WOOO!! THESE FUTURE SUITS GOT ME SO HYPED!!!
IT'S SO LIGHT!!
AND CUTE!♡
BUT IT'S ALL OKAY, BECAUSE NAMI AND ROBIN LOOK SO GOOD!♡
I'VE NEVER SEEN FASHION LIKE THIS BEFORE.♡
NICE OUTFIT, ROBIN!! YOU LOOK TOUGH!!
I DO?

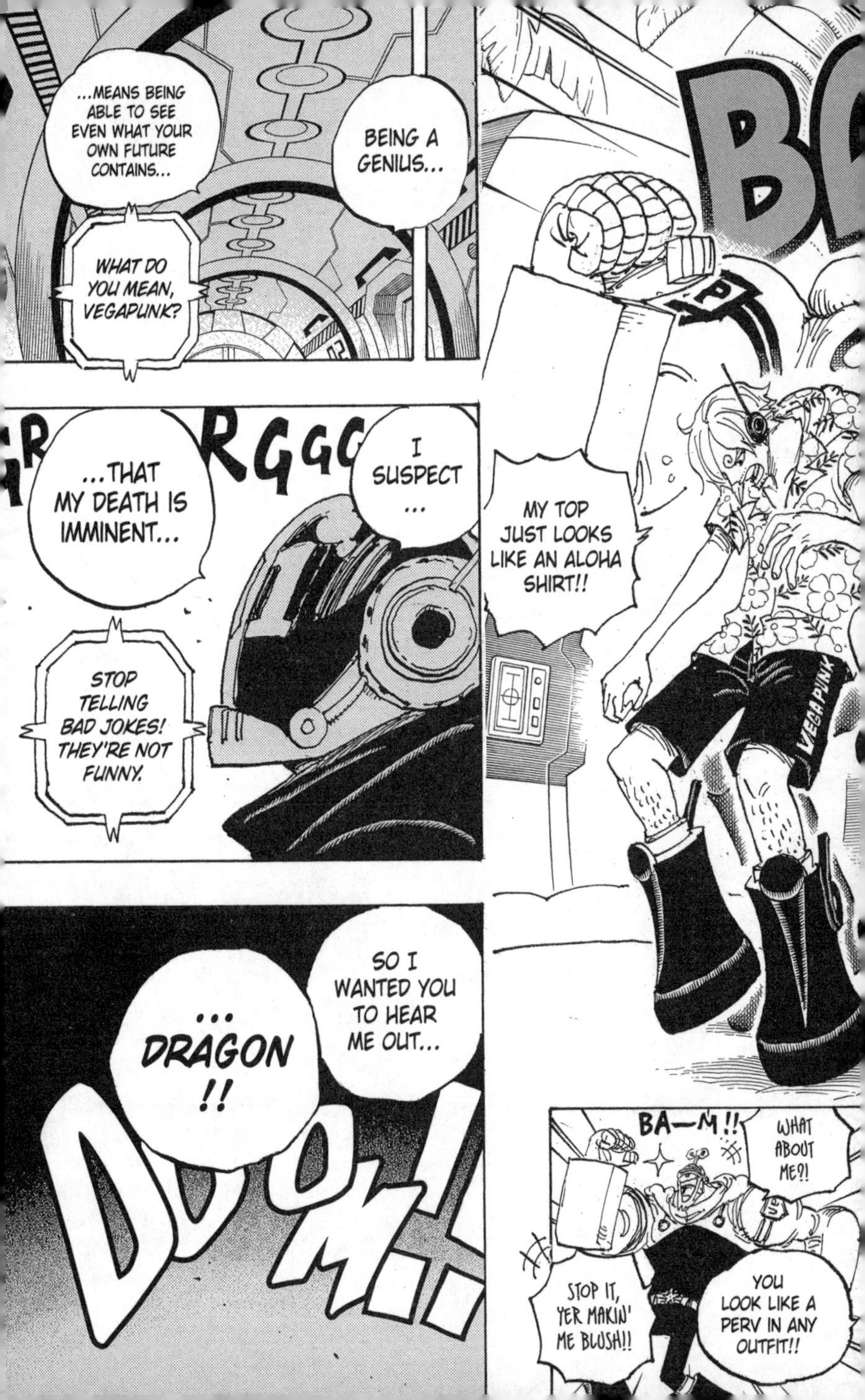
MY TOP JUST LOOKS LIKE AN ALOHA SHIRT!!
BA—M!!
WHAT ABOUT ME?!
YOU LOOK LIKE A PERV IN ANY OUTFIT!!
STOP IT, YER MAKIN' ME BLUSH!!
BEING A GENIUS...
...MEANS BEING ABLE TO SEE EVEN WHAT YOUR OWN FUTURE CONTAINS...
WHAT DO YOU MEAN, VEGAPUNK?
I SUSPECT...
...THAT MY DEATH IS IMMINENT...
STOP TELLING BAD JOKES! THEY'RE NOT FUNNY.
SO I WANTED YOU TO HEAR ME OUT...
...DRAGON!!

Chapter 1065: SIX VEGAPUNKS

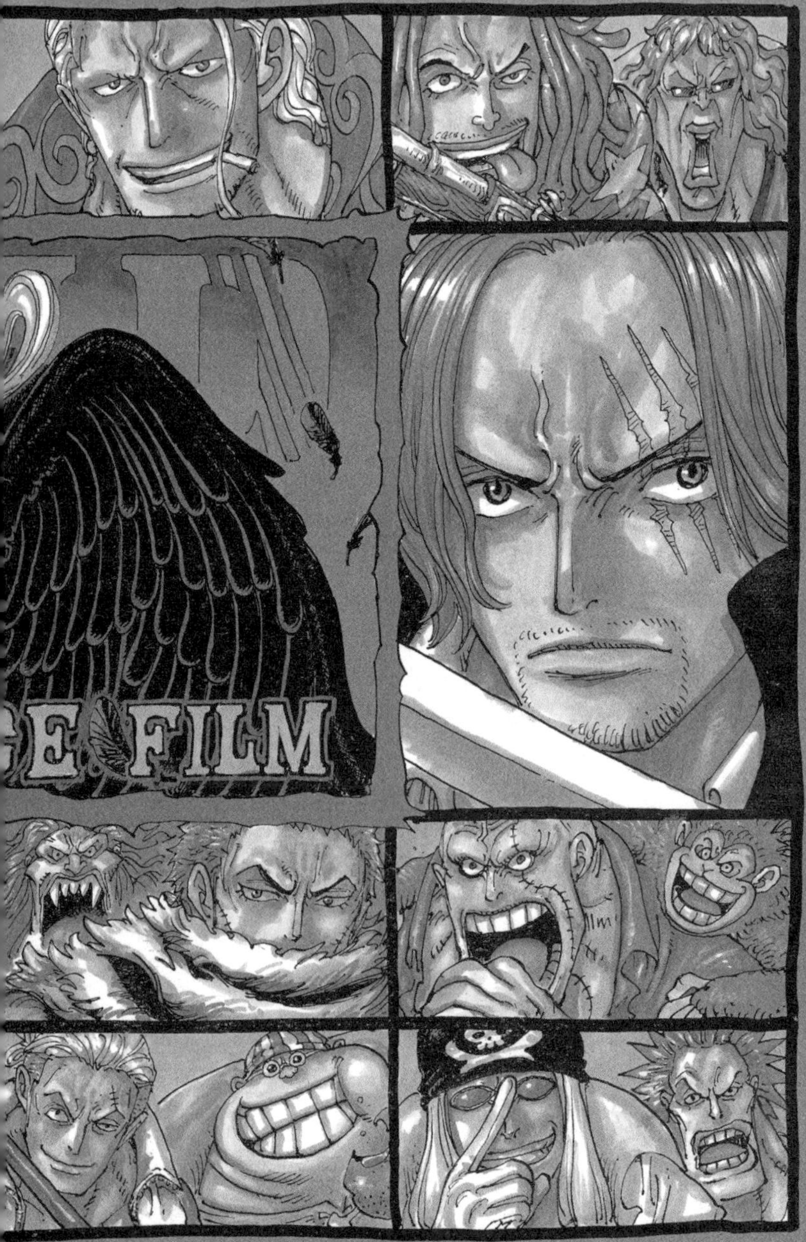
E FILM

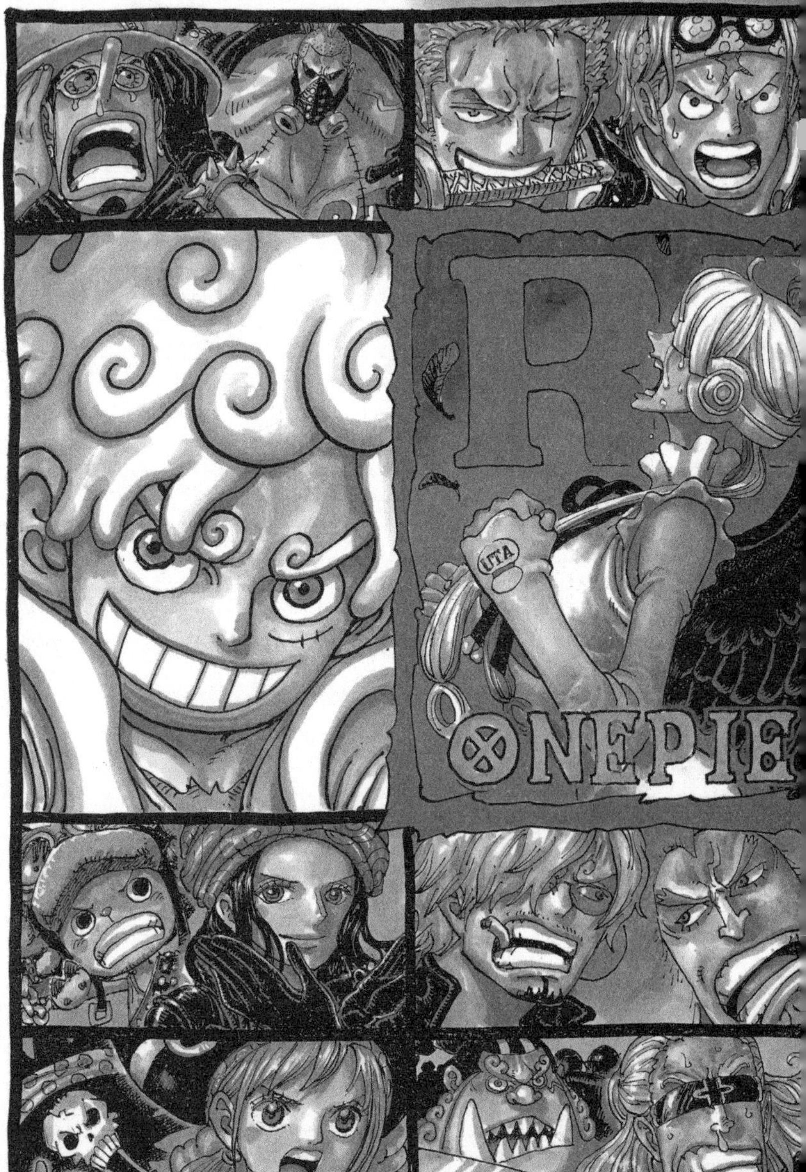
R
UTA
ONEPIE

vol.105
ONE PIECE

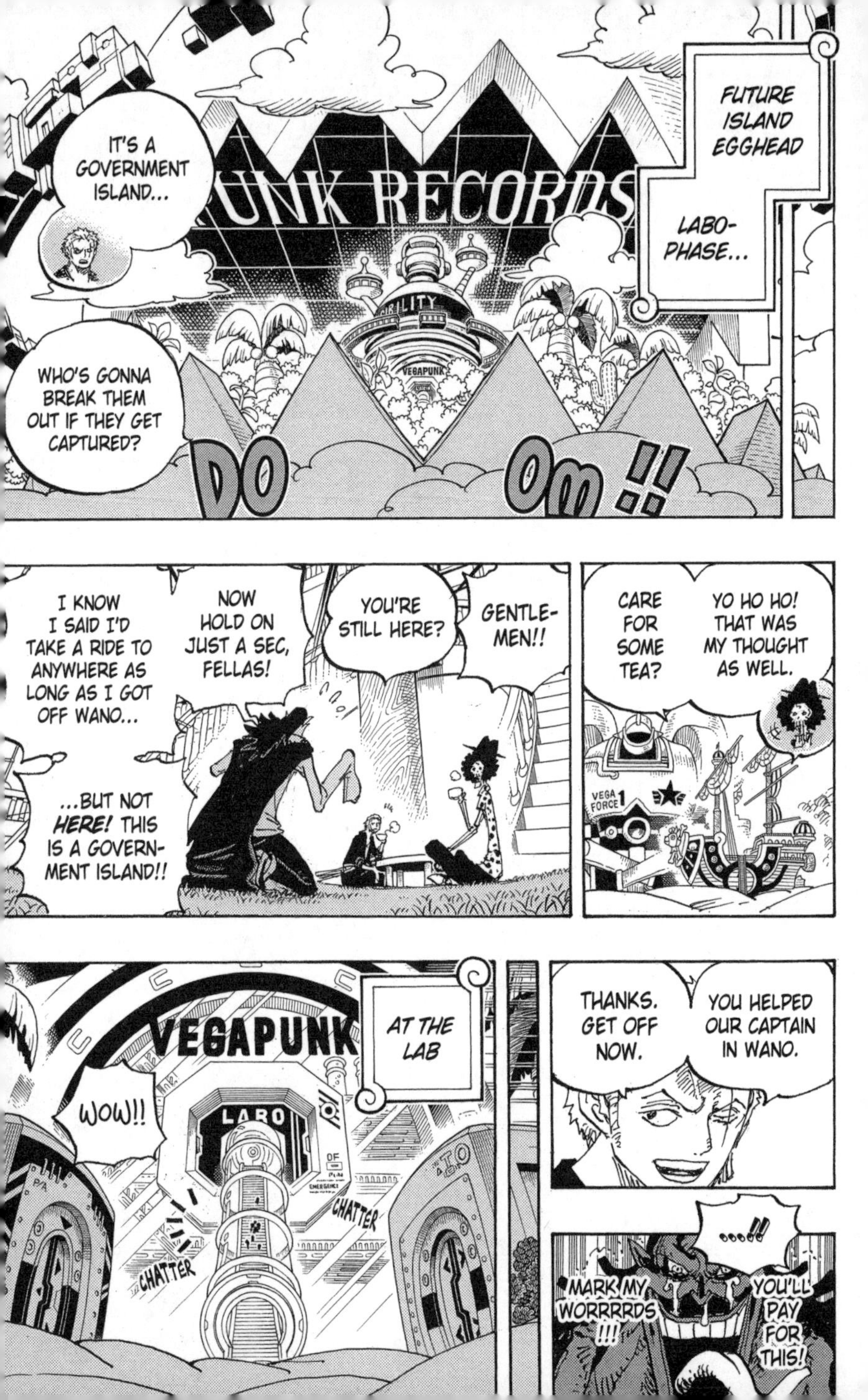
FUTURE ISLAND EGGHEAD
LABO-PHASE...
UNK RECORDS
IT'S A GOVERNMENT ISLAND...
WHO'S GONNA BREAK THEM OUT IF THEY GET CAPTURED?
VEGAPUNK
DOOM!!
YO HO HO! THAT WAS MY THOUGHT AS WELL.
CARE FOR SOME TEA?
VEGA FORCE 1
GENTLEMEN!!
YOU'RE STILL HERE?
NOW HOLD ON JUST A SEC, FELLAS!
I KNOW I SAID I'D TAKE A RIDE TO ANYWHERE AS LONG AS I GOT OFF WANO...
...BUT NOT HERE! THIS IS A GOVERNMENT ISLAND!!
YOU HELPED OUR CAPTAIN IN WANO.
THANKS. GET OFF NOW.
...!!
YOU'LL PAY FOR THIS!
MARK MY WORRRRDS!!!
AT THE LAB
VEGAPUNK
WOW!!
LABO
CHATTER
CHATTER

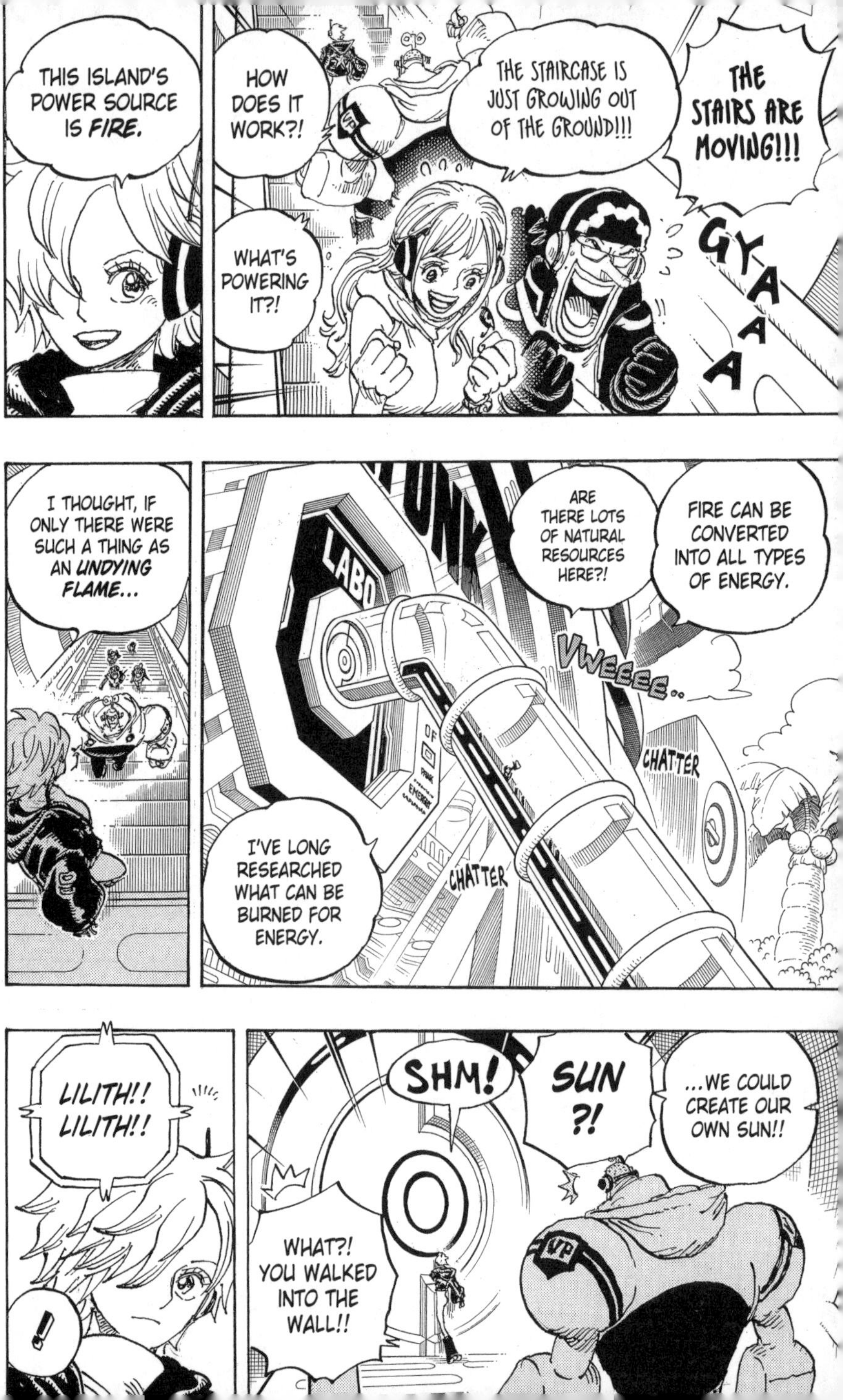
THE STAIRS ARE MOVING!!!
GYAAAA
THE STAIRCASE IS JUST GROWING OUT OF THE GROUND!!!
HOW DOES IT WORK?!
WHAT'S POWERING IT?!
THIS ISLAND'S POWER SOURCE IS *FIRE.*
FIRE CAN BE CONVERTED INTO ALL TYPES OF ENERGY.
ARE THERE LOTS OF NATURAL RESOURCES HERE?!
VWEEEE..
LABO
CHATTER
I'VE LONG RESEARCHED WHAT CAN BE BURNED FOR ENERGY.
CHATTER
I THOUGHT, IF ONLY THERE WERE SUCH A THING AS AN *UNDYING FLAME...*
...WE COULD CREATE OUR OWN SUN!!
SUN?!
SHM!
WHAT?! YOU WALKED INTO THE WALL!!
LILITH!! LILITH!!
!

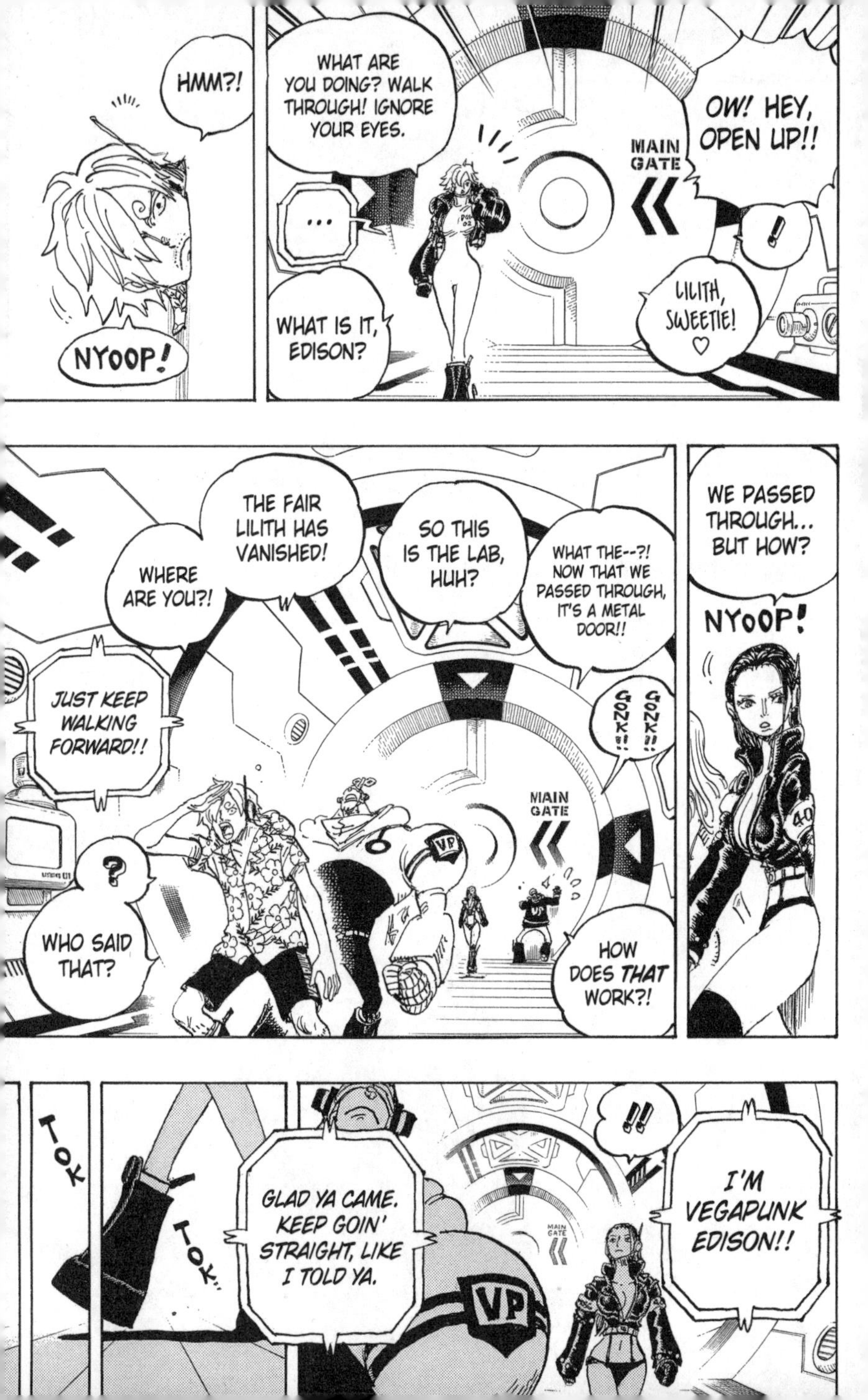
OW! HEY, OPEN UP!!
MAIN GATE
!
LILITH, SWEETIE! ♡
WHAT ARE YOU DOING? WALK THROUGH! IGNORE YOUR EYES.
...
WHAT IS IT, EDISON?
HMM?!
NYOOP!
WE PASSED THROUGH... BUT HOW?
NYOOP!
WHAT THE--?! NOW THAT WE PASSED THROUGH, IT'S A METAL DOOR!!
SO THIS IS THE LAB, HUH?
THE FAIR LILITH HAS VANISHED!
WHERE ARE YOU?!
GONK!! GONK!!
JUST KEEP WALKING FORWARD!!
MAIN GATE
HOW DOES THAT WORK?!
?
WHO SAID THAT?
!!
I'M VEGAPUNK EDISON!!
MAIN GATE
GLAD YA CAME. KEEP GOIN' STRAIGHT, LIKE I TOLD YA.
TOK
TOK..

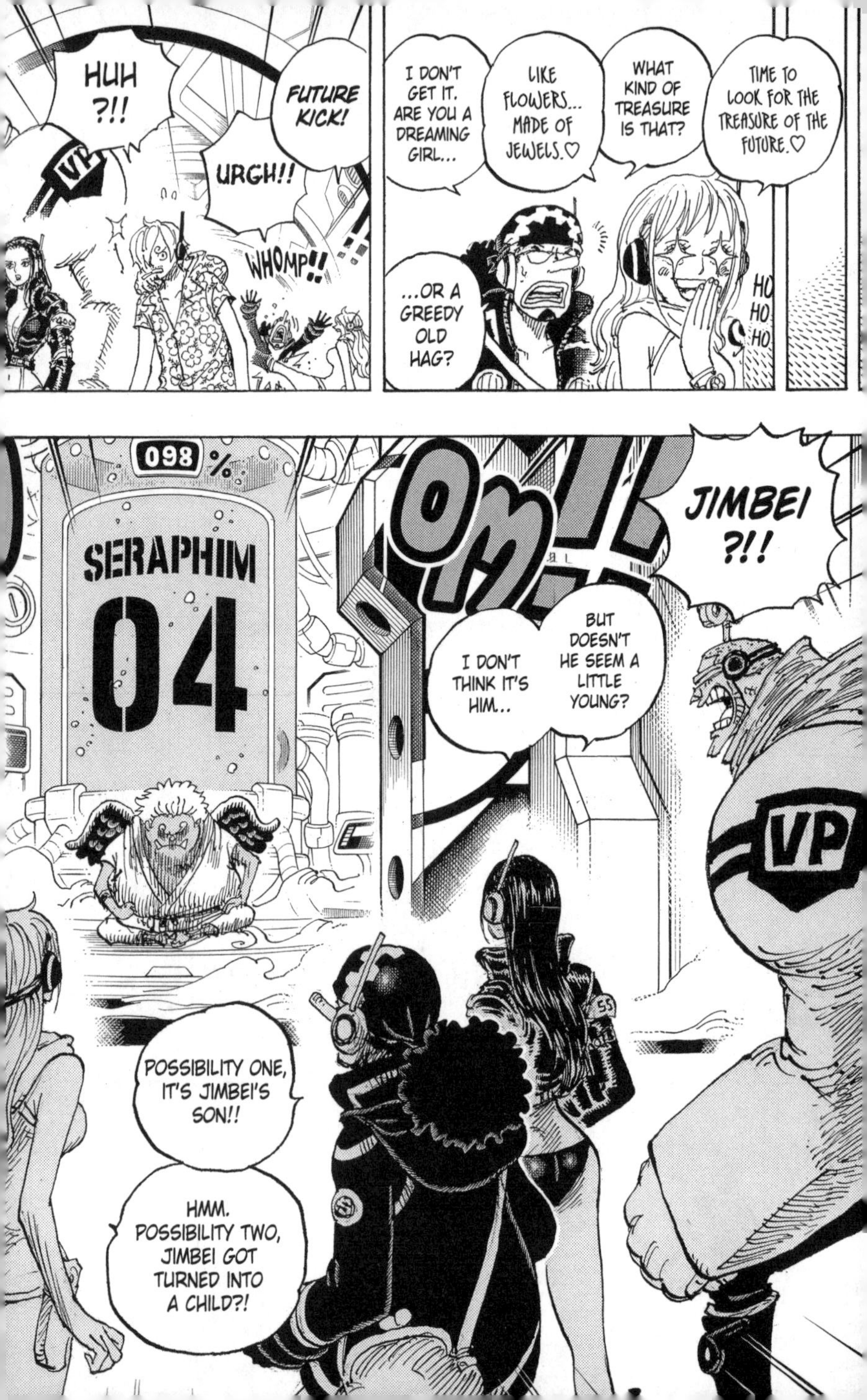
TIME TO LOOK FOR THE TREASURE OF THE FUTURE.♡
WHAT KIND OF TREASURE IS THAT?
LIKE FLOWERS... MADE OF JEWELS.♡
I DON'T GET IT. ARE YOU A DREAMING GIRL...
...OR A GREEDY OLD HAG?
HO HO HO
FUTURE KICK!
HUH ?!!
URGH!!
VP
WHOMP!!
JIMBEI ?!!
BUT DOESN'T HE SEEM A LITTLE YOUNG?
I DON'T THINK IT'S HIM...
098 %
SERAPHIM
04
VP
POSSIBILITY ONE, IT'S JIMBEI'S SON!!
HMM. POSSIBILITY TWO, JIMBEI GOT TURNED INTO A CHILD?!

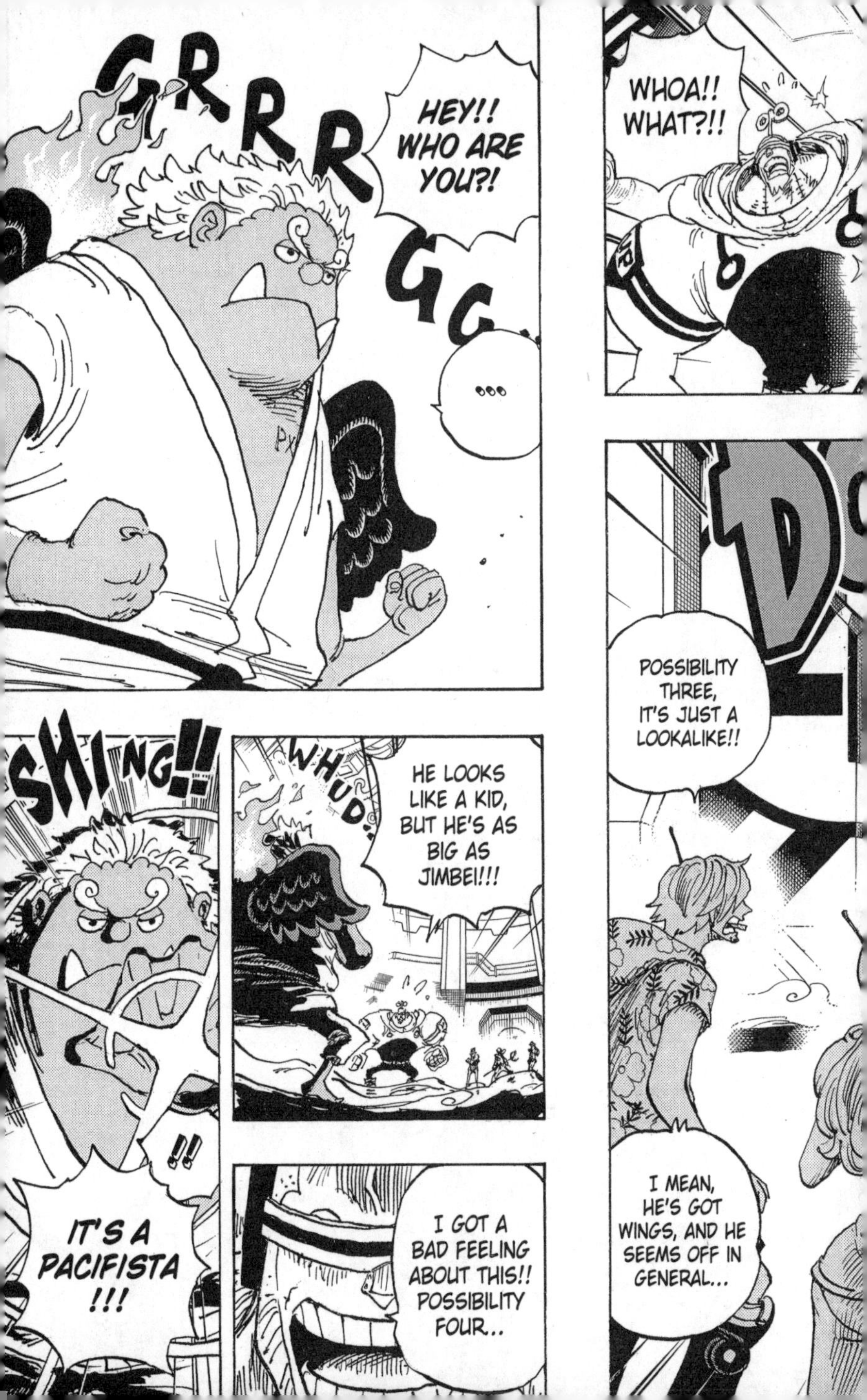
WHOA!! WHAT?!!
POSSIBILITY THREE, IT'S JUST A LOOKALIKE!!
I MEAN, HE'S GOT WINGS, AND HE SEEMS OFF IN GENERAL...
GRRRR
HEY!! WHO ARE YOU?!
GG...
...
WHUD
HE LOOKS LIKE A KID, BUT HE'S AS BIG AS JIMBEI!!!
I GOT A BAD FEELING ABOUT THIS!! POSSIBILITY FOUR...
SHING!!
!!
IT'S A PACIFISTA!!!

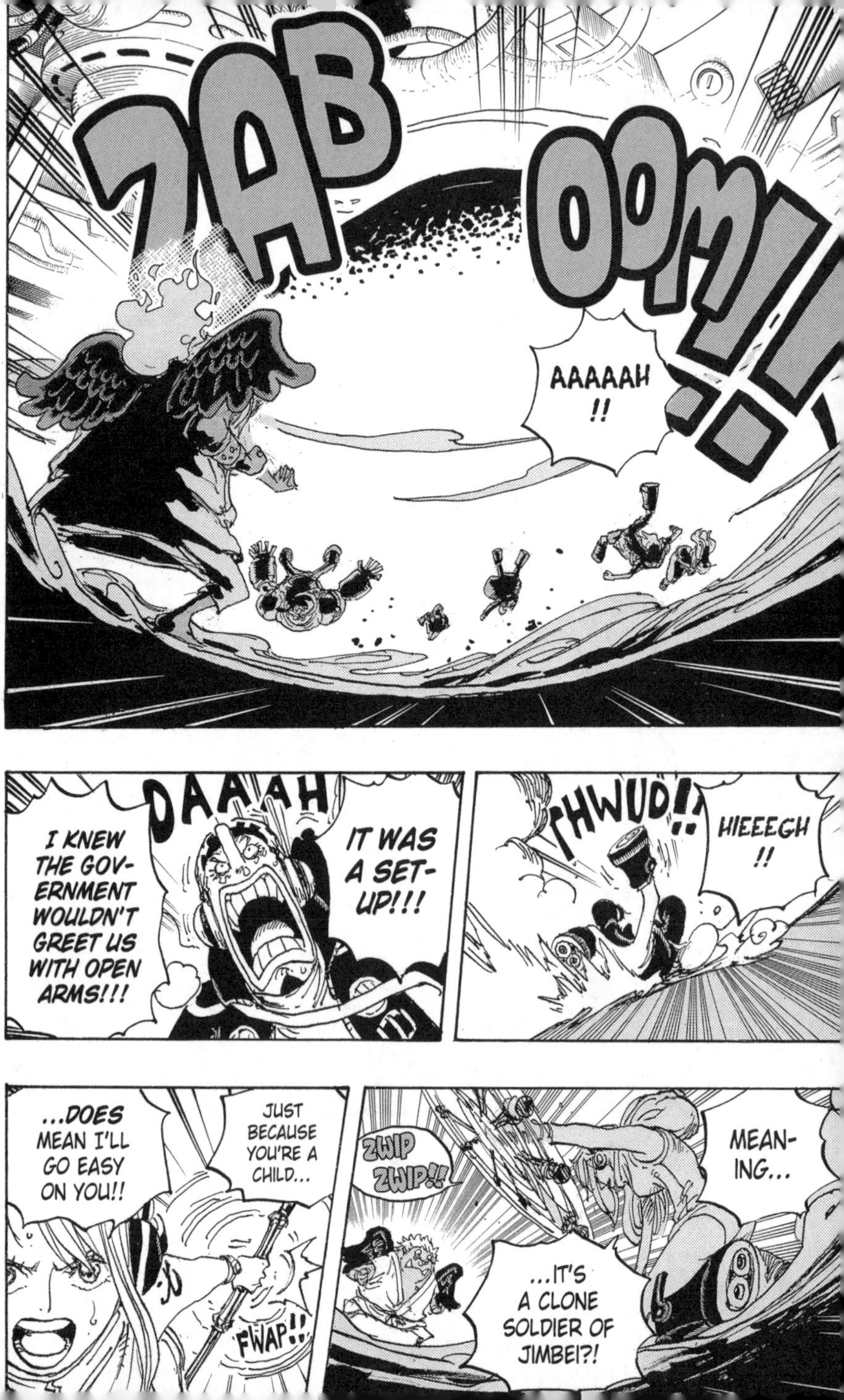
ZABOOM!!
AAAAAH!!
HIEEEGH!!
THWUD!!
IT WAS A SET-UP!!!
DAAAH
I KNEW THE GOV-ERNMENT WOULDN'T GREET US WITH OPEN ARMS!!!
MEAN-ING...
ZWIP ZWIP!!
...IT'S A CLONE SOLDIER OF JIMBEI?!
JUST BECAUSE YOU'RE A CHILD...
...DOES MEAN I'LL GO EASY ON YOU!!
FWAP!!

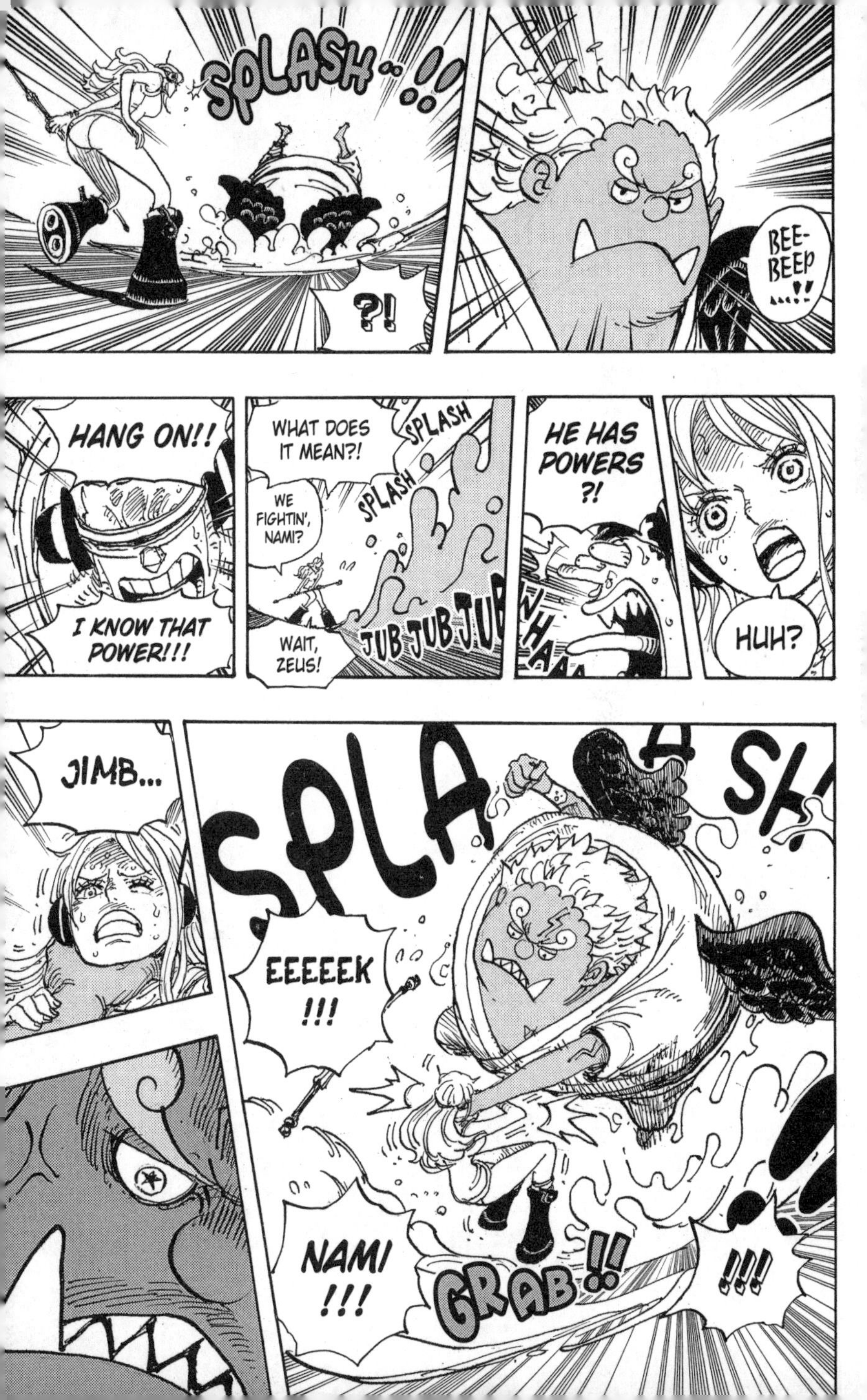
BEE-BEEP...!!
SPLASH..!!
?!
HUH?
HE HAS POWERS ?!
WHAAA
WHAT DOES IT MEAN?!
SPLASH
SPLASH
WE FIGHTIN', NAMI?
JUB JUB JUB
WAIT, ZEUS!
HANG ON!!
I KNOW THAT POWER!!!
SPLASH!
EEEEEK !!!
GRAB!!
!!!
NAMI !!!
JIMB...

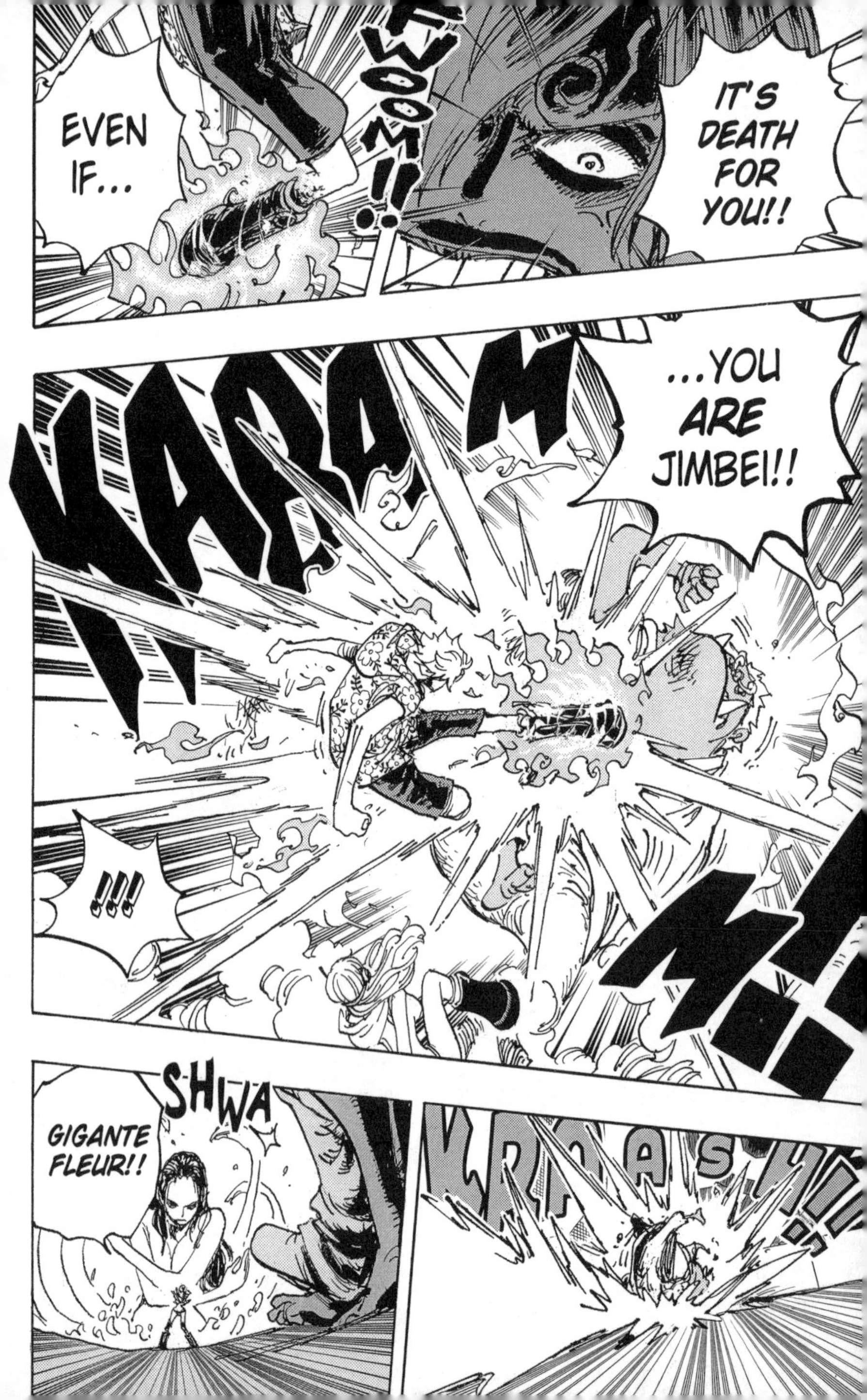
IT'S DEATH FOR YOU!!
FWOOM!!
EVEN IF...
...YOU ARE JIMBEI!!
!!!
SHWA
GIGANTE FLEUR!!

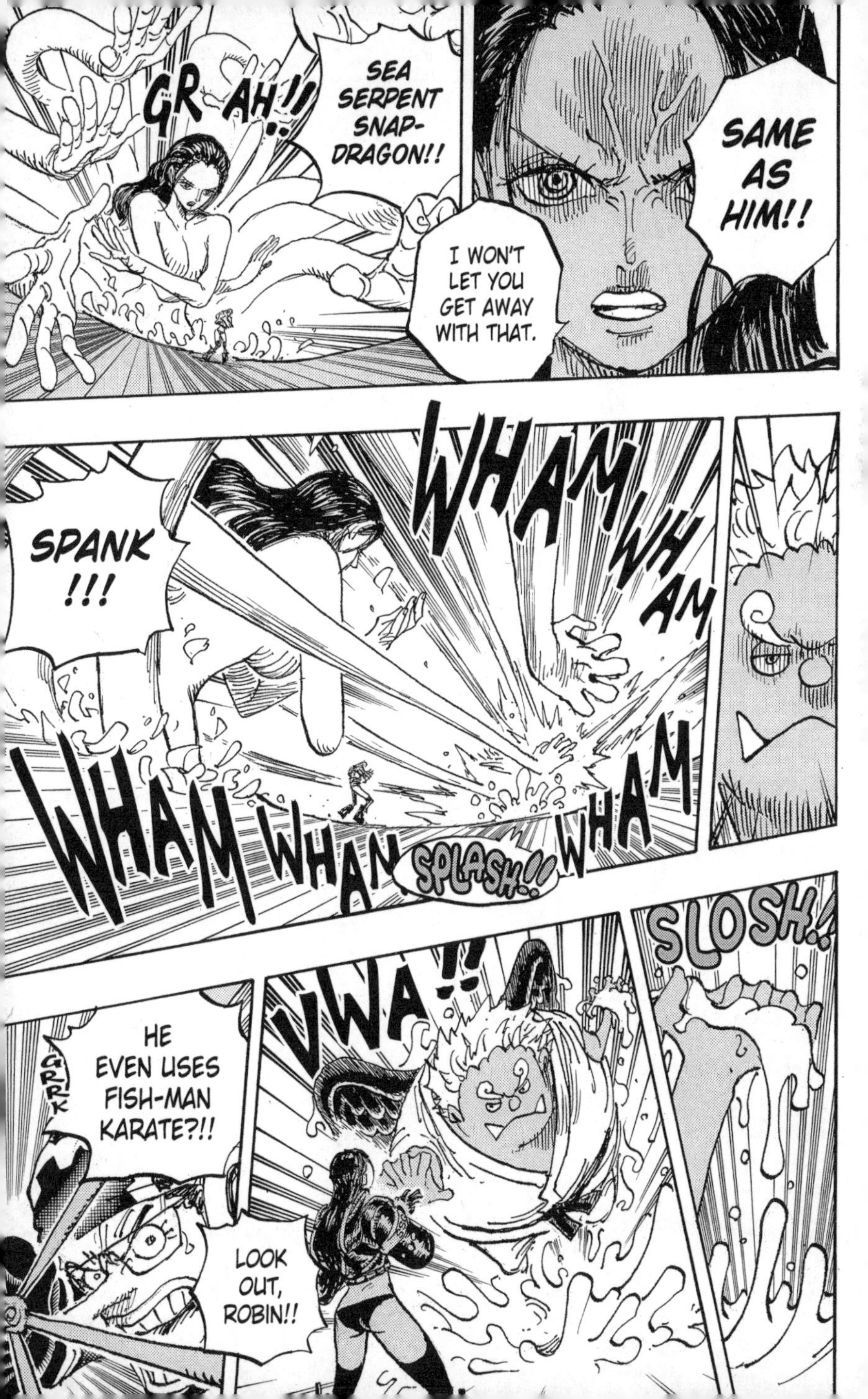
SAME AS HIM!!
I WON'T LET YOU GET AWAY WITH THAT.
SEA SERPENT SNAP-DRAGON!!
GRAH!!
WHAM
WHAM
SPANK!!!
WHAM
WHAM
SPLASH!!
WHAM
SLOSH!!
VWA!!
LOOK OUT, ROBIN!!
HE EVEN USES FISH-MAN KARATE?!!
GRRK

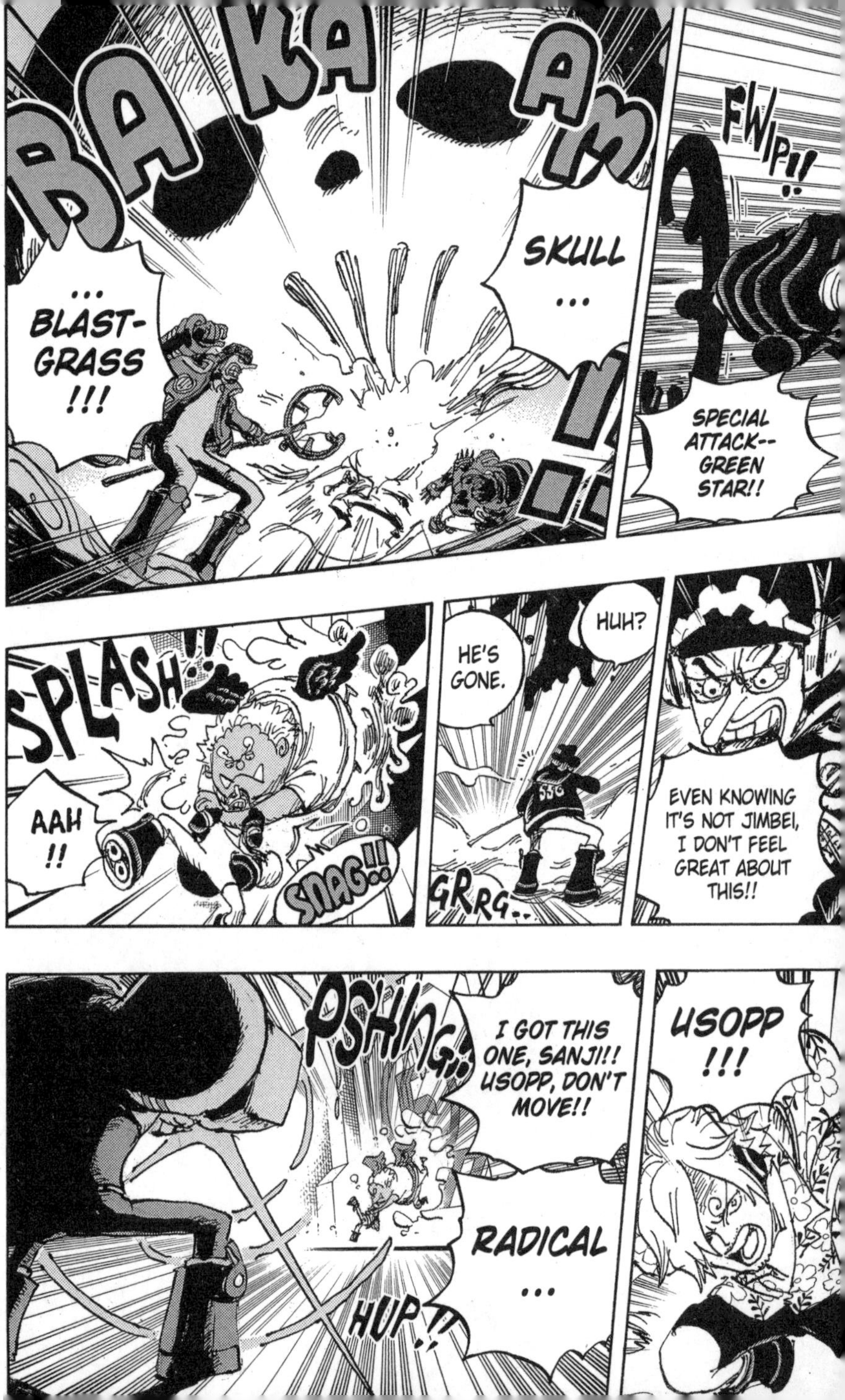
FWIP!!
SPECIAL ATTACK--GREEN STAR!!
BAKAAM!!
SKULL ...
... BLAST-GRASS!!!
EVEN KNOWING IT'S NOT JIMBEI, I DON'T FEEL GREAT ABOUT THIS!!
HUH?
HE'S GONE.
GRRG...
SPLASH!!
SNAG!!
AAH!!
USOPP!!!
PSHING!!
I GOT THIS ONE, SANJI!! USOPP, DON'T MOVE!!
RADICAL ...
HUP!!

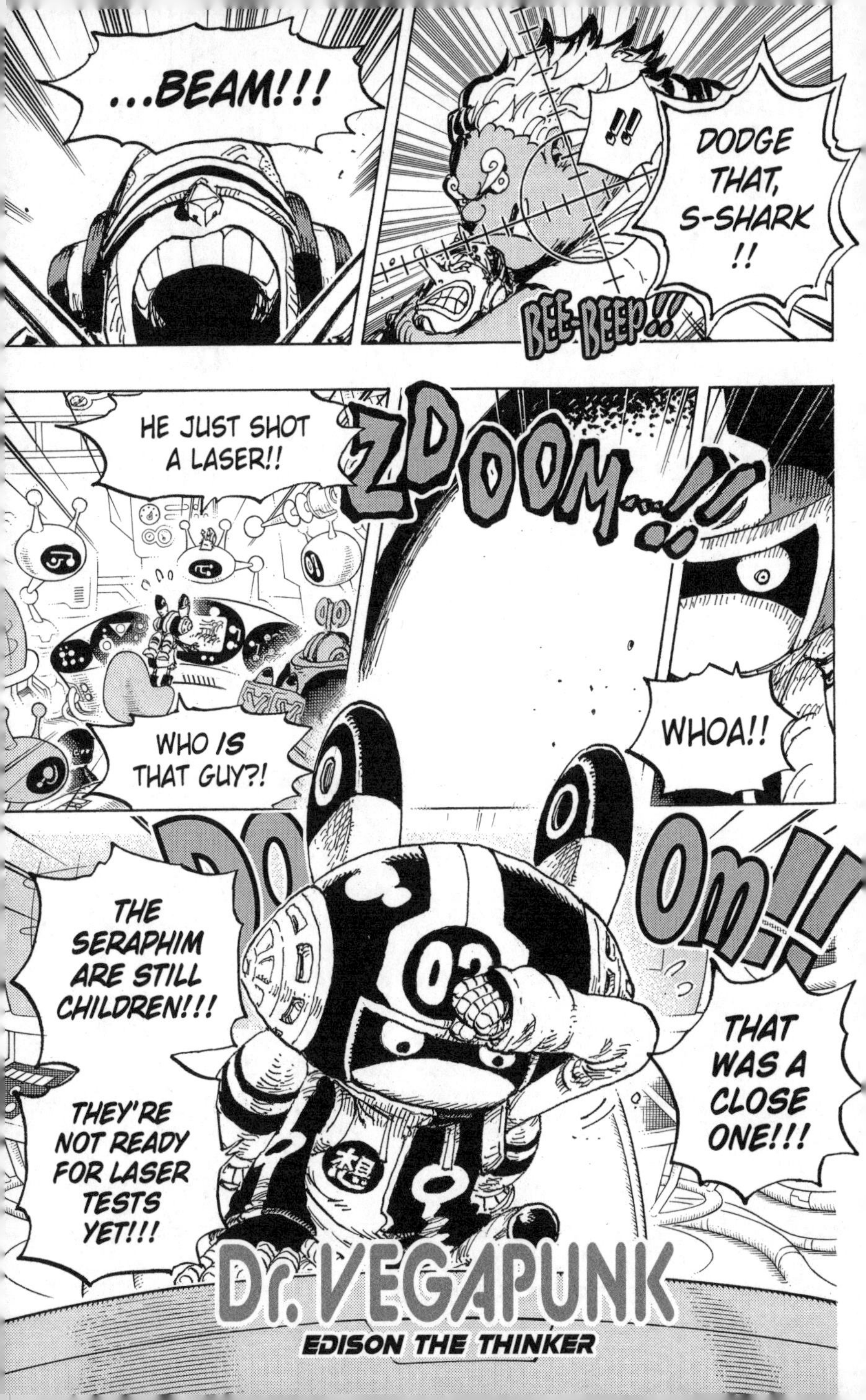
!!
DODGE THAT, S-SHARK !!
BEE-BEEP!!
...BEAM!!!
WHOA!!
ZDOOM...!!
HE JUST SHOT A LASER!!
WHO *IS* THAT GUY?!
DO
OM!!
THAT WAS A CLOSE ONE!!!
THE SERAPHIM ARE STILL CHILDREN!!!
THEY'RE NOT READY FOR LASER TESTS YET!!!
Dr. VEGAPUNK
EDISON THE THINKER

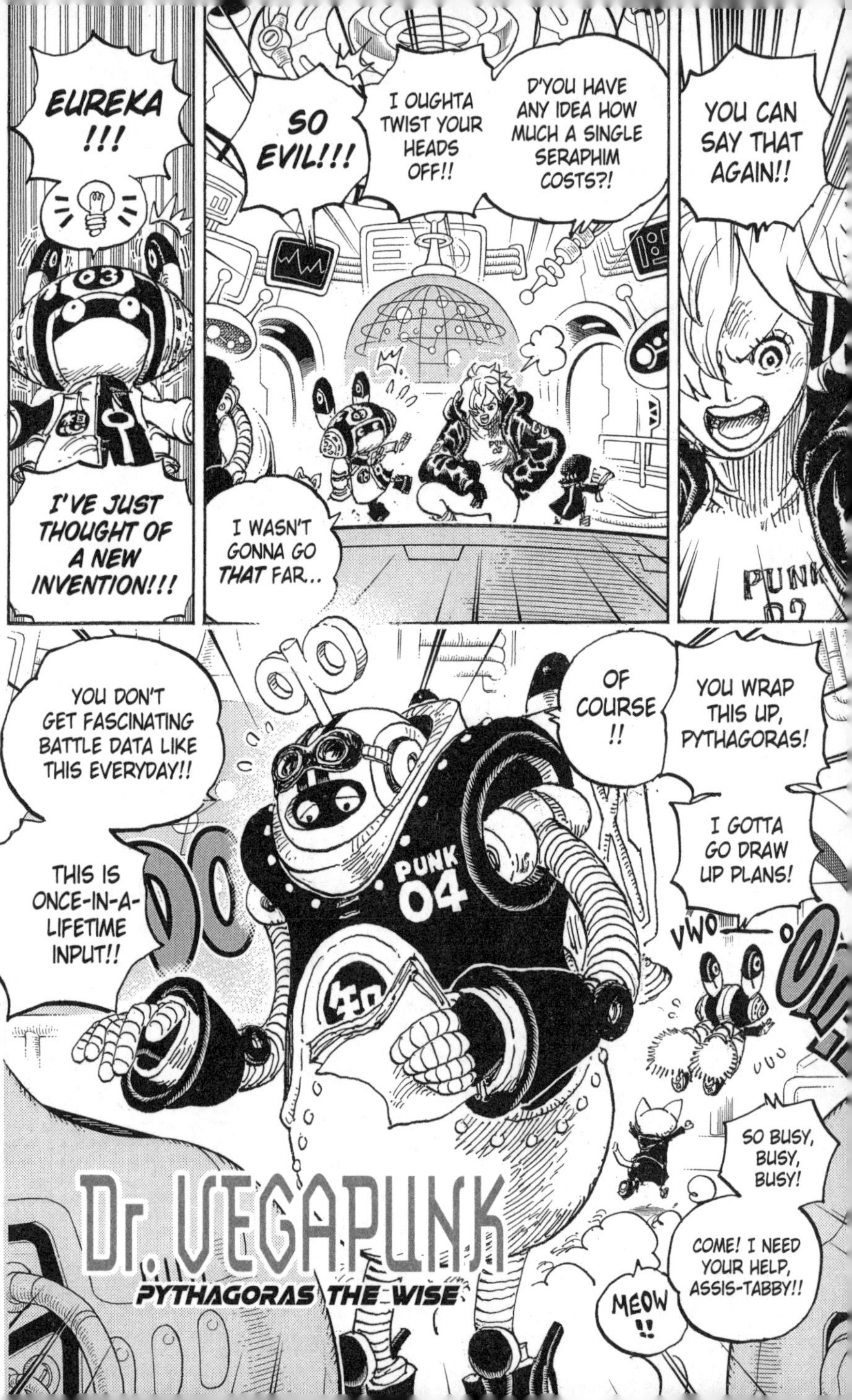
YOU CAN SAY THAT AGAIN!!
D'YOU HAVE ANY IDEA HOW MUCH A SINGLE SERAPHIM COSTS?!
I OUGHTA TWIST YOUR HEADS OFF!!
SO EVIL!!!
I WASN'T GONNA GO THAT FAR...
EUREKA!!!
I'VE JUST THOUGHT OF A NEW INVENTION!!!
YOU WRAP THIS UP, PYTHAGORAS!
I GOTTA GO DRAW UP PLANS!
OF COURSE!!
VWO
SO BUSY, BUSY, BUSY!
COME! I NEED YOUR HELP, ASSIS-TABBY!!
MEOW!!
PUNK 04
YOU DON'T GET FASCINATING BATTLE DATA LIKE THIS EVERYDAY!!
THIS IS ONCE-IN-A-LIFETIME INPUT!!
Dr. VEGAPUNK
PYTHAGORAS THE WISE

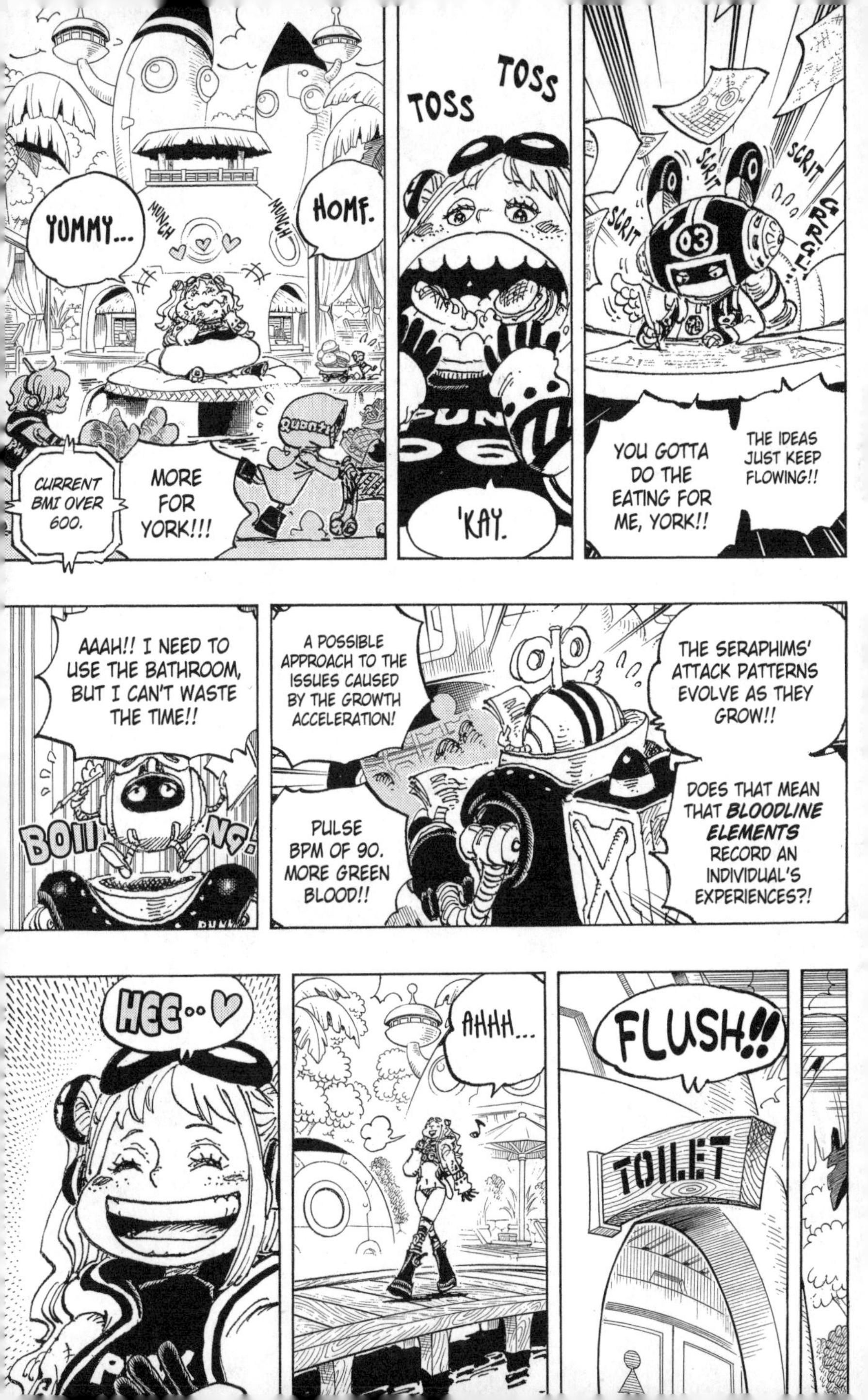
SCRIT
SCRIT
SCRIT
GRRGL!!
THE IDEAS JUST KEEP FLOWING!!
YOU GOTTA DO THE EATING FOR ME, YORK!!
TOSS
TOSS
'KAY.
HOMF.
MUNCH
MUNCH
YUMMY...
MORE FOR YORK!!!
CURRENT BMI OVER 600.
THE SERAPHIMS' ATTACK PATTERNS EVOLVE AS THEY GROW!!
DOES THAT MEAN THAT ***BLOODLINE ELEMENTS*** RECORD AN INDIVIDUAL'S EXPERIENCES?!
A POSSIBLE APPROACH TO THE ISSUES CAUSED BY THE GROWTH ACCELERATION!
PULSE BPM OF 90. MORE GREEN BLOOD!!
AAAH!! I NEED TO USE THE BATHROOM, BUT I CAN'T WASTE THE TIME!!
BOIIING!
FLUSH!!
TOILET
AHHH...
HEE..♡

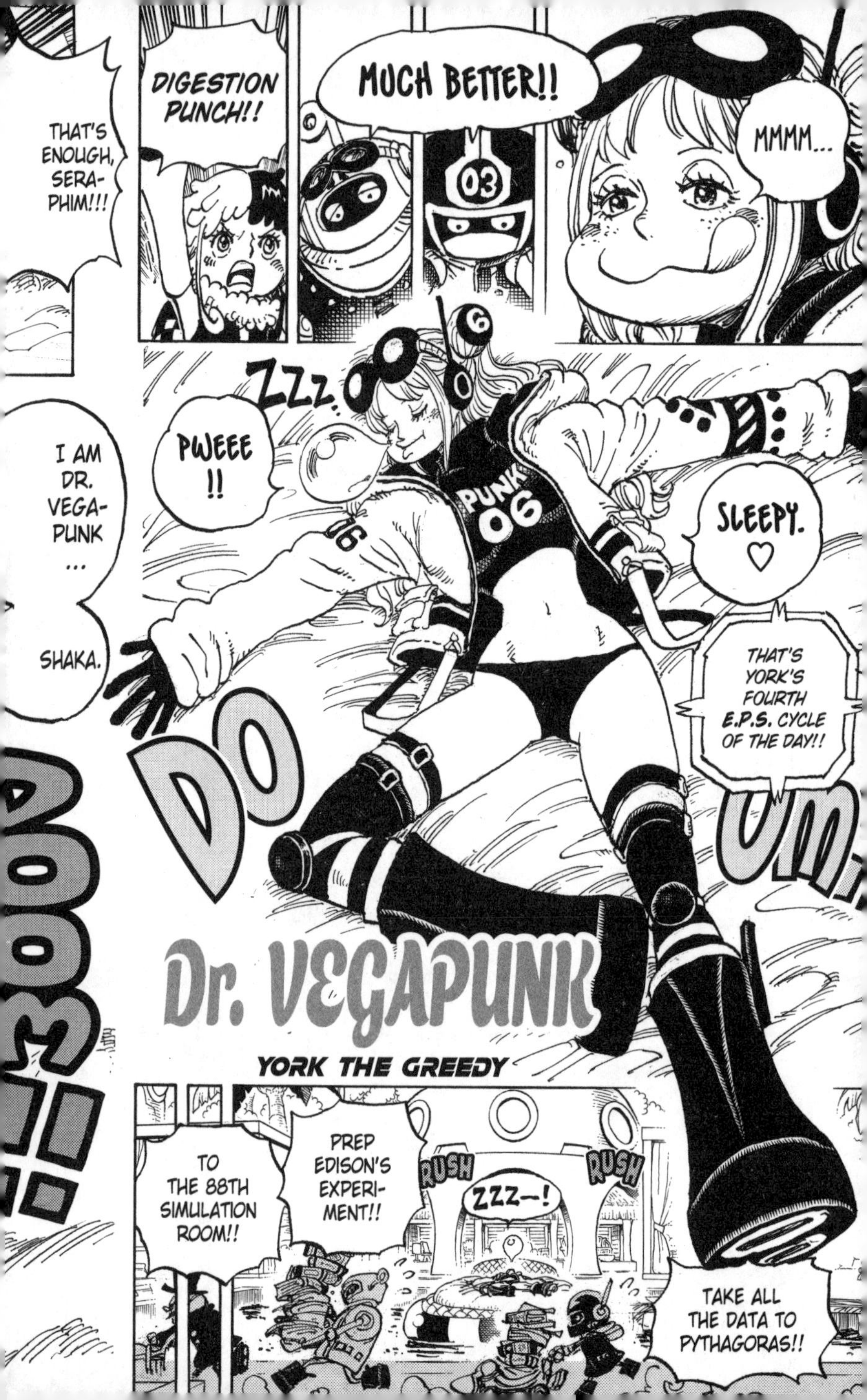
MMMM...
MUCH BETTER!!
DIGESTION PUNCH!!
SLEEPY. ♡
THAT'S YORK'S FOURTH E.P.S. CYCLE OF THE DAY!!
PWEEE!!
ZZZ
DO
OM
Dr. VEGAPUNK
YORK THE GREEDY
TAKE ALL THE DATA TO PYTHAGORAS!!
RUSH
RUSH
ZZZ-!
PREP EDISON'S EXPERIMENT!!
TO THE 88TH SIMULATION ROOM!!
THAT'S ENOUGH, SERAPHIM!!!
I AM DR. VEGAPUNK...
SHAKA.
OOM!!

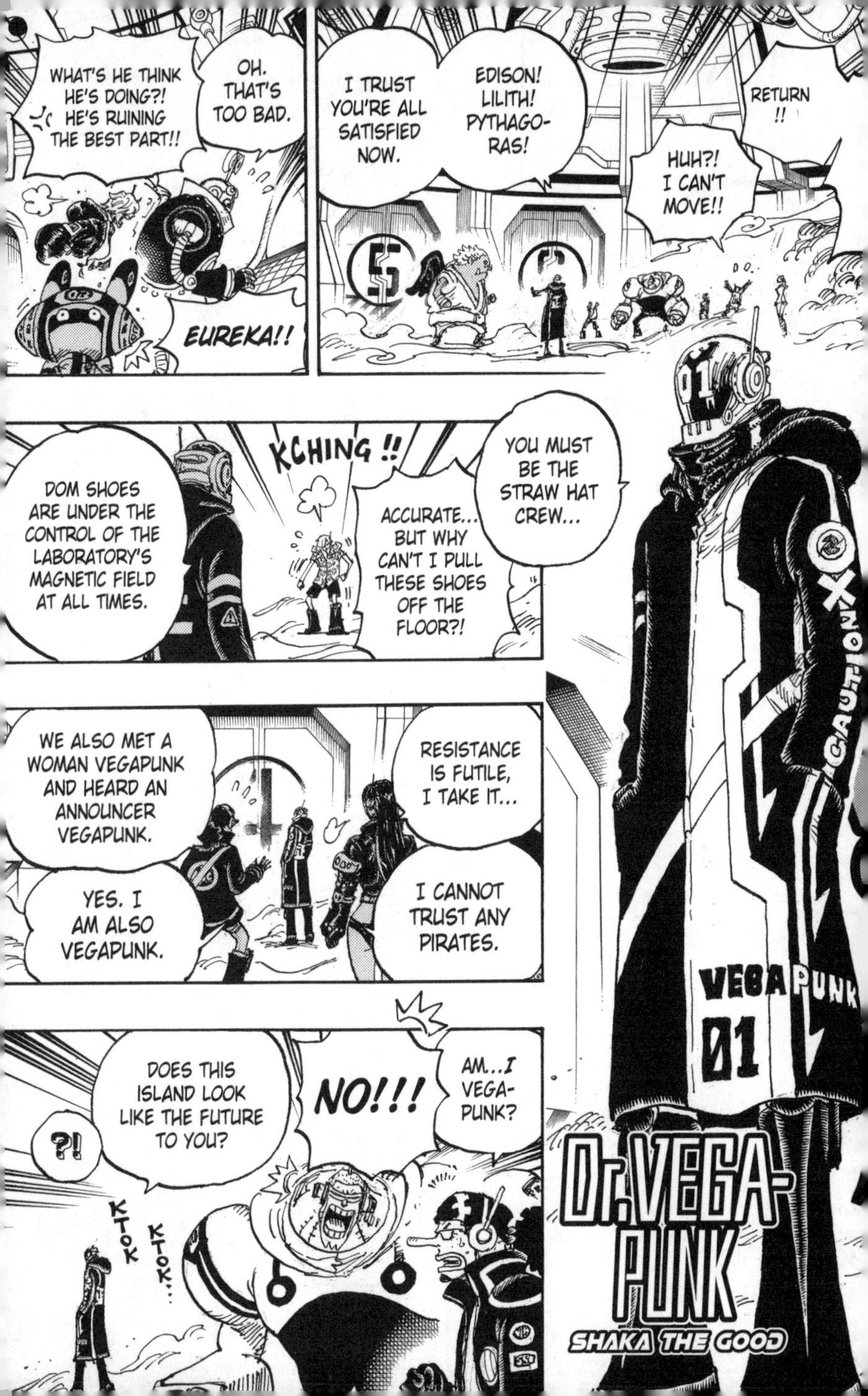
RETURN!!
HUH?! I CAN'T MOVE!!
EDISON! LILITH! PYTHAGO-RAS!
I TRUST YOU'RE ALL SATISFIED NOW.
OH. THAT'S TOO BAD.
WHAT'S HE THINK HE'S DOING?! HE'S RUINING THE BEST PART!!
EUREKA!!
CAUTION
VEGAPUNK
01
Dr. VEGA-PUNK
SHAKA THE GOOD
YOU MUST BE THE STRAW HAT CREW...
KCHING!!
ACCURATE... BUT WHY CAN'T I PULL THESE SHOES OFF THE FLOOR?!
DOM SHOES ARE UNDER THE CONTROL OF THE LABORATORY'S MAGNETIC FIELD AT ALL TIMES.
RESISTANCE IS FUTILE, I TAKE IT...
WE ALSO MET A WOMAN VEGAPUNK AND HEARD AN ANNOUNCER VEGAPUNK.
I CANNOT TRUST ANY PIRATES.
YES. I AM ALSO VEGAPUNK.
AM...I VEGA-PUNK?
NO!!!
DOES THIS ISLAND LOOK LIKE THE FUTURE TO YOU?
?!
KTOK
KTOK...

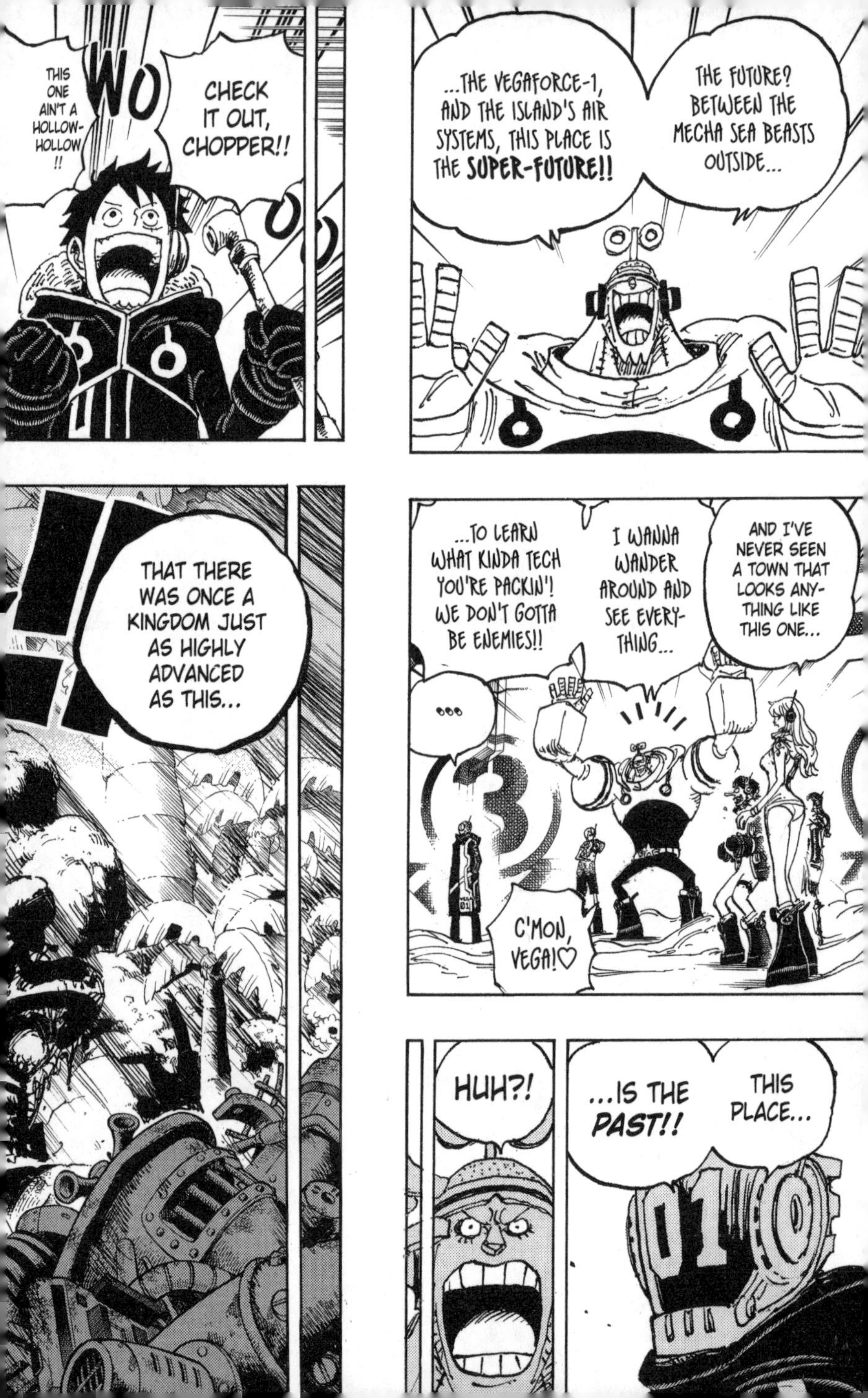
THE FUTURE? BETWEEN THE MECHA SEA BEASTS OUTSIDE...
...THE VEGAFORCE-1, AND THE ISLAND'S AIR SYSTEMS, THIS PLACE IS THE SUPER-FUTURE!!
CHECK IT OUT, CHOPPER!!
WO
THIS ONE AIN'T A HOLLOW-HOLLOW!!
AND I'VE NEVER SEEN A TOWN THAT LOOKS ANY-THING LIKE THIS ONE...
I WANNA WANDER AROUND AND SEE EVERY-THING...
...TO LEARN WHAT KINDA TECH YOU'RE PACKIN'! WE DON'T GOTTA BE ENEMIES!!
...
C'MON, VEGA!♡
THIS PLACE...
...IS THE PAST!!
HUH?!
THAT THERE WAS ONCE A KINGDOM JUST AS HIGHLY ADVANCED AS THIS...

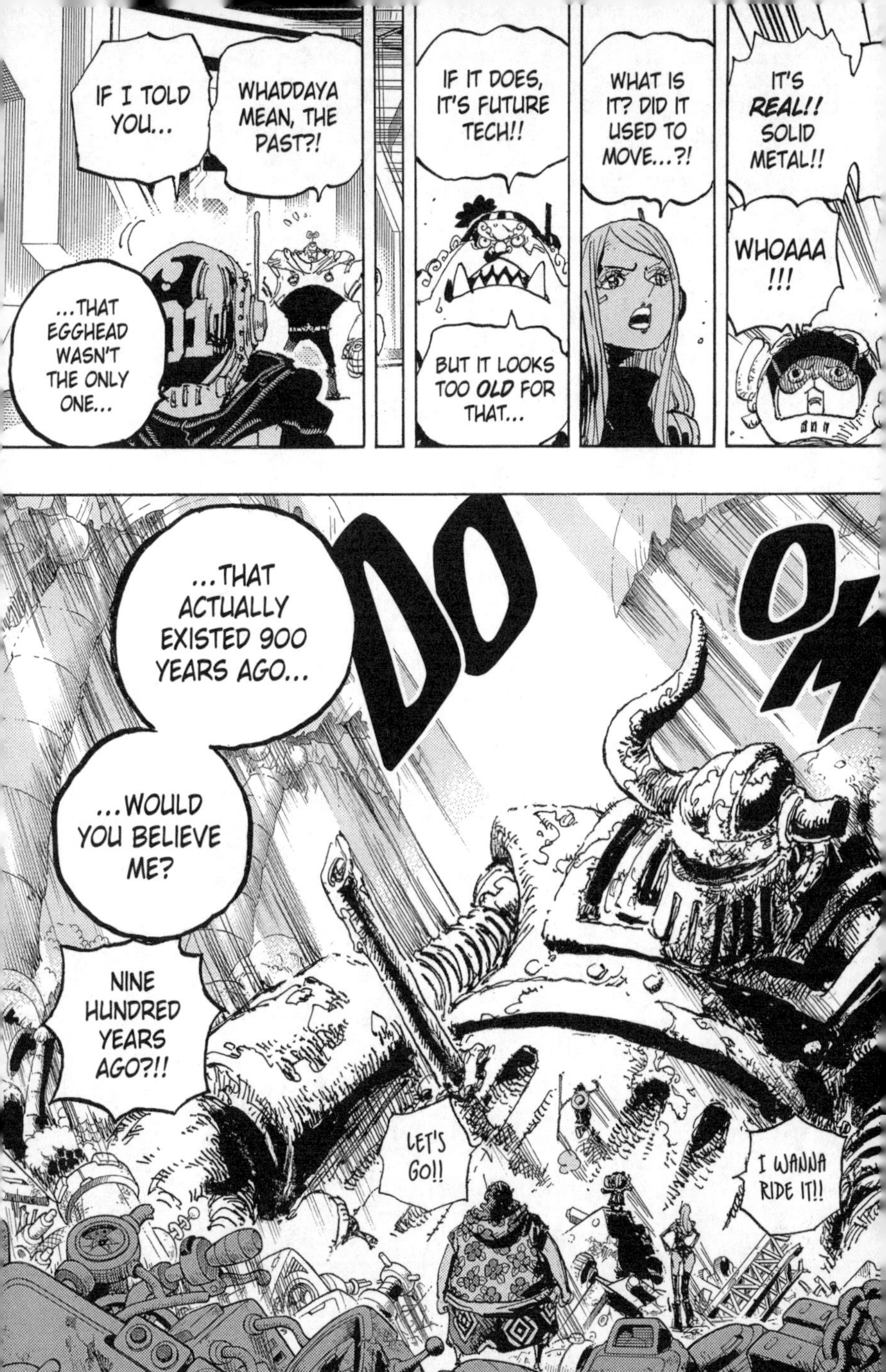
IT'S REAL!! SOLID METAL!!
WHOAAA!!!
WHAT IS IT? DID IT USED TO MOVE...?!
IF IT DOES, IT'S FUTURE TECH!!
BUT IT LOOKS TOO OLD FOR THAT...
WHADDAYA MEAN, THE PAST?!
IF I TOLD YOU...
...THAT EGGHEAD WASN'T THE ONLY ONE...
DOOM
...THAT ACTUALLY EXISTED 900 YEARS AGO...
...WOULD YOU BELIEVE ME?
I WANNA RIDE IT!!
LET'S GO!!
NINE HUNDRED YEARS AGO?!!
TO BE CONTINUED IN ONE PIECE, VOL. 106!

COMING NEXT VOLUME:

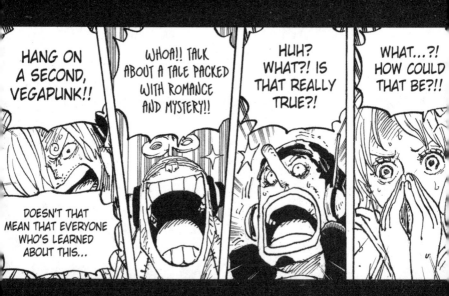

WHAT...?! HOW COULD THAT BE?!!
HUH? WHAT?! IS THAT REALLY TRUE?!
WHOA!! TALK ABOUT A TALE PACKED WITH ROMANCE AND MYSTERY!!
HANG ON A SECOND, VEGAPUNK!!
DOESN'T THAT MEAN THAT EVERYONE WHO'S LEARNED ABOUT THIS...

The Straw Hats crew's adventures on Egghead continue as new secrets are revealed. And when the real Dr. Vegapunk finally makes his appearance, the state of the world may be about to change in a major way!

ON SALE JULY 2024!

尾田栄一郎

"When I tell people I'm a *One Piece* fan, they get excited and want to talk about everything, but then I can't keep up. Odacchi! I might be a light reader, but do I have the right to stand up and claim, 'I love One Piece! I'm a *One Piece* fan too!'?"
—From P.N. Suzune

You sure do!!!

When people say, "I've only read this far," I'm actually thinking, "Wow, you read all the way to there?! Thanks!" So let the volume 105 gratitude party begin!!

—Eiichiro Oda, 2023

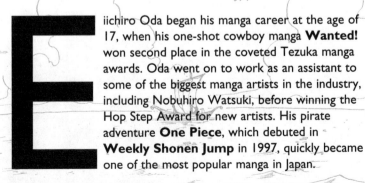

E iichiro Oda began his manga career at the age of 17, when his one-shot cowboy manga **Wanted!** won second place in the coveted Tezuka manga awards. Oda went on to work as an assistant to some of the biggest manga artists in the industry, including Nobuhiro Watsuki, before winning the Hop Step Award for new artists. His pirate adventure **One Piece**, which debuted in **Weekly Shonen Jump** in 1997, quickly became one of the most popular manga in Japan.

ONE PIECE VOL. 105
WANO PART 16

SHONEN JUMP Edition

STORY AND ART BY EIICHIRO ODA

Translation/Stephen Paul
Touch-Up Art & Lettering/Vanessa Satone
Design/Yukiko Whitley
Editor/Alexis Kirsch

Printed in the U.S.A.

Published by VIZ Media, LLC
P.O. Box 77010
San Francisco, CA 94107

10 9 8 7 6 5 4 3 2 1
First printing, March 2024

viz.com

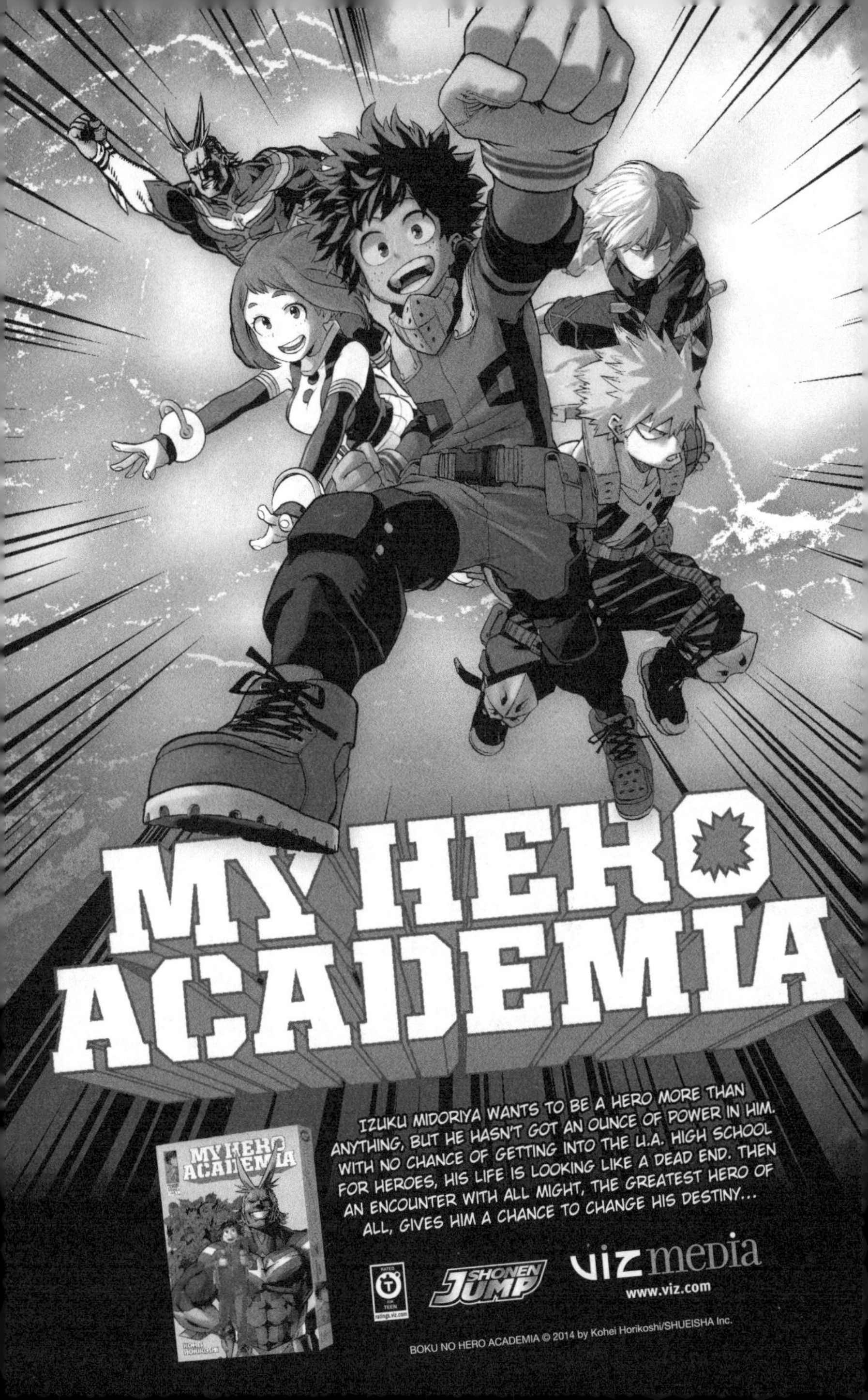
MY HERO ACADEMIA
IZUKU MIDORIYA WANTS TO BE A HERO MORE THAN ANYTHING, BUT HE HASN'T GOT AN OUNCE OF POWER IN HIM. WITH NO CHANCE OF GETTING INTO THE U.A. HIGH SCHOOL FOR HEROES, HIS LIFE IS LOOKING LIKE A DEAD END. THEN AN ENCOUNTER WITH ALL MIGHT, THE GREATEST HERO OF ALL, GIVES HIM A CHANCE TO CHANGE HIS DESTINY...
MY HERO ACADEMIA
RATED T FOR TEEN ratings.viz.com
SHONEN JUMP
viz media
www.viz.com
BOKU NO HERO ACADEMIA © 2014 by Kohei Horikoshi/SHUEISHA Inc.

Story and Art by
KOYOHARU GOTOUGE

In Taisho-era Japan, kindhearted Tanjiro Kamado makes a living selling charcoal. But his peaceful life is shattered when a demon slaughters his entire family. His little sister Nezuko is the only survivor, but she has been transformed into a demon herself! Tanjiro sets out on a dangerous journey to find a way to return his sister to normal and destroy the demon who ruined his life.

BORUTO
=NARUTO NEXT GENERATIONS=

CREATOR/SUPERVISOR **Masashi Kishimoto**
ART BY **Mikio Ikemoto** SCRIPT BY **Ukyo Kodachi**

A NEW GENERATION OF NINJA IS HERE!

Naruto was a young shinobi with an incorrigible knack for mischief. He achieved his dream to become the greatest ninja in his village, and now his face sits atop the Hokage monument. But this is not his story... A new generation of ninja is ready to take the stage, led by Naruto's own son, Boruto!

You're Reading in the Wrong Direction!!

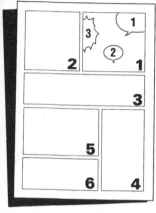

Whoops! Guess what? You're starting at the wrong end of the comic!

...It's true! In keeping with the original Japanese format, **One Piece** is meant to be read from right to left, starting in the upper-right corner.

Unlike English, which is read from left to right, Japanese is read from right to left, meaning that action, sound effects, and word-balloon order are completely reversed...something which can make readers unfamiliar with Japanese feel pretty backwards themselves. For this reason, manga or Japanese comics published in the U.S. in English have sometimes been published "flopped"— that is, printed in exact reverse order, as though seen from the other side of a mirror.

By flopping pages, U.S. publishers can avoid confusing readers, but the compromise is not without its downside. For one thing, a character in a flopped manga series who once wore in the original Japanese version a T-shirt emblazoned with "M A Y" (as in "the merry month of") now wears one which reads "Y A M"! Additionally, many manga creators in Japan are themselves unhappy with the process, as some feel the mirror-imaging of their art skews their original intentions.

We are proud to bring you Eiichiro Oda's **One Piece** in the original unflopped format. For now, though, turn to the other side of the book and let the journey begin...!

—Editor